ST GREGORY OF NYSSA

On Death and Eternal Life

ST VLADIMIR'S SEMINARY PRESS
Popular Patristics Series
Number 64

The Popular Patristics Series published by St Vladimir's Seminary Press provides readable and accurate translations of a wide range of early Christian literature to a wide audience—students of Christian history to lay Christians reading for spiritual benefit. Recognized scholars in their fields provide short but comprehensive and clear introductions to the material. The texts include classics of Christian literature, thematic volumes, collections of homilies, letters on spiritual counsel, and poetical works from a variety of geographical contexts and historical backgrounds. The mission of the series is to mine the riches of the early Church and to make these treasures available to all.

ST GREGORY OF NYSSA

On Death and Eternal Life

Translation and Introduction by

BRIAN E. DALEY

ST VLADIMIR'S SEMINARY PRESS

YONKERS, NEW YORK

2022

Library of Congress Cataloging-in-Publication Data

Names: Gregory, of Nyssa, Saint, approximately 335-approximately 394, author. | Daley, Brian E., 1940- translator. | Gregory, of Nyssa, Saint, approximately 335-approximately 394. Works. Selections. 2022. | Gregory, of Nyssa, Saint, approximately 335-approximately 394. Works. Selections. English. 2022.
Title: On death and eternal life / St Gregory of Nyssa ; translation and introduction by Brian E. Daley.
Description: Yonkers, NY : St Vladimir's Seminary Press, 2022. | Series: Popular patristics series ; 64 | Includes bibliographical references. | English and Greek on facing pages. | Summary: "The seven works in this volume (some translated for the first time) explore the great human mystery of death and the promise of eternal life. They present-along with On the Soul and the Resurrection (PPS 12)-a vision that is consistent, philosophically profound, and characteristic of Gregory's wider theology. The first three works (On the Dead, On Infants Taken Away before Their Time, and On the "Final Subjection" of Christ) might be termed thematic essays; the fourth is a sermon celebrating Christ's resurrection (On the Holy Pascha); and the remaining three are funeral homilies given for prominent people in Constantinople (Meletius, Pulcheria, and Flaccilla). This volume includes the critical Greek text"-- Provided by publisher.
Identifiers: LCCN 2022041156 (print) | LCCN 2022041157 (ebook) | ISBN 9780881417098 (paperback) | ISBN 9780881417104 (kindle edition)
Subjects: LCSH: Death--Early works to 1800. | Future life--Christianity--Early works to 1800.
Classification: LCC BT825 .G684 2022 (print) | LCC BT825 (ebook) | DDC 236/.1--dc23/eng/20221103
LC record available at https://lccn.loc.gov/2022041156
LC ebook record available at https://lccn.loc.gov/2022041157

575 Scarsdale Road, Yonkers, NY 10707
1-800-204-2665
www.svspress.com

ISBN 978-088141-709-8 (paper)
ISBN 978-088141-710-4 (electronic)
ISSN 1555-5755

PRINTED IN THE UNITED STATES OF AMERICA

I would like to offer this set of translations as a modest but heartfelt token of congratulations to my friend and fellow student of early Christianity, Fr John Anthony McGuckin, on his retirement from teaching at the Union Theological Seminary in New York. May the years ahead offer him the freedom to keep reading and reflecting, to keep writing, and to keep sharing his wisdom with us all.

~ ~ ~

The publication of this book was made possible in part by a generous grant from the Brewer Charitable Fund in memory of Daniel L. Banner.

Contents

Abbreviations

Brill Dictionary	*The Brill Dictionary of Gregory of Nyssa*. Edited by Lucas Francisco Mateo-Seco and Giulio Maspero and translated by Seth Cherney. Supplements to *Vigiliae Christianae* 99. Leiden and Boston: Brill, 2010.
GNO	Gregorii Nysseni Opera. 10 vols in 17 plus supplement. Edited by Werner Jaeger, Herman Langerbeck, Hadwiga Hörner, et al. Leiden: Brill, 1952–2014.
NPNF²	A Select Library of Nicene and Post-Nicene Fathers of the Christian Church. Second Series. New York: The Christian Literature Company, 1886–1900, and many reprints.
PG	Patrologiae Cursus Completus. Series Graeca. 161 volumes. Edited by J.-P. Migne. Paris, 1857–1866.
PPS	Popular Patristics Series. Crestwood/Yonkers, NY: St Vladimir's Seminary Press, 1996–
SC	Sources chrétiennes. Paris: Les Éditions du Cerf, 1942–

Introduction

The Humanist Theologian

In a number of ways, St Gregory of Nyssa shares in the beginning of something new in early Christian literature and thought. Like several of his late-fourth-century contemporaries in both the Latin- and Greek-speaking worlds—his own brother Basil of Caesaraea and their friend Gregory of Nazianzus in the East, Ambrose of Milan and Augustine of Hippo in the West—Gregory was no cultural outsider, but was born in a Christian family of comfortable means and considerable social standing, and was given a thorough classical education. After three and a half centuries of gradual growth in membership and public acceptance within the Roman Empire, the Christian community in the second half of the fourth century suddenly found itself recognized as the center of the religious movements of the Mediterranean world, steadily growing in favor with Emperor Constantine and most of his descendants, protected by the laws, increasingly dominant in the culture. By the 350s, a new generation of Christian intellectuals was emerging, trained in the disciplines that were traditionally thought of as forming a person to take an active role in public life: linguistic ability and a knowledge of the literary tradition of Greece and Rome; a nodding acquaintance, at least, with the principles and lore of the natural sciences and the law; and usually also a deeper familiarity with the practice of classical philosophy, which enabled a person to reason clearly and argue forcefully. Yet while their education was broadly humanistic, similar to what had been enjoyed by non-Christian Greek and Latin speakers for centuries, this new Christian generation of educated citizens found the heart of their understanding of reality in the

message of the Christian Scriptures, and in the liturgy and creeds of the Christian Church; so they were confronted now with the challenge to understand and express this faith in terms that were both authentically Christian and classically comprehensible. They were challenged, in other words, to be Christian humanists, Christian rhetoricians, Christian philosophers—and so, with new fullness, to be Christian theologians.

Despite this common opportunity, however, educated Christians of the late fourth century responded to these challenges in different ways. Basil accepted the call to be metropolitan bishop of Caesaraea, the provincial capital of Cappadocia in central Asia Minor, in 370, and spent the next nine years or so until his death largely playing the role of unifier and peacemaker in a Church still divided over the Nicene definition of Jesus' divinity. Basil's companion in early studies, Gregory of Nazianzus, the son of a small-town bishop from western Cappadocia, was persuaded by his friend in the early 370s to be ordained a bishop himself, as part of a campaign to populate the Church with outspoken leaders who could defend the theology of Nicaea. But Gregory of Nazianzus, an introverted intellectual, always resisted the demands of office; after a few months as *de facto* bishop of Constantinople in 381, and even a few weeks as chairman of the ecumenical council held in the capital that spring, he resigned his responsibilities and retired to his rural villa to spend his final decade as a thoughtful outsider, a prolific Christian poet, and classical *littérateur*.

Ambrose, in the West, had been trained, like his Cappadocian contemporaries, in classical rhetoric, and began his career as a lawyer and imperial politician; while serving in Milan as governor of the province of Aemilia-Liguria, he was chosen by acclamation to be bishop of that busy city late in 374, even though he was not yet himself baptized; he spent the rest of his life preaching on biblical books in classical style, interpreting the Church's sacramental practices, and boldly administering his part of the Western Church. Augustine, himself baptized at the age of thirty-three by Ambrose

in 387, soon returned to his native North Africa and became bishop of the port city of Hippo in 395, where he spent thirty-five years engaged in a prodigious amount of correspondence, preaching, and controversial writing, along with his own administrative duties. All of these men were clearly people of extraordinary talent and energy; all were professional rhetoricians, trained to varying degrees in the classical art of persuasive speech, before their election as bishops; all were humanists in the classical mold, delighting in the eloquent and subtle use of their own language. And although it is often difficult to determine just what ancient thinkers they had studied, all had received considerable training in the eclectic ongoing conversation of late antique philosophy. They were trained, in other words, to be capable speculative thinkers, as well as men of affairs and men of letters.

Among these late-fourth-century Christian writers, it seems fair to say that Gregory of Nyssa, Basil of Caesaraea's younger brother, holds a special place as the most philosophically enterprising, and perhaps the most broadly learned, of them all. Although he has left us a few homilies for church feasts, as well as letters, sermons on the Lord's Prayer, the Beatitudes, and the Book of Ecclesiastes, and a masterful set of lectures commenting on the Song of Songs, many of Gregory's best-known writings are, rather, occasional pieces of a more philosophical character: essays on a problem encountered in thinking through the Christian faith, often written in answer to a request from an acquaintance. In all of these, the guiding norm for his reflections is clearly the received faith of the Christian community as he understands it, grounded in the biblical text and celebrated in the liturgy. But Gregory's approach is usually not to begin directly with exegesis, but to discuss the problem at hand in the style of an ancient academic lecture or philosophical treatise: dealing with difficulties that traditional Christian faith presents to his educated contemporaries, arguing for his own position through analysis and philosophical persuasion, and in the process referring to biblical texts as confirmation that his argument stands rooted in Christian

tradition. While Augustine's theological positions seem to spring directly from his constant reading and preaching of the biblical text for African congregations, Gregory prefers to approach issues from the perspective of his own unified vision of Christian theology, and to bolster his arguments, once advanced, by showing that they resonate accurately with the Scripture that anchors the Church's mainstream faith. As a result, Gregory's thought is often original and speculative, and develops challenging positions—on the relations of the persons of the Trinity, for instance, and on the nature and universal inclusiveness of the salvation achieved for humanity by Christ—that were received somewhat uncomfortably by later Christian theologians in the Greek-speaking world. He occasionally sounded, it seems, too much like a Platonist to be convincing to ordinary Christians. So, it is really only in the twentieth century that he came to be recognized as a major patristic thinker in his own right, largely because of the pioneering efforts of Werner Jaeger—himself a German Protestant and primarily a scholar of ancient culture and Greek philosophy—to publish and promote his works.

Gregory's Life

In contrast to his brother Basil and his friend Gregory of Nazianzus, we know relatively few details of the shape of Gregory of Nyssa's life and career. He is usually thought to have been born in Caesaraea, the provincial capital of Cappadocia in central Asia Minor, between 335 and 340, one of the younger children in a large Christian family. His father, Basil the elder, was a teacher of rhetoric—part of the rapidly expanding class of educated Christians who made it their profession to accept and promote the tradition of Hellenistic thought. His mother, Emmelia, came from a family that had been converted to Christianity, a century before, by Gregory "the Wonderworker," himself an enthusiastic disciple of Origen and the original evangelizer of Cappadocia. We do not know whether our Gregory, like his older brother Basil, went abroad for any part of his own education.

Clearly, however, he acquired a wide range of learning: not only knowledge of the Greek language and classical literature, and of the science of rhetoric and argument, but a deep familiarity with later Greek philosophy, and an unusual knowledge of what we would call natural science, including anatomy and medicine, zoology, botany, astronomy, and physics. Of all early Christian writers, Gregory of Nyssa is one of the most prone to draw on this body of secular learning, in his theological arguments, for detailed illustrations and analogies.[1] He seems to have been especially fascinated by organic life, in a universe governed by laws of growth and change. Change, for Gregory, was the natural presupposition for the gradual perfection of the creature.

By the late 360s or early 370s, when he seems to have written his treatise *On Virginity*, Gregory was apparently married and had a daughter;[2] he seems also to have been ordained as a reader at an early stage of his life, since Gregory of Nazianzus, by now a family friend, criticized him in a letter of the late 360s for abandoning his work in the Church to pursue a secular career as a teacher of rhetoric.[3] In 371 or 372, however, that situation was permanently changed: his brother Basil, now bishop of Caesaraea, ordained Gregory bishop of the newly-created see of Nyssa, as part of an effort to staff the churches of Cappadocia with bishops faithful to the Nicene profession, in opposition to the Emperor Valens' promotion of non-Nicene "Homoeans" to church office. In 375 or 376, Gregory was accused by officials in his local church of financial mismanagement (probably out of theological motives, as Gregory himself suggests in his *Life of Macrina* [GNO VIII/1:393]), and was forced to go into exile for a few

[1] Among Greek theologians of the period, the only competitor to Gregory for an interest in the natural world is Nemesius of Emesa, author of a treatise, *On Human Nature*, which attempts to link what is known about the human person with orthodox faith in Christ. This treatise seems to have been written about 400, and shows similar interests on the author's part to those of Gregory himself. Nemesius may, in fact, have been an acquaintance of the Cappadocian Fathers, since Gregory of Nazianzus exchanged letters with someone of that name (*Ep.* 198–201).

[2] See *On Virginity* 3.

[3] Gregory of Nazianzus, *Ep.* 11.

years, possibly in Cilicia, in southern Asia Minor near Antioch. In those years, like his friend Gregory of Nazianzus, he seems to have become part of the circle of Meletius, the embattled but increasingly beloved bishop of the major Christian community in that city. Even in his years of exile, too, Gregory seems to have continued writing theological essays.

In late 378, with the accession of Theodosius—a Nicene Christian and successful military officer from Spain—as emperor, Gregory was able to return to his own see. Influenced by Meletius of Antioch and by the brilliant and sensitive Gregory of Nazianzus, who had been made bishop of the Nicene party in Constantinople, Theodosius summoned an ecumenical council to meet in the capital in late May of 381, mainly to produce a definitive reaffirmation of Nicaea's understanding of the full divinity of Christ, and also to deal with other disputed theological issues of the day, notably the status of the Holy Spirit. During the early days of that council, Meletius (its first president) died suddenly; Gregory of Nazianzus—never at ease in public office—succeeded him, but for canonical reasons was forced to resign from his roles, both as local bishop and as chair of the council's sessions, a few weeks later. Gregory of Nyssa remained in Constantinople, however, active and influential, and was clearly close to the emperor. He was chosen, for instance, to deliver the funeral oration for Meletius, as the departed patriarch's remains were about to be sent back to Antioch for burial; and in a decree recognizing the normative character of the council's theology a few months later, Theodosius named Gregory as one of eleven well-known bishops from the Greek world whose faith might now be seen as the standard for orthodoxy.[4] For the emperor, at least, Gregory—rather than his late older brother or his retiring namesake of Nazianzus—had taken on the public role of an articulate, exemplary spokesman for the Christian faith.

After the council, we know from his letters that Gregory travelled—probably at the emperor's behest—to visit the churches and

[4]See *Codex Theodosianus* 17.1.3

holy sites of Palestine and Arabia, where his mission apparently was to promote doctrinal unity and disciplinary reform in the wake of the council's decrees. When and for how long he returned to his own church of Nyssa is not known, but Gregory seems at least to have spent a good deal of his later years in Constantinople, where he continued to preach and to write theological and spiritual works. The date and place of his death are also unknown, but he is usually assumed to have lived until the mid-390s.

Like the particulars of his life, the exact dating of Gregory's works remains largely a matter of guesswork. In attempting to develop a chronology for them, modern scholars sometimes lay hold of the few of his works that offer some hint of their historical setting—*On the Soul and the Resurrection*, for instance, which Gregory tells us was inspired by a conversation with his older sister Macrina, shortly after their brother Basil's death in late 378 or early 379; from these, modern scholars have developed a general outline, on the basis of what appears to be more or less his "mature thought." But such an approach clearly remains somewhat arbitrary, and must be used with caution. Gregory is not a systematic writer, and the differences in style and content among his works may be due as much to their intended audiences, and to the rhetorical genre of the works themselves, as to his own intellectual or theological development.

Works on Death and Eternal Life

In this context, it may be helpful to say something about the seven works of Gregory of Nyssa we have translated here. All of them deal with the great human mystery of death and the promise, affirmed by Christian believers, of eternal life. Some of them have not previously been translated into English, others are available only in obscure or very old versions. And while they do not quite offer together a comprehensive theology of the Christian hope in the face of death, they still present—along with Gregory's larger, better-known treatise *On the Soul and the Resurrection*, a translation of which already appears

in this series—a portrait of that hope that is consistent, philosophically profound, and characteristic of Gregory's wider theology. The first three works presented here might be termed thematic essays; the fourth is an elaborate and formal sermon or address commemorating the paschal feast of the resurrection of Christ; and the remaining three are memorial homilies or addresses delivered on the occasion of the deaths of prominent people in Constantinople, and carefully constructed to echo these themes while embodying the rhetorical genre of the funeral oration (ἐπιτάφιος λόγος, *epitaphios logos*).

Let us consider these works in more detail.

A Discourse on the Dead (De mortuis)

This elaborate essay is written in the style of a free-standing lecture or treatise on the subject of death, and sets out to persuade its hearers or readers that death is *not*, as many suppose, the ultimate human misfortune. Its style is clearly philosophical, first of all, and only moves in the direction of specifically Christian teaching on death and eternal life toward the end of the work (18–20)[5]—a feature that suggests it may have been composed before the more expressly scriptural treatise *On the Soul and the Resurrection*, perhaps in the mid-370s. Gregory begins by asking what is the ultimate Good for the human person, and concludes that it cannot simply be identified with some aspect of our present physical well-being. Human life here in the world, the life of embodied souls, is inescapably also a process of consumption, of "filling and emptying" the stomach or the lungs (5)—a continuing cycle on which our existence depends. The true Good must be a permanent and unchanging form of life enjoyed by the soul alone, a life open to everyone, peaceful and effortless, free from danger and fluctuation. In that life,

[5]Numbers given in parentheses, here and elsewhere in the introduction, refer to the section numbers we have introduced into the translations in this volume. [References to the GNO page numbers are given in the text below.—*Ed.*]

> the soul will live as one unburdened from all such things and free, neither having nor losing property, through which servitude and lordship are determined. . . . The freedom from want, the immateriality of that life will make all these things, and everything like them, no longer inevitable. In that life, what supports the personal survival of the soul will not be its share in anything dry or moist, but knowledge of the divine nature; and we will know unmistakably that what we inhale is a share not in the air we breathe here, but in the true, Holy Spirit. (6)

With such a concept of human spiritual fulfillment as the ideal, the death of our bodies can only be a liberation (7–9).

So Gregory goes on to identify the intellectual soul as the center of human identity. When freed from its needy attachment to matter, the soul comes to recognize itself as formed in the image of God: "immaterial and without shape, intellectual and incorporeal" (10). So Gregory reflects on the soul's present embodied state in terms reminiscent of Plato's *Phaedo*:

> For the matter of the body is truly an alien thing, foreign to the incorporeal nature; the mind is necessarily intermingled with it in this present life, and passes its time in wretchedness, sharing the fate of a different kind of life altogether. The shared relationship of elements woven together with each other has something forced and jarring about it. . . . But the mind, which is mingled with these elements, not being composite, lives on in its simple and uniform nature in the midst of strange, foreign objects. . . . [And] with the war within us ended by death, the soul lives on in peace, having left the battlefield (that is, the body), and the opposition between the elements, behind. Moving away from them, it lives for itself, recovering in rest its own strength, which had become worn out by its involvement with the body. (11)

Gregory then argues, however, that the whole human person, soul and body, is naturally constructed to grow and change. This prepares

us for our final healing, "our restoration to our original state, which is nothing else than likeness to what God is" (14). For this transformation to take place, a refinement of our present composite state must occur, a transformation of what is ugly and deformed in us, through ascetical practices in this life and ultimately through the "purifying fire" of death itself (15).

In the final part of the treatise, Gregory adjusts this unabashedly Platonic picture of death and eternal life to include an explicit hope in bodily resurrection. Our present problem, he argues, is not embodiment itself, but the choices that the embodied soul makes to be dominated by bodily needs and desires (15). The use of a body, in fact, is "indispensable" for the soul in its present state, as its locus of free choice and self-mastery (16). The soul must simply learn ways of purifying its own vision of the world and its own desires. "It is not the body, but free choice that acts as the starting-point for vices" (17). "Let not the body, then, be vilified by thoughtless people; after this life the soul will be adorned by a body that is transformed into a more divine state through regeneration, when death has purified it of what is superfluous and useless for the enjoyment of the life to come" (18). Citing 1 Corinthians 15.51—the first direct reference to Scripture in this work—Gregory insists that "we shall be changed": the risen body will be different in form and quality from the present one—perhaps (but not definitely) losing even its sexual characteristics (20)—and will be "transformed into something more divine." In the end all of us will be reshaped by "one and the same grace," and will finally be formed anew in the image of God, as God originally intended (20). So a consciousness of our future state, even now, can "purify our grieving" in the face of death, by reminding us of what lies ahead of us all (20). Salvation through transformation is the key to God's plan for human life.

On Infants Taken Away before Their Time (De infantibus praemature abreptis)

This treatise is also a formal, highly ornate essay on death and the afterlife, and is addressed to a certain Hierius, whom Gregory flatteringly characterizes as a "philosopher," a man of high moral principles and modest life-style, who has served in the past as an important government official. Gregory hints (1 and 3) that he has been invited, along with other public intellectuals, to contribute an essay on the puzzling question of how a good and powerful God, the just judge of human affairs, can allow some human beings to die in infancy, when their life has scarcely begun. Attempts have been made to identify the addressee; the most likely candidate is a certain "Prefect Hierius"—probably prefect or governor of Egypt in the early 360s—to whom Gregory wrote an early letter (*Ep.* 7), asking for pardon for a young acquaintance who had been sentenced to death. This Hierius is identified in other sources—Libanius' Letter 195, for instance, written in 364—as a man of philosophical temper and admirable virtue, who may well have been a pagan;[6] his request for philosophical reflection on the divine justice of infant mortality, by Gregory and other thinkers, could suggest that he has lost a child of his own. If this identification is correct, it would be significant that one of the "philosophers" from whom Hierius requests such a reflection is the Christian bishop of Nyssa. The only difficulty here is the dating: Gregory stresses in the beginning of the work (1 and 3) that he is an "old man," which suggests a date in the late 380s or early 390s, twenty years and more after the Prefect Hierius's known tenure as administrator. If he wrote the work at an earlier date, closer to that of Letter 7, would Gregory have referred to himself in this way? Conversely, if it is a late work of Gregory's, the Prefect Hierius would by then be elderly as well; one wonders then why a

[6]For a list of the available ancient sources referring to this Hierius and others of the same name, see A. H. M. Jones, J. R. Martindale, and J. Morris, *The Prosopography of the Later Roman Empire* 1 (Cambridge: Cambridge University Press, 1971), 430–31, especially the entry "Hierius 4."

long-retired official would still be so keenly interested in the question of infant mortality?

Puzzles remain. Whoever the addressee may be, Gregory treats him with much respect, and throughout the work interweaves allusions to the Hebrew Bible, the Gospels, and Paul with philosophical reflection. Gregory begins his argument, after several paragraphs complimenting Hierius himself on his virtues, with a statement of the issue that has been raised: if death is normally followed by God's judgment of our deeds and then by reward or purgative suffering, how should we imagine the death of one who has not lived long enough to be judged in this way (5)? Would it be just for God to admit infants who die to the same full beatitude as those tested by a long life (6)?

Gregory acknowledges that this is a great mystery (7), then insists that God's goal in creating intelligent creatures is clearly to allow them to share his life through contemplation (8–10). In our present state of alienation and ignorance, this clearly requires that God first heal and restore each of us; but the end of the process—what we call the "beatific vision"—is still presented here as "the necessary consequence of our natural disposition" (10), made possible by the mediation of Christ. So a person who dies in early infancy must still grow inwardly until he or she is mature enough to share fully in the vision of God (12). Gregory clearly assumes this growth can take place after death, as well as before it.

The more troubling question, and presumably the question Hierius has posed to begin with, is why God allows infants to die before they have matured humanly in a normal way. Gregory's answer, proposed tentatively but at some length, is that God, who is always benevolent and just, may do this because he foresees the person who dies in infancy would have "engaged himself in vice in a still more damaging way than those who have been notorious for wickedness while they lived" (17). Like the host at a dinner party, who ushers out guests who he foresees will get drunk and disgrace themselves if they stay, God may simply be "foreclosing the indiscipline of vice for those inclined to live this way" (20). It is a bold speculation, but one

that fits closely with some of Gregory's principal assumptions about creation and redemption.

On the "Final Subjection" of Christ (In illud: Tunc et ipse filius)

The next text translated here is an interpretation of Paul's somewhat challenging text in 1 Corinthians 15.24–28, which asserts that after all things have been providentially subjected to Christ, at the end of history, "then the Son will be made subject to the one who has subjected all things to him, and God will be all in all." This passage from Paul was a key text in the debates between Marcellus of Ancyra and his critics, from the mid-fourth to early fifth centuries, over the status of the Son, our Savior, within the eternal Mystery of God. Did Paul here suggest, as Marcellus was charged with saying, that the Word who became flesh in Jesus simply embodied a divine function, a phase in that saving Mystery, expressing God's merciful outreach into time, but that he and those who belong to him would, in the end, be simply absorbed into the life and providence of God? Did 1 Corinthians 15.24–28 suggest, in other words, what had come to be known as a "Sabellian" or modalist understanding of the God who is Trinity, and so an unacceptable model of human salvation?

For Gregory, too, in this essay, the central concern in discussing the passage from Paul is clearly Christological and soteriological: what is Paul saying about the person of the Son of God, and about the salvation he has brought to the human race? The implied connection of the passage in 1 Corinthians 15 with the debates over Marcellus and his theology also suggests a date of composition: Marcellus and his followers were condemned, with other groups of major Christological heretics, by the Council of Constantinople in 381 (Canons 1 and 7),[7] and Gregory may well have been consulted, shortly before or after that gathering, on the normative value of this passage in Paul

[7]No acts or decrees have survived directly from the Council of 381. The dogmatic declaration and canons associated with it are taken from the synodal letter of the local council that met in Constantinople the following year, which conveyed and expounded these decisions. See Theodoret, *Church History* 5.9.

for evaluating Marcellus' understanding of Christ and his work, and on how one might take the passage in an orthodox way.[8] This essay seems, in any case, to have been written in response to an inquiry from an unknown correspondent, whom Gregory addresses in the second person singular in the final sentence of the work.

Gregory begins by discussing the various meanings of being "subject" (2–5), and insists that no suggestion of inferiority or domination should be ascribed to the relationship of Father and Son within the Trinity. His eventual interpretation of this passage is to see in it instead a primarily ecclesial and eschatological meaning: to recognize that "subjection" here refers not to the relationship of Son and Father as divine persons, but to those "who belong to Christ" (1 Cor 15.23), and who will be raised from the dead at the end of history to share in his eternal life. So he sums up his interpretation:

> What, then, is the heart of the doctrine that the divine Apostle is teaching us in this passage? It is that at some point the nature of evil will be transformed into non-existence, completely made to disappear from reality, and pure divine goodness will contain all rational nature within itself; nothing of all that has come into being from God will fall outside the boundaries of God's Kingdom, but when all the evil that has been mingled with existing things is consumed, like some material impurity, by the melting-process of purifying fire, everything will become just as it was when it had its origin from God . . . (8)

[8]Reinhard Hübner has argued that Marcellus modified his position on the distinctness of the Son in the course of his career in a more orthodox direction; he sees the Pseudo-Athanasian *De incarnatione et contra Arianos,* which Martin Tetz ("Zur Theologie des Markell von Ankyra I. Eine Markellische Schrift 'De incarnatione et contra Arianos'," *Zeitschrift für Kirchengeschichte* 75 [1964]: 215–70) argued is really a work of Marcellus, as representing, in chapters 20–21, Marcellus' later understanding of the Pauline text: adopting essentially a position similar to what Gregory is arguing for here. See Hübner, "Gregor von Nyssa und Markell von Ancyra," in M. Harl, *Écriture et culture philosophique dans las pensée de Grégoire de Nysse* (Leiden: Brill, 1971), 210–19. Pointing to similarities in exegesis of this passage in Gregory's *Contra Eunomium* I, composed in 381, Hübner dates this present work between 381 and 383/4. See also Joseph T. Lienhard, "The Exegesis of I Cor. 15.24–28 from Marcellus of Ancyra to Theodoret of Cyrus," *Vigiliae Christianae* 17 (1983): 340–59, esp. 348–50.

The purification of fallen human nature has begun with the incarnation, Gregory explains, when God the Son became fully human and lived a human life of perfect virtue among us. It continued still further in Jesus' death and resurrection, revealing the risen Jesus to be "a kind of first-fruit of the mixture [of divine and human] that will include us all" (9). The goal is the complete transformation of humanity, in union with Christ, beginning with the Church:

> When, then, all of us come to be outside the realm of evil, in imitation of our "first-fruit," the whole mix that is nature, blended in with the first-fruit and becoming one body in its solidarity, will receive within itself the rule of the Good alone; so with the whole body of our nature mingled with the divine, immortal nature, that subjection here ascribed to the Son will become reality through us, as subjection is brought to fulfillment in his Body and is referred to him who works in us the grace of submission. (10)

The "subjection of the Son" to God, in other words, really means the return of all humanity, through the Church that is Christ's Body, to the obedient, life-giving union with God that humans were created to enjoy, so that ultimately "there will be nothing outside the realm of what is saved" (13). Subjection, for Gregory here, points directly to universal salvation.

An Oration on the Holy Pascha (In sanctum Pascha III)[9]

The fourth treatise of Gregory's that develops his understanding of the life promised us after death is his sermon *On the Holy Pascha*, a formal, rhetorically elaborate address or treatise on the resurrection of Christ as the model for the resurrection Christians hope for.

[9]Five discourses on the Easter feast are attributed to Gregory and included in modern editions. Of them, the "first" simply deals with the question of how Jesus' time in the tomb can be construed as lasting "three days," and the "fourth" seems to be the concluding section of that same treatise. The so-called "second" is actually Severus of Antioch's Homily 77, and the "fifth" is now identified as a work of Amphilochius of Iconium, Gregory of Nazianzus' cousin.

Much of this work is an apologetic for the plausibility of this central Christian hope, in terms that echo passages in the second-century Greek apologists, and that anticipate the broader, more philosophically nuanced treatment in Gregory's dialogue *On the Soul and the Resurrection.* If this is a "rehearsal" of the arguments in that longer work, it would suggest a date of composition no later than 379.

Like Gregory of Nazianzus in his first sermon celebrating the birth of Christ (Or. 38), our Gregory begins by evoking the paschal festival as a day of unity, joy, and rest for Christians and for all creation (1–4). The heart of the day's celebration is the proclamation that death is not the end of human existence (5). After referring briefly to Jesus' death as the full expression of his share in our mortal nature, Gregory argues that the human person, in all our wisdom and complexity, must have been made for more than decomposition. Gregory then compares the process of re-forming the disintegrated human body with the even more wonderful process of creating it (8–9). His focus is on change and development: in human gestation (11), in the growth of an ear of wheat from a tiny grain (12–13), in the changes exhibited by trees in the course of the seasons (13), in the waking of snakes from hibernation (14), and even in our own experience of sleep and waking (15). To re-create a living body from its scattered parts is also a kind of organic transformation. Gregory then emphasizes the resurrection's importance for the moral life, since the actions for which we will eventually be held responsible are all actions done as embodied creatures in the world; the whole human person must, in the end, stand before Christ—"for if there is no resurrection, there is no judgment, and if judgment is removed, fear of God will be eliminated with it" (17). Gregory concludes his apologetic for the resurrection by referring to Ezekiel 37 and 1 Corinthians 15.52, where Paul reminds his readers that "we shall be changed." The framework is biblical faith, but the argument, for virtually all of the work, has been broadly philosophical.

The three other works we have translated here are all homilies in a stricter sense: sermons given by Gregory in the setting of a

liturgy or memorial service for a distinguished person who has recently died. In each of them, Gregory is apparently speaking on behalf of the imperially-recognized Church in Constantinople, as a distinguished ecclesiastical voice—as the Emperor Theodosius' appointed preacher, perhaps. In each of them, the hope Gregory expresses in the face of a tragic recent death is put in decidedly biblical terms—more explicitly biblical terms, certainly, than he employs in the other, more occasional pieces we have been discussing—but the form of each of them is still masterfully shaped by the standards of Hellenistic rhetoric. These are moving works of late classical eloquence, as well as testimonies of faith.

In the widely used third-century Greek handbook of rhetorical forms and techniques attributed to "Menander Rhetor"—which may in fact be a hybrid of two works by different Hellenistic authors—the "funeral speech" (*epitaphios logos*) is discussed as a particular genre of discourse, appropriate both to a ceremony held over the body of the deceased and to a memorial service several months later.[10] The main point of this kind of oration, "Menander" suggests, is to praise the person who has died by "pure encomium," though it is also intended to console those grieving; its tone throughout should be markedly but tastefully emotional. It usually begins with the speaker's admission of his own sense of difficulty, even hopelessness, about speaking adequately on such a sad occasion. He then should refer to the distinguished family of the deceased, to his or her privileged birth, physical beauty, and mental gifts, and to move on to his or her education and accomplishments. One may even compare the person with heroes of the past. Finally, after evoking the recent sad circumstances of the person's death, one is expected to address to the family of the deceased some form of religious consolation: a depiction of the Elysian Fields, perhaps, or a prayer to the gods to reward the departed and comfort the grieving. In adapting this traditional

[10]Menander, *Treatise* 2.11; English translation in *Menander Rhetor: A Commentary*, ed. and trans. Donald A. Russell and Nigel G. Wilson (Oxford: Oxford University Press, 1981), 170–79.

format to an unequivocally Christian context, Gregory frames each of his homilies in scriptural allusions, and emphasizes the Church's hope for the departed soul's immediate sharing in the life of God, and expresses the eventual expectation of bodily resurrection.

A Funeral Oration for Meletius, Bishop of Antioch (Oratio funebris in Meletium)

Meletius, as we have already said, was one of the most influential churchmen in the Eastern Mediterranean world in the second half of the fourth century. Over some twenty-five years as bishop in various places, he emerged gradually as a cautious but unequivocal supporter of Nicene theology—in clear opposition to the more ambiguous religious policy of several emperors—and as a patron of those who wished to preserve the earlier liturgical and theological traditions of a Church that was rich in them.[11] Apparently influential with the new emperor Theodosius after his accession in 378, the elderly Meletius seems to have played a role in persuading the emperor to summon an ecumenical council at Constantinople in late May of 381. He was asked by the emperor to be its president, but died during the first week of its deliberations.

Gregory's funeral homily for Meletius seems to have been delivered at a crowded memorial service of some kind, perhaps a liturgy marking the sending of the dead bishop's body back to his Church in Antioch. From his allusion to the words of other "noble brethren" on the occasion (1; cf. 4), Gregory seems not to have been the only speaker. He begins, as was customary, by confessing the difficulty he faces in finding language adequate to express the grief shared by everyone present, contrasting it dramatically with the euphoria of the capital city only a few days before, when Meletius' arrival had signaled the start of the council (2). Alluding to the funeral celebrations

[11]See my article, "The Enigma of Meletius of Antioch," in Ronnie J. Rombs and Alexander Y. Hwang, eds, *Tradition and the Rule of Faith in the Early Church: Essays in Honor of Joseph T. Lienhard, SJ* (Washington: The Catholic University of America Press, 2010), 128–50.

for the biblical patriarch Jacob in Egypt, mentioned in Genesis 50, as his body was being sent back to Israel for burial, Gregory evokes the grief of the Church of Constantinople at the death of this contemporary patriarch, the head of their own synodal gathering, and their sympathy for his ecclesial "family" in Antioch (4–5). Skillfully interweaving various allusions to the death of God's holy ones in the Old Testament, Gregory evokes Meletius' many years of struggle in his early career, as he tried to unite a number of competing factions in his own Church in the long and turbulent aftermath of Nicaea. Through it all, as Gregory emphasizes, Meletius remained gracious, humble, and conciliatory, and came to be loved deeply in the Church of Antioch as a result (6). Near the end of his homily, Gregory turns to the consolations of Christian hope, describing Meletius now as having entered the heavenly sanctuary with Christ, to share in his priestly intercession. Alluding to the impressive sight of this funeral liturgy in the imperial capital, Gregory concludes with an apparent exhortation to those who grieve for Meletius to find consolation in the Scriptures and the Eucharist.

A Discourse of Consolation for the Princess Pulcheria (Oratio consolatoria in Pulcheriam)

A second funeral homily of Gregory's is that delivered for the imperial princess Pulcheria, the young middle child of Theodosius and his wife Flaccilla, who died in August, 385, at the age of six. Characterizing the death of the little girl as an "earthquake" parallel in magnitude to the one that had devastated the nearby city of Nicomedia thirty years earlier, Gregory evokes the pain and grief shared by all who knew of her (1–2), and describes the muted but impressive sadness of her funeral procession (3). Gregory then turns to Scripture: first, to Paul's exhortation to the Thessalonians not to "grieve as those who have no hope" (1 Thess 4.13) (4), then to Jesus' command, "Let the little children come to me" (Mt 19.14) (5). Pulcheria has now been "transplanted," Gregory insists, to another kingdom and lives

in another, better royal palace (5), more radiantly beautiful than ever. Gregory then reflects on the regrets some may have that she has been deprived of the experiences of a normal life, and argues that her present state—espoused to her heavenly Bridegroom—is far more secure and blessed (6). Gregory moves on to compare the situation of Pulcheria's parents to that of Abraham and Sarah in Genesis, when asked to offer their only son, Isaac, in sacrifice (7–8), and describes Job's serene reaction to the news of the death of his children (9). Finally, Gregory reminds his hearers that our present nature was created to live forever, ultimately to be transformed by resurrection to a more splendid life, which will really be "the formation of our nature once again in its original condition" as God's image (10). Death is the necessary step toward that final reshaping.

A Funeral Oration for the Empress Flaccilla (Oratio funebris in Flaccillam)

Gregory's third extant funeral homily was probably given some six months later, during the winter of 386, to commemorate Theodosius' first wife, Aelia Flavia Flaccilla, who had died at the age of thirty while seeking a cure at a spa named Skotoume in Thrace. Invited by Nectarius, bishop of Constantinople, to speak at her funeral liturgy in the capital (1), Gregory again begins by evoking the general grief of the population, and confesses the difficulty of putting such grief into words. He begins by emphasizing the role the empress has played in sharing not only the public affection but the charitable projects of Theodosius (3). Turning to the unexpected tragedy of her death, he characterizes it as a massive loss for the imperial city, coming so soon after the death of her daughter Pulcheria (4–5). Gregory then attempts to describe in dramatic terms the procession that brought the empress's body, in the midst of a thunderstorm, back to Constantinople (6). Turning to the Scriptures for the consolation of Christian faith, Gregory next emphasizes (7–9) the joy, freedom, and security of life with Christ in the heavenly Kingdom, and insists that Flaccilla—known for her active works of charity—has surely

been judged worthy of that inheritance (10). In conclusion, Gregory describes three other virtues for which Flaccilla has been known: her humility, her devotion to her husband (11), and, most importantly, her zeal for Nicene orthodoxy (12). "By this," Gregory confidently asserts, "she has been brought safely to the bosom of Abraham, the father of faith, by the spring of paradise . . . under the shade of the tree of life" (12). Flaccilla has embodied, in Gregory's view, the qualities rooted in Christian faith that lead to the beginning of eschatological transformation.

Some Common Themes

The seven short works translated here, most of them quite different in character from each other, do not offer a comprehensive or systematic treatment of Christian hope. Nevertheless—along with Gregory's longest work on death and eternal life, the dialogue *On the Soul and the Resurrection*—they do present details of such a hope, which are consistent with the rest of his theology, and characteristic of his work as a profound and original Christian philosopher and rhetorician. Here are some characteristic features of Gregory's vision:

Change

In many of his works, Gregory emphasizes that all created beings, having come into existence from nothing, live constantly, by their nature, in a state of change, which can be toward either good or evil. "If they should act according to nature," he comments in his *Catechetical Discourse* (8.18), "the alteration is always for the better for them, but if they should turn aside from the straight path, a movement toward opposite things takes its place."[12] So salvation, the healing of the results of sin in human beings, is a communication

[12]Gregory of Nyssa, *Catechetical Discourse: A Handbook for Catechists*, trans. Ignatius Green, Popular Patristics Series 60 (Yonkers, NY: St Vladimir's Seminary Press, 2019), 89 (GNO III/4:35.18–23).

to humanity by Christ of a new form of such change: steady, positive growth toward greater union with God. In our present life, this comes about through constant increase in the virtues, which make us like God; after death it takes place through individual purification of the soul's choices and habits, and eventually through the resurrection of the body, the call for it to join the soul again in a renewed, spiritualized state. Even the existence of the saved in the life to come will be, as Gregory famously insists, not a state of completed goodness and happiness but of our constant growth toward an increasing share in God's perfections. "For this is truly perfection," as he suggests elsewhere: "never to stand still in growing toward what is better, nor to circumscribe perfection by any limit."[13]

Christ as the Beginning

The definitive key to this transformation of a fallen humanity toward participation in the life of God is the person, teaching, and work of *Christ*, God's incarnate Son. Gregory suggests in a number of places that God is himself archetypal virtue, and therefore that human virtue is a share in the perfection of God.[14] Jesus began the process of the transformation of humanity by living a life free from sin, as a man perfectly formed in virtue. After offering himself to the Father for humanity on the cross, Jesus is raised from the dead in his material human body, now immortal and glorious. This transformation toward a greater share in God's qualities of virtue and life is first accomplished in Jesus as the "first-fruits" of redeemed humanity, and it spreads "outward" from him to us.[15]

[13]*On Perfection* (GNO VIII/1:214.4–6); cf. also *Life of Moses*, Preface 9 (SC 1:50) and 225–26 (SC 1:262).

[14]See *Contra Eunomium* II:7.60–64 (GNO II:236.10–237.18); *On the Soul and the Resurrection* (GNO III/3:76.13–14.); *On the Beatitudes* 4 (GNO III/1:122); *Life of Moses*, Prologue 7 (SC 150.6–8); *On the Song of Songs* 9 (GNO VI:285.17).

[15]See my article, "'Heavenly Man' and 'Eternal Christ': Apollinarius and Gregory of Nyssa on the Personal Identity of the Savior," *Journal of Early Christian Studies* 10 (2002): 469–88.

Soul and Body

For this reason, however much Gregory argues at times for the role of a non-material *soul as the center* and dominating force in the life of the human person, the complete human who is to be saved always includes the body as well. In *On the Soul and the Resurrection*, he argues that the soul—which continues in existence after death, even while the body disintegrates into the material elements that originally composed it—has left its distinctive stamp on all those component fragments, and will play a key role in reassembling them at the time of resurrection.[16] The final form and condition of our material body is still unknown to us, but it will be shaped by our purified, wholly virtuous soul, and will be related to the present body as the ripe ear of corn, not yet visibly in existence, is related to its present seed.

Human Fulfillment

In Gregory's view, the goal of our existence as created, embodied intellects, made in God's image, is to be *united with God* in contemplation and love, since "everyone who pursues true virtue," as Gregory insists in the *Life of Moses*, "participates in nothing else than God."[17] So Meletius, set free from the weakness of age and the struggles of his office, is now able to "lead the philosophic life"—a life of contemplative self-restraint, focus, and dedication—in God's presence, as he joins in Christ's priestly intercession. "He has loosened the sandal of his soul, so that he might tread with pure step on the holy ground of understanding, where God is seen directly."[18] Pulcheria, as a little girl, has already recovered the original beauty of human existence in the company of Jesus, who loves children.[19] Flaccilla, the virtuous and self-effacing spouse of the emperor, shares now in Christ's kingly rule, because of her virtues and her concern

[16]See especially GNO III/3:52.3–56.5.
[17]*Life of Moses*, Prologue 7.
[18]*Homily for Meletius* 8.
[19]*Homily for Pulcheria* 5.

for orthodox faith.[20] To be united with God in such a way that one has no further wants is to become more fully oneself, and to fulfill Paul's prophecy that eventually "God will be all in all."[21]

Return to our Original Form

Gregory also clearly asserts that the final form of the human person, still unknown to us, will be *the form God originally intended* in creating us. As an enthusiastic student of Origen's works, he seems to have been inspired by Origen's sense of a dynamically developing creation, guided by God's constant providence, and by Origen's Christ-centered way of reading Scripture as a single story of salvation. But Gregory was also aware of the mounting criticisms in the late fourth century—led by Epiphanius of Salamis in the Greek-speaking world—of some aspects of Origen's theological speculation, and was careful to distance himself from what were then thought of as doctrinally suspect Origenist positions: notably from a strongly subordinationist understanding of God the Son in his relation to the Father, from the notion that the human soul is eternal—or at least that it pre-existed the material body it now animates—and from the idea that the souls of the dead might come later on to animate other bodies. Gregory clearly sees each human life as on a single, unique trajectory toward union with God, modeled on the incarnate divine existence of God the Son. Although we may not now fully guess what it entails, perfection, for each human being, is to become what God intended us to be, fully conformed to the risen Christ.[22]

Growth and Purification

Gregory assumes, in several of these works, that the progress of human beings toward union with God and bodily resurrection

[20] *Homily for Flaccilla* 10–12.
[21] See *On the Final Subjection of Christ* 12–13.
[22] See *On the Dead* 20.

necessarily involves *personal growth*, and a *purification* of our moral state and consciousness, which may need to take place after death as well as during this present life.[23] *On the Dead* insists that such purification of human affections and habits must take place either during the present life, by thoughtful self-restraint and asceticism, or else after death "by fire" (see 1 Cor. 3.13–15)—which he seems to understand here primarily as an image for the violence of death itself.[24] Like the elimination of slag from iron, such "fire" purges our minds and wills of the impurities of mixed motivation. In the treatise *On Infants*, Gregory also points to our need to have our spiritual senses purged, our inner vision healed, if we are to participate in the life of God,[25] a process that takes place either during this life or after death. So, too, the souls of infants who die without acquiring virtue, and who have shared only in "the beginning stage" of life,[26] will need to mature further "by a nourishment appropriate to contemplation"[27] before they will be able to share in the full knowledge of God. Human growth, in Gregory's view, cannot cease with bodily death.

Universal Salvation

In the judgment of many modern scholars, Gregory believes that *all human beings* will be included in this final transformation—will together be "subject" to God in the incarnate Son, as part of his Body, in the midst of a redeemed cosmos. "We have no doubt," he writes in *On the Dead* 20, "that then there will be one race including all, when all of us will become one body of Christ, formed by one shape, since the divine image will illumine us all equally." In *On the*

[23]See *On Infants* 20, where the main component of human purification and growth is seen as "acquiring every kind of virtue."

[24]*On the Dead* 18–19. Later on, he suggests that our grief over the necessity of death is itself part of the purification of our desires (21). In other works, however, Gregory emphasizes that purification from the effects of sin also can take place after death, and may last for a long time before the soul is freed to enter beatitude.

[25]*On Infants* 11.

[26] Ibid. 12.

[27]Ibid.

Final Subjection of Christ 13, Gregory elaborates on Paul's familiar image of the community as Christ's Body, taking it in a way that will include the whole of humanity and presenting this as implied by the incarnation itself:

> The one, then, who has united all of us to himself, and who is both united to us and has become one with us all in his relationship to us, makes everything that is ours his own. And the chief of all the blessings he bestows on us will be submission to God, when all creation comes to be in harmony with itself, and "Every knee will bend to him, of those in heaven and on earth and under the earth, and every tongue will confess that Jesus Christ is Lord" (Phil 2.10–11). Then, when all creation has become one body, and all have come together in him by their obedience, he will offer to the Father the obedience of his own Body to himself.

In the midst of a transformed and reconciled creation, Gregory suggests here, all humanity will become "sons and daughters in the Son," and in their submission to Christ as their head will share—consciously, dynamically, and ever more fully—in the life of God.

Brian E. Daley, S.J.

A Discourse on the Dead
(*De mortuis*)

A Note on the Text

The critical edition of the Greek text of this discourse, by Günther Heil, appears in the series *Gregorii Nysseni Opera* [GNO] IX, pp. 28–93. It draws on the preliminary editorial work of Hermann Langerbeck, who also edited other works in the GNO collection. I have also made use of the Italian translation and commentary on Heil's Greek text by Giuseppe Lozza (Torino: Società Editrice Internazionale, 1991), and I have adopted Lozza's numbering of sections in the text, for convenience in reference. For a discussion of the predominantly philosophical argumentation of the work, as well as its date, rhetorical structure, and genre, see Monique Alexandre, "Le *De mortuis* de Grégoire de Nysse," *Studia Patristica* 10 (1970): 35–43. It is difficult to assign a precise date to the work; Daniélou and Alexandre place it just before 379, while Lozza suggests "around 380" (see Maraval, "Chronology of Works," *The Brill Dictionary of Gregory of Nyssa*, 161).

GNO IX:28 PG 46:497

ΓΡΗΓΟΡΙΟΥ ΕΠΙΣΚΟΠΟΥ ΝΥΣΣΗΣ ΛΟΓΟΣ ΕΙΣ ΤΟΥΣ ΚΟΙΜΗΘΕΝΤΑΣ

Οἱ τὴν ἀναγκαίαν τῆς φύσεως ἡμῶν ἀκολουθίαν ἐν τοῖς ἐξιοῦσιν ἀπὸ τοῦ βίου συμφορὰν ποιούμενοι καὶ βαρυπενθοῦντες ἐπὶ τοῖς μεθισταμένοις ἀπὸ τοῦ τῇδε βίου πρὸς τὸν νοερὸν καὶ ἀσώματον οὔ μοι δοκοῦσιν ἐπεσκέφθαι τὴν ζωὴν ἡμῶν ἥτις ἐστίν, ἀλλὰ τὸ τῶν πολλῶν πάσχειν, οἳ διά τινος ἀλόγου συνηθείας τὸ παρὸν αὐτοῖς ὡς καλὸν ἀγαπῶσιν, οἷον δ' ἂν εἴη. καίτοι γε τὸν λόγῳ καὶ διανοίᾳ τῆς ἀλόγου φύσεως προτεταγμένον πρὸς τοῦτο μόνον τὴν ῥοπὴν ἔχειν προσῆκεν, ὃ τῇ τοῦ λόγου κρίσει καλόν τε καὶ αἱρετὸν ἀναφαίνεται, καὶ μὴ τοῦτο πάντως αἱρεῖσθαι, ὅπερ ἂν αὐτοῖς ἐκ συνηθείας τινὸς καὶ ἀκρίτου προσπαθείας ἡδύ τε καὶ καταθύμιον φαίνηται. διό μοι δοκεῖ καλῶς ἔχειν ἐπινοίᾳ τινὶ τῆς πρὸς τὸ σύνηθες αὐτοὺς διαθέσεως ἀποστήσαντα μεταγαγεῖν ὡς ἔστι δυνατὸν ἐπὶ τὴν ἀμείνω τε καὶ πρέπουσαν τοῖς λελογισμένοις
GNO 29 διάνοιαν. οὕτω γὰρ ἂν ἐξορισθείη τῆς | ἀνθρωπίνης ζωῆς ἡ σπουδαζομένη περὶ τὰ πάθη τοῖς πολλοῖς ἀλογία. γένοιτο δ' ἂν ἡμῖν ἀκόλουθος ἡ τοῦ λόγου σπουδὴ πρὸς τὴν ὑποκειμένην ὑπόθεσιν, εἰ πρῶτον μὲν τὸ ἀληθῶς ἀγαθὸν οἷόν ἐστιν ἐξετασθείη, ἔπειτα δὲ τὸ ἴδιον τῆς ἐν σώματι ζωῆς θεωρήσαιμεν, πρὸς τούτοις δὲ εἰ διὰ συγκρίσεως ἀντιπαρατεθείη τοῖς παροῦσι τὰ δι' ἐλπίδος ἡμῖν ἀποκείμενα. οὕτω γὰρ ἂν προέλθοι πρὸς τὸν σκοπὸν τοῦ λόγου ἡ θεωρία, ὥστε μετατεθῆναι τῶν πολλῶν ἀπὸ τοῦ συνήθους ἐπὶ τὸ καλὸν τὴν διάνοιαν. ἐπειδὴ γὰρ πᾶσιν ἀνθρώποις φυσική τις πρὸς τὸ καλὸν ἔγκειται σχέσις καὶ πρὸς τοῦτο κινεῖται πᾶσα

A Discourse on the Dead
(*De mortuis*)

1 Those who consider the necessary tendency of our nature, in people who have departed from this life, to be a misfortune, and who grieve deeply for those who have moved on, from living here on earth, to a spiritual life without the body, seem to me not to have examined what this life of ours is, but to be in the same state of mind as most people are, who through some irrational habit of thinking love best what is immediately before them, whatever that might be. Yet surely it befits a person who surpasses irrational nature in reason and critical understanding to be inclined toward that alone, which seems good and preferable in reason's judgment, and not just to choose what appears to them pleasant and congenial, by custom and irrational attraction. So it seems to me a good idea to try, by some sort of argument, to lead them away, as far as we can, from this inclination toward customary thinking toward a better set of assumptions—toward a kind of thinking more appropriate for rational beings. In this way, the unreasonable thoughts that preoccupy most people, as we consider the things we immoderately desire, may be banished from human life.

2 The argument we will be trying to use to realize this plan might be developed most consistently, if first of all we examine what the truly Good is, then consider what characterizes our life in the body, and then, by comparison, contrast the features of this present life with the things stored up for us in hope. In this way, our reflection may achieve the purpose of our argument, and convert popular understanding from its customary pattern toward what is best. For since a kind of natural relationship toward the Good is innate in everyone,

προαίρεσις τὸν τοῦ καλοῦ σκοπὸν πάσης τῆς κατὰ τὸν βίον
σπουδῆς προβαλλομένη, τούτου χάριν ἡ περὶ τὸ ὄντως καλὸν
ἀκρισία τὰ πολλὰ τῶν ἁμαρτανομένων εἴωθεν ἐξεργάζεσθαι, ὡς
εἴ γε πρόδηλον πᾶσιν ἦν τὸ ἀληθῶς ἀγαθόν, οὐκ ἂν ἐκείνου ποτὲ
διημάρτομεν ᾧ φύσις ἡ ἀγαθότης ἐστίν, οὐδ᾽ ἂν ἑκουσίως τῇ τῶν
PG 500 κακῶν συνηνέχθημεν πείρᾳ, | εἴπερ μὴ ἐπεκέχρωστο τὰ πράγματα
διεψευσμένῃ τινὶ τοῦ καλοῦ φαντασίᾳ. οὐκοῦν πρὸ πάντων τοῦτο
τῷ λόγῳ κατανοήσωμεν τί τὸ ἀληθῶς ἀγαθόν, ὡς ἂν μὴ τῇ περὶ
τούτου πλάνῃ σπουδασθείη ποτὲ τὸ χεῖρον ἀντὶ τοῦ κρείττονος.
φημὶ τοίνυν χρῆναι καθάπερ ὅρισμόν τινα καὶ χαρακτῆρα τοῦ
ζητουμένου προϋποθέσθαι τῷ λόγῳ, δι᾽ οὗ γένοιτ᾽ ἂν ἡμῖν ἀσφαλὴς
ἡ τοῦ καλοῦ κατανόησις.

Τίς οὖν ὁ χαρακτὴρ τῆς ἀληθινῆς ἀγαθότητος; τὸ μὴ μόνον
GNO 30 πρός τι τὸ ὠφέλιμον ἔχειν μηδὲ κατὰ καιρούς τινας ἢ | ἐπωφελὲς ἢ
ἄχρηστον φαίνεσθαι μηδέ τινι μὲν εἶναι καλὸν ἑτέρῳ δὲ οὐ τοιοῦτον,
ἀλλ᾽ ὅπερ καὶ ἐφ᾽ ἑαυτοῦ κατὰ τὴν ἰδίαν φύσιν ἐστὶ καλὸν καὶ παντὶ
καὶ πάντοτε ὡσαύτως ἔχει. οὗτός ἐστι κατά γε τὴν ἐμὴν κρίσιν
τῆς τοῦ καλοῦ φύσεως ὁ χαρακτὴρ ἀπλανής τε καὶ ἀδιάψευστος.
ὃ γὰρ μήτε πᾶσι μήτε πάντοτε μήτε ἐφ᾽ ἑαυτοῦ δίχα τῆς ἔξωθεν
περιστάσεώς ἐστι καλόν, οὐκ ἂν κυρίως ἐν τῇ τοῦ καλοῦ κρίνοιτο
φύσει. διόπερ πολλοὶ τῶν ἀνεξετάστως προσεχόντων τοῖς οὖσιν ἐν
τοῖς τοῦ κόσμου στοιχείοις εἶναι τὸ καλὸν ἐφαντάσθησαν, ὧν οὐδὲν
εὕροι τις ἂν διεξετάζων καὶ ἐφ᾽ ἑαυτοῦ καὶ πάντοτε καὶ παντὶ καλὸν
εὑρισκόμενον. μέμικται γὰρ τῷ ἀφ᾽ ἑκάστου τούτων χρησίμῳ καὶ
ἡ πρὸς τὸ ἐναντίον ἐνέργεια. οἷον τὸ ὕδωρ σωτήριον μὲν τοῖς ἐν
αὐτῷ τρεφομένοις ἐστὶν ὀλέθριον δὲ τοῖς χερσαίοις, εἰ ἐπικλύσειεν·
ὡσαύτως δὲ καὶ ὁ ἀὴρ τοῖς μὲν ἐν αὐτῷ ζῆν πεφυκόσιν ἐστὶ σωτήριος,
τοῖς δὲ τὸν ἔνυδρον εἰληχόσι βίον φθαρτικὸς εὑρίσκεται καὶ ὀλέθριος,

and since every choice we make is directed toward this, as we put the goal of the Good ahead of all the other interests in our lives, our failure to judge rightly what is truly good is therefore the usual cause of our misdeeds.[1] If what is truly good were perfectly clear to everyone, we would never be mistaken about the One who is by nature Goodness itself,[2] nor would we willingly be enticed by our experience of evil things, if they were not colored by the deceptive appearance of being good. Therefore, let us try first of all to establish by rational argument what is truly good, lest, through our being mistaken about this, we seek what is less good in place of what is better. So I suggest that we need to lay down at the start of the essay a kind of definition or description of what we are looking for, through which we can be assured of a clear recognition of the Good.

3 What, then, is the mark of true goodness? It is not simply to be useful for some purpose, nor just to seem useful at some times and useless at others, nor to be good for one person but not so for someone else; rather, it is to be something good in itself and for everyone, by its own nature, and something that always remains this way. In my judgment, at least, this is the unchanging, unmistakable mark of the nature of goodness; for what is *not* good for everyone, or always, or by itself, apart from external circumstances, cannot properly be thought to share in the nature of the Good. That is why many people who focus on things in an unreflective way imagine that the Good is to be found among the material elements of the world—none of which a careful investigator would discover to be good in itself, or always good, or good for everyone. For mixed in with the useful results of each of these things is also the opposite effect. Water, for example, a source of life for beings nurtured in it, is destructive for land-dwelling creatures if they are immersed in it. Similarly, air is life-giving for creatures who normally live in it, but damaging and

[1]Gregory here articulates the classical Greek philosophical understanding—going back to Plato (e.g., *Protagoras* 352c), of why humans consciously do wrong: they are mistaken about where the really good option lies, in a particular situation.

[2]Presumably God, who is the author of the moral law.

ὅταν ἐν αὐτῷ τι γένηται τῶν ὑποβρυχίων· οὕτω καὶ τὸ πῦρ πρός τι
χρήσιμον ἡμῖν γινόμενον φθαρτικόν ἐστιν ἐν τοῖς πλείοσι, καὶ αὐτὸν
δὲ τὸν ἥλιον εὕροι τις ἂν οὔτε παντὶ οὔτε πάντοτε οὔτε κατὰ πάντα
καλὸν τοῖς μετέχουσιν· ἔστι γὰρ ἐν οἷς καὶ σφόδρα γίνεται βλαπτικὸς
ὑπερζέων τε τοῦ καθήκοντος μέτρου καὶ ξηραίνων ἐν ἀμετρίᾳ τὸ
ὑποκείμενον καὶ νοσώδεις αἰτίας πολλάκις ἐξεργαζόμενος καὶ τοῖς
ἐμπαθεστέροις τῶν ὀφθαλμῶν προσεπιτρίβων τὴν νόσον καὶ διὰ
τῆς σήψεως τῶν ὑγρῶν βλαβερά τε καὶ ἀηδῆ τινα ζωογονῶν ἐν τῇ
κατεφθαρμένῃ τῶν ὑγρῶν σηπεδόνι. οὐκοῦν καθὼς εἴρηται μόνον
GNO 31 ἐκ πάντων ὡς καλὸν προαιρεῖσθαι χρὴ ὃ | πάντοτε καὶ πᾶσιν ὁμοίως
ἐν τῇ τοῦ καλοῦ καθορᾶται φύσει ἀεὶ τοιοῦτον ὂν καὶ οὐ πρὸς τὰς
ἔξωθεν περιστάσεις μεταβαλλόμενον. περὶ γὰρ τῶν ἄλλων ὅσα
κατά τινα πρόληψιν ἀλογωτέραν καλὰ τοῖς ἀνθρώποις δοκεῖ, περὶ
σῶμά τέ φημι καὶ τὰ ἔξωθεν οἷον ἰσχύς τε καὶ κάλλος καὶ γένους
λαμπρότης χρήματά τε καὶ δυναστεῖαι καὶ περιφάνειαι καὶ πάντα τὰ
τοιαῦτα, ὡς αὐτόθεν πᾶσιν ὄντα φανερὰ σιωπᾶν οἶμαι χρῆναι καὶ
μὴ μάτην διὰ τῶν ὁμολογουμένων ὄχλον ἐπεισάγειν τῷ λόγῳ. τίς
γὰρ οὐκ οἶδε τοῦ κάλλους τε καὶ τῆς δυνάμεως τὸ ὠκύμορον ἢ τῆς
δυναστείας τὸ εὐμετάπτωτον ἢ τῆς δόξης τὸ ἀνυπόστατον ἢ τὴν
ματαίαν πρὸς τὰ χρήματα τῶν ἀνθρώπων προσπάθειαν, παρ᾽ ὧν διὰ
τὸ εὔχρουν τε καὶ τὸ σπάνιον ἐν ποιαῖς ὕλαις τὸ καλὸν ἐνομίσθη;
τούτων δὲ οὕτως ἡμῖν διηρθρωμένων σκεπτέον ἂν εἴη περὶ τῆς
παρούσης ζωῆς (ταύτης φημὶ δὴ τῆς διὰ σαρκὸς ἐνεργουμένης)
PG 501 εἴτε τοιοῦτόν ἐστιν ὡς ἐν τῷ χαρα|κτῆρι τοῦ καλοῦ θεωρεῖσθαι εἴτε
καὶ ὡς ἑτέρως ἔχει. τὸ γὰρ εὑρισκόμενον περὶ αὐτῆς ὑπὸ τοῦ λόγου
ὁδηγήσει πάντως τὴν τῶν ἐπεσκεμμένων διάνοιαν ὅπως χρὴ περὶ
τὴν ἐνθένδε μετάστασιν ἔχειν.

fatal for creatures whose lot is life in the water, if any of these swimmers should come into it. So fire, too, which is so useful to us for certain purposes, is still destructive in most situations. One might say that even the sun is not good for everything exposed to it, nor good at all times, or in every way; for in some situations it becomes very harmful, heating material beyond the appropriate limit and drying it out by its excess, often acting as a source of disease or inflicting irritation on the more sensitive parts of the eyes, or through the putrefaction of moist bodies giving rise to harmful and disgusting organisms in the resulting rotten wetness.

4 Therefore, as we have said, we must choose as good, from all the possibilities, only what is recognized to display the nature of goodness always and to all alike—what always remains so, and does not alter according to external circumstances. Concerning the other things, which seem good to people by some less-than-reasonable preconceptions—concerning the body, I mean, and externals like strength and beauty and distinguished ancestry, money and power and fame and all such things—we should, I think, be silent, as being points obvious to everyone from the start, and not add unnecessary complication to our argument by speaking of things we already agree on. For who does not realize how short-lived beauty or power is, how easily power collapses, how insubstantial glory is, how vain the human attachment is to wealth—even though goodness is attributed to some material things simply because of their lovely color and rarity?[3]

But since we have made these distinctions, we ought to examine this present life—I mean the life realized now through the flesh: whether it is the kind of thing that should be recognized as characterized by the Good, or whether it, too, is something else. For what our reason discovers about the present life will probably guide our critical understanding of the subject under discussion toward the attitude we should properly have concerning our departure from this world.

[3]Gregory seems to be thinking here of gold, silver, and precious stones.

Ἔστι τοίνυν ἡ τοῦ σώματος ἡμῶν ζωὴ πλήρωσίς τε καὶ κένωσις διχόθεν ἐνεργουμένη, ἡ μὲν διὰ βρώσεώς τε καὶ πόσεως, ἡ δὲ διὰ τῆς τοῦ ἀέρος ὁλκῆς τε καὶ ἀποποιήσεως, ὧν ἄνευ ἡ κατὰ σάρκα ζωὴ συστῆναι φύσιν οὐκ ἔχει. τότε γὰρ τοῦ ζῆν ὁ ἄνθρωπος παύεται, ὅταν ἡ τῶν ἐναντίων τούτων διαδοχὴ μηκέτι διοχλῇ
GNO 32 τὴν φύσιν· ἵσταται | γὰρ μετὰ τοῦτο καθόλου ἡ τοιαύτη ἐνέργεια οὐδενὸς τῶν ἔξωθεν ἐν τοῖς νεκρωθεῖσιν οὔτε εἰσρέοντος οὔτε ἀπογινομένου, ἀλλὰ πρὸς τὰ συγγενῆ στοιχεῖα τοῦ ἐκ τούτων συνεστηκότος σώματος διακριθέντος καὶ ἀναλύσαντος. ἠρεμεῖ τὸ λοιπὸν δι᾽ ἡσυχίας ἡ φύσις τῷ οἰκείῳ στοιχείῳ προσαναπαύσασα τὸ συγγενὲς καὶ ὁμόφυλον, τῇ γῇ τὸ γεῶδες καὶ τῷ ἀέρι τὸ ἴδιον καὶ τῷ ὑγρῷ τὸ οἰκεῖον καὶ τῷ θερμῷ τὸ κατάλληλον. μηκέτι γὰρ τοῦ ὄγκου τοῦ ἐκ τῶν ἑτερογενῶν συνεστηκότος βιαίως τε καὶ κατηναγκασμένως συμπεπλεγμένου, ἀλλὰ κατ᾽ ἐξουσίαν ἑκάστου τῶν ἐν ἡμῖν πρὸς τὴν οἰκείαν ἑστίαν ἐπανελθόντος παύεται τὸ ἀπὸ τούτου ἡ φύσις συνέχουσα βιαίως ἐν ἑαυτῇ τῶν ἀλλοφύλων τὴν συμφυΐαν. εἰ δέ τις καὶ τὸν ὕπνον καὶ τὴν ἐγρήγορσιν πρὸς τὸ τῆς ζωῆς ταύτης εἶδος μετὰ τῶν εἰρημένων παραλαμβάνοι, οὐκ ἔξω τῆς ἀληθείας τὸν λόγον ποιήσεται. κάμνει γὰρ καὶ διὰ τούτων ἡ φύσις ἀεὶ πρὸς τὰ ἐναντία μεθελκομένη καὶ νῦν μὲν λυομένη τῷ ὕπνῳ πάλιν δὲ τονουμένη διὰ τῆς ἐγρηγόρσεως, δι᾽ ὧν ἀμφοτέρων πρὸς τὸ κενοῦσθαι καὶ πληροῦσθαι παρασκευάζεται. εἰ τοίνυν πλήρωσίς τε καὶ κένωσις τῆς ζωῆς ἡμῶν ἐστι τὸ ἰδίωμα, καλῶς ἂν ἔχοι τὸν προρρηθέντα περὶ τῆς τοῦ καλοῦ κρίσεως χαρακτῆρα νῦν ἀντεξετάσαι τοῖς τῆς ζωῆς ἰδιώμασιν, ὥστε κατιδεῖν εἴτε τὸ ἀληθινόν ἐστιν ἀγαθὸν ἡ ζωὴ αὕτη εἴτε καὶ ἄλλο παρὰ τοῦτο.

5 The life of our body, in fact, is a matter of filling and emptying, realized in two distinct ways: one focused on food and drink, the other on the drawing-in and breathing-out of air; without either of them, life in the flesh cannot maintain our nature in existence. A human being ceases to live when these opposing functions we have inherited no longer offer resistance to the forces of nature. For when that happens, the active working of the body stops completely; nothing from outside enters or leaves a dead person, but his body, composed of material elements, is broken up and dissolved into the related matter around it. From then on, its nature is still and at rest, allowing each element to settle in with what belongs to its own genus and species—the earthy to the earth, and the corresponding elements to air and water and heat. Our bulk, which has come together from a variety of components, is at present knit into a single entity by a kind of [inner] force and compulsion; but each part of us later returns, however it can, to its own position [in the cosmos], and nature, from then on, ceases to hold together this unity of different elements in dynamic cohesion.[4] And if one considers sleep and waking in their relationship to this form of life as we have described it, one will not be directing one's reasoning away from the truth. For nature is strained by constantly being drawn by these tensions in opposite directions, and now is relaxed in sleep, now braced for action by waking; it is prepared by both of them for the process of emptying and filling.

If, then, filling and emptying [the stomach and lungs] is the characteristic mark of our life, it would be a good idea to examine now the shape of what we have already said about judging the Good by these familiar features of life, so as to determine whether this present life is the true Good, or whether it is something else besides this.

[4]Gregory gives a similar, if somewhat more detailed, description of the dissolution of the elements of the material body at death in his dialogue *On the Soul and the Resurrection* (GNO III/3:27.19–31.15; PG 46:44A ln. 12–48B ln. 13; PPS 12:67–69). Clearly the soul is that "alien force" that holds the fragments of various material elements in the living body together in a single organic, functioning whole (GNO III/3:13.14–15).

ὅτι μὲν οὖν καθ' ἑαυτὴν ἡ πλήρωσις οὐκ ἂν εἰκότως ἐν τῇ τοῦ
GNO 33 καλοῦ φύσει κριθείη, | πᾶσι δῆλον τὸ τοιοῦτόν ἐστιν ἐκ τοῦ καὶ
τὸ ἐναντίον αὐτῇ (λέγω δὲ τὸ κενοῦσθαι) καλὸν εἶναι νομίζεσθαι.
ἐπὶ γὰρ τῶν ἀλλήλοις ἐκ τοῦ ἐναντίου ἀντικαθεστηκότων οὐκ
ἔστι δυνατὸν τὸν τοῦ καλοῦ λόγον ἐπίσης τοῖς ἀντικαθεστῶσιν
ἁρμόζεσθαι, ἀλλ' εἰ τοῦτο καλὸν εἴη κατὰ τὴν ἑαυτοῦ φύσιν, τὸ
ἀντικείμενον αὐτῷ πάντως ἔσται κακόν. ἀλλὰ μὴν ἐνταῦθα ἐπίσης
παρ' ἑκατέρου τούτων τὸ χρήσιμον ἡ φύσις ἔχει. οὐκ ἄρα τὸν
τοῦ καλοῦ ὁρισμὸν δέξασθαι δυνατῶς ἔχει οὔτε ἡ πλήρωσις οὔτε
ἡ κένωσις. οὐκοῦν ἄλλο τι παρὰ τὸ ἀγαθὸν ἀποδέδεικται εἶναι
ἡ πλήρωσις. οὔτε γὰρ παντὶ οὔτε πάντοτε οὔτε κατὰ πᾶν εἶδος
αἱρετὸν εἶναι τὸ τοιοῦτον παρὰ πάντων ὡμολόγηται. οὐ μόνον γὰρ
τὸ ἐν τοῖς βλαπτικοῖς γενέσθαι τὸν κόρον ἐστὶν ὀλέθριον, ἀλλὰ
καὶ τὸ ἐν τοῖς καταλλήλοις παρελθεῖν τῇ ἀμετρίᾳ τὸ χρήσιμον
κινδύνων πολλάκις καὶ διαφθορᾶς αἴτιον γίνεται. καὶ εἴ ποτε
πληθωρικῆς καταστάσεως ἐπιζητούσης τὴν κένωσιν ἄλλη τις
πληθώρα τὴν οὖσαν ἐπιφορτίσειεν, σωρεία γίνεται κακῶν τὸ
τοιοῦτον εἰς ἀνήκεστα προιοῦσα πάθη. οὐκοῦν οὔτε παντὶ οὔτε
πάντως ἀγαθόν τί ἐστιν ἡ πλήρωσις, ἀλλὰ καὶ πρός τι καί ποτε
καὶ κατὰ τὸ ποσόν τε καὶ τὸ ποιὸν τὸ ἐξ αὐτοῦ γίνεται χρήσιμον.
PG 504 | οὕτω δ' ἄν τις εὕροι καὶ τὸ ἐξ ἐναντίου νοούμενον (τὸ κατὰ τὴν
κένωσιν λέγω) καὶ κινδυνῶδες τοῖς ὑπομένουσιν, εἰ παρέλθοι τῇ
ἀμετρίᾳ τὸ χρήσιμον, καὶ πάλιν οὐκ ἀνονήτως γινόμενον, εἰ πρός τι
τῶν ὠφελούντων συμβαίνοι τοῦ τε καιροῦ καὶ τοῦ ποσοῦ καὶ τοῦ
ποιοῦ συμπαραλαμβανομένου πρὸς τὸ τῆς κενώσεως χρήσιμον.
ἐπειδὴ τοίνυν οὐ συμβαίνει πρὸς τὸν τοῦ καλοῦ χαρακτῆρα τὸ τῆς
GNO 34 ζωῆς ταύτης εἶδος ᾧ | βιοτεύομεν, ὁμολογούμενον ἂν εἴη διὰ τῆς
τῶν εἰρημένων ἀκολουθίας ὅτι οὐδενὸς ἀγαθοῦ χωρισμός ἐστιν ἡ
ἐκ τοῦ τοιούτου βίου μετάστασις. φανερὸν γὰρ ὅτι τὸ ἀληθινῶς
καὶ κυρίως καὶ πρώτως ἀγαθὸν οὔτε κένωσίς ἐστιν οὔτε πλήρωσις,

That being filled, by itself, would probably not be judged to be this in nature as a whole—this should be clear to everyone from the fact that its opposite (I mean being emptied) is also considered a good thing. For with things that are related to each other as opposites, it is impossible to apply the term "good" equally to both opposed things; if one thing is good by its very nature, surely what is opposed to it is evil. But in this case, nature benefits equally from both alternatives. So neither filling nor emptying [ourselves] can possibly constitute the definition of the Good. Being full, then, is necessarily something else than the Good itself; everyone would agree that it should not be thought of as the chief goal for everyone, at all times, and in every way. Not only is the sense of surfeit caused by eating dangerous foods harmful, but even going beyond healthy limits, by lack of moderation in appropriate foods, often endangers health and causes damage. And if one is in a full state, one that calls for evacuation, but then, by eating another full meal, instead adds to the burden already felt, this sets in motion a chain of ills, leading to unbearable suffering. So then, filling oneself is clearly not a good thing for everyone, or in all circumstances, but what is in itself beneficial comes to be a good in relation to the circumstances: at certain times, and depending on its quantity and quality.[5] In the same way, one might find that what is thought to be the opposite (I speak of evacuation) is also harmful to those who experience it, when this action, which is itself beneficial, becomes excessive; but again, it turns out to be not unprofitable, if it should coincide with those beneficial circumstances of time and quantity and quality that join with it to produce evacuation's useful effect.

When, therefore, the form of this life we lead does not reflect the shape of the Good, all would agree, as a consequence of what we have been saying, that departure from such a life is not in itself a separation from anything good. For it is obvious that what is truly and precisely and primordially Good is neither emptying nor filling

[5]Gregory alludes here to Aristotle's famous list of the "categories" of predication: see *Categories* 4 (1b25–2a3), and passim.

ἅπερ καί ποτε καὶ πρός τι καὶ ἐπί τινων ἀποδέδεικται χρήσιμα, οἷς οὐκ ἔπεστιν ὁ τοῦ ἀληθῶς ὄντος ἀγαθοῦ χαρακτήρ.

Ἐπεὶ οὖν τῷ ἀληθῶς ἀγαθῷ πρὸς τὸ μὴ ἀληθῶς ἀγαθόν ἐστιν ἡ ἀντίθεσις, ἄμεσος δὲ τῶν δύο τούτων ἡ ἐναντίωσις, ἀκόλουθον ἂν εἴη τοῖς χωριζομένοις τοῦ μὴ ἀληθῶς ὄντος καλοῦ πρὸς τὸ τῇ φύσει καλὸν ἐνθένδε πιστεύειν τὴν μετάστασιν γίνεσθαι, ὃ πάντοτε καὶ παντὶ καὶ διὰ πάντων ἐστὶν ἀγαθὸν οὔτε κατὰ καιροὺς οὔτε πρός τι οὔτε ἐπί τινων οὔτε διά τι, ἀλλ' ἀεὶ κατὰ τὰ αὐτὰ καὶ ὡσαύτως ἔχον. πρὸς τοῦτο τοίνυν μέτεισιν ἀπὸ τῆς σαρκώδους ζωῆς ἡ ἀνθρωπίνη ψυχή, ἄλλην τινὰ βίου κατάστασιν ἀντὶ τῆς παρούσης μεταλαμβάνουσα, ἣν δι' ἀκριβείας μὲν ἰδεῖν ἥτις ἐστὶ τοῖς ἔτι τῇ σαρκὶ συγκεκραμένοις ἀμήχανον, ἐκ δὲ τῆς τῶν κατὰ τὸν βίον τοῦτον γνωριζομένων ὑπεξαιρέσεως δυνατόν ἐστι στοχασμόν τινα δι' ἀναλογίας ἀναλαβεῖν. οὐκέτι γὰρ ἔσται σωματικῇ παχύτητι συμπεπλεγμένη οὔτε τῇ ἰσοκρατίᾳ τῶν ἀντιστοιχούντων ἐμβιοτεύουσα, ὧν ἡ ἰσόρροπος πρὸς ἄλληλα μάχη τὴν σύστασίν τε ἡμῶν καὶ τὴν ὑγίειαν ποιεῖ (ὁ γὰρ πλεονασμὸς
GNO 35 | τῶν ἐναντίων τινὸς καὶ ἡ ὕφεσις πάθος καὶ ἀρρώστημα τῆς φύσεως γίνεται), ἐν ᾗ οὐδὲν οὔτε συστέλλεται κενούμενον οὔτε δυσφορεῖ φορτιζόμενον, ἀλλὰ καὶ τῶν ἐκ τοῦ ἀέρος ἀηδῶν ἔξω παντάπασι γίνεται (κρύους τε λέγω καὶ θάλπους) καὶ πάντων τῶν κατὰ τὸ ἐναντίον νοουμένων ἀπηλλαγμένη, ἐν ἐκείνοις δὲ γινομένη, ὅπου πάντων τῶν ἀναγκαίων καμάτων ἐλευθέρα τε καὶ ἄνετός ἐστιν ἡ ζωή, οὐ διὰ γεωργίας κακοπαθοῦσα οὐ τοὺς διαποντίους ὑπομένουσα πόνους οὐ διὰ τῆς ἐμπορίας <τε καὶ> καπηλείας ἀσχημονοῦσα οἰκοδομικῆς τε καὶ ὑφαντικῆς καὶ τῆς τῶν βαναύσων τεχνῶν ταλαιπωρίας κεχωρισμένη Ἤρεμόν τινα καὶ ἡσύχιον διάγει βίον καθὼς ὁ Παῦλός φησιν, οὐχ ἱππομαχοῦσα οὐ ναυμαχοῦσα οὐ συστάδην διὰ τῆς πεζικῆς παρατάξεως

ourselves. We have shown them simply to be beneficial for certain people, depending on time and circumstances; these things do not share in the characteristics of what is truly Good.

6 Since, then, there is direct opposition between what is truly good and what is *not* truly good, and the antithesis of the two is absolute, it would be logical to believe that for those who are removed from what is not truly good, there immediately takes place a transferal to what *is* naturally good—what is good always and for everyone and in every situation, not just at certain times or relatively to something else, or for some people or some reason, but which always remains as it is, and in the same way. The human soul, then, moves on to this from life in the flesh, receiving another level of life in place of the present one;[6] it is impossible for those still mingled with flesh to see exactly what this is, but one can construct a kind of proportioned guess, by imagining away those features that we recognize as belonging to this present life. For it [i.e., the soul] will no more be bound by the clumsiness of the body, nor have to live among elements that oppose each other with equal force, and struggle to balance each other in the way that constitutes our survival and health—for the dominance of one of the opposites and the defeat of the other makes for disease and natural weakness. In that [future] life, the soul will not be reduced by emptying, nor will it suffer because of excess, and it will also be completely untouched by the noxious qualities of the atmosphere, such as cold and heat. Liberated from everything that can be thought to oppose it, it will find itself in circumstances where life is free and unburdened by all necessary labors; it will suffer no harm from working in the fields, will not undergo the labors of the seaman's life, will not be troubled by the merchant's trade, will be free from the pressure of the builder's or the weaver's or the mechanic's art, but will live "a calm and peaceful way of life," as Paul puts it (1 Tim 2.2), not fighting on horseback or on a ship, not engaging

[6]Gregory here begins to imagine what eternal life might be like, mainly by describing it in negative terms as a life free from the evils and limitations of present human existence.

συμπλεκομένη οὐ πρὸς κατασκευὴν ὅπλων ἀσχολουμένη οὐ φόρους ἐκλέγουσα οὐ τάφρους καὶ τείχη κατασκευάζουσα, ἀλλὰ πάντων τῶν τοιούτων ἀτελής τίς ἐστι καὶ ἐλευθέρα μήτε ἔχουσα πράγματα μήτε παρέχουσα, ἐν ᾗ δουλεία τε καὶ κυριότης καὶ πενία καὶ πλοῦτος εὐγένειά τε καὶ δυσγένεια καὶ ἰδιωτικὴ ταπεινότης καὶ ἀξιωματικὴ δυναστεία καὶ πᾶσα τοιαύτη ἀνωμαλία χώραν οὐκ ἔχει. παραιρεῖται γὰρ πάντων τούτων καὶ τῶν τοιούτων τὴν ἀνάγκην τὸ ἀνενδεὲς τῆς ζωῆς ἐκείνης καὶ ἄϋλον, ἐν ᾗ τὸ διακρατοῦν τῆς ψυχῆς τὴν ὑπόστασιν οὐ ξηροῦ τε καὶ ὑγροῦ τινός ἐστι μετουσία, ἀλλ᾽ ἡ τῆς θείας φύσεως κατανόησις, ἀντὶ δὲ τοῦ ἐναερίου
PG 505 πνεύματος | τοῦ | ἀληθινοῦ τε καὶ ἁγίου πνεύματος εἶναι τὴν
GNO 36 κοινωνίαν οὐκ ἀμφιβάλλομεν. ὧν ἡ ἀπόλαυσις οὐκ ἐνηλλαγμένη καθ᾽ ὁμοιότητα τοῦ τῇδε βίου διὰ ἕξεως καὶ στερήσεως γίνεται εἰσκρινομένη τε καὶ ἀποποιουμένη, ἀλλ᾽ ἀεὶ πληρουμένη καὶ οὐδέποτε περιγράφουσα κόρῳ τὴν πλήρωσιν. ἀβαρὴς γὰρ ἡ νοερὰ τρυφὴ καὶ ἀπλήρωτος πάντοτε ταῖς ἐπιθυμίαις τῶν μετεχόντων ἀκορέστως ἐπιπλημμυροῦσα. διὰ τοῦτο μακαρία τίς ἐστιν ἐκείνη ἡ ζωὴ καὶ ἀκήρατος μηκέτι ταῖς τῶν αἰσθητηρίων ἡδοναῖς πρὸς τὴν τοῦ καλοῦ κρίσιν ἐμπλανωμένη. τί τοίνυν ἐστὶ σκυθρωπὸν ἐν τῷ πράγματι δι᾽ ὃ τῇ μεταστάσει τῶν ἐπιτηδείων ἐπιστυγνάζομεν; εἰ μὴ τοῦτό τις ἄρα λυπηρὸν ἡγεῖται ὅτι πρὸς τὸν ἀπαθῆ τε καὶ ἀνενόχλητον βίον αὐτοῖς ἡ μετάστασις γίνεται, ὃς οὔτε πληγῶν ὀδύνας προσίεται οὐ πυρὸς δέδοικεν ἀπειλὴν οὐ τὰ διὰ σιδήρου τραύματα οὐ τὰς ἀπὸ σεισμῶν καὶ ναυαγιῶν καὶ αἰχμαλωσιῶν συμφορὰς οὐ τὰς τῶν ὠμοβόρων θηρίων προσβολὰς οὐ τὰ τῶν ἑρπυστικῶν τε καὶ ἰοβόλων κέντρα καὶ δήγματα, ἐν ᾧ οὐδεὶς οὔτε ἐξογκοῦται τῷ τύφῳ οὔτε πατεῖται ἐν ταπεινότητι οὔτε ὑπὸ θράσους ἐκθηριοῦται οὔτε ὑπὸ δειλίας καταπτοεῖται οὔτε τῇ ὀργῇ περιοιδαίνει ζέων τῷ θυμῷ καὶ μαινόμενος οὔτε κλονεῖται ὑπὸ τοῦ φόβου ἀντισχεῖν πρὸς τὴν τοῦ κρατοῦντος ὁρμὴν οὐ δυνάμενος,

in hand-to-hand combat in an infantry formation, not laboring to keep weapons ready, not paying taxes, not digging ditches or building walls. Rather, the soul will live as one unburdened from all such things and free, neither having nor losing property—through which servitude and lordship are determined, poverty and wealth, noble and base birth, the ordinary citizen's humble state and the aristocrat's power—all such inequality will have no more place! The freedom from want, the immateriality of that life will make all these things, and everything like them, no longer inevitable. In that life, what supports the personal survival of the soul will not be its share in anything dry or moist, but knowledge of the divine nature; and we will know unmistakably that what we inhale is a share not in the air we breathe here, but a share in the true, Holy Spirit.

The enjoyment of those blessings will not be experienced in give-and-take, as in this life, or marked by passionate desire and deprivation, as things enter us and leave us; it will always be complete, and will never limit its own fullness by the experience of excess. Our spiritual nourishment there will not weigh us down, and without leading to satiation will always overflow the insatiable appetites of those who share in it. For this reason, that life will be something blessed and pure, something never distracted, in its judgments of the Good, by the pleasures of the senses. What is there, then, that truly should make us downcast, what reason is there for being distressed, about this change in the conditions of life? Think, at least, of this: who would consider it sad that a transition is being offered them to a life free of suffering and trouble, a life not open to painful blows; which has no fear of the threat of fire, nor of wounds from the sword, nor of being harmed by earthquakes or shipwrecks or captivity, nor of the attacks of carnivorous beasts, nor of the stings and bites of serpents or venomous creatures; where no one is puffed up by pride[7] or walks in humble obscurity; where no one is made savage by rashness or cowers back in fear; where no one swells in fury,

[7]Gregory turns now to imagine the moral freedom of life after death, in which virtue will be at the heart of a transformed human existence.

ἐν ᾧ φροντὶς οὐκ ἔστιν, οἷα τῶν βασιλέων τὰ ἤθη τίνες αἱ νομοθεσίαι
GNO 37 οἷοι τὸν τρόπον οἱ ἐπὶ τῶν ἀρχῶν τεταγμένοι οἷα τὰ διαγράμ-|
ματα πόσος ὁ ἐτήσιος φόρος οὔτε εἰ πολλὴ γέγονεν ἐπομβρία
κατακλύζουσα τῇ ἀμετρίᾳ τὸ γεωργούμενον οὔτε εἰ χάλαζα τὰς
ἐλπίδας τῶν γεωπόνων ἠχρείωσεν οὔτε εἰ αὐχμὸς ἐπικρατήσας
ἀποξηραίνει πᾶν τὸ φυόμενον. ἀλλὰ καὶ τῶν λοιπῶν τοῦ βίου
κακῶν πᾶσαν ἄδειαν ἔχει· ὀρφανίας τε γὰρ τὸ σκυθρωπὸν οὐ λυπεῖ
τὴν ζωὴν ἐκείνην, τὰ ἐκ χηρείας κακὰ χώραν οὐκ ἔχει, ἀργοῦσι δὲ
καὶ αἱ πολύτροποι τοῦ σώματος ἀρρωστίαι, οἵ τε κατὰ τῶν
εὐημερούντων φθόνοι καὶ αἱ κατὰ τῶν δυσπραγούντων ὑπεροψίαι
καὶ πάντα τὰ τοιαῦτα τῆς ζωῆς ἐκείνης ἐξώρισται, ἰσηγορία δέ τις
καὶ ἰσονομία διὰ πάσης ἐλευθερίας εἰρηνικῆς τῷ τῶν ψυχῶν δήμῳ
συμπολιτεύεται ἐκεῖνο ἑκάστου ἔχοντος ὅπερ ἂν ἑαυτῷ ἑτοιμάσῃ
ἐκ προαιρέσεως. εἰ δέ τι χεῖρον ἔκ τινος ἀβουλίας τινὶ
παρασκευασθείη ἀντὶ τοῦ κρείττονος, ἀναίτιος τῶν τοιούτων ὁ
θάνατος κατ᾽ ἐξουσίαν τὸ δοκοῦν ἑλομένης τῆς προαιρέσεως.
ὑπὲρ τίνος οὖν δυσχεραίνουσιν οἱ θρηνοῦντες τὸν ἀποιχόμενον;
καὶ μὴν εἰ μὴ παντάπασιν ἐκαθάρευεν πάσης ἐμπαθοῦς διαθέσεως
ὁ συναποδυσάμενος τὴν ἡδονήν τε καὶ τὴν λύπην μετὰ τοῦ
σώματος, ἐκεῖνος ἂν δικαιότερον τοὺς περιόντας ἐθρήνησεν, οἳ
ταὐτὸν πάσχουσιν τοῖς ἐν δεσμωτηρίῳ διάγουσιν, οὓς ἡ πρὸς τὰ
σκυθρωπὰ συνήθεια καὶ ἡ συντροφία τοῦ ζόφου προσηνές τε καὶ
GNO 38 ἄλυπον τὸ παρὸν νομίζειν ἐποίησεν. καὶ | τυχὸν κἀκεῖνοι τοῖς τῆς
φυλακῆς ἐκβαλλομένοις ἐπιστυγνάζουσιν ἀγνοίᾳ τῆς φαιδρότητος
τῆς ἐκδεχομένης τοὺς ἀπαλλάγεντας τοῦ ζόφου. εἰ γὰρ ᾔδεσαν τὰ
ἐν ὑπαίθρῳ θεάματα τό τε αἰθέριον κάλλος καὶ τὸ οὐράνιον ὕψος
καὶ τὰς τῶν φωστήρων αὐγὰς τήν τε τῶν ἀστέρων χορείαν καὶ

boiling with rage, and no one shakes with terror, unable to resist the attack of the powerful? Where there is no need to worry about the moods of kings; about the laws that have been passed, or the integrity of bureaucrats, or of calculating one's annual taxes; or whether heavy rains will flood the crops in their excess, or hailstorms nullify the hopes of husbandmen, or a dominant drought parch all growing things? It will also be a life marked by complete freedom from fearing life's other misfortunes: the sadness of being orphaned does not cloud that life, the evils of widowhood have no place there, and the many forms of bodily illness are no longer a threat; envy of the prosperous, contempt for the impoverished, and all such attitudes are banned from that life; equal right to speak and equal protection of the law, enjoyed in full and peaceful freedom, will characterize the common life of that city of souls, and each one will possess what he has chosen to acquire for himself. And if some person's lot there should seem to him, through a kind of thoughtlessness, to be less good than it might be, death is not the cause of such a fate; our free choice can embrace at will what seems best.[8]

7 Why, then, do mourners lament the one who has passed away? Surely if the one who has stripped off pleasure and pain, along with the body, has not completely purged himself of the ability to share others' sorrow, *he* would have a better right to grieve for his survivors, whom, like long-term prisoners, habitual sadness and familiarity with darkness lead to consider their situation easy and not unpleasant. Perhaps, too, mourners are sad for those who have been released from detention, because they [i.e., the mourners] are themselves unaware of the splendor that awaits people freed from the darkness. If they knew what is to be seen in the region above the earth—its ethereal beauty, the height of the heavenly spaces and the rays of the heavenly lights, the dancing of the stars, the sun's orbits

[8]In this eloquent and powerful reflection on the ideal human life, Gregory visualizes the existence of the blessed as one of individual virtue, peaceful and egalitarian community life, and radical freedom, as well as of personal satisfaction. Many of the Cappadocian Fathers' longstanding ethical and political ideals are echoed here.

<τὰς> περιόδους ἡλιακὰς καὶ τὸν σεληναῖον δρόμον καὶ τὴν
PG 508 πολυειδῆ | τῆς γῆς ἐν τοῖς βλαστήμασιν ὥραν καὶ τὴν ἡδεῖαν τῆς
θαλάσσης ὄψιν ἐν ἡλιοειδεῖ τῇ αὐγῇ δι' ἠρεμαίου τοῦ πνεύματος
γλαφυρῶς ἐπιφρίσσουσαν τῶν τε κατὰ τὰς πόλεις οἰκοδομημάτων
τὰ κάλλη τά τε ἴδια καὶ τὰ δημόσια, δι' ὧν αἵ λαμπραί τε καὶ
πολυτελεῖς τῶν πόλεων καλλωπίζονται, εἰ ταῦτα τοίνυν ᾔδεσαν
καὶ τὰ τοιαῦτα οἱ ἐντεχθέντες τῷ δεσμωτηρίῳ, οὐκ ἂν τοὺς ἐκ τῆς
φυλακῆς προαγομένους ὡς ἀγαθοῦ τινος χωριζομένους
ἀπωλοφύροντο. ὅπερ οὖν εἰκὸς τοὺς ἔξω τοῦ δεσμωτηρίου περὶ
τῶν ἔτι καθειργμένων διανοεῖσθαι ὡς ἐλεεινῇ προσταλαιπωρούντων
ζωῇ, τοῦτο μοι δοκοῦσι καὶ οἱ τῆς τοῦ βίου τούτου φυλακῆς ἔξω
γενόμενοι, εἴπερ ὅλως δυνατὸν ἦν αὐτοῖς διὰ δακρύων ἐνδείξασθαι
τὴν πρὸς τοὺς κακοπαθοῦντας συμπάθειαν, θρηνεῖν καὶ δακρύειν
τῶν ἐν ταῖς ὀδύναις τοῦ βίου τούτου παρατεινομένων ὅτι μὴ ὁρῶσι
τὰ ὑπερκόσμιά τε καὶ ἄϋλα κάλλη, θρόνους τε καὶ ἀρχὰς καὶ
GNO 39 ἐξουσίας καὶ κυριότητας καὶ στρατιὰς ἀγγελικὰς καὶ | ἐκκλησίας
ὁσίων καὶ τὴν ἄνω πόλιν καὶ τὴν ὑπερουράνιον τῶν
ἀπογεγραμμένων πανήγυριν. τὸ γὰρ ὑπερκείμενον τούτων κάλλος,
ὃ τοὺς καθαροὺς τῇ καρδίᾳ βλέπειν ὁ ἀψευδὴς ἀπεφήνατο λόγος,
κρεῖττόν τε πάσης ἐλπίδος ἐστὶ καὶ τῆς ἐκ στοχασμῶν εἰκασίας
ἀνώτερον. οὐ τοῦτο δὲ μόνον στεναγμῶν τε καὶ λύπης ἄξιον ἀφ'
ἡμῶν τοῖς μεταστᾶσιν ἂν ἐνομίσθη, ἀλλ' ὅτι τοσούτων ἀλγεινῶν
περικειμένων τῷ βίῳ τοσαύτη τις ἐνέστηκεν αὐτοῖς ἡ περὶ τὰ
μοχθηρὰ συνδιάθεσις, ὥστε οὐχ ὡς ἀναγκαίαν τινὰ λειτουργίαν
τὴν προσβολὴν αὐτῶν φέρουσιν, ἀλλ' ὅπως ἂν εἰς τὸ διηνεκὲς
παραμένοι ταῦτα τὴν σπουδὴν ποιοῦνται. ἡ γὰρ περὶ τὰς δυναστείας
τε καὶ πλεονεξίας καὶ τὰς ἀπολαυστικὰς ταύτας λαιμαργίας
ἐπιθυμία καὶ εἴ τι ἄλλο τοιοῦτον σπουδάζεται ὧν χάριν καὶ ὅπλα
καὶ πόλεμοι καὶ ἀλληλοφονίαι καὶ πᾶσα ἡ ἑκουσίως ἐνεργουμένη

and the moon's course; and if they knew the multiform beauty of the earth in its fruits, the lovely sight of the sea in brilliant sunlight, subtly stirred by a gentle breeze, the beauty of buildings, public and private, in our cities, which adorn the most illustrious and splendid of them—if they kept these things in mind, and others like them, while locked in their prisons, they would not be loudly lamenting those released from prison, as if they had been deprived of some good thing.[9]

What those who have come out of prison probably think about the ones still confined there—as people made miserable by a wretched way of life—seems to me, in all likelihood, to be what those will think who have gone beyond this life's confinement (provided it is possible at all for them to show compassion by their tears for those suffering misfortune, or to mourn and weep for those held fast in the miseries of this life), because those here do not see the immaterial beauty beyond this world: the thrones and dominations and lordships,[10] the angelic armies and gatherings of the saints, the city on high and the assembly of those whose names are written down there, above the heavens.[11] For the beauty that lies beyond all this, which the Word that cannot deceive has told us the pure of heart will gaze at,[12] is better than all our hope and higher than all comparisons we might guess at. This is not the only thing that those who have left us might have thought worthy of groans and sadness in our case; there is also the fact that despite the great woes surrounding this present life, still such a deep attraction toward these evils has been imbued in us human beings that we do not simply put up with their threats, as a kind of necessary servitude, but keep eagerly trying to make them last forever. Lust for power and possessions and other forms of sensuous self-indulgence, and desire for whatever else of this sort people strive after, for the sake of which there are arms and war and

[9]Gregory seems to be inspired here, and in the following paragraph, by Plato's famous "allegory of the cave," in Book 7 of the *Republic* (514b–521b).

[10]See Col 1.16.

[11]See Heb 12.23.

[12]See Mt 5.8.

ταλαιπωρία καὶ δολιότης, οὐδὲν ἄλλο ἢ σωρεία τίς ἐστι συμφορῶν
ἐκ προαιρέσεως μετὰ σπουδῆς τε καὶ προθυμίας ἐπεισαγομένη τῷ
βίῳ. ἀλλὰ δακρύων μὲν ἐν τοῖς κατοιχομένοις πάθος οὐκ ἔστιν ὅτι
μηδ᾽ ἄλλο τι πάθος, νοῦς δὲ καὶ πνεῦμα τυγχάνοντες οἱ σαρκὸς
ἀπηλλαγμένοι καὶ αἵματος τοῖς τῇ παχύτητι τοῦ σώματος
ἐγκεχωσμένοις ὀφθῆναι φύσιν οὐκ ἔχουσιν οὐδὲ νουθετῆσαι δι᾽
ἑαυτῶν τοὺς ἀνθρώπους ἀποστῆναι τῆς πεπλανημένης περὶ τῶν
ὄντων κρίσεως. οὐκοῦν ὁ νοῦς ἡμῖν ὁ ἡμέτερος ἀντ᾽ ἐκείνων
διαλεχθήτω καὶ εἴπωμεν ὡς ἔστι δυνατὸν ἔξω τῶν σωμάτων τῇ
διανοίᾳ γενόμενοι καὶ τῆς πρὸς τὴν ὕλην προσπαθείας τὴν ψυχὴν
GNO 40 ἀποστήσαντες ὅτι | „Ὦ ἄνθρωπε, πᾶς ὁ μετέχων τῆς φύσεως,
Πρόσεχε σεαυτῷ κατὰ τὸ Μωυσέως παράγγελμα καὶ γνῶθι
σεαυτὸν ἀκριβῶς τίς εἶ, διαστείλας τῷ λογισμῷ τί μὲν ἀληθῶς εἶ
σύ, τί δὲ περὶ σὲ καθορᾶται. μήποτε τὰ ἔξω σοῦ βλέπων σεαυτὸν
καθορᾶν νομίσῃς. μάθε παρὰ τοῦ μεγάλου Παύλου τοῦ δι᾽
ἀκριβείας ἐπεσκεμμένου τὴν φύσιν, ὅς φησι τὸν μὲν ἔξωθεν ἡμῶν
εἶναι ἄνθρωπον τὸν δὲ ἔσωθεν, κἀκείνου φθειρομένου τοῦτον
ἀνακαινίζεσθαι. μὴ τοίνυν τὸ φθειρόμενον βλέπων σεαυτὸν οἰηθῇς
PG 509 βλέπειν (ἔσται | μὲν γάρ ποτε κἀκεῖνο φθορᾶς ἐλεύθερον, ὅταν ἐν
τῇ παλιγγενεσίᾳ τὸ θνητόν τε καὶ διαλυτὸν μετασκευασθῇ πρὸς τὸ
ἀθάνατόν τε καὶ ἀδιάλυτον, ἀλλὰ τό γε νῦν ῥέει καὶ διαπίπτει, καὶ
φθείρεται τὸ ἔξωθεν ἡμῶν προφαινόμενον). οὐκοῦν οὐ πρὸς τοῦτο
χρὴ βλέπειν, ὅτι μηδὲ πρὸς ἄλλο τι προσήκει τῶν βλεπομένων
ὁρᾶν οὕτως εἰπόντος τοῦ Παύλου ὅτι Μὴ σκοπούντων ἡμῶν τὰ
βλεπόμενα ἀλλὰ τὰ μὴ βλεπόμενα· τὰ γὰρ βλεπόμενα πρόσκαιρα

---

[13]From here through the end of chapter 20, Gregory makes his point about the relationship of soul and body by means of the rhetorical device of "personification" (προσωποποιΐα, *prosōpopoiia*)—an imagined address by the rational soul (νοῦς, *nous*) to all of embodied humanity.

[14]See Deut 15.9.

murder, and all the trouble and deceit we willingly set in motion, is all nothing but a kind of chain of misfortunes, introduced into our life by our free choice and pursued with eager seriousness. But the propensity for tears no longer remains in those who have departed, nor indeed any other passion; and those who have been freed from flesh and blood, being now simply mind and spirit, do not have a nature that can be seen by those cast in the thick mold of a body, nor can they, on their own, urge human beings to move away from making an erroneous judgment about what is real.

8 In their stead, then, let our Mind engage us in conversation, and let us affirm that it is possible for us to move outside our bodies in critical thought, and so to separate our souls from attachment to matter:[13]

"O humans, each of you who shares this nature, examine yourself according to the command of Moses,[14] and know yourselves[15] accurately as you are—distinguishing in your reflection between what you truly are, and what can be perceived as connected with you. Never think that by looking at what is outside of you, you will see into yourself. Learn from the great Paul, when he examined our nature precisely, and said there is in us an 'outer man' and an 'inner man,' and while the former decays, the latter is renewed.[16] Do not imagine, then, that in looking at the decaying man you are looking at yourself (even though there will be a time when that [outer man], too, will be free from decay—when, in the restoration, what is mortal and corruptible will be changed into what is immortal and incorruptible; but for now, it flows away and collapses, and our outward appearance is corrupted). So we must not look to this existence, but rather it behooves us to look toward another reality; so Paul says, 'We look not to the things that are seen, but to what is unseen; for what is seen

[15]Gregory here uses the familiar Greek phrase attributed to the Pythagorean school of philosophy: "Know yourself" (γνῶθι σαυτόν, *gnōthi sauton*). He seems to be deliberately placing the Greek tradition of philosophical wisdom alongside Moses' call for self-examination in Deuteronomy.

[16]2 Cor 4.16.

τὰ δὲ μὴ βλεπόμενα αἰώνια, ἀλλ' ἐπὶ τὸ ἀόρατον τῶν ἐν ἡμῖν τρέψαντας τὴν θεωρίαν ἐκεῖνο πιστεύειν ἀληθῶς εἶναι ἡμᾶς, ὃ διαφεύγει τὴν αἰσθητικὴν κατανόησιν.

Γενώμεθα τοίνυν κατὰ τὸν παροιμιώδη λόγον Ἑαυτῶν ἐπιγνώμονες. τὸ γὰρ ἑαυτὸν γνῶναι καθάρσιον τῶν ἐκ τῆς ἀγνοίας πλημμελημάτων γίνεται. ἀλλ' οὐκ ἔστι ῥᾴδιον ἑαυτὸν κατιδεῖν τόν γε ἀληθῶς ἑαυτὸν ἰδεῖν βουλόμενον μή τινος ἐπινοίας δυνατὸν
GNO 41 ποιούσης ἡμῖν τὸ ἀδύνατον. ὅπερ γὰρ | ἐπὶ τῶν σωματικῶν ὀφθαλμῶν ἡ φύσις ἐποίησεν, οἳ πάντα τὰ ἄλλα βλέποντες ἑαυτῶν ἀθέατοι μένουσιν, τὸν αὐτὸν τρόπον καὶ ἡ ψυχὴ πάντα τὰ ἄλλα διερευνωμένη καὶ τὰ ἔξω ἑαυτῆς πολυπραγμονοῦσα καὶ ἀνιχνεύουσα ἑαυτὴν ἰδεῖν ἀδυνάτως ἔχει. οὐκοῦν ὅπερ ἐπὶ τῶν ὀφθαλμῶν γίνεται τοῦτο καὶ ἡ ψυχὴ μιμησάσθω. καὶ γὰρ κἀκεῖνοι ἐπειδὴ οὐκ ἔστιν αὐτοῖς ἐκ φύσεως δύναμις πρὸς τὴν ἑαυτῶν θεωρίαν τὴν ὀπτικὴν ἐνέργειαν ἐπαναστρέψαι καὶ ἑαυτοὺς κατιδεῖν ἐν κατόπτρῳ τὸ εἶδός τε καὶ τὸ σχῆμα τοῦ ἰδίου θεασάμενοι κύκλου διὰ τῆς εἰκόνος ἑαυτοὺς καθορῶσιν. οὕτως χρὴ καὶ τὴν ψυχὴν πρὸς τὴν ἰδίαν ἀπιδεῖν εἰκόνα καὶ ὅπερ ἂν ἴδῃ ἐν τῷ χαρακτῆρι ᾧ ἀφωμοίωται, ὡς ἴδιον ἑαυτῆς τοῦτο θεάσασθαι. ἀλλὰ μικρὸν ὑπαλλάξαι τι προσήκει τοῦ ὑποδείγματος, ἵνα οἰκειωθῇ τῷ λόγῳ τὸ νόημα· ἐπὶ μὲν γὰρ τῆς ἐν τῷ κατόπτρῳ μορφῆς ἡ εἰκὼν πρὸς τὸ ἀρχέτυπον σχηματίζεται, ἐπὶ δὲ τοῦ τῆς ψυχῆς χαρακτῆρος τὸ ἔμπαλιν νενοήκαμεν· κατὰ γὰρ τὸ θεῖον κάλλος τὸ τῆς ψυχῆς εἶδος ἀπεικονίζεται. οὐκοῦν ὅταν πρὸς τὸ ἀρχέτυπον ἑαυτῆς βλέπῃ ἡ ψυχή, τότε δι' ἀκριβείας ἑαυτὴν καθορᾷ.

Τί τοίνυν ἐστὶ τὸ θεῖον ᾧ ἡ ψυχὴ προσωμοίωται; οὐ σῶμα οὐ σχῆμα οὐκ εἶδος οὐ πηλικότης οὐκ ἀντιτυπία οὐ βάρος οὐ τόπος οὐ χρόνος οὐκ ἄλλο τι τοιοῦτον οὐδὲν δι' ὧν ἡ ὑλικὴ κτίσις γνωρίζεται, ἀλλὰ πάντων τούτων καὶ τῶν τοιούτων ὑφαιρεθέντων

is transient, but what is not seen is eternal.'[17] So in turning our contemplation toward the invisible reality that is in us, we should believe that this is truly what we are: what escapes the grasp of our senses.

9 "Let us become, then, according to the proverb, people who 'know themselves.'[18] For knowing ourselves is a way of purifying ourselves of the mistakes that arise from ignorance. But it is not easy for one who truly wants to know himself to achieve that self-knowledge completely, unless some mental construction makes the impossible possible for us. For as nature has done in the case of our physical eyes, which see everything else but cannot see themselves, so the soul, too, investigates all other things, researching and tracking down things outside itself, but it remains incapable of seeing itself. Therefore, the soul must imitate what happens with the eyes. For since they do not have the power by nature to turn their optic activity within and see themselves, in order to contemplate what they are, they gaze on their form, their rounded shape, in a mirror, and see themselves by means of an image. So the soul, too, must gaze at its own image, and see as proper to itself what it sees in that shape by which it is represented.

"But it seems appropriate to change our example briefly, so that the idea can be adapted better to our argument. For in the case of the shape in a mirror, the image is formed to correspond to the original; but we recognize that the opposite happens with the shaping of the soul: the form of the soul, in fact, is an imitation of the divine beauty. So when the soul gazes on its own archetype, it sees itself in an accurate way.

10 "What, then, is this divine reality that the soul resembles? It is not a body, not a shape, not a form, not magnitude, not resistance, not weight, not place, not time, not any other thing of this kind, by which material creation is recognized; but with all of these and

[17] 2 Cor 4.18.

[18] For a thorough study of the long use of this phrase in the later Greek philosophical and theological tradition, see Pierre Courcelle, *Connais-toi toi-même: de Socrate à saint Bernard*, 3 vols (Paris: Études augustiniennes, 1974–1975).

νοερόν τι καὶ ἄϋλον καὶ ἀναφὲς καὶ ἀσώματον καὶ ἀδιάστατον χρὴ
πάντως νοεῖν τὸ λειπόμενον. εἰ τοίνυν τοιοῦτος ὁ χαρακτὴρ τοῦ
ἀρχετύπου καταλαμβάνεται, ἀκόλουθον πάντως κατὰ τὸ εἶδος
GNO 42 ἐκεῖνο μεμορφωμένην | τὴν ψυχὴν διὰ τῶν αὐτῶν χαρακτήρων
ἐπιγνωσθῆναι, ὥστε καὶ ταύτην ἄϋλόν τε εἶναι καὶ ἀειδῆ καὶ
νοερὰν καὶ ἀσώματον.

Λογισώμεθα τοίνυν πότε μᾶλλον τῷ ἀρχετύπῳ κάλλει
προσεγγίζει ἡ ἀνθρωπίνη φύσις, ἐν τῷ διὰ σαρκὸς ζῆν ἢ ὅταν ἔξω
ταύτης γενώμεθα. ἀλλὰ παντὶ δῆλον τὸ τοιοῦτόν ἐστιν, ὅτι ὥσπερ
PG 512 ἡ σὰρξ | ὑλώδης οὖσα τῇ ὑλικῇ ταύτῃ ζωῇ προσῳκείωται, οὕτω καὶ
ἡ ψυχὴ τότε μετέχει τῆς νοερᾶς καὶ ἀΰλου ζωῆς, ὅταν τὴν
περιέχουσαν αὐτὴν ὕλην ἀποτινάξηται. τί οὖν ἐν τούτοις συμφορᾶς
ἐστιν ἄξιον; εἰ μὲν γὰρ σῶμα ἦν τὸ ἀληθῶς ἀγαθὸν, δυσχεραίνειν
ἡμᾶς ἔδει πρὸς τὴν τῆς σαρκὸς ἀλλοτρίωσιν ὡς ἐκπιπτόντων ἡμῶν
ἐκείνου συναποβαλλομένης πάντως μετὰ τοῦ σώματος καὶ τῆς
πρὸς τὸ ἀγαθὸν οἰκειότητος. ἐπειδὴ δὲ νοερόν τε καὶ ἀσώματον τὸ
ὑπὲρ πᾶσαν ἔννοιαν ἀγαθὸν οὗ κατ' εἰκόνα γεγόναμεν, ἀκόλουθον
ἂν εἴη πεπεῖσθαι, ὅταν διὰ τοῦ θανάτου πρὸς τὸ ἀσώματον
μεταβαίνωμεν, προσεγγίζειν ἐκείνῃ τῇ φύσει ἣ πάσης σωματικῆς
παχυμερείας κεχώρισται, καὶ οἷόν τι προσωπεῖον εἰδεχθὲς τὴν
σαρκώδη περιβολὴν ἐκδυομένους εἰς τὸ οἰκεῖον ἐπανιέναι κάλλος,
ἐν ᾧ κατ' ἀρχὰς ἐμορφώθημεν κατ' εἰκόνα τοῦ ἀρχετύπου
γενόμενοι. ἡ δὲ τοιαύτη διάνοια εὐφροσύνης οὐ κατηφείας γένοιτ'
ἂν τοῖς λεγομένοις ὑπόθεσις, ὅτι τὴν ἀναγκαίαν ταύτην λειτουργίαν

[19]Gregory develops this same comparison of the soul's presence in the body—the human "microcosm"—to God's presence and activity within the whole universe (the "macrocosm") in *On the Soul and the Resurrection* (PG 46:28B ln. 10–C ln. 15; GNO III/3:13.10–14.6). On the insufficiency of the term, "microcosm" to denote the human soul, see *De hominis opificio* 16.1

[20]In one of the earliest Greek manuscripts of this work—*Vaticanus Graecus* 2066, from the ninth or tenth century (which the editor, Günther Heil, designates as manuscript F)—the text from here to the first sentence of chapter 17 below is replaced

all things like them removed, one must surely understand what remains to be something intelligible, immaterial, impalpable, bodiless, and without extension. If, then, the character of the original is understood to be of this kind, surely it follows that the soul, formed in that image, must be recognized by the same characteristics: so it, too, must be immaterial and without shape and intellectual and incorporeal.[19]

11 "Let us consider, then, when human nature will come closer to the beauty of its archetype: through its fleshly life, or when it lives apart from the flesh.[20] But something like this will be clear to everyone: just as the flesh, being material, is adapted to this fleshly existence, so the soul, too, will then share in the intelligible and immaterial life, when it shakes off the matter that contains it. What should we consider a misfortune, when this happens? For if the body were what is truly Good, we would have to lament our being distanced from it, because, in departing from it, our relationship to the Good would surely be destroyed, along with the body. But since that Good beyond all comprehension, in whose image we are formed, is intelligible and incorporeal, it would be a logical consequence to believe that when, through death, we are transferred to a bodiless existence, we will approach that nature that is separated from all bodily clumsiness; and putting off the wrapping of flesh like an ugly mask, we will ascend to our own proper beauty, in which we were formed in the beginning, and come to be conformed to the shape of our archetype.

"This understanding ought to be a joyful, not a sad discovery for those left behind:[21] that the human person, having fulfilled this

by a much briefer summary, apparently intended to "sanitize" Gregory's doctrine by affirming the bodily resurrection in a more traditional form, while eliminating his allusion to universal salvation in chapter 15. See the introduction to Lozza's translation, pp. 22–24.

[21]I have followed here editor Hermann Langerbeck's suggested emendation of τοῖς λεγομένοις (*tois legomenois*), "in what we have said"—the reading that appears in the manuscripts—to τοῖς λειπομένοις (*tois leipomenois*), "for those left behind," which seems to fit the context better.

ἀποπληρώσας ὁ ἄνθρωπος οὐκέτι ἐν ἀλλοτρίοις ζῇ ἀποδοὺς μὲν ἑκάστῳ τῶν στοιχείων τὸ ἴδιον ὃ παρ' αὐτῶν ἠρανίσατο, εἰς δὲ τὴν οἰκείαν αὐτῷ καὶ κατὰ φύσιν ἐπανελθὼν ἑστίαν τὴν καθαρὰν καὶ
GNO 43 ἀσώματον. ξένη γάρ τίς ἐστιν ὄντως καὶ ἀλλοδαπὴς τῇ | ἀσωμάτῳ φύσει ἡ τοῦ σώματος ὕλη, ᾗ κατ' ἀνάγκην ὁ νοῦς ἐν τῇ ζωῇ ταύτῃ συμπεπλεγμένος ἐνταλαιπωρεῖ τῷ ἀλλοφύλῳ βίῳ συνδιαιτώμενος. τῆς γὰρ τῶν στοιχείων πρὸς ἄλληλα συμπλοκῆς ὥσπερ τινῶν ἀλλογλώσσων τε καὶ ἀπεξενωμένων τοῖς ἤθεσιν ἀνθρώπων ἐκ διαφόρων ἐθνῶν ἕνα δῆμον ἀναπληρούντων βεβιασμένη τε καὶ ἀσύμφωνος γίνεται ἡ κοινωνία, ἑκάστου πρὸς τὸ συγγενὲς καὶ οἰκεῖον ὑπὸ τῆς ἰδίας φύσεως ἀφελκομένου. ὁ δὲ νοῦς ὁ τούτοις ἐγκεκραμένος ἀσύνθετος ὢν ἐν ἁπλῇ τε καὶ μονοειδεῖ τῇ φύσει ἐν ξένοις καὶ ἀλλοτρίοις ζῇ ἀσύμφυλος ὢν τῷ περιέχοντι αὐτὸν ἐκ τῶν στοιχείων δήμῳ, ὃς τῇ πολυμερείᾳ τῇ σωματικῇ δι' ἀνάγκης τινὸς ἐνσπειράμενος τὴν ἑαυτοῦ φύσιν βιάζεται τοῖς ἀλλοφύλοις ἑνούμενος. τῶν δὲ στοιχείων πρὸς τὴν ἀπ' ἀλλήλων διάλυσιν φυσικῶς ἐπὶ τὸ συγγενές τε καὶ οἰκεῖον ἀφελκομένων ἀνιᾶται κατ' ἀνάγκην λυομένης τε καὶ σχιζομένης τῆς συμφυΐας ἡ αἴσθησις· συνανιᾶται δὲ τῇ αἰσθήσει τὸ διανοητικὸν τῆς ψυχῆς πρὸς τὸ ἀεὶ λυποῦν ἐκ συνηθείας ἐπικλινόμενον. τότε οὖν ὁ νοῦς δυσφορῶν τε καὶ ἀνιώμενος παύεται, ὅταν ἔξω γένηται τῆς μάχης τῆς ἐν τῇ συμπλοκῇ τῶν ἀντιστοιχούντων συνισταμένης. ἐπειδὰν γὰρ ἢ τὸ ψυχρὸν ἡττηθῇ τοῦ θερμοῦ κατισχύσαντος ἢ τὸ ἔμπαλιν φύγῃ τὸν πλεονασμὸν τῆς ψύξεως ἡ θερμότης, τῷ τε ξηρῷ διὰ τῆς ἐπικρατήσεως τὸ ὑγρὸν ὑποχωρήσῃ ἢ διαλυθῇ τοῦ ξηροῦ τὸ

necessary time of service, no longer lives in a foreign land, but is giving back to each of the elements the particular materials it has borrowed from them, and is ascending to the pure and bodiless region that is naturally its home. For the matter of the body is truly an alien thing, foreign to the incorporeal nature; the mind is necessarily intermingled with it in this present life, and passes its time in wretchedness, sharing the fate of a different kind of life altogether. The shared relationship of elements woven together with each other has something forced and jarring about it, like human beings of different native languages and foreign customs, coming from different ethnic backgrounds, who must live as one people; each of them is naturally drawn back to what is properly its own kind.[22] But the mind, which is mingled with these elements, not being composite, lives on in its simple and uniform nature in the midst of strange, foreign objects, not belonging to the same tribe as the crowd of material elements that contains it; being sown into bodily composition by some necessity, it undergoes stress in its own nature when living together with things of alien origin. But when the elements, at the moment of [the body's] dissolution, are naturally drawn away, each to what is related to it and proper to its own kind, sense-perception necessarily grieves, since their unity is being destroyed and broken up; and the rational part of the soul, too, grieves then along with the senses, being inclined, by force of its long habit, to grieve forever. The soul only ceases to mourn and grieve at that point when it comes to be outside the struggle caused by the engagement of opposing forces. For when cold is overcome by the superior strength of the warm, or—conversely—when warmth flees the dominance of coolness; when what is moist yields place to the dry because of its dominance, or the solidity of the dry is dissolved in an excess of moisture; then,

[22]See above, chapter 5 and n. 6 (p. 7). In this treatise, Gregory seems to assume that the present constitution of the human person, as a soul coordinating and ordering a body made of many material components, has something strained and artificial about it. This is not the impression he gives in *On the Soul and the Resurrection*, where the harmony of both aspects of the human person is constantly stressed, and where each is seen as incomplete without the other..

πάγιον ἐν τῷ πλεονασμῷ τῆς ὑγρότητος—τότε τοῦ ἐν ἡμῖν
πολέμου διὰ τοῦ θανάτου λυθέντος εἰρήνην ὁ νοῦς ἄγει καταλιπὼν
GNO 44 | τὸ τῆς μάχης μεταίχμιον, τὸ σῶμα λέγω, καὶ τῆς τῶν στοιχείων
πρὸς ἄλληλα παρατάξεως ἔξω γενόμενος καθ' ἑαυτὸν ζῇ
PG 513 πεπονηκυῖαν ἐν τῇ τοῦ σώ|ματος συμπλοκῇ τὴν ἰσχὺν ἑαυτοῦ δι'
ἡσυχίας ἀναλαμβάνων. "Ταῦτα τοίνυν καὶ τὰ τοιαῦτα τοῖς ἐν τῷ
σώματι ζῶσιν ὁ νοῦς διαλέγεται μονονουχὶ φωνὴν ἀφιεὶς ὅτι „Ὦ
ἄνθρωποι, οὔτε ἐν οἷς ἐστε ἀκριβῶς οἴδατε, καὶ εἰς ὅτι μεταχωρήσετε
οὔπω ἐπίστασθε. τὸ μὲν γὰρ παρὸν οἷον τῇ φύσει ἐστὶν, οὔπω
ἐξευρεῖν ὁ λόγος δεδύνηται, ἀλλὰ πρὸς μόνην τὴν τοῦ ζῆν
συνήθειαν βλέπει μὴ δυνάμενος γνῶναι, τίς ἡ τοῦ σώματος φύσις
τίς ἡ τῶν αἰσθήσεων δύναμις τίς ἡ τῶν ὀργανικῶν μελῶν διασκευὴ
τίς ἡ τῶν σπλάγχνων οἰκονομία τίς ἡ αὐτοκίνητος τῶν νεύρων
ἐνέργεια πῶς τῶν ἐν ἡμῖν τὸ μὲν εἰς ὀστέου πήγνυται φύσιν, τὸ δὲ
εἰς τὴν φωτοειδῆ τοῦ ὀφθαλμοῦ αὐγὴν οὐσιοῦται πῶς ἐκ τῆς αὐτῆς
τροφῆς καὶ τοῦ αὐτοῦ πόματος τὸ μὲν εἰς τρίχας λεπτύνεται, τὸ δὲ
εἰς ὄνυχας τοῖς ἀκροῖς τῶν δακτύλων ἐπιπλατύνεται ἢ πῶς ἀεὶ τὸ
ἐγκάρδιον ἀναφλέγεται πῦρ διὰ τῶν ἀρτηριῶν ἐφ' ἅπαν τὸ σῶμα
διαφερόμενον ἢ πῶς τὸ πινόμενον, ἐπειδὰν ἐν τῷ ἥπατι γένηται,
μεταβάλλει καὶ τὸ εἶδος καὶ τὴν ποιότητα διά τινος ἀλλοιώσεως
αὐτομάτως ἐξαιματούμενον. ὧν ἁπάντων ἡ γνῶσις μέχρι τοῦ
παρόντος ἐστὶν ἀπόρρητος, ὡς ἀγνοεῖν ἡμᾶς τὴν ζωὴν ἐν ᾗ
βιοτεύομεν. τὸν δὲ τῆς αἰσθήσεως κεχωρισμένον βίον οἱ τῇ
αἰσθήσει συζῶντες ἀδυνατοῦσι καθόλου θεάσασθαι. πῶς γὰρ ἄν
τις δι' αἰσθήσεως ἴδοι τὸ ἔξω τῆς αἰσθήσεως; ἀμφοτέρων τοίνυν
τῶν βίων ὁμοίως ἀγνοουμένων, τούτου μὲν διὰ τὸ πρὸς μόνον τὸ
GNO 45 φαινόμενον | βλέπειν ἡμᾶς, ἐκείνου δὲ διὰ τὸ μὴ καθικνεῖσθαι τὴν
αἴσθησιν, τί πεπόνθατε, ὦ ἄνθρωποι, τούτου μὲν ὡς ἀγαθοῦ

---

[23]The notion of a constant tension, even a dynamic conflict, between tiny particles of the basic elements of material reality was common to many schools of philosophy in the ancient world, and was first popularized by the speculative fifth-century Sicilian poet Empedocles.

with the war within us ended by death, the soul lives on in peace, having left the battlefield (that is, the body), and the opposition between the elements, behind. Moving beyond them, it lives for itself, recovering in rest its own strength, which had become worn out by its involvement with the body."[23]

12 This is the kind of address the Mind makes to those living in the body, speaking almost audibly in words like these: "Human beings, you do not precisely realize the conditions you are living in, and have not yet grasped that reality into which you will be transformed. Reason cannot yet fully investigate what our present existence naturally is, but considers only the life to which it is accustomed; it cannot understand what the nature of the body is,[24] or the power of the senses, the arrangements of our various organic parts, the functioning of our intestines, the spontaneous activity of our nervous system; it cannot grasp how part of our growing material structure takes on the form of bone, another part is shaped into the light-transmitting ray of the eye, or how—from the same food and the same drink—some matter is spun out into hair, some is spread out over the ends of fingers as nails, or how the heart constantly spreads heat through the arteries to reach the whole body, or how what we drink, when it reaches the liver, changes form and quality, by some transformative process, and on its own becomes blood. Knowledge of all of this cannot be fully explained, up to now, so that we are ignorant of the life in which we spend our days.

"Those whose life is constantly associated with sense-perception are generally unable to imagine a life apart from sensation. How can one know through perception what lies outside of its range? And since both forms of life are equally unknown to us—the unseen because we look only at appearances, the seen because our senses are insufficient for the task—what is the effect on you, O men and women? You cling to the one [i.e., sensible reality] as a good, even

[24]Gregory embarks here on a detailed reflection on how the body functions, showing—as in many of his works—an extensive acquaintance with the Greek medical literature of his time.

περιεχόμενοι καίτοι ἀγνοουμένου, ἐκεῖνον δὲ δεδοικότες καὶ
φρίττοντες ὡς χαλεπὸν καὶ φόβου ἄξιον δι᾽ οὐδὲν ἄλλο ἢ διὰ
τοῦτο μόνον ὅτι ἀγνοεῖται οἷόν ἐστι; καίτοι πολλὰ καὶ ἄλλα καὶ
τῶν κατ᾽ αἴσθησιν ἡμῖν προφαινομένων καὶ ἀγνοουμένων οὐ
δεδοίκαμεν. τίς γὰρ ἡ φύσις τῶν κατ᾽ οὐρανὸν φαινομένων ἢ τί τὸ
περιάγον τῶν πόλων ἐξ ἐναντίου τὴν κίνησιν ἢ τί τὸ ἐρεῖδον τὴν
τῆς γῆς παγιότητα, πῶς δὲ ἡ ῥευστὴ τῶν ὑδάτων φύσις ἀεὶ γίνεται
ἐκ τῆς γῆς καὶ οὐ δαπανᾶται ἡ γῆ καὶ ἄλλα τοιαῦτα πολλὰ οὔτε
ἐγνώκαμεν οὔτε φόβων ἀξίαν τὴν ἄγνοιαν κρίνομεν. ἀλλὰ καὶ
αὐτὴν τὴν πάντα νοῦν ὑπερβαίνουσαν φύσιν τὴν θείαν τε καὶ
μακαρίαν καὶ ἀκατάληπτον ὅτι μὲν ἔστι πεπιστεύκαμεν, ἐν τίνι δὲ
αὐτῆς τὸ εἶναι καταλαμβάνεται οὔπω τις εὑρέθη διὰ στοχασμοῦ
κατανόησις, καὶ ὅμως ἀγαπῶμεν τὸ ἀγνοούμενον ἐξ ὅλης καρδίας
τε καὶ ψυχῆς καὶ δυνάμεως τὸ καταληφθῆναι τοῖς λογισμοῖς οὐ
δυνάμενον. διὰ τί τοίνυν ἐπὶ μόνου τοῦ μετὰ τὴν ζωὴν ταύτην
ἐκδεχομένου ἡμᾶς βίου ὁ ἄλογος οὗτος συνίσταται φόβος διὰ
μόνην τὴν ἄγνοιαν δεδοικότων ἡμῶν ὃ οὐκ οἴδαμεν, καθάπερ ἐπὶ
τῶν νηπίων γίνεται τῶν πρὸς τὰς ἀνυποστάτους ὑπονοίας
δειματουμένων; ὁ γὰρ πρὸς τὴν ἀλήθειαν τῶν ὄντων ἐθέλων
βλέπειν πρῶτον ἐν περινοίᾳ τοῦ πράγματος γίνεται, εἶτα οἷόν ἐστι
κατὰ τὴν φύσιν ἐπιλογίζεται εἴτε τι χρηστὸν καὶ εὐπρόσιτον εἴτε
GNO 46 χαλεπόν τι καὶ ἀποτρόπαιον· | τὸ δὲ ἄδηλον καθόλου καὶ
ἀγνοούμενον πῶς ἄν τις τῶν νοῦν ἐχόντων χαλεπὸν εἶναι κρίνοι
PG 516 τὴν τῆς συνηθείας | ἀναχώρησιν μόνην ὡς πυρός τινος ἢ θηρίου
προσβολὴν ὑποπτεύων; καίτοι παιδευόμεθα διὰ τοῦ βίου σαφῶς
μὴ πάντοτε πρὸς τὴν συνήθειαν βλέπειν, ἀλλὰ πρὸς τὸ καλὸν ταῖς
ἐπιθυμίαις ἀεὶ μετατίθεσθαι. οὔτε γὰρ διὰ παντὸς ἐν ἐμβρύῳ τοῖς
πλασσομένοις ἐστὶν ἡ ζωή, ἀλλ᾽ ἕως ἂν ἐν τοῖς σπλάγχνοις ὦσιν,

---

[25]I.e., the life of the soul by itself, after the death of the body.

[26]Gregory here alludes to the understanding of the motions of the earth current in the Greek cosmology of his day; see Aristotle, *On the Heavens* 285b9.

though you don't understand it, while you fear and shrink from the other[25] as something hard and frightening, for no other reason but that its nature is unknown. Yet many other things, even things that appear in our sense world, which we still do not understand, we do not fear. What, after all, is the nature of heavenly phenomena? What regulates the opposing motion of the poles?[26] What keeps in its place the solid mass of the earth, and how is it that the fluid nature of water always comes out of the earth, while earth is not consumed by it? There are many other such things that we do not understand, yet we do not judge our ignorance of them a reason to fear. But as for the divine and blessed nature, which exceeds all understanding and is beyond our grasp, we believe that it exists, but no explanation, even an approximate one, has yet been found for what its nature is understood to be. Even so, we love this Unknown 'with all our heart and soul and strength,'[27] although it cannot be grasped by our reasoning.

"Why, then, does this irrational fear arise only in connection with the life that awaits us after this life? We fear, through ignorance, only what we do not know—just as happens to children frightened by insubstantial fantasies. But the person who wishes to gaze on the truth of things first tries to develop a general understanding of the object before him,[28] then reasons out what kind of thing it is in its nature—whether it is something useful and worth approaching, or harmful and to be avoided. How, then, could a rational person judge something so generally vague and not known to be harmful, suspecting what is just its unaccustomed character to be like the threat of fire or of a wild animal? And yet we are taught clearly by everyday life not always to consider just what we are accustomed to, but also to be constantly transformed by our yearnings toward the Good. Life, for humans after conception, does not always remain in the fetal stage; yet for as long as [fetuses] remain in the womb,

[27]See Deut 6.5; Mk 12.30; Mt 22.37; Lk 10.27.

[28]Gregory is giving a general description of how we come to know what the objects we perceive really are.

ἡδεῖαν αὐτοῖς καὶ κατάλληλον ἡ φύσις ποιεῖ τὴν ἐν τῇ νηδύϊ ζωήν, οὔτε ἐπειδὰν ἔξω γένωνται, τῇ θηλῇ διὰ παντὸς παραμένουσιν, ἀλλ᾽ ἐφ᾽ ὅσον τῷ ἀτελεῖ τῆς ἡλικίας καλὸν τὸ τοιοῦτόν ἐστι καὶ κατάλληλον. μετὰ τοῦτο δὲ πρὸς ἄλλην ἀκολουθίαν βίου μετέρχονται οὐδὲν ὑπὸ τῆς συνηθείας τῷ μαζῷ συμπαραμένειν ἀναπειθόμενοι· εἶτα μετὰ τὴν νηπιώδη κατάστασιν ἄλλα τῶν μειρακίων καὶ ἄλλα τῶν παρηλικεστέρων ἐπιτηδεύματα γίνεται, πρὸς ἃ μεταβαίνει δι᾽ ἀκολουθίας ὁ ἄνθρωπος ἀλύπως συμμεταβάλλων ταῖς ἡλικίαις καὶ τὴν συνήθειαν. ὥσπερ τοίνυν, εἰ φωνή τις ἦν τῷ ἐντρεφομένῳ τῇ μητρῴᾳ νηδύϊ, ἠγανάκτησεν ἂν διὰ γεννήσεως τῶν σπλάγχνων ἐξοικιζόμενον καὶ δεινὰ πάσχειν ἐβόα τῆς καταθυμίου διαγωγῆς ἀποσπώμενον, (ὅπερ δὴ καὶ ποιεῖ τῇ πρώτῃ ἀναπνοῇ συνεκβάλλον ἅμα τῇ γεννήσει τὸ δάκρυον ὥσπερ ἀγανακτοῦν τε καὶ ὀδυρόμενον ἐπὶ τῷ χωρισμῷ τῆς συνήθους ζωῆς) οὕτω μοι δοκοῦσιν οἱ πρὸς τὴν μεταβολὴν τοῦ παρόντος δυσχεραίνοντες βίου τὸ τῶν ἐμβρύων πάσχειν ἐν τῷ διὰ
GNO 47 παντὸς ἐθέλειν τῷ χωρίῳ τῆς ὑλικῆς ταύτης ἀηδίας ἐμβιο|τεύειν.
ἐπειδὰν γὰρ ἡ ὠδὶς τοῦ θανάτου πρὸς ἕτερον βίον τοὺς ἀνθρώπους μαιεύηται, αὐτοὶ μὲν ὅταν εἰς τὸ φῶς ἐκεῖνο προέλθωσιν καὶ τοῦ καθαροῦ σπάσωσι πνεύματος, τῇ πείρᾳ γινώσκουσιν ὅσον ἐστὶ τῆς ζωῆς ἐκείνης πρὸς τὴν νῦν τὸ διάφορον, οἱ δὲ ὑπολειφθέντες τῷ ὑγρῷ τούτῳ καὶ πλαδῶντι βίῳ ἔμβρυα ὄντες ἀτεχνῶς καὶ οὐκ ἄνθρωποι ταλανίζουσι τὸν προεξελθόντα τῆς περιεχούσης ἡμᾶς συνοχῆς ὡς ἀγαθοῦ τινος ἔξω γενόμενον, οὐκ εἰδότες ὅτι ἐκείνῳ καθ᾽ ὁμοιότητα τοῦ τεχθέντος βρέφους ἀνοίγεται μὲν ὁ ὀφθαλμός, ὅταν ἔξω τοῦ νῦν συνέχοντος γένηται (νοεῖν δὲ χρὴ πάντως τὸν ὀφθαλμὸν τῆς ψυχῆς ᾧ διορᾷ τὴν τῶν ὄντων ἀλήθειαν), ἀνοίγεται δὲ τὸ ἀκουστικὸν αἰσθητήριον, δι᾽ οὗ τῶν ἀρρήτων ἐπακούει ῥημάτων Ἃ οὐκ ἐξὸν ἀνθρώπῳ λαλῆσαι καθώς φησιν ὁ ἀπόστολος, ἀνοίγεται δὲ τὸ στόμα καὶ ἕλκει τὸ καθαρόν τε καὶ ἄϋλον πνεῦμα, δι᾽ οὗ τονοῦται πρὸς τὴν νοητὴν φωνὴν καὶ τὸν ἀληθινὸν λόγον, ὅταν καταμιχθῇ τῷ ἤχῳ τῶν ἑορταζόντων ἐν τῷ τῶν ἁγίων χορῷ·

nature makes life within their mother's bodies pleasant and suitable. Nor, once they have been born, do they cling to the breast forever, but only as long as this is good and proper for their early stage of development. After this, they move on to another period of life, and are not persuaded to go on clinging to the breast simply because they are accustomed to it; so after the stage of infancy, young children have other needs and activities suitable to their age, and the human person moves from one to another in sequence, painlessly changing his or her accustomed practices to fit their time of life. So, then, just as if the fetus in his mother's womb had a voice, he would complain at being pushed out of her body by birth, and would shout that he was going to suffer severely by being wrenched away from the form of life he had grown used to (which surely is what causes a newborn infant to cry as soon as he draws his first breath, as if complaining and lamenting at this break in his accustomed form of life), so those who lament the change in this present pattern of life seem to me to be doing what fetuses do: they want always to continue living in this disgusting material place.

"When, then, the birth-pangs of death deliver people into another life, when they advance into that light and breathe in that pure spiritual air, they will know by experience how great the difference is between that life and our present state; but those who remain behind in this moist and flaccid realm, being still simply fetuses and not mature persons, will think that the one who has been released from the conflicts that presently entrap us has left some good thing behind, not realizing that for him or her the eye has been opened like that of a newborn child, who has been released from what presently restrains him. This means, of course, the eye of the *soul*, by which it sees clearly the truth of things. And the organ of hearing will be opened up, by which it hears unspoken 'words impossible for a human to utter' (2 Cor 12.4), as the Apostle says; and the mouth will be opened to draw in the pure and immaterial air, by which it will echo the spiritual voice and the true word, when it mingles with the song of those feasting in the country of the saints. And so they will

οὕτω δὲ καὶ γεύσεως ἀξιοῦται θείας, δι' ἧς γινώσκει κατὰ τὴν
ψαλμῳδίαν, Ὅτι χρηστὸς ὁ κύριος, καὶ διὰ τῆς ὀσφραντικῆς
ἐνεργείας τῆς τοῦ Χριστοῦ εὐωδίας ἀντιλαμβάνεται, καὶ τὴν
ἁπτικὴν προσλαμβάνει δύναμιν ἐφαπτομένη τῆς ἀληθείας ἡ ψυχὴ
καὶ ψηλαφῶσα τὸν λόγον κατὰ τὴν Ἰωάννου μαρτυρίαν. εἰ ταῦτα
τοίνυν καὶ τὰ τοιαῦτα μετὰ τὸν διὰ τοῦ θανάτου τόκον τοῖς
ἀνθρώποις ἀπόκειται, τί βούλεται τὸ πένθος καὶ ἡ σκυθρωπότης
PG 517 καὶ ἡ κατήφεια; νῦν ἡμῖν ὁ πρὸς τὴν τῶν πραγμά|των φύσιν
GNO 48 βλέπων ἀποκρινέσθω, εἰ | προτιμότερον οἴεται τὸ τοῖς σωματικοῖς
αἰσθητηρίοις περὶ τὴν τοῦ καλοῦ κρίσιν διαπλανᾶσθαι τοῦ γυμνῷ
τῷ τῆς ψυχῆς ὀφθαλμῷ πρὸς αὐτὴν τὴν τῶν πραγμάτων βλέπειν
ἀλήθειαν. ἐνταῦθα γὰρ ἀνάγκη τις ἔπεστι τῇ ψυχῇ ἀλλοτρίᾳ κρίσει
δουλεύειν ἐν τῇ περὶ τοῦ καλοῦ ὑπονοίᾳ. ἐπειδὴ γὰρ ἡ τελεία τῆς
ψυχῆς δύναμις ἀχώρητός ἐστιν ἔτι τῷ νηπιάζοντι σώματι, ἡ δὲ τῶν
αἰσθητηρίων ἐνέργεια εὐθὺς τελεία τῷ βρέφει συναποτίκτεται,
τούτου χάριν προλαμβάνεται ὑπὸ τῆς αἰσθήσεως ἡ διάνοια ἐν τῇ
τοῦ καλοῦ κρίσει καὶ τὸ τοῖς αἰσθητηρίοις φανὲν ἤδη καὶ νομισθὲν
εἶναι καλὸν καὶ διὰ συνηθείας προειλημμένον ἀβασανίστως
δέχεται ἡ ψυχή, ἐκεῖνο καλὸν εἶναι πεισθεῖσα ὅπερ ἂν προλαβοῦσα
προσμαρτυρήσῃ ἡ αἴσθησις, ἐν χρώμασί τισι καὶ χυμοῖς καὶ τοῖς
τοιούτοις λήροις τὸ καλὸν θεωροῦσα. ὧν μηκέτι προφαινομένων
μετὰ τὴν ἐκ τοῦ σώματος ἔξοδον ἀνάγκη πᾶσα τὸ ἀληθῶς ἀγαθὸν
τῇ ψυχῇ φανῆναι, πρὸς ὃ κατὰ φύσιν ᾠκείωται. οὔτε γὰρ πρὸς τὸ
εὔχρουν ἔτι ἡ ὄψις δελεασθήσεται τοῦ ὀφθαλμοῦ τούτου μηκέτι
ὄντος οὔτε πρὸς ἄλλο τι τῶν καταγλυκαινόντων τὰ αἰσθητήρια ἡ
ῥοπὴ τῆς προαιρέσεως ἔσται πάσης σωματικῆς αἰσθήσεως
ἀποσβεσθείσης, μόνης δὲ τῆς νοερᾶς ἐνεργείας ἀΰλως τε καὶ
ἀσωμάτως τοῦ νοητοῦ κάλλους ἐφαπτομένης ἀκωλύτως ἡ φύσις

become worthy of that divine taste, by which, according to the Psalm, they 'see that the Lord is good' (Ps 33.8), and through the activity of smell they share in 'the fragrance of Christ' (2 Cor 2.15). So the soul, laying hold of truth, will in the end acquire the power of touch, and will 'handle the Word' (1 Jn 1.1)—as John bears witness.[29]

13 "If these and similar experiences are in store for human beings after the birth-pangs that take place through death, what does our grieving and sorrow and dejection mean? Let the person who considers the nature of things tell us now whether he thinks it more valuable to be deceived in judging what is good by our bodily senses than to gaze at the very truth of things with the naked eye of the soul. In this life it is, in a way, unavoidable, after all, that the soul should be held captive by inauthentic judgments on what it considers to be good. For since the perfect power of the soul is not yet developed in the immature body, yet the activity of the senses is immediately born complete in a baby, our use of reason is therefore preceded by sensation in our judgment of the good; and what appears to our senses and seems to be good, what normally comes first to our consciousness, this the soul also uncritically accepts—considering whatever our proactive senses first present us with to be beautiful, imagining beauty to consist in colors and flavors and other forms of mere show.

"But when such things are no longer in our view, after [the soul's] departure from the body, it is also inevitable that what is truly good—that to which the soul is naturally drawn—will become clear to the soul. Our sense of sight will no longer be attracted to beautiful colors, since this eye will no longer exist, nor will the activity of choice be drawn toward any other of the things that now so delight our senses, since all bodily sensation will be extinguished. But when the activity of the mind alone grasps intelligible beauty, free from

[29]Gregory here concisely sums up the classical Christian conception of our eschatological acquisition of "spiritual senses." See Paul Gavrilyuk and Sarah Coakley, eds, *The Spiritual Senses: Perceiving God in Western Christianity* (Cambridge: Cambridge University Press, 2012).

τὸ ἴδιον ἀπολήψεται ἀγαθόν, ὃ μήτε χρῶμα μήτε σχῆμα μήτε διάστασις μήτε πηλικότης ἐστίν, ἀλλ' ὃ πᾶσαν στοχαστικὴν εἰκασίαν παρέρχεται.

Τί οὖν ἴσως ἐρεῖ τις δυσχεραίνων πρὸς τὴν παροῦσαν ζωήν; ἵνα
GNO 49 τί τὸ σῶμα καὶ ἀντὶ τίνος ἡμῖν, εἴπερ ἀμείνων ὁ | χωρὶς τούτου βίος
ἀπεδείχθη τῷ λόγῳ; πρὸς ὃν ἐροῦμεν ὅτι οὐ μικρόν ἐστι οὐδὲ τὸ ἐκ
τούτων κέρδος τοῖς δυναμένοις εἰς πᾶσαν βλέπειν τὴν οἰκονομίαν
τῆς φύσεως. μακάριος μὲν γὰρ ὄντως ἐκεῖνος τῶν ἀγγέλων ὁ βίος
ὁ μηδὲν τοῦ σωματικοῦ προσδεόμενος βάρους. οὐ μὴν οὐδὲ οὗτος
ἀσυντελὴς ὡς πρὸς ἐκεῖνόν ἐστιν· ὁδὸς γὰρ πρὸς τὸ ἐλπιζόμενον
ὁ παρὼν γίνεται βίος, καθάπερ ἐπὶ τῶν βλαστημάτων ἔστιν ἰδεῖν,
ἐφ' ὧν ὁ καρπὸς ἀπὸ τοῦ ἄνθους ἀρξάμενος δι' αὐτοῦ πρόεισιν εἰς
τὸ γενέσθαι καρπὸς κἂν μὴ καρπὸς ᾖ τὸ ἄνθος. ἀλλὰ καὶ τὰ λήια
τῶν σπερμάτων ἐκφυόμενα οὐκ εὐθὺς ἐν τῷ στάχυι φαίνεται, ἀλλὰ
χόρτος τὸ πρῶτον γίνεται βλάστημα, εἶτα ἀπὸ τούτου καλάμη
συνίσταται περιφθαρέντος τοῦ χόρτου καὶ οὕτω τῇ κεφαλῇ
τοῦ ἀστάχυος ὁ καρπὸς ἐμπεπαίνεται. πλὴν οὐκ αἰτιᾶται τὴν
ἀναγκαίαν ταύτην περίοδόν τε καὶ ἀκολουθίαν ὁ γεωπόνος διὰ τί
λέγων πρὸ τοῦ καρποῦ τὸ ἄνθος, ἢ ὑπὲρ τίνος ὁ ἐκ τοῦ σπέρματος
προανατέλλων χόρτος, εἴ γε καὶ τὸ ἄνθος ἀπορρέει καὶ ὁ χόρτος
μάτην ξηραίνεται πρὸς οὐδὲν συντελῶν τῇ ἀνθρωπίνῃ τροφῇ·
οἶδεν γὰρ ὁ πρὸς τὴν θαυματοποιΐαν βλέπων τῆς φύσεως ὅτι
οὐκ ἂν ἄλλως ἐκ τῶν σπερμάτων τε καὶ βλαστημάτων ὁ καρπὸς
τελειωθείη μὴ τῆς τεχνικῆς ταύτης ἀκολουθίας ὁδοποιούσης
αὐτοῦ τὴν τελείωσιν. οὐ γὰρ ἐπειδὴ πρὸς ἀπόλαυσιν ἡμετέραν
ὁ προεκβαλλόμενος ἐκ τῶν σπερμάτων χόρτος ἀχρήστως ἔχει,
διὰ τοῦτο περιττόν τε καὶ παρέλκον ἐστὶ τὸ γινόμενον. ὁ μὲν
PG 520 γὰρ τῆς τρο|φῆς χρῄζων πρὸς τὴν ἑαυτοῦ χρείαν ὁρᾷ, ὁ δὲ τῆς
φύσεως λόγος οὐ πρὸς ἄλλο τι βλέπει, ἀλλ' ὅπως ἂν προαγάγοι
τὴν καρπογονίαν διὰ τῆς τεταγμένης ἀκολουθίας ἐπὶ τὸ τέλειον.

matter and the body, nature will recover its own proper good unhindered, which is neither color nor shape nor extension nor size, but which lies beyond all the conjectures we can possibly form.

14 "'What, then?' someone may ask, complaining about this present life. 'What is the purpose of the body, and at what price is it given to us, if indeed it has been shown by our argument that life without the body is better?' We would answer such a person that the benefit even of these bodily functions is no small one, for those who are able to reflect on the whole arrangement of nature. The life of the angels is truly blessed, since it has no need of the weight of a body. But even this life is not without its value in comparison to theirs; for our present life comes to be a way toward what we hope for—just as we can see with plants, where the fruit begins from the flower, and gradually progresses through it to become a fruit, even though the flower is not a fruit. Crops that grow from seeds, too, do not immediately appear as full-grown ears, but first the green shoot appears, then from this the stalk grows while the leaves die down, and finally, at the head of the whole stalk, the fruit comes to maturity. But the farmer does not raise questions about this necessary process and sequence, asking why the flower must come before the fruit, or seeking a reason why leaves sprout up from the seed first, or wondering if the flower fades and the leaves wither to no purpose, since they contribute nothing to human nourishment. In fact, anyone who considers the miraculous working of nature knows that fruit would not otherwise reach full perfection from seeds and sprouts, if this artful sequence were not opening the way toward completion. For one cannot say that since the green foliage that issues first from seed itself remains useless for human nourishment, therefore what grows out of it is superfluous and extraneous.

"After all, the person who consumes food considers his or her own need, but the structure of nature looks toward nothing else but how it might bring about the production of fruit, through an orderly sequence of steps moving toward full ripeness. Thus [a plant]

GNO 50 διὸ πρῶτον | πολυμερῶς διὰ ῥιζῶν τῷ ὑποκειμένῳ ἐμφύεται, δι'
ὧν ἕλκει τὴν κατάλληλον ἑαυτῷ διὰ τῆς ἰκμάδος τροφήν, εἶτα
χόρτον βλαστάνει [διὰ τὴν ἐκ τοῦ ἀέρος βλάβην προκάλυμμα τῆς
ῥίζης τὴν πόαν ποιούμενος] ὅπερ καρπὸς μὲν οὐκ ἔστι συνεργία
δέ τις καὶ ὁδὸς γίνεται τῆς τοῦ καρποῦ τελειώσεως πρῶτον μὲν
ἐκκαθαίρων δι' ἑαυτοῦ τὴν ἐγκειμένην τῷ σπέρματι δύναμιν (οἷόν
τι περίττωμα τοῦ καρποῦ τὸν χόρτον προαποσκευαζομένης τῆς
φύσεως), εἶτα σκέπασμα γίνεται τῇ ῥίζῃ πρὸς τὰς ἐκ τοῦ ἀέρος
βλάβας τὰς διὰ κρύους τε καὶ θάλπους ἐγγινομένας. εὐτονώτερον
δὲ ἤδη διὰ βάθους ἐν ταῖς ῥίζαις ὑποσκευασθέντος τοῦ σπέρματος
τότε τοῦ χόρτου λοιπὸν ἀμεληθέντος διὰ τὸ μηκέτι δεῖσθαι τὴν
ῥίζαν τοῦ προκαλύμματος πρὸς τὴν τῆς καλάμης ἀναδρομὴν πᾶσα
συνδίδοται δύναμις μηχανικῇ τινι σοφίᾳ τὴν αὐλοειδῆ κατασκευὴν
φιλοτεχνούσης τῆς φύσεως, ἧς εὐθυτενὴς μὲν ἡ βλάστη χιτῶσιν
ἐπαλλήλοις ἐν κύκλῳ διειλημμένη· χρὴ γὰρ τούτοις ὑγρὰν οὖσαν
καὶ ἄτονον τὴν καλάμην παρὰ τὴν πρώτην ἐντρέφεσθαι τοῖς διὰ
μέσου συνδέσμοις ἀσφαλείας χάριν ὑπεζωσμένην. εἰ δὲ πρὸς τὸ
σύμμετρον ἀναδράμοι μῆκος, τότε κομᾷ ἡ καλάμη τοῦ τελευταίου
χιτῶνος ἀφ' ἑαυτοῦ τὸν στάχυν προδείξαντος, ὃς εἰς πολλοὺς
ἀθέρας τριχοειδῶς διαιρούμενος κρύπτει τὸν κόκκον τὸν κατὰ τὴν
βάσιν τῶν ἀθέρων τοῖς ἐλύτροις ὑποτρεφόμενον. εἰ τοίνυν οὔτε
πρὸς τὰς ῥίζας τῶν σπερμάτων ὁ γεωργὸς δυσχεραίνει οὔτε πρὸς
GNO 51 τὸν προεκβαλλόμενον ἐκ τοῦ σπέρματος χόρτον | οὔτε εἰς τοὺς
ἀθέρας τοῦ στάχυος, ἀλλ' ἐν ἑκάστῳ τούτων ἐνθεωρεῖ τινα χρείαν
ἀναγκαίαν, δι' ἧς τεχνικῶς ἡ φύσις ὁδεύουσα προάγει τὸν καρπὸν
εἰς τελείωσιν διὰ τῆς τῶν ἀχρείων ἀποποιήσεως τὴν γόνιμον
ἐκκαθαίρουσα δύναμιν, ὥρα καὶ σοὶ μὴ δυσχεραίνειν διὰ τῶν
ἀναγκαίων ὁδῶν προιούσης ἡμῶν τῆς φύσεως ἐπὶ τὸ ἴδιον τέλος
ἀλλ' ἡγεῖσθαι κατὰ τὴν ἐν τοῖς σπέρμασιν ἀναλογίαν τὸ ἀεὶ παρὸν
πρός τι πάντως χρησίμως τε καὶ ἀναγκαίως ἔχειν, οὐ μὴν τοῦτο
εἶναι οὗ χάριν εἰς γένεσιν ἤλθομεν. οὐ γὰρ ἐπὶ τὸ ἔμβρυον γενέσθαι

begins to emerge from the soil by developing a complex system of roots, through which it draws in nourishment appropriate to itself, in liquid form. Then it sends forth leaves, creating foliage as a covering for the roots, because of possible damage from the weather. This is not the grain itself, but is a kind of helper and path toward the grain's final growth: first purifying, through its own presence, the power inherent in the seed (for nature produces foliage from a seed as a kind of preliminary by-product of the fruit), it then becomes a protective canopy for the root, in view of the dangers that can be offered by the weather—dangers of cold and heat. And when the seed is more vigorously supported by greater depth in the roots, the leaf tends to be neglected from then on, because the root no longer needs a canopy for the growing shoot. All the power of the plant now contributes, with its nature working—in a kind of inventive wisdom—toward the formation of a tubular structure, whose straight shoot is marked by wrappings that reciprocally surround it. For it is necessary that the spear [of grain], being moist and weak, should be supported throughout its first stages by being wrapped in these central connective coverings, for the sake of its own safe growth. And if it reaches the appropriate height, then the stalk becomes a plume, with the final wrapping showing forth the ear from within itself; and the ear, dividing itself into many hairy spines, conceals the grain, which, at the base of the spines, is protected by these coverings.

"If, then, the farmer does not complain about the roots sent down by the seed, nor about the leafy growth that shoots up from the seed, nor about the spines at the end of the ear, but sees in each of these a certain necessary usefulness, through which nature, plotting out its way, brings the fruit to full maturity and then purifies the plant's life-giving power by discarding what is unnecessary, it makes sense for you, too, not to complain because our nature goes forward by its own necessary paths to its proper goal. Consider, instead, that what always takes place [in us] with another goal in view is itself completely useful and necessary, along the lines of what happens with seeds; yet this is still not that for whose sake we

παρὰ τοῦ δημιουργήσαντος ἡμᾶς ὑπέστημεν οὐδὲ πρὸς τὸν
βρεφώδη βίον ὁ σκοπὸς τῆς φύσεως βλέπει οὐδὲ πρὸς τὰς ἐφεξῆς
ἡλικίας ὁρᾷ ἃς ἀεὶ διὰ τῆς ἀλλοιώσεως μετενδύεται τῷ χρόνῳ
τὸ εἶδος συνεξαλλάσσουσα, οὐδὲ πρὸς τὴν ἐπιγινομένην διὰ τοῦ
θανάτου λύσιν τῷ σώματι, ἀλλὰ πάντα ταῦτα καὶ τὰ τοιαῦτα τῆς
ὁδοῦ δι᾽ ἧς πορευόμεθα, μέρη ἐστίν. ὁ δὲ σκοπὸς καὶ τὸ πέρας τῆς
διὰ τούτων πορείας ἡ πρὸς τὸ ἀρχαῖον ἀποκατάστασις, ὅπερ οὐδὲν
ἕτερον ἢ ἡ πρὸς τὸ θεῖόν ἐστιν ὁμοίωσις. καὶ ὥσπερ ἐπὶ τῆς κατὰ
τὸν στάχυν εἰκόνος ἀναγκαῖος μὲν ἐφάνη τῷ λόγῳ τῆς φύσεως καὶ
ὁ προεκβαλλόμενος χόρτος, οὐ μὴν δὲ δι᾽ ἐκεῖνόν ἐστιν ἡ γεωργία
οὐδὲ χιτῶνες καὶ ἀθέρες καὶ καλάμη καὶ ὑποζώματα πρόκεινται τῇ
τῆς γεωργίας σπουδῇ ἀλλ᾽ ὁ τρόφιμος καρπὸς ὁ διὰ τούτων προϊὼν
PG 521 εἰς τελείωσιν, οὕτω καὶ τῆς ζωῆς τὸ μὲν προσδοκώ|μενον πέρας
μακαριότης ἐστίν, τὰ δὲ ὅσα περὶ τὸ σῶμα νῦν καθορᾶται, θάνατος
καὶ γῆρας καὶ νεότης καὶ νηπιότης καὶ ἡ ἐν ἐμβρύῳ διάπλασις,
πάντα ταῦτα οἷόν τινες χόρτοι καὶ ἀθέρες καὶ κάλαμοι ὁδὸς καὶ
GNO 52 ἀκολουθία | καὶ δύναμις τῆς ἐλπιζομένης ἐστὶ τελειώσεως. πρὸς
ἣν βλέπων ἐὰν εὐφρονῇς, οὔτε ἀπεχθῶς ἕξεις πρὸς ταῦτα οὔτε μὴν
ἐμπαθῶς τε καὶ ἐπιθυμητικῶς διατεθήσῃ ὡς ἢ χωριζόμενος αὐτῶν
ἀνιᾶσθαι ἢ αὐτομολεῖν πρὸς τὸν θάνατον.

Εἰ δὲ χρὴ προσθεῖναι καὶ τοῦτο τῷ λόγῳ, οὐκ ἄχρηστον ἴσως ἐστίν, κἂν ἔξω τῆς ἀκολουθίας εἶναι δοκῇ, ὅτι ἐμμελετᾷ τῷ θανάτῳ διὰ παντὸς ἡ φύσις καὶ συμπέφυκε διὰ τοῦ χρόνου προιούσῃ τῇ ζωῇ πάντως ὁ θάνατος. πρὸς γὰρ τὸ μέλλον ἐκ τοῦ παρῳχηκότος τῆς ζωῆς πάντοτε κινουμένης καὶ οὐδέποτε πρὸς τὸ κατόπιν ἀναλυούσης θανατός ἐστι τὸ πάντοτε τῇ ζωτικῇ ἐνεργείᾳ συνημμένως ἑπόμενον. ἐν γὰρ τῷ παρῳχηκότι τοῦ χρόνου παύεται

have come into being. For we have not come into existence, at the hand of the one who created us, in order to become a fetus, nor is the purpose of our nature summed up in a baby's life, nor does it look toward those succeeding phases in which it constantly clothes itself through change, altering its form along with time, nor even toward the dissolution that comes upon the body through death; all these stages, and others like them, are parts of the path by which we make our way forward. And the goal and final limit of this process is restoration (ἀποκατάστασις, *apokatastasis*) to our original state,[30] which is nothing else than likeness to the divine. As with the image of the ear of wheat, the first growth of leaves appeared to be necessary, by the inner logic of nature, but cultivation is not undertaken for that reason; nor do the wrappings or the spines or the stalk or the membranes serve as the ultimate purpose of the farmer's labor, but it is rather the nourishing fruit that comes forth through these things to full maturity; so, too, the end of life that we look forward to is blessedness, and all the things we now recognize as associated with our bodies—death and old age and youth and infancy and formation in the womb—all these things, like leaves and spines and stalks, are the path and sequence and dynamism leading to the perfection we hope for. If then you look toward this end with a good heart, you will not be hostile to all these stages, or be so affected by passions and desires that you either grieve to be separated from them, or that you hasten by your own will toward death.

"And if I might add this, also, to our argument, perhaps it would not be useless, even if it may seem to lie outside the chain of our reasoning: that nature constantly seems to be preparing for death, and surely death is a part of life as it moves forward through time. If life, after all, is always moving toward what is to come, and away from what has gone by, if it is never unraveled by moving in a backward direction, then death is something that always follows on the activity of life, and is interwoven with it. In the passing of

[30]Gregory seems to be referring here especially to Genesis 1.27: "And God created man in his own image . . ." This is the "beginning" of the biblical story of humanity, to which the human race is destined to return.

πάντως πᾶσα κίνησις ζωτικὴ καὶ ἐνέργεια. ἐπεὶ οὖν ἴδιόν ἐστι θανάτου τὸ ἄπρακτόν τε καὶ ἀνενέργητον, τοῦτο δὲ κατόπιν ἀεὶ τῇ ζωτικῇ ἐνεργείᾳ πάντως ἐφέπεται, οὐκ ἔξω τῆς ἀληθείας ἐστὶ τὸ συμπεπλέχθαι τῇ ζωῇ ταύτῃ τὸν θάνατον λέγειν. καὶ ἄλλως δ' ἄν τις εὕροι τὸ τοιοῦτον νόημα διὰ τῆς ἀληθείας ἡμῖν κρατυνόμενον αὐτῆς τῆς πείρας μαρτυρούσης τῷ δόγματι ὅτι οὐχ ὁ αὐτός ἐστι τῷ χθιζῷ ὁ σήμερον ἄνθρωπος κατὰ τὸ ὑλικῶς ὑποκείμενον, ἀλλά τι πάντως αὐτοῦ διὰ παντὸς νεκροῦται καὶ ὄζει καὶ διαφθείρεται καὶ ἐκβάλλεται καθάπερ οἰκίας τινὸς τῆς τοῦ σώματος λέγω κατασκευῆς, τὴν νεκρώδη δυσωδίαν ἐκφερούσης τῆς φύσεως καὶ τῇ γῇ παραδιδούσης τὸ ἤδη τῆς ζωτικῆς δυνάμεως ἔξω γενόμενον. διὸ κατὰ τὴν τοῦ μεγάλου φωνὴν Παύλου Καθ' ἡμέραν
GNO 53 ἀποθνήσκομεν οὐχ οἱ αὐτοὶ διὰ παντὸς ἐν τῷ αὐτῷ διαμένοντες | οἴκῳ τοῦ σώματος ἀλλ' ἑκάστοτε ἄλλοι ἐξ ἄλλου γινόμενοι, διὰ προσθήκης τε καὶ ἀποποιήσεως ὡς πρὸς καινὸν σῶμα διὰ παντὸς ἀλλοιούμενοι. τί οὖν ξενιζόμεθα πρὸς τὸν θάνατον, οὗ ἀπεδείχθη μελέτη διηνεκὴς καὶ γυμνάσιον ἡ διὰ σαρκὸς οὖσα ζωή; κἂν τὸν ὕπνον εἴπῃς καὶ τὴν ἐγρήγορσιν, ἄλλην θανάτου λέγεις πρὸς τὴν ζωὴν συμπλοκὴν κατασβεννυμένης ἐν τοῖς καθεύδουσι τῆς αἰσθήσεως καὶ πάλιν τῆς ἐγρηγόρσεως ἐνεργούσης ἡμῖν ἐν ἑαυτῇ τὴν ἐλπιζομένην ἀνάστασιν.

Ἀλλ' οὔπω τὸ προκείμενον ἡμῖν ἐσαφηνίσθη διὰ τῶν εἰρημένων τοῦ ἐπεισοδίου νοήματος πρὸς ἑτέραν θεωρίαν παραγαγόντος τὸν λόγον. πάλιν τοίνυν τὸ προτεθὲν ἀναλάβωμεν ὅτι οὐκ ἀχρήστως πρὸς τὴν προσδοκωμένην τῶν ἀγαθῶν ἐλπίδα οὐδὲ ἡ τοῦ σώματος φύσις ἔχει. εἰ μὲν γὰρ ἦμεν ὅπερ ἐξ ἀρχῆς ἐγενόμεθα, οὐκ ἂν πάντως τοῦ δερματίνου χιτῶνος προσεδεήθημεν ἐπιλαμπούσης ἡμῖν τῆς πρὸς τὸ θεῖον ὁμοιώσεως. ὁ δὲ θεῖος χαρακτὴρ ὁ ἐπιφαινόμενος ἡμῖν τὸ κατ' ἀρχὰς οὐ ποιὰ σχήματός τινος ἢ

time, surely, all of life's movement and energy will come to a stop. Since, then, not-doing and not-acting are proper to death, and this stoppage always follows living activity from behind, as it were, it is not outside the realm of truth to say that death is intermingled with this life.

"Put another way, this idea is reinforced for us by what we know of the truth, with our very experience bearing witness to this teaching: that the human person today is not the same as he or she was yesterday in material substructure, but that something of the human person, as it were, is always dying, always smells rotten and is decayed and discarded—thrown out of the house, by which I mean out of the structure of the body—as nature rids herself of the stink of death, and hands over again to earth what has already come to be outside the realm of her living power. Therefore, according to the saying of the great Paul, 'we die day by day' (1 Cor 15.31), not always remaining the same, in the same bodily dwelling, but constantly becoming different, starting from different points of origin—constantly being changed into a new body by adding and discarding. Why, then, are we surprised at death, since our fleshly life has been proved to be a constant preparation for it, the place where we wrestle with it? Or if you wish to consider sleep and waking, you might call them yet another interweaving of death with life: sensation is quenched in those who sleep, but waking once again realizes in us, by itself, the resurrection we hope for.

15 "We have attempted to clarify the subject by what we have been saying—yet perhaps this point we have just come to has led the argument off toward a different consideration! Let us, then, take up once more our proposed theme: that even our bodily nature is not wasting its time in holding out a hope for the good things we look forward to. For if we *were* what we were made to be from the beginning, we surely would have had no need of this garment of skin (Gen 3.21),[31] since our likeness to the Divine would be shining

[31]See Lucas Mateo-Seco, "Tunics of Hide," in *The Brill Dictionary of Gregory of Nyssa*, 768–70.

χρώματος ἦν ἰδιότης, ἀλλ' οἷς τὸ θεῖον θεωρεῖται κάλλος τοιούτοις
ἐκαλλωπίζετο καὶ ὁ ἄνθρωπος δι' ἀπαθείας τε καὶ μακαριότητος
καὶ ἀφθαρσίας τὴν ἐν τῷ ἀρχετύπῳ χάριν ἀπομιμούμενος. ἐπειδὴ
δὲ δι' ἀπάτης τοῦ ἐχθροῦ τῆς ζωῆς ἡμῶν πρὸς τὸ κτηνῶδες καὶ
ἄλογον ἑκουσίως τὴν ῥοπὴν ἔσχεν ὁ ἄνθρωπος, τὸ μὲν ἄκοντας
PG 524 ἀποστῆσαι τοῦ | χείρονος καὶ πρὸς τὸ κρεῖττον ἀναγκαστικῶς
μεταθεῖναι τοῖς μὲν ἀνεξετάστοις χρήσιμον ἴσως δοκεῖ, τῷ δὲ
πλάστῃ τῆς φύσεως ἀλυσιτελὲς ἐφάνη καὶ ἄδικον τὴν τοῦ μεγίστου
GNO 54 τῶν ἀγαθῶν ζημίαν διὰ | τῆς τοιαύτης οἰκονομίας ἐμποιῆσαι τῇ
φύσει. ἐπειδὴ γὰρ θεοειδὴς ὁ ἄνθρωπος ἐγένετο καὶ μακάριος τῷ
αὐτεξουσίῳ τετιμημένος (τὸ γὰρ αὐτοκρατές τε καὶ ἀδέσποτον
ἴδιόν ἐστι τῆς θείας μακαριότητος), τὸ δι' ἀνάγκης αὐτὸν ἐπί τι
μεταχθῆναι βιαίως ἀφαίρεσις τοῦ ἀξιώματος ἦν. εἰ γὰρ ἑκουσίως
τὴν ἀνθρωπίνην φύσιν κατὰ τὴν αὐτεξούσιον κίνησιν ἐπί τι τῶν
οὐ δεόντων ὁρμήσασαν βιαίως τε καὶ κατηναγκασμένως τῶν
ἀρεσάντων ἀπέστησεν, ἀφαίρεσις ἂν ἦν τοῦ προέχοντος ἀγαθοῦ
τὸ γινόμενον καὶ τῆς ἰσοθέου τιμῆς ἀποστέρησις. (ἰσόθεον γάρ
ἐστι τὸ αὐτεξούσιον.) ὡς ἂν οὖν καὶ ἡ ἐξουσία μένοι τῇ φύσει καὶ
τὸ κακὸν ἀπογένοιτο, ταύτην εὗρεν ἡ σοφία τοῦ θεοῦ τὴν ἐπίνοιαν
τὸ ἐᾶσαι τὸν ἄνθρωπον ἐν οἷς ἐβουλήθη γενέσθαι, ἵνα γευσάμενος
τῶν κακῶν ὧν ἐπεθύμησεν καὶ τῇ πείρᾳ μαθὼν οἷα ἀνθ' οἵων
ἠλλάξατο, παλινδρομήσῃ διὰ τῆς ἐπιθυμίας ἑκουσίως πρὸς τὴν
πρώτην μακαριότητα ἅπαν τὸ ἐμπαθές τε καὶ ἄλογον ὥσπερ τι
ἄχθος ἀποσκευάσας τῆς φύσεως ἤτοι κατὰ τὴν παροῦσαν ζωὴν
διὰ προσοχῆς τε καὶ φιλοσοφίας ἐκκαθαρθεὶς ἢ μετὰ τὴν ἐνθένδε

in us. And the divine form that appeared in us from the beginning was not some peculiar kind of shape or color, but the human person was made beautiful by those features in which the divine beauty could be contemplated, imitating the grace of the Archetype in his freedom from passion, his blessedness, his incorruptibility. But when, through the deceit of the enemy of our life, the human person willingly took possession of his own urge toward what is bestial and irrational, perhaps the solution would seem to be, to those who have not thought much about it, [for God] simply to turn [humans] away from evil, even against their will, and to transfer them forcibly toward what is better. But to the Creator of our nature, it would have seemed unprofitable, even unjust, to deprive our nature, by a measure such as this, of the greatest of goods. For since the human person had been created like God, and had been made blessed by the ability to determine his own acts (for being autonomous and independent is what is proper to the divine blessedness), for him to be led forcefully, by constraint, would deprive him of his dignity. Surely if [God] led human nature—which, using its own power of self-determination, had voluntarily reached out for something it should have avoided—away from what pleased it by using force and compulsion, this step would be a deprivation of [humanity's] most outstanding good, a loss of the honor that made them like God. For to be self-determining is to be godlike.

"So that this power, then, might remain in our nature, and so that evil might still be done away with, God's wisdom devised this plan: to let the human person remain in the state where he had chosen to be, so that, having tasted the evil things he had yearned for, and having learned by experience what he had given up to gain them, he might turn again voluntarily, through his own desires, toward his first blessedness—shaking off everything passionate and irrational from his nature like some burden, and either being purified during this present life by attentive and ascetic living,[32] or after

[32]Greek: διὰ προσοχῆς τε καὶ φιλοσοφίας (*dia prosochēs te kai philosophias*). "Attention" (προσοχή, *prosochē*) is a classical Greek term—also used by Origen—for

μετάστασιν διὰ τῆς τοῦ καθαρσίου πυρὸς χωνείας. ὥσπερ γὰρ
εἴ τις ἰατρικὸς ὢν καὶ πᾶσαν ἐπιστήμην τῶν τε σωτηρίων καὶ
τῶν δηλητηρίων ἐκ τέχνης ἔχων συμβουλεύων τῷ μειρακίῳ τὰ
δέοντα μὴ δυνηθείη διὰ συμβουλῆς κωλῦσαι τὸν ἀτελῆ κατὰ τὴν
ἡλικίαν τε καὶ τὴν φρόνησιν ἐπιθυμητικῶς πρός τινα φθοροποιὸν
καρπὸν ἢ πόαν διατεθέντα, ἔχων δὲ παντοίαν τῶν ἀλεξιφαρμάκων
GNO 55 παρασκευὴν ἐπιτρέ|ψειε τῷ παιδὶ μετασχεῖν τῶν βλαπτόντων,
ἐφ᾽ ᾧτε διὰ τῆς τῶν ἀλγεινῶν πείρας τὸ χρήσιμον τῆς πατρῴας
συμβουλῆς μαθόντα καὶ ἐν ἐπιθυμίᾳ τῆς ὑγιείας γενόμενον πάλιν
διὰ τῶν ἀλεξητηρίων ἐπαναγάγῃ πρὸς εὐεξίαν τὸν παῖδα ἧς διὰ
τῆς ἀτόπου τῶν δηλητηρίων ἐπιθυμίας ἐξέπεσεν, οὕτως ὁ γλυκύς
τε καὶ ἀγαθὸς τῆς φύσεως ἡμῶν πατὴρ ὁ εἰδὼς καὶ δι᾽ ὧν σῳζόμεθα
καὶ δι᾽ ὧν ἀπολλύμεθα, ἐγνώρισε μὲν τῷ ἀνθρώπῳ τὸ δηλητήριον
καὶ τὸ μὴ μετασχεῖν συνεβούλευσεν, κρατησάσης δὲ τῆς ἐπιθυμίας
τοῦ χείρονος οὐκ ἠπόρησε τῶν ἀγαθῶν ἀντιφαρμάκων, δι᾽ ὧν
ἐπαναγάγῃ πάλιν πρὸς τὴν ἐξ ἀρχῆς εὐεξίαν τὸν ἄνθρωπον. τὴν
γὰρ ὑλικὴν ταύτην ἡδονὴν πρὸ τῆς ψυχικῆς εὐφροσύνης τοῦ
ἀνθρώπου προελομένου συντρέχειν μέν πως ἔδοξεν αὐτῷ τῇ ὁρμῇ
διὰ τοῦ δερματίνου χιτῶνος, ὃν διὰ τὴν πρὸς τὸ χεῖρον αὐτῷ ῥοπὴν
περιέθηκεν, δι᾽ οὗ τῆς ἀλόγου φύσεως [ἐπεμίχθη τῷ ἀνθρώπῳ] τὰ
ἰδιώματα [ὧν τῶν ἀλόγων ζῴων] τῆς λογικῆς φύσεως ἔνδυμα
κατεσκευάσθη τῇ σοφίᾳ τοῦ διὰ τῶν ἐναντίων οἰκονομοῦντος τὰ

---

an intentional concern with the central object of our desires. "Philosophy" (φιλοσοφία, *philosophia*), for fourth-century Christians, meant primarily an ascetical lifestyle, consciously focused on higher goods.

[33]This is an early suggestion of what would later, in the more juridically oriented culture of the Latin Middle Ages, be conceived of as the post-mortem *state* of Purgatory; see Jacques Le Goff, *La naissance du Purgatoire* (Paris: Gallimard, 1981), English translation: *The Birth of Purgatory* (Chicago: University of Chicago Press, 1984). In the writings of the Greek Fathers—especially those of Origen and his followers, such as Gregory—the idea of a *purgative process* for the soul after death was certainly fairly common, but often identified with the "fiery" experience of judgment itself—an apocalyptic notion drawing on Paul's somewhat obscure remarks in 1 Corinthians 3.13–15. See, for example, Justin, *Dialogue with Trypho* 116; Lactantius, *Institutes* 7.21; Augustine, Sermon 362.9.9; *Enarrations on the Psalms* 3 on Psalm 103.3.5. The

his departure from here by the purgation of a purifying fire.[33] For just as if someone who is a doctor and has, by training in his art, complete knowledge of what heals and what harms, were to advise his teenage son on proper behavior, but be unable, simply by advice, to keep him—immature as he is in age and understanding—from being attracted in his desires toward some harmful fruit or drink; but then if, having all kinds of curative drugs prepared, he still were to allow the lad to try out what would harm him, so that when, through experience of painful things, he should learn what is profitable in his father's advice and come on his own to desire health, the father might bring his son once again by his remedies to a healthy state, which he had lost by his destructive yearning for things that harmed him; so the kind, good Father of our nature, who knows both the things that will heal us and those that will destroy us, made known to humanity what would harm us and advised us not to partake of it, but when our yearning for what is evil overpowered us, he was not at a loss for good counter-medications, through which he might lead the human person back to the state of health he enjoyed from the beginning. So, when the human person preferred this material pleasure to the soul's happiness, [God] decided, one might say, to let him yield to the impulse that he felt through the garment of skin, which God had wrapped around him because of his impulse toward evil; through this, the characteristics of irrational nature, like those of the mute beasts, were made into a wrapping[34] for his rationality, by the wisdom of him who brings about good things by their opposites. For

association of the idea of post-mortem purification with Origen, however, and with the possibility that even those who die with unexpurgated sins may ultimately be saved, is probably what made medieval Byzantine and modern Orthodox theology somewhat uncomfortable with the idea. At the end of chapter 18 here, Gregory hints that this "purifying fire" may simply be the experience of death itself. The arguments offered by tradition for and against the notion of a post-mortem purification by fire were discussed intensely at the "reunion" Council of Florence in 1439–41. See Ivan Ostroumev, *The History of the Council of Florence* (London, 1861); Joseph Gill, *The Council of Florence* (Cambridge, 1959).

[34]We have followed the conjecture of the editor, Hermann Langerbeck, here, and omitted what seems to be a doubling of the phrase "through which qualities of an irrational nature were mingled for the human person."

κρείττονα· πάντα γὰρ φέρων ἐν ἑαυτῷ τὰ ἰδιώματα ὁ δερμάτινος
ἐκεῖνος χιτὼν ὅσα εἶχε περιέχων τὴν ἄλογον φύσιν, ἡδονήν τε καὶ
θυμὸν καὶ γαστριμαργίαν καὶ ἀπληστίαν καὶ τὰ ὅμοια, ὁδὸν δίδωσι
τῇ ἀνθρωπίνῃ προαιρέσει τῆς καθ' ἑκάτερον ῥοπῆς εἰς ἀρετήν τε
καὶ κακίαν ὕλη γινόμενος. τούτοις γὰρ ἐμβιοτεύων κατὰ τὸν τῇδε
PG 525 βίον ὁ ἄνθρωπος | τῇ αὐτεξουσίῳ κινήσει εἰ μὲν διακρίνοι τοῦ
ἀλόγου τὸ ἴδιον καὶ πρὸς ἑαυτὸν βλέποι διὰ τῆς ἀστειοτέρας ζωῆς,
GNO 56 καθάρσιον τῆς ἐμμιχθείσης κακίας τὸν παρόντα βίον | ποιήσεται,
κρατῶν διὰ τοῦ λόγου τῆς ἀλογίας· εἰ δὲ πρὸς τὴν ἄλογον τῶν
παθημάτων ῥοπὴν ἐπικλιθείη τῷ τῶν ἀλόγων δέρματι συνεργῷ
χρησάμενος πρὸς τὰ πάθη, ἄλλως μετὰ ταῦτα βουλεύσεται πρὸς
τὸ κρεῖττον μετὰ τὴν ἐκ τοῦ σώματος ἔξοδον γνοὺς τῆς ἀρετῆς
τὸ πρὸς τὴν κακίαν διάφορον ἐν τῷ μὴ δύνασθαι μετασχεῖν τῆς
θειότητος μὴ τοῦ καθαρσίου πυρὸς τὸν ἐμμιχθέντα τῇ ψυχῇ ῥύπον
ἀποκαθάραντος.

Ταῦτά ἐστιν ἃ τὴν τοῦ σώματος χρείαν ἀναγκαίαν ἡμῖν ἐποίησεν, δι' οὗ τό τε αὐτεξούσιον σῴζεται καὶ ἡ πρὸς τὸ ἀγαθὸν πάλιν ἐπάνοδος οὐ κωλύεται· ἀλλὰ τῇ περιοδικῇ ταύτῃ ἀκολουθίᾳ διὰ τοῦ ἑκουσίου γίνεται ἡμῖν ἡ πρὸς τὸ κρεῖττον ῥοπὴ τῶν μὲν ἐντεῦθεν ἤδη διὰ τῆς ἐν σαρκὶ ζωῆς τὸν πνευματικὸν ἐν ἀπαθείᾳ κατορθούντων βίον, οἵους γεγενῆσθαι τοὺς πατριάρχας τε καὶ τοὺς προφήτας ἀκούομεν καὶ τοὺς σὺν αὐτοῖς τε καὶ μετ' ἐκείνους δι' ἀρετῆς τε καὶ φιλοσοφίας ἀναδραμόντας ἐπὶ τὸ τέλειον (μαθητὰς λέγω καὶ ἀποστόλους καὶ μάρτυρας καὶ πάντας τοὺς τὴν ἐνάρετον ζωὴν πρὸ τοῦ ὑλικοῦ τετιμηκότας βίου, οἳ κἂν ἐλάττους ὦσι τῷ ἀριθμῷ τοῦ πλήθους τῶν πρὸς τὸ χεῖρον ἀπορρεόντων, οὐδὲν ἧττον τὸ δυνατὸν εἶναι διὰ σαρκὸς τὴν ἀρετὴν κατορθῶσαι μαρτυροῦνται), τῶν δὲ λοιπῶν διὰ τῆς εἰς ὕστερον ἀγωγῆς ἐν τῷ καθαρσίῳ πυρὶ ἀποβαλλόντων τὴν πρὸς τὴν ὕλην προσπάθειαν

that garment of skin, bearing in itself all the characteristics that it had acquired through being wrapped around an irrational nature—pleasure and anger and gluttony and greed and the like—opens up for human choice a way to be drawn in either direction, having become the raw material for both virtue and vice.

"By living in the midst of these conflicting inclinations in this present life, then, the human person, if he discerns what is characteristic of irrational nature and struggles to care for himself in a more thoughtful way of living, will construct, by the dynamism of his own self-determination, a means of purging this present existence of the evil that is mingled with it, using reason to gain control of his irrationality. But if he should be inclined toward diseased, mindless impulses, relying on 'the skin of the irrational beasts' as his support for his passion, he will form other, better choices afterward—after his departure from the body—having now come to know the difference of virtue from vice in his inability to participate in divinity, as long as the cleansing fire has not fully purged away the impurities that have become mingled with his soul.

16 "All these things have made the use of the body indispensable for us; by it, our free choice is preserved, and our way to ascend back toward the Good is not hindered. But by this circuitous passage through the range of things we willingly do, an impulse toward the Good develops in us: either by our choices here, already in this fleshly life, bringing about a spiritual life free from passion—a life such as we hear the patriarchs and prophets led, and those with and after them, who ran in the way of virtue and self-discipline[35] toward perfection (I mean the disciples and apostles and martyrs, and all who valued the virtuous life above the material one; even if they are fewer in number than the multitude of those who declined toward evil, they nonetheless bear witness to the fact that it is possible to achieve virtue while in the flesh)—or else, with the rest of humanity, through our training later on in the purifying fire, casting away our

[35]Greek: φιλοσοφία (*philosophia*).

GNO 57 καὶ πρὸς τὴν ἐξ ἀρχῆς ἀποκληρωθεῖσαν | τῇ φύσει χάριν διὰ τῆς τῶν ἀγαθῶν ἐπιθυμίας ἑκουσίως ἐπανιόντων. οὐ γὰρ εἰς ἀεὶ παραμένει τῶν ἀλλοτρίων ἡ ἐπιθυμία τῇ φύσει, διότι πλήσμιον ἑκάστῳ καὶ προσκορές ἐστι τὸ μὴ ἴδιον οὗ μὴ κατ᾽ ἀρχὰς ἔσχεν ἐν ἑαυτῇ τὴν κοινωνίαν ἡ φύσις, μόνον δὲ τὸ συγγενὲς καὶ ὁμόφυλον ποθεινὸν καὶ ἐράσμιον εἰς ἀεὶ διαμένει, ἕως ἂν ἐφ᾽ ἑαυτῆς ἡ φύσις ἀπαράτρεπτος μένῃ. εἰ δέ τινα ἐκτροπὴν πάθοι διὰ μοχθηρᾶς προαιρέσεως, τότε αὐτῇ τῶν ἀλλοτρίων ἡ ἐπιθυμία ἐγγίνεται, ὧν ἡ ἀπόλαυσις ἡδύνει οὐχὶ τὴν φύσιν ἀλλὰ τὸ πάθος τῆς φύσεως, ἐκχωρήσαντος δὲ τοῦ πάθους καὶ ἡ τῶν παρὰ φύσιν ἐπιθυμία συνανεχώρησεν καὶ γίνεται πάλιν αὐτῇ τὸ οἰκεῖον ποθεινὸν καὶ κατάλληλον. τοῦτο δέ ἐστι τὸ καθαρόν τε καὶ ἄϋλον καὶ ἀσώματον, ὅπερ ἴδιον τῆς ὑπερκειμένης τῶν πάντων θεότητος εἰπών τις οὐχ ἁμαρτήσεται. ὡς γὰρ τοῖς σωματικοῖς ὀφθαλμοῖς ῥεύματός τινος δριμυτέρου τὸ ὀπτικὸν πνεῦμα θολώσαντος ἴδιον ὁ ζόφος γίνεται διὰ τὴν τῆς παχύτητος πρὸς τὸ σκότος συγγένειαν, εἰ δὲ δαπανηθείη διά τινος θεραπείας τὸ διοχλῆσαν τῷ πνεύματι, πάλιν τὸ φῶς οἰκεῖον καὶ κατάλληλον γίνεται τῷ καθαρῷ τε καὶ αὐγοειδεῖ τῆς κόρης καταμιγνύμενον, τὸν αὐτὸν τρόπον ἐπειδὴ ῥεύματός τινος δίκην δι᾽ ἀπάτης τοῦ ἀντικειμένου ἐπερρύη τῷ ὀπτικῷ τῆς ψυχῆς ἡ κακία, ἑκουσίως πρὸς τὸν σκοτεινὸν βίον ὁ λογισμὸς ἐπεκλίθη διὰ τοῦ πάθους οἰκειωθεὶς τῷ ζόφῳ (Πᾶς γὰρ
PG 528 | ὁ τὰ φαῦλα πράσσων μισεῖ τὸ φῶς καθώς φησιν ἡ θεία φωνή), ἐκδαπανηθέντος δὲ τοῦ κακοῦ ἐκ τῶν ὄντων καὶ εἰς τὸ μὴ ὂν αὖθις μεταχωρήσαντος πάλιν μεθ᾽ ἡδονῆς ἀναβλέπει πρὸς τὸ φῶς ἡ φύσις τοῦ ἐπιθολοῦντος τὸ καθαρὸν τῆς ψυχῆς ἐκχωρήσαντος. |

---

[36]Literally, "the optic spirit." Ancient medicine believed that the eye contained and directed outward a positive energy, like a ray of light from within the head, which focused on some external object and then was reflected back into the eye in the form of an image of the object itself. Cataracts—which Gregory seems to be describing here—prevented this energy from leaving the eye efficiently, as well as from returning to it unhindered.

attraction toward matter, and through our yearning for good things ascending willingly toward the grace allotted to our nature from the beginning.

"For the desire for things foreign to itself will not always remain in [human] nature, because what is not proper to it can satiate and even be excessive for each of us, since our nature did not have a relationship to these things at the beginning. Only that which we yearn for and love as related to us, as being of the same family as we are, remains always, as long as our nature remains unaltered in itself. But if nature should suffer some diversion through a bad choice, then the yearning for foreign things begins to grow in it, and the enjoyment of these things gives pleasure—not to nature, but to a diseased state of nature; yet when the pathological condition subsides, unnatural desire withdraws along with it, and proper and appropriate yearning comes to function in it again. This is something pure and immaterial and bodiless, something that one would be right to call proper to the divinity that is above all things. For in the eyes of our body some acrid discharge can cloud the eye's proper ability to see,[36] and sight tends to become foggy because of the similarity of the cataract to external darkness; but if what blocks the power of sight is then lessened through some kind of therapy, the proper and appropriate degree of light is restored once again, mingled with the pure and luminous character of the pupil. So in the same way, when vice flows over the optic center of the soul, by the deceit of the enemy, like some kind of effluvium, our reason willingly leans toward a shadowy form of life, growing more like darkness because of passion ('for everyone who does evil things hates the light' [Jn 3.20] as the voice of God says); but when evil is spent from beings and is transformed again into simple nothingness,[37] nature will once again gladly gaze upward to the light, with what had clouded the soul's purity now removed.

[37]Since evil, in the view of most ancient philosophers, was essentially the lack of some aspect of reality rather than a positive entity, it was natural to conceive of the defeat of evil as its transformation into total nothingness, as Gregory suggests here.

GNO 58 Μάταιον τοίνυν δέδεικται διὰ τῶν εἰρημένων τὸ δυσμενῶς πρὸς τὴν τῆς σαρκὸς ἔχειν φύσιν· οὐ γὰρ ταύτης ἤρτηται τῶν κακῶν ἡ αἰτία (ἢ γὰρ ἂν κατὰ πάντων ἐπίσης ἔσχε τὸ κράτος τῶν τὸν σωματικὸν εἰληχότων βίον), ἀλλ' ἐπειδὴ τῶν ἐπ' ἀρετῇ μνημονευομένων ἕκαστος καὶ ἐν σαρκὶ ἦν καὶ ἐν κακίᾳ οὐκ ἦν, φανερὸν διὰ τούτων ἐστὶν ὅτι οὐ τὸ σῶμα τῶν παθημάτων αἴτιον ἀλλ' ἡ προαίρεσις ἡ δημιουργοῦσα τὰ πάθη. τὸ μὲν γὰρ σῶμα καταλλήλως τῇ ἰδίᾳ κινεῖται φύσει, δι' ὧν συντηρεῖται πρὸς τὴν ἑαυτοῦ σύστασιν καὶ διαμονὴν πρὸς ταῦτα ταῖς ἰδίαις ὁρμαῖς διοικούμενον. οἷόν τι λέγω· βρώσεώς ἐστιν αὐτῷ χρεία καὶ πόσεως ὥστε τὸ διαπνευσθὲν τῆς δυνάμεως πάλιν ἀντεισαχθῆναι τῷ λείποντι. πρὸς τοῦτο κινεῖται ἡ ὄρεξις. πάλιν διὰ τῆς τῶν γινομένων διαδοχῆς θνητὴ οὖσα ἡ τοῦ σώματος φύσις ἀθανατίζεται. διὰ τοῦτο καὶ πρὸς ταύτην τὴν ὁρμὴν ἐπιτηδείως ἔχει. ἔτι πρὸς τούτοις γυμνὸν τοῦ ἐκ τῶν τριχῶν σκεπάσματος τὸ σῶμα πεποίηται, οὗ χάριν τῆς ἔξωθεν περιβολῆς ἐδεήθημεν. ἀλλὰ καὶ πρὸς φλογμόν τε καὶ κρύος καὶ ἐπομβρίαν ἀντισχεῖν οὐ δυνάμενοι τὴν ἐκ τῶν οἴκων σκέπην ἐπεζητήσαμεν. ταῦτα καὶ τὰ τοιαῦτα ὁ μὲν λελογισμένως πρὸς τὴν χρείαν βλέπων δέχεται τούτων ἕκαστον ἀπραγμόνως ὅρον τῆς ὀρέξεως τὸν σκοπὸν τῆς χρείας ποιούμενος· οἶκον ἱμάτιον συζυγίαν τροφήν, δι' ἑκάστου τούτων θεραπεύων τὸ ἐνδέον τῆς φύσεως. ὁ δὲ τῶν ἡδονῶν ὑπηρέτης ὁδοὺς παθημάτων τὰς ἀναγκαίας χρείας ἐποίησεν ἀντὶ μὲν τῆς τροφῆς τὴν τρυφὴν ἐπιζητῶν, ἀντὶ δὲ τῆς περιβολῆς τὸν καλλωπισμὸν προαιρούμενος, ἀντὶ δὲ τῆς τῶν
GNO 59 οἴκων χρείας | τὴν πολυτέλειαν, ἀντὶ δὲ τῆς παιδοποιΐας πρὸς τὰς παρανόμους τε καὶ ἀπηγορευμένας ἡδονὰς βλέπων. διὰ τοῦτο ἥ τε πλεονεξία πλατείαις ταῖς πύλαις τῇ ἀνθρωπίνῃ ζωῇ εἰσεκώμασεν,

[38]Gregory is talking about the sexual urge, which is naturally directed toward reproduction and the continuity of the human species. Some ancient Greek thought linked the sexual urge to a longing for immortality; for example, Aristotle claims that a plant or animal reproduces "in order that, as far as its nature allows, it may partake

17 "What we have said shows, then, how foolish it is to resent the nature of the flesh. For the cause of our ills cannot be identified with it—otherwise it would have had an equal dominance over all who share this life in the body. But since each of those whom we remember for their virtue also had a fleshly life, but did not live dominated by vice, it is clear from this that it is not the body that causes our damaged state, but choice, which shapes our passions. For the body is made to work in a way that corresponds to its own nature, managing, through its particular drives, the operations that lead to its nurture and, beyond that, to its further existence. What I mean is this: it needs food and drink, so that whatever of its energy has been used up might be restored to the one who lacks it. This is the reason why appetite is set in motion. Moreover, by the succession of people being born, the nature of the body, which is mortal, becomes immortal. For this reason, nature is favorably adapted to this [reproductive] urge, as well.[38] And beyond this, the body is formed without the protection that is provided by fur, which is why we need outer garments. We have also sought out the refuge of housing, since we cannot protect ourselves from heat, cold, and storms.

"The person who considers these and similar urges in a reasonable way, in relation to our needs, will accept each of these explanations without difficulty, sketching out a definition of appetite in terms of the goals of our needs—housing, clothing, sex, food, and the rest of them—and through each of these making up for the deficiencies of our nature. But the servant of pleasure has turned necessary needs into pathways for the passions, seeking culinary delight instead of nourishment, choosing style instead of simply clothing, a wealthy residence rather than just appropriate housing, looking for illegitimate, even forbidden, [sexual] pleasures rather than procreation. So it is that greed has come barging into human nature through these

in the eternal and divine." *On the Soul* II.4 (415a29); English translation: J. A. Smith, in *The Complete Works of Aristote: The Revised Oxford Translation*, ed. Jonathan Barnes, vol. 1, Princeton/Bollingen Series 71:2 (Princeton, NJ: Princeton University Press, 1984), 661.

καὶ ἡ μαλακία καὶ ὁ τῦφος καὶ ἡ χαυνότης καὶ ἡ πολυειδὴς ἀσωτία καὶ τὰ τοιαῦτα ὥσπερ τινὲς ὄζοι καὶ ξηράδες τῶν ἀναγκαίων χρειῶν παρεβλάστησαν διὰ τὸ παρελθεῖν τοὺς τῆς χρείας ὅρους τὴν ὄρεξιν καὶ τοῖς ἐπ᾽ οὐδενὶ χρησίμῳ σπουδαζομένοις ἐπιπλατύνεσθαι. τί γὰρ κοινὸν ἔχει πρὸς τὸ τῆς τροφῆς χρήσιμον ὁ διάγλυφος ἄργυρος χρυσῷ καὶ λίθοις ἐπανθιζόμενος; ἢ τίνος χάριν ἐπεδεήθη τὸ ἱμάτιον τοῦ χρυσοῦ νήματος καὶ τῆς εὐανθοῦς πορφυρίδος καὶ τῆς ὑφαντικῆς ζωγραφίας, δι᾽ ἧς πόλεμοι καὶ θῆρες καὶ τὰ τοιαῦτα τοῖς χιτῶσί τε καὶ τοῖς ἐπενδύμασι παρὰ τῶν ὑφαινόντων ἐνζωγραφοῦνται, οἷς συμμαχοῦσα ἡ τῆς πλεονεξίας ἐνεφύη νόσος; ἵνα γὰρ ἐπιτύχωσι τῆς πρὸς ταῦτα παρασκευῆς καὶ δυνάμεως, τὰς τῶν ἐπιθυμουμένων ὕλας παρὰ τῆς πλεονεξίας πορίζονται. ἡ δὲ
PG 529 | πλεονεξία τῇ ἀπληστίᾳ τὴν εἴσοδον ἤνοιξεν, ἥτις ἐστὶ κατὰ τὸν Σολομῶνα ὁ τετρημένος πίθος ἀεὶ τοῖς ἐπαντλοῦσι λείπων καὶ κενὸς εὑρισκόμενος. οὐκοῦν οὐ τὸ σῶμα τὰς τῶν κακῶν ἀφορμὰς ἀλλ᾽ ἡ προαίρεσις ἐμποιεῖ τὸν σκοπὸν τῆς χρείας εἰς τὴν τῶν ἀτόπων ἐπιθυμίαν ἐκτρέπουσα.

Μὴ τοίνυν κακιζέσθω παρὰ τῶν ἀπερισκέπτων τὸ σῶμα, ᾧ μετὰ ταῦτα διὰ τῆς παλιγγενεσίας μεταστοιχειωθέντι πρὸς τὸ θειότερον
GNO 60 ἡ ψυχὴ καλλωπίσεται τὰ περιττά τε καὶ | ἄχρηστα ὡς πρὸς τὴν ἀπόλαυσιν τῆς μελλούσης ζωῆς τοῦ θανάτου ἀποκαθάραντος. οὐ γὰρ πρὸς ἃ νῦν ἐπιτηδείως ἔχει τὰ αὐτὰ καὶ ἐν τῷ μετὰ ταῦτα χρησιμεύσει βίῳ, ἀλλ᾽ οἰκεία καὶ κατάλληλος ἔσται τῇ ἀπολαύσει τῆς ζωῆς ἐκείνης ἡ τοῦ σώματος ἡμῶν παρασκευὴ ἁρμοδίως πρὸς τὴν τῶν ἀγαθῶν μετουσίαν διατεθεῖσα. οἷόν τι λέγω (κρεῖττον γὰρ ὑποδείγματι τῶν γνωρίμων τινὶ διασαφηνίσαι τὸ νόημα)· ἡ τοῦ σιδήρου βῶλος χρησιμεύει τῇ χαλκευτικῇ τέχνῃ καὶ ἀκατέργαστος ἄκμων γενομένη τοῦ τεχνιτεύοντος. ἀλλ᾽ ὅταν δέῃ πρός τι λεπτότερον μετεργασθῆναι τὸν σίδηρον, τότε δι᾽ ἐπιμελείας τὴν

broad gates, and with it softness and arrogance and vanity and wastefulness in all their forms; and all of these things, like shoots and dried-out branches, have sprung up as by-products of genuine needs, because appetite has gone beyond what our needs specify and has broadened out into pursuits that have no useful purpose. What relationship to essential nourishment is there in an embossed silver vessel, ornamented with gold and gems? Or why does a robe need threads of gold and bright purple, and woven figures in which battles and beasts are depicted by weavers on tunics and shawls? Is it not by association with these things that the disease of avarice is born within us? For in order to provide these things for themselves and have access to them, people seek out the means for what they want out of sheer greed.[39] And greed opens the way for insatiable desire, which is, in Solomon's words, 'a leaky wine-jar'[40]—never holding enough for those who want a drink, always found to be empty. So, then, it is not the body, but free choice that acts as the starting-point for vices, perverting our intention to satisfy needs into a yearning for ridiculous things.

18 "Let not the body, then, be vilified by thoughtless people; after this life the soul will be adorned by a body that is transformed into a more divine state through regeneration, when death has purified it of what is superfluous and useless so that it can enjoy the life to come. For the same things that it finds suitable for this present life will not all be needed in the life after this one, but the organization of our body will instead be appropriate for the enjoyment of that life, fittingly ordered toward our sharing in its blessings. I mean something like this—for it is best to clarify our thought by an example from everyday life: a lump of iron is useful for the blacksmith's craft, since even in an unwrought state it can serve as an anvil for the forger. But when he needs to transform the iron into something more

[39]Literally, "people provide from greed the materials of the things they desire."

[40]See Prov 23.27 (LXX): "Another man's house is a leaky wine-jar." Gregory also refers to this verse in his *Funeral Oration for the Empress Flaccilla* 9. Plato uses the same image in *Gorgias* 493 b–e.

βῶλον τοῦ πυρὸς ἐκκαθάραντος ἅπαν ἀποτίθεται τὸ γεῶδες καὶ ἄχρηστον, ὃ δὴ σκωρίαν οἱ τεχνῖται τῆς ἐργασίας ταύτης κατονομάζουσι, καὶ οὕτως ὁ ποτὲ ἄκμων λεπτουργηθεὶς ἢ θώραξ ἢ ἄλλο τι τῶν λεπτῶν κατασκευασμάτων ἐγένετο τοῦ τοιούτου περιττώματος ἐκκαθαρθεὶς διὰ τῆς χωνείας, ὅπερ ἕως ὅτε ἄκμων ἦν οὐκ ἐνομίζετο πρὸς τὴν τότε χρείαν εἶναι περίττωμα. συνετέλει γάρ τι καὶ ἡ σκωρία πρὸς τὸν ὄγκον τοῦ σιδήρου ἐγκαταμεμιγμένη τῇ βώλῳ. εἰ δὴ νενόηται ἡμῖν τὸ ὑπόδειγμα, μετακτέον ἤδη πρὸς τὸ προκείμενον νόημα τὴν ἐν τῷ ὑποδείγματι θεωρηθεῖσαν διάνοιαν. τί οὖν ἐστι τοῦτο; πολλὰς ἔχει νῦν σκωριωδεῖς ποιότητας ἡ τοῦ σώματος φύσις, αἳ κατὰ μὲν τὴν παροῦσαν ζωὴν πρός τι χρήσιμον συντελοῦσιν, ἀχρήστως δὲ παντάπασι καὶ ἀλλοτρίως ἔχουσι πρὸς
GNO 61 τὴν μετὰ ταῦτα προσδοκωμένην | μακαριότητα. ὅπερ οὖν ἐν τῷ πυρὶ περὶ τὸν σίδηρον γίνεται τὸ ἄχρηστον ἅπαν τῆς χωνείας ἀποποιούσης, τοῦτο διὰ τοῦ θανάτου κατορθοῦται τῷ σώματι παντὸς περιττώματος ἀποποιουμένου διὰ τῆς ἐν τῇ νεκρότητι λύσεως. φανερὰ μὲν οὖν ἐστι πάντως τοῖς ἐπεσκεμμένοις ποῖα ταῦτά ἐστιν ὧν ἀποκαθαίρεται τὸ σῶμα εἰς ὕστερον, ἅπερ εἰ μὴ παρείη κατὰ τὴν παροῦσαν ζωὴν ζημία γίνεται τοῦ βίου τούτου.

Πλὴν ἀλλὰ καὶ παρ' ἡμῶν σαφηνείας χάριν δι' ὀλίγων εἰρήσεται· ἔστω καθ' ὑπόθεσιν ἀντὶ μὲν τῆς βώλου ἡ ὄρεξις ἡ φυσικῶς ἐπὶ πάντων ἐνεργουμένη, ἀντὶ δὲ τῆς σκωρίας ταῦτα πρὸς ἃ νῦν τὰς ὁρμὰς ἔχει ἡ ὄρεξις· ἡδοναὶ καὶ πλοῦτοι καὶ φιλοδοξίαι καὶ δυναστεῖαι καὶ θυμοὶ καὶ τῦφοι καὶ τὰ τοιαῦτα. τούτων ἁπάντων καὶ τῶν τοιούτων καθάρσιον ἀκριβὲς ὁ θάνατος γίνεται· ὧν γυμνωθεῖσά τε καὶ καθαρθεῖσα πάντων ἡ ὄρεξις πρὸς τὸ μόνον ὀρεκτόν τε καὶ ἐπιθυμητὸν καὶ ἐράσμιον τῇ ἐνεργείᾳ
PG 532 τραπήσεται οὐκ ἀποσβέσασα | καθόλου τὰς ἐγκειμένας φυσικῶς ἡμῖν ἐπὶ τὰ τοιαῦτα ὁρμὰς ἀλλὰ πρὸς τὴν ἄϋλον τῶν ἀγαθῶν μετουσίαν μεταποιήσασα. ἐκεῖ γὰρ ὁ ἔρως τοῦ ἀληθινοῦ κάλλους ὁ ἄπαυστος, ἐκεῖ ἡ ἐπαινετὴ τῶν τῆς σοφίας θησαυρῶν πλεονεξία

finely crafted, then fire is used to purify the lump, and it sheds all that is earthy and useless—what craftsmen in this kind of work call *slag*. So what once was an anvil is now finely worked, and becomes a breastplate or some other piece of light equipment, purified by the smelting away of all that is excessive—which, while [the iron] was an anvil, was not thought to be excessive for its use at that time. For the slag, too, contributed something toward the bulk of the iron, while it was mixed into the lump.

"If one thinks, then, about this example, one will transfer the idea one finds in the image to the thought before us. And what is that? The nature of our body has many slag-like qualities, which make their useful contributions during the present life, but will be completely useless and foreign in relation to the blessed state we look forward to after this. What happens, then, in the fire to the iron, when smelting does away with all that is useless, is achieved for the body by death, as all excessive material is eliminated by the annihilation of dying.

19 "Surely it is obvious, then, to those who consider the matter, what these things are, of which the body will later be purified, but the absence of which, if they were not available in this present existence, would constitute a loss for our way of life. For the sake of clarity, though, we will also say a few more words about this.

"Let us suppose, instead of the lump of iron, appetite naturally reaching out in all directions; instead of slag, those things toward which appetite is driven—pleasure and wealth and the desire for reputation, power and strong feelings and self-promotion, and all such things. Death will be an accurate purifier of all these things, and of whatever is like them. Stripped and purged of them all, our appetite will be actively redirected toward what alone is to be desired and yearned for and loved—not quenching completely the drives that are naturally inscribed in us toward such [earthly] things, but transforming them toward an immaterial participation in the Good. For in that life, love of true Beauty will be what is unceasing; there [we will have a] praiseworthy desire to acquire the treasures of Wisdom,

καὶ ἡ καλή τε καὶ ἀγαθὴ φιλοδοξία ἡ τῇ κοινωνίᾳ τῆς τοῦ θεοῦ βασιλείας κατορθουμένη καὶ τὸ καλὸν πάθος τῆς ἀπληστίας <τὸ> οὐδέποτε κόρῳ τῶν ὑπερκειμένων πρὸς τὸν ἀγαθὸν <ἀνιὸν> πόθον ἐπικοπτόμενον. οὐκοῦν μαθὼν ὅτι τοῖς καθήκουσι χρόνοις ὁ τοῦ παντὸς τεχνίτης τὴν τοῦ σώματος βῶλον εἰς ὅπλον εὐδοκίας μεταχαλκεύσει Θώρακα δικαιοσύνης καθώς φησιν ὁ ἀπόστολος
GNO 62 καὶ Μάχαιραν πνεύματος καὶ Περικεφαλαίαν | ἐλπίδος καὶ πᾶσαν τὴν τοῦ θεοῦ Πανοπλίαν κατεργασάμενος, ἀγάπα τὸ ἴδιον σῶμα κατὰ τὸν τοῦ ἀποστόλου νόμον, ὅς φησιν ὅτι Οὐδεὶς τὸ ἑαυτοῦ σῶμα ἐμίσησεν.

Τὸ σῶμα δὲ τὸ κεκαθαρμένον ἀγαπᾶσθαι χρή, οὐ τὴν ἀποποιουμένην σκωρίαν. ἀληθὲς γάρ ἐστιν ὥς φησιν ἡ θεία φωνὴ Ὅτι ἐὰν ἡ ἐπίγειος ἡμῶν οἰκία τοῦ σκήνους καταλυθῇ, τότε αὐτὴν εὑρήσομεν οἰκοδομὴν ἐκ θεοῦ γενομένην οἰκίαν ἀχειροποίητον αἰώνιον ἐν τοῖς οὐρανοῖς, ἀξίαν τοῦ εἶναι αὐτὴν θεοῦ Κατοικητήριον ἐν πνεύματι. καί μοι μηδεὶς χαρακτῆρα καὶ σχῆμα καὶ εἶδος ὑπογραφέτω τῆς ἀχειροποιήτου ἐκείνης οἰκίας καθ' ὁμοιότητα τῶν νῦν ἐπιφαινομένων ἡμῖν χαρακτήρων καὶ διακρινόντων ἡμᾶς ἀπ' ἀλλήλων τοῖς ἰδιώμασιν. οὐ γὰρ μόνης τῆς ἀναστάσεως ἡμῖν παρὰ τῶν θείων λογίων κεκηρυγμένης ἀλλὰ καὶ τὸ δεῖν ἀλλαγῆναι τοὺς ἀνακαινισθέντας διὰ τῆς ἀναστάσεως τῆς θείας διεγγυωμένης γραφῆς, ἀνάγκη πᾶσα κεκρύφθαι παντάπασι καὶ ἀγνοεῖσθαι πρὸς ὅ τι ἀλλαγησόμεθα τῷ μηδὲν ὑπόδειγμα τῶν ἐλπιζομένων ἐν τῷ νῦν καθορᾶσθαι βίῳ. νῦν μὲν γὰρ πᾶν τὸ παχὺ καὶ στερέμνιον ἐκ φύσεως ἔχει τὴν ἐπὶ τὸ κάτω φοράν, τότε δὲ πρὸς τὸ ἀνωφερὲς ἡ μεταποίησις τοῦ σώματος γίνεται οὕτως εἰπόντος τοῦ λόγου ὅτι μετὰ τὸ ἀλλαγῆναι τὴν φύσιν ἐν πᾶσι τοῖς ἀναβεβιωκόσι διὰ τῆς ἀναστάσεως Ἁρπαγησόμεθα ἐν νεφέλαις εἰς ἀπάντησιν τοῦ κυρίου εἰς ἀέρα καὶ οὕτως πάντοτε σὺν κυρίῳ ἐσόμεθα. εἰ τοίνυν

---

[41]Gregory may be alluding here to Origen's famous conjecture (see *On First Principles* 1.8.1; 2.8.3; 9.5–6) that souls originally existed in a state of blissful union with God and each other, but voluntarily turned away from God because they had become sated with their own happiness. One of the frequent criticisms leveled against Origen

there a wholly upright love of honor that is reoriented by our sharing in the Kingdom of God, and there the virtuous passion of insatiability, never to be cut short on the path of its longing for the Good by a surfeit of the blessings that come from above us.[41] So then, learning that at the appropriate time the maker of the universe will re-forge the lump that is the body into the armor of holy desires, shaping 'the breastplate of righteousness,' as the Apostle says, and 'the sword of the Spirit,' and 'the helmet of hope,' and all the rest of the 'full armor of God' (Eph 6.13–17)—love your own body, according to the Apostle's rule, who says, 'No one hates his own body' (Eph 5.29).

20 "But we must love the purified body, not the slag that is cast away. For it is true, as the Word of God puts it, that 'if the earthly house of our dwelling is destroyed,' then we will find that it has itself become a dwelling place made by God, 'an eternal house not made by hands in the heavens' (2 Cor 5.1), worthy of being itself God's 'dwelling place in the Spirit' (Eph 2.22). And let no one describe to me the type and shape and form of that 'house not made by hands' along the lines of the marks and characteristics that [now] distinguish us from one another. For the resurrection is not only proclaimed to us by the Word of God, but Holy Scripture also pledges that those renewed by the resurrection will be *changed* (see 1 Cor 15.51); so it is completely necessary that what we shall be changed to remains [now] wholly hidden and unknown (see 1 Jn 3.2), because no example of what we hope for can be seen in this present life. Now, everything thick and solid naturally has a downward trajectory, but in the future the transformation of the body will direct it upward. So Scripture says that after nature is changed in all who have been raised up by resurrection, 'we shall be caught up in the clouds to meet the Lord in the air, and so we shall always be with the Lord' (1 Thess 4.17).

and his followers in succeeding centuries was that this theory suggested beatitude itself can never be permanent. Gregory, who always takes pains to distance himself from such an idea, here insists that the strong desires and satisfactions of our eschatological state can never lead to surfeit, or to the desire to turn away.

ἐπὶ τῶν ἀλλαγέντων τὸ βάρος οὐ παραμένει τῷ σώματι, ἀλλὰ
συμμετεωροποροῦσι τῇ ἀσωμάτῳ φύσει οἱ πρὸς τὴν θειοτέραν
GNO 63 μεταστοιχειωθέντες κατάστασιν, πάντως ὅτι καὶ τὰ λοιπὰ τῶν |
ἰδιωμάτων τοῦ σώματος πρός τι τῶν θεωτέρων συμμετατίθεται·
τὸ χρῶμα τὸ σχῆμα ἡ περιγραφὴ καὶ τὰ καθ' ἕκαστον πάντα.
τούτου χάριν οὐδεμίαν ἀνάγκην ὁρῶμεν τοῖς ἀλλαγεῖσι διὰ τῆς
ἀναστάσεως ἐνθεωρεῖσθαι τὴν τοιαύτην διαφορὰν ἣν νῦν διὰ τὴν
τῶν ἐπιγινομένων ἀκολουθίαν ἀναγκαίως ἔσχεν ἡ φύσις (οὔτε μὴν
ὅτι οὐκ ἔσται σαφῶς ἔστιν ἀποφήνασθαι ἀγνοούντων ἡμῶν εἰς ὅ
τι ταῦτα διὰ τῆς ἀλλαγῆς μεταβήσεται), ἀλλ' ὅτι μὲν γένος ἔσται
τῶν πάντων ἕν, ὅταν ἓν σῶμα Χριστοῦ οἱ πάντες γενώμεθα τῷ ἑνὶ
χαρακτῆρι μεμορφωμένοι, οὐκ ἀμφιβάλλομεν πᾶσι κατὰ τὸ ἴσον
τῆς θείας εἰκόνος ἐπιλαμπούσης, τί δὲ ἡμῖν ἀντὶ τῶν τοιούτων
ἰδιωμάτων ἐν τῇ ἀλλαγῇ τῆς φύσεως προσγενήσεται, κρεῖττον
PG 533 | εἶναι πάσης στοχαστικῆς ἐννοίας ἀποφαινόμεθα. ὡς δ' ἂν μὴ
καθ' ὅλου ἀγύμναστος ἡμῖν ὁ περὶ τούτου λόγος καταλειφθείη,
τοῦτό φαμεν ὅτι εἰς οὐδὲν ἕτερον τῆς κατὰ τὸ ἄρρεν καὶ θῆλυ
διαφορᾶς συνεργούσης τῇ φύσει πλὴν τῆς παιδοποιΐας τάχα
τινὰ στοχασμὸν ἔστιν ἀναλαβεῖν τῆς ἐπηγγελμένης τοῦ θεοῦ
τῶν ἀγαθῶν εὐλογίας ἐπάξιον ἐν τῷ περὶ τούτου λόγῳ, ὅτι εἰς
τὴν ἐκείνου τοῦ τόκου ὑπηρεσίαν μεταβήσεται ἡ γεννητικὴ τῆς
φύσεως δύναμις, οὗ μετέσχεν ὁ μέγας Ἠσαΐας εἰπὼν ὅτι Ἀπὸ
τοῦ φόβου σου, κύριε, ἐν γαστρὶ ἐλάβομεν καὶ ὠδινήσαμεν καὶ
ἐτέκομεν· πνεῦμα σωτηρίας σου ἐκυήσαμεν ἐπὶ τῆς γῆς. εἰ γὰρ
ἀγαθὸς ὁ τοιοῦτος τόκος καὶ σωτηρίας αἰτία γίνεται ἡ τεκνογονία
καθώς φησιν ὁ ἀπόστολος, οὐδέποτε τὸ πνεῦμα τῆς σωτηρίας

---

[42]Gregory is more agnostic here about the future of sexual differentiation in the risen human body than he is in his much-discussed treatment in *De hominis opificio* 16–17. There he argues, on the basis of Genesis 1.27–28, that the differentiation of male and female was not part of God's original plan for the human being who was made in God's image as a unity of the spiritual and the corporeal, but was introduced at the

"If, then, heaviness will not remain in the bodies of those who are changed, but those who are transformed into a more divine state will move through the air along with bodiless nature, probably the other characteristics of the body will also be transformed into something more divine—color, shape, external form, and all the particular details. For this reason, let us not feel we must imagine in those changed by resurrection the kind of [sexual] differentiation that human nature now necessarily has, in view of the succession of our descendants (although it is not possible to prove clearly that this will *not* be so, since we do not know what these things will be changed to by our transformation).[42] But we have no doubt that then there will be one race including all, when all of us will become one body of Christ, formed by the one shape, since the divine image will illuminate us all equally; and we shall make it clear that what will be given to us in that change of our nature, in place of these present characteristics, will be better than any idea we can form by guesswork.

"And so that what we have said about these things might not be left generally untested, let us also say this: since the distinction into male and female does not aid nature to accomplish anything else but the generation of children, perhaps it is possible to make a worthy guess about the future blessings promised by God for our benefit in biblical texts dealing with this. For we read that in order to serve the purpose of that procreation, the generative power of nature will change—[an idea] in which the great Isaiah shared, when he said, 'Out of fear of you, O Lord, we have conceived in our belly and have gone into labor and given birth; we have spread the spirit of your salvation over the earth' (Is 26.17–18, LXX). For if this present kind of childbirth is good, and this form of procreation is the source of salvation, as the Apostle says (1 Tim 2.15), then no one who once has

moment of creation to express and accompany the mortality and continuing conflicts that God foresaw would be the result of humanity's fall. In that view, a resurrected and restored humanity would also no longer be divided into male and female. Here, however, Gregory claims to be less certain about the eschatological future and purpose of sexual differentiation.

γεννῶν τις παύεται ὁ ἅπαξ διὰ τοῦ τοιούτου τόκου τὸν πληθυσμὸν
GNO 64 τῶν ἀγαθῶν ἑαυτῷ τεκνωσάμενος. ἀλλὰ κἂν τὸν | χαρακτῆρά
τις λέγῃ ᾧ μεμορφώμεθα, πάλιν ἡμῖν ἐν τῇ ἀναβιώσει τὸν αὐτὸν
συμπαρέσεσθαι, οὐδὲ πρὸς τοῦτο πρόχειρος ἡμῶν ἐστιν ἡ διάνοια
οὕτως ἢ ἑτέρως ἔχειν ὑπονοῆσαι. εἴτε γὰρ ἐπὶ τοῦ αὐτοῦ λέγοι τις
εἴδους τὴν ἀναβίωσιν ἔσεσθαι, εἰς πολλὴν ἀμηχανίαν ἐκπεσεῖται ὁ
λόγος διὰ τὸ μὴ τὸν αὐτὸν ἑαυτῷ κατὰ τὸ εἶδος τοῦ χαρακτῆρος
πάντοτε διαμένειν τὸν ἄνθρωπον ὑπό τε τῶν ἡλικιῶν καὶ τῶν
παθημάτων ἄλλοτε πρὸς ἄλλο εἶδος μεταπλασσόμενον. ἄλλως
γὰρ μορφοῦται τὸ νήπιον καὶ τὸ μειράκιον, ἄλλως ὁ παῖς ὁ
ἀνὴρ ὁ μεσῆλιξ ὁ παρῆλιξ ὁ γηραιὸς ὁ πρέσβυς· οὐδὲν τούτων
ὡσαύτως ἔχει πρὸς τὸ ἕτερον. ἀλλὰ καὶ ὁ τῷ ἰκτέρῳ κατιωθεὶς
καὶ ὁ ἐξῳδηκὼς τῷ ὑδέρῳ ὅ τε ξηρανθεὶς ἐν τηκεδόνι καὶ ὁ
πολυσαρκήσας ἔκ τινος δυσκρασίας, ὁ κατάχολος ὁ αἱματώδης ὁ
φλεγματίας ἑκάστου τούτων πρὸς τὴν ἐπικρατοῦσαν δυσκρασίαν
συμμορφουμένου οὔτε παραμένειν ταῦτα μετὰ τὸ ἀναβιῶναι
καλῶς ἔχει λογίσασθαι τῆς ἀλλαγῆς πάντα μετασκευαζούσης
πρὸς τὸ θειότερον οὔτε οἷον ἡμῖν ἐπανθήσει τὸ εἶδος εὔκολόν
ἐστιν ἀναλογίσασθαι τῶν κατ᾽ ἐλπίδα ἡμῖν προκειμένων ἀγαθῶν
ὑπὲρ ὀφθαλμὸν καὶ ἀκοὴν καὶ διάνοιαν εἶναι πεπιστευμένων. ἢ
τάχα γνωριστικὸν εἶδος ἑκάστου τὴν ποιὰν ἰδιότητα τῶν ἠθῶν
εἰπών τις οὐ τοῦ παντὸς ἁμαρτήσεται. καθάπερ γὰρ νῦν ἡ κατά
τι παραλλαγὴ τῶν ἐν ἡμῖν στοιχείων τὰς τῶν χαρακτήρων ἐν
ἑκάστῳ διαφορὰς ἐξεργάζεται κατὰ πλεονασμὸν ἢ ἐλάττωσιν τῶν
ἀντιστοιχούντων τινὸς σχηματιζομένου τε καὶ χρωννυμένου τοῦ
GNO 65 κατὰ τὴν μορφὴν ἰδιώματος, οὕτω μοι | δοκεῖ τὰ εἰδοποιοῦντα
τότε τὴν ἑκάστου μορφὴν οὐ ταῦτα τὰ στοιχεῖα γίνεσθαι ἀλλὰ τὰ
τῆς κακίας ἢ τῆς ἀρετῆς ἰδιώματα, ὧν ἡ ποιὰ πρὸς ἄλληλα μίξις
ἢ οὕτως ἢ ἑτέρως τὸ εἶδος παρασκευάζει, χαρακτηρίζεσθαι, οἷον
δή τι σχεδὸν καὶ ἐπὶ τοῦ παρόντος γίνεται βίου, ὅταν ἡ ἔξωθεν

given birth for himself to a multitude of blessings by a childbirth such as this will ever stop generating the spirit of salvation. But if someone should insist that the form into which we are changed will be just the same for us in our new existence [as it is now], our reasoning has no easy way to decide in response whether they will be this in the same way or in another. For if one argues that we will come to life again in the same form [that we have now], our reasoning will encounter great difficulty, since even now the human person does not always remain the same, as far as outward form goes, but is reshaped at various times into different forms under the influence of age or disease. The baby, after all, has a different form from the teenager, the young man is different again, [and similarly] the adult, the middle-aged person, the person past his prime, the elderly person, the very old; none of these times in life is identical [in shape] with the others. So also the person who has come down with jaundice, the person swollen with dropsy, the person wasted by some consuming disease, the person who is obese because of overeating, the bilious person, the sanguine person, the phlegmatic person—each of them is physically conformed to his or her dominant disorder. It does not seem right to suppose that they will continue to be this way after being raised, when change has reshaped them into a more divine form, nor can one guess that they will even be as our form now flourishes best, since we believe that the blessings stored up for our hope will be above and beyond [the powers of] eye and hearing and imagination.[43]

"Perhaps, though, one is not wholly mistaken in saying that the recognizable form of each person will be the particular shape of his or her character. Just as now the variations, in some respect, of the elements that constitute us bring about the differences in our external form, and our characteristic shape is being sketched out and colored by an excess or deficiency of some of our various components, so, too, it seems to me that what will eventually give each of us form in the next life will not be these material elements, but that

[43]See 1 Cor 2.9.

τοῦ προσώπου διάθεσις τὴν ἐν τῷ κρυπτῷ τῆς ψυχῆς καταμηνύῃ
διάθεσιν, ὅθεν ῥᾳδίως ἐπιγινώσκομεν τόν τε τῇ λύπῃ κρατούμενον
καὶ τὸν τῷ θυμῷ διανεστηκότα καὶ τὸν ἐν ἐπιθυμίᾳ λυόμενον
καὶ ἐκ τοῦ ἐναντίου τὸν φαιδρὸν τὸν ἀόργητον τὸν τῷ σεμνῷ
PG 536 χαρακτῆρι τῆς σωφροσύνης καλλωπιζόμενον. | ὥσπερ τοίνυν
κατὰ τὴν ἐνεστῶσαν ζωὴν μορφὴ γίνεται ἡ ποιὰ διάθεσις τῆς
καρδίας καὶ πρὸς τὸ ἐγκείμενον πάθος τὸ τοῦ ἀνθρώπου εἶδος
ἀπεικονίζεται, οὕτω μοι δοκεῖ πρὸς τὸ θειότερον ὑπαλλαγείσης
τῆς φύσεως εἰδοποιεῖσθαι διὰ τοῦ ἤθους ὁ ἄνθρωπος οὐκ ἄλλο τι
ὢν καὶ ἄλλο φαινόμενος, ἀλλ’ ὅπερ ἐστὶ τοῦτο καὶ γινωσκόμενος
ὡς ὁ σώφρων ὁ δίκαιος ὁ πρᾶος ὁ καθαρὸς ὁ ἀγαπητικὸς ὁ
φιλόθεος, καὶ πάλιν ἐν τούτοις ἢ ὁ πάντα ἔχων τὰ ἀγαθὰ ἢ ὁ ἑνὶ
μόνῳ κοσμούμενος ἢ ὁ ἐν τοῖς πλείοσιν εὑρισκόμενος ἢ ὁ ἐν τῷδε
μὲν ἐλαττούμενος πλεονεκτῶν δὲ κατὰ τὸ ἕτερον. ἐκ τούτων
γὰρ καὶ τῶν τοιούτων, τῶν τε κατὰ τὸ κρεῖττον καὶ τῶν κατὰ τὸ
ἐναντίον ἐπιθεωρουμένων ἰδιωμάτων, οἷον εἰς διαφόρους ἰδέας
οἱ καθ’ ἕκαστον ἀπ’ ἀλλήλων μερίζονται, ἕως ἂν τοῦ ἐσχάτου
GNO 66 ἐχθροῦ καταργηθέντος ὥς φησιν ὁ | ἀπόστολος καὶ τῆς κακίας
καθόλου πάντων τῶν ὄντων ἐξοικισθείσης ἓν τὸ θεοειδὲς κάλλος
ἐπαστράψῃ τοῖς πᾶσιν, ᾧ κατ’ ἀρχὰς ἐμορφώθημεν. τοῦτο δέ ἐστι
φῶς καὶ καθαρότης καὶ ἀφθαρσία καὶ ζωὴ καὶ ἀλήθεια καὶ τὰ
τοιαῦτα, [οὐδὲ γὰρ ἀπεικός ἐστιν ἡμέρας τέκνα καὶ φωτὸς εἶναί τε
καὶ φαίνεσθαι] φωτὸς δὲ καὶ καθαρότητος καὶ ἀφθαρσίας οὐδεμία
παραλλαγὴ οὐδὲ διαφορὰ πρὸς τὸ ὁμογενὲς εὑρεθήσεται, ἀλλὰ μία
χάρις ἐπιλάμψει τοῖς πᾶσιν, ὅταν υἱοὶ φωτὸς γενόμενοι λάμψωσιν
ὡς ὁ ἥλιος κατὰ τὴν ἀψευδῆ τοῦ κυρίου φωνήν. ἀλλὰ καὶ τὸ
πάντας ἔσεσθαι τετελειωμένους εἰς τὸ ἓν κατὰ τὴν ἐπαγγελίαν τοῦ
θεοῦ λόγου τῆς αὐτῆς ἔχεται διανοίας τῷ μίαν καὶ τὴν αὐτὴν τοῖς
πᾶσιν ἐπιφανήσεσθαι χάριν, ὡς τὴν αὐτὴν εὐφροσύνην ἕκαστον τῷ
πέλας ἀντιχαρίζεσθαι, δι’ οὗ ἕκαστος καὶ εὐφραίνεται τοῦ ἑτέρου

rather the characteristics of vice and virtue—the particular mix of them with each other, this way or that, bringing about our particular form—will be stamped on us. Something like this even happens in the present life, when the external expression on our faces hints at the disposition hidden in our souls. So we easily recognize the person bowed down by sorrow, and the person roused by anger, and the person consumed by desire—and on the other side, the person radiant with joy, the person free of rage, the person adorned with the seriousness of balance. As in this present life, then, a particular attitude of the heart takes shape, and visibly forms the human appearance according to what is experienced within, so, it seems to me, when our nature is transformed into something more divine, the human person will be given shape by his or her character: not being one thing and appearing to be something else, but recognized to be what one is—balanced, just, gentle, pure, lovable, devout—and moreover will either be found to have all these qualities (or most of them), or to be lacking in one but abounding in another.

"From these qualities and others like them—recognized in various visible characteristics, for better or for worse—individuals are to be distinguished from each other, as it were, into different types, until, 'with the last enemy destroyed' (as the Apostle says [1 Cor 15.26]), and with evil completely driven out of all beings, a single godlike Beauty will shine forth in all people, the Beauty according to which we were formed at the beginning. This is light and purity and incorruptibility and life and truth and all such things; for it is likely we will be, and will seem to be, 'children of day and of the light' (1 Thess 5.5); and no change or difference will be found in light and purity and incorruption, as far as their internal likeness goes, but one grace will radiate on all when, having become 'children of light,' they will 'shine like the sun' (Mt 13.43), according to the Lord's word, which cannot deceive. But the fact that all will also be perfected as one, according to the promise of God's Word, means the same thing as the promise that one and the same grace will appear in all, so that each will find joy in sharing in the same happiness as his neighbor.

κάλλος βλέπων καὶ ἀντευφραίνει μηδεμιᾶς κακίας μεταμορφούσης τὸ εἶδος εἰς εἰδεχθῆ χαρακτῆρα.

Ταῦτα ἡμῖν ὁ νοῦς ὁ ἡμέτερος ἀντὶ τῶν κατοιχομένων διείλεκται τὰς φωνὰς ἐκείνων ὡς δυνατὸν ἡμῖν ὑποκρινόμενος. ἡμεῖς δὲ τῇ τοῦ μεγάλου Παύλου φωνῇ τὴν πρὸς τοὺς βαρυπενθοῦντας συμβουλὴν περιγράψωμεν ὅτι Οὐ θέλω ὑμᾶς ἀγνοεῖν, ἀδελφοί, περὶ τῶν κεκοιμημένων, ἵνα μὴ λυπῆσθε ὡς καὶ οἱ λοιποὶ οἱ μὴ ἔχοντες ἐλπίδα.

Εἰ οὖν τι μεμαθήκαμεν σπουδῆς ἄξιον περὶ τῶν κεκοιμημένων
δι᾽ ὧν ἡμῖν ὁ λόγος τὰ περὶ τούτων ἐφιλοσόφησε, μηκέτι τὴν
GNO 67 δυσγενῆ ταύτην καὶ ἀνδραποδώδη λύπην | παραδεξώμεθα, ἀλλ᾽
εἰ χρὴ καὶ λυπεῖσθαι, ἐκείνην ἑλώμεθα τὴν λύπην τὴν ἐπαινετὴν
καὶ ἐνάρετον. ὡς γὰρ τῆς ἡδονῆς τὸ μέν ἐστι κτηνῶδες καὶ ἄλογον
τὸ δὲ καθαρόν τε καὶ ἄϋλον, οὕτω καὶ τὸ ἀντικείμενον τῇ ἡδονῇ
πρὸς κακίαν καὶ ἀρετὴν διαστέλλεται. ἔστιν οὖν τι καὶ πένθους
εἶδος μακαριζόμενον καὶ πρὸς κτῆσιν ἀρετῆς οὐκ ἀπόβλητον,
ὅπερ ἐναντίως ἔχει πρὸς τὴν ἄλογον ταύτην καὶ ἀνδραποδώδη
κατήφειαν. ὁ μὲν γὰρ ἐν ταύτῃ γενόμενος ἑαυτοῦ μετὰ ταῦτα
διὰ μεταμελείας καθάψεται ὡς ἔξω τοῦ καθεστῶτος παρενεχθείς,
ὅτε τοῦ πάθους ἥττων ἐγένετο. τὸ δὲ μακαριζόμενον πένθος
ἀμεταμέλητον καὶ ἀνεπαίσχυντον ἔχει τὴν σκυθρωπότητα τοῖς δι᾽
PG 537 αὐτοῦ τὸν ἐν ἀρετῇ κατορθοῦσι βίον. | πενθεῖ γὰρ ὡς ἀληθῶς ὁ
ἐν συναισθήσει τῶν ἀγαθῶν ἐκείνων γενόμενος ὧν ἀποπέπτωκεν,
ἀντιπαραθεὶς τὴν ἐπίκηρον ταύτην καὶ ῥυπῶσαν ζωὴν τῇ ἀκηράτῳ
ἐκείνῃ μακαριότητι, ἧς ἐν ἐξουσίᾳ ἦν πρὶν τῇ ἐξουσίᾳ εἰς κακὸν
ἀποχρήσασθαι, καὶ ὅσῳ πλέον ἐπὶ τῷ τοιούτῳ βίῳ βαρύνει τὸ

Because of this, each will rejoice in gazing on his neighbor's beauty, and the neighbor will rejoice in return at the form the other has received, with no ill will ever changing the shape of this into that of hatred."[44]

21 This is what our Mind tells us, on behalf of the departed, personifying their voices to us as far as possible. But let us, with the words of the great Paul, offer some hints of advice to those weighed down by grief: "I do not wish you to be ignorant, brothers and sisters, about those who have fallen asleep, so that you might not grieve like the rest, who have no hope" (1 Thess 4.13). If we have learned anything worth taking seriously about those who have died, from what our reason has argued for us about them, let us no longer give place to a low-minded, servile grief; but if it is necessary to grieve, let us choose a form of grief that is praiseworthy and virtuous. Just as some forms of pleasure are bestial and unthinking, others pure and immaterial, so the opposite of pleasure is distinguished into the vicious and the virtuous. There is a form of mourning, then, that is called blessed[45] and that we must not overlook in acquiring virtue; it is the opposite of an irrational and slavish dejection. The person who experiences [such dejection] later will have a change of heart and get hold of him- or herself, having moved beyond the state he was in when overcome by grief. The mourning that is called blessed, on the other hand, involves a sadness that does not call for a change of heart or repentance in those who, because of it, live their lives in virtue. For the person who truly grieves has become aware of those blessings from which he has fallen, by putting this soiled, mortal existence in the place of that undying blessedness, in whose power we lived before we misused our freedom for evil; the more a grief over losing such a blessed life weighs

[44]Here Gregory ends the imagined address of Mind to the reader, analyzing our bodily life in the present world and the Christian hope for resurrection from the perspective of those who have already experienced death. He returns now to a more straightforward homiletic style.

[45]See Mt 5.4.

πένθος, τοσούτῳ μᾶλλον ἐπιταχύνει ἑαυτῷ τὴν τῶν ποθουμένων
ἀγαθῶν κτῆσιν. ἡ γὰρ τῆς τοῦ καλοῦ ζημίας συναίσθησις τῆς περὶ
τὸ ποθούμενον σπουδῆς ὑπέκκαυμα γίνεται. οὐκοῦν ἐπειδήπερ
ἔστιν καὶ σωτήριόν τι πένθος καθὼς ὁ λόγος ὑπέδειξεν, ἀκούσατε,
οἱ πρὸς τὸ τῆς λύπης πάθος εὐκόλως καταφερόμενοι, ὅτι οὐ
κωλύομεν τὴν λύπην, ἀλλ᾽ ἀντὶ τῆς κατεγνωσμένης τὴν ἀγαθὴν
συμβουλεύομεν. μὴ λυπεῖσθε τοίνυν τὴν τοῦ κόσμου λύπην τὴν
κατεργαζομένην τὸν θάνατον, καθώς φησιν ὁ ἀπόστολος, ἀλλὰ
τὴν κατὰ θεόν, ἧς τὸ πέρας ἡ τῆς ψυχῆς ἐστι σωτηρία. τὸ γὰρ
εἰκῇ καὶ μάτην τοῖς κεκοιμημένοις ἐπιχεόμενον δάκρυον τάχα καὶ
GNO 68 κατακρίσεως αἴτιον | γίνεται τῷ κακῶς οἰκονομοῦντι τὸ χρήσιμον.
εἰ γὰρ ἐπὶ τούτῳ τὴν λυπηρὰν ταύτην διάθεσιν ἐνετεκτήνατο τῇ
φύσει ὁ πάντα ἐν σοφίᾳ ποιήσας ἐφ᾽ ᾧτε καθάρσιον μὲν αὐτὴν
εἶναι τῆς προκατασχούσης κακίας ἐφόδιον δὲ τῆς τῶν ἐλπιζομένων
ἀγαθῶν μετουσίας, τάχα ὁ μάτην καὶ ἀνωφελῶς ἐκχέων τὸ δάκρυον
διαβληθήσεται τῷ ἰδίῳ δεσπότῃ κατὰ τὸν εὐαγγελικὸν λόγον ὡς
κακὸς οἰκονόμος διασπείρων ἀχρήστως τὸν πιστευθέντα πλοῦτον.
πᾶν γὰρ τὸ ἐπ᾽ ἀγαθῷ χρησιμεῦον πλοῦτός ἐστι τοῖς τιμίοις τῶν
κειμηλίων ἐναριθμούμενος. οὐ θέλω οὖν ὑμᾶς ἀγνοεῖν, ἀδελφοί,
περὶ τῶν κεκοιμημένων ταῦτα ἃ μεμαθήκαμεν, καὶ εἴ τι ἄλλο
πρὸς τούτοις παρὰ τοῦ πνεύματος τοῦ ἁγίου τοῖς τελειοτέροις
ἀποκαλύπτεται μάθημα, Ἵνα μὴ λυπῆσθε ὡς καὶ οἱ λοποὶ οἱ μὴ
ἔχοντες ἐλπίδα. μόνων γάρ ἐστι τῶν ἀπίστων τὸ τῷ παρόντι
βίῳ τὰς τοῦ ζῆν ἐλπίδας περιορίζειν, καὶ διὰ τοῦτο συμφορᾶς
ἄξιον ποιοῦνται τὸν θάνατον, ὅτι αὐτοῖς τὸ πιστευόμενον παρ᾽
ἡμῖν οὐκ ἐλπίζεται. ἡμεῖς δὲ τῷ μεγάλῳ ἐγγυητῇ τῆς ἐκ νεκρῶν
ἀναστάσεως πεπιστευκότες αὐτῷ τῷ δεσπότῃ πάσης τῆς κτίσεως,
ὃς διὰ τοῦτο καὶ ἀπέθανεν καὶ ἀνέστη, ἵνα τῷ ἔργῳ τὸν περὶ τῆς
ἀναστάσεως λόγον πιστώσηται, ἀναμφιβόλως ἔχομεν τῶν ἀγαθῶν

one down, so much the more quickly does one regain for oneself the blessings one longs for. A perception of the loss of the Good, after all, becomes combustible fuel for serious striving toward our real goal.

Since, then, grief can be a healthy thing, as our argument has shown, listen, you who are easily carried away toward the passion of sorrow: we do not prohibit mourning, but we recommend to you the right kind, rather than the kind we have criticized. Do not mourn, then, with "the world's kind of mourning," which "works death," as the Apostle says, but with God's kind, whose end is the salvation of the soul (2 Cor 7.10). Tears poured forth pointlessly and vainly over those who have fallen asleep can perhaps even become a cause for condemnation, in that one has made poor use of a good opportunity. For if the wise creator of all things has built the affection of grief into our nature for this purpose, that it might be a purgative for the vice that previously dominated us, and so a support toward our sharing in the good things we hope for, perhaps the person who sheds tears vainly and without purpose will stand accused before his own master, as the Gospel passage says, for wasting the wealth entrusted to him without gaining any benefit.[46] For all that we put to good use will be counted as wealth, and deposited with the most precious goods in the treasury.

"I do not want you to be ignorant, brothers and sisters, about those who have fallen asleep"—ignorant of these things that we have learned here, and any other doctrine beyond them that is revealed by the Holy Spirit to the perfect—"so that you might not grieve like the rest, who have no hope" (1 Thess 4.13). For it belongs simply to those without faith to limit their hopes of living to this present life; for that reason, they consider death to constitute a great misfortune, because what we all believe does not give them hope. But *we* have come to believe in the great Guarantor of our resurrection from the dead—in him who is the Lord of all creation, and who for this reason both died and rose, that by his action he might make credible the good

[46]See Lk 16.1.

τὴν ἐλπίδα, ἧς παρούσης ἡ ἐπὶ τοῖς κατοιχομένοις λύπη χώραν οὐχ ἕξει. ὁ δὲ θεὸς ἡμῶν καὶ κύριος Ἰησοῦς Χριστὸς ὁ παρακαλῶν τοὺς ταπεινοὺς παρακαλέσει ὑμῶν τὰς καρδίας καὶ στηρίξει εἰς τὴν ἑαυτοῦ ἀγάπην διὰ τῶν οἰκτιρμῶν αὐτοῦ. [ὅτι] αὐτῷ ἡ δόξα εἰς τοὺς αἰῶνας τῶν αἰώνων. Ἀμήν.

news of the resurrection.[47] We hope unambiguously for good things; and because we do, grief for those who have departed has no place among us. And our God and Lord, Jesus Christ, who comforts the lowly, will comfort your hearts, and in his compassion strengthen them to love him. To him be glory unto the ages of ages. Amen.

[47] See 1 Thess 5.10.

On Infants Taken Away before Their Time
(*De infantibus praemature abreptis*)

A Note on the Text

This translation is based on the critical edition of this work by Hilda Pollack, as corrected by Hadwig Hörner, in *Gregorii Nysseni Opera* [GNO] III/2:61–99. An earlier translation, by W. Moore and H. A. Wilson, based on the text in the *Patrologia Graeca*, appears in the series *Nicene and Post-Nicene Fathers*, Series 2, vol. 5:372–82. I have added section numbers to the text, for ease and consistency of reference.

This ornate, complex treatise seems to have been written as a kind of rhetorical set piece, perhaps as part of a literary and philosophical competition (sections 1 and 3), on a challenging question at the heart of religious faith: how can belief in a God who is all-good and all-powerful be reconciled with the death of newborn children? It is, at the core, a question of theodicy. Hierius, to whom the essay is addressed, is not otherwise known with certainty, although two philosophers and several imperial officials by that name flourished in the Middle East in the mid-fourth century.[1] One of them ("Hierius 4") was prefect (governor) of Egypt around 360, and is characterized by Libanius, in his Letter 195 (dated 364), as a thoughtful and religious pagan, who, "while he occupied a governor's seat . . . mingled philosophy with government."[2] One manuscript (V) of Gregory's

[1]See p. xix, n. 6 above.

[2]*Libanius: Autobiography and Selected Letters*, vol. 2, trans. A. E. Norman, Loeb Classical Library 479 (Cambridge, MA: Harvard University Press, 1992), 57.

Life of Macrina includes a dedication of that work to a person of this name. Gregory also addressed his own Letter 7 to "the Prefect Hierius," who seems to have had the right to condemn or spare the life of a young man, named Synesius, with whom Gregory was connected.

The Hierius to whom this profound, rather formal work is dedicated may well have been this same official. He is, for example, identified in the first two sections of this work as a leader; as an influential patron and a man of cultivated tastes, of noble bearing, intelligent and well-educated, yet living in material simplicity; and as winning people's affection by his public activity (2). One wonders, too, whether he had himself suffered the untimely loss of an infant child (see 15). Whoever he was, Hierius seems to have invited Gregory—already recognized, it seems, as a rhetorician and a Christian philosopher—along with other thinkers, to write something for him about the mysteries of theodicy and divine Providence, as exemplified by the question of the salvation of children who die at birth, even though he was apparently not formally involved in the rhetorical competition. With great tact, Gregory makes the effort to present his essay on the subject not simply as a showpiece or as part of an intellectual debate, but as a serious reflection on a difficult theological subject (see 7). Although he alludes to biblical texts, especially in the latter part of the essay, Gregory's treatment draws even more from the classical philosophical tradition—an approach that would be especially appropriate if the addressee were not himself a Christian.

The date of the work is uncertain, but Gregory's insistence on his own advanced age suggests it is a late work; so Daniélou dates it after 386 (see Maraval, "Chronology of Works," *Brill Dictionary,* 155) If, however, the addressee is the Hierius we have been discussing, that identification may suggest a somewhat earlier date, perhaps sometime in the 370s.

GNO III/2:67
PG 46:161

ΓΡΗΓΟΡΙΟΥ ΕΠΙΣΚΟΠΟΥ ΝΥΣΣΗΣ ΠΡΟΣ ΙΕΡΙΟΝ ΠΕΡΙ ΤΩΝ ΠΡΟ ΩΡΑΣ ΑΝΑΡΠΑΖΟΜΕΝΩΝ ΝΗΠΙΩΝ

Σοὶ μέν, ὦ ἄριστε, πάντες σοφισταί τε καὶ λογογράφοι τὴν τοῦ
λέγειν πάντως ἐπιδείξονται δύναμιν, οἷόν τινι σταδίῳ τῷ πλάτει τῶν
σῶν θαυμάτων ἐνδιαθέοντες· καὶ γάρ πως οἶδεν μεγαλοφωνότερον
ποιεῖν τὸν λόγον γενναία τις καὶ ἀμφιλαφὴς προτεθεῖσα τοῖς
δυναμένοις ὑπόθεσις, περὶ ἣν ὑψοῦται ὁ λόγος τῷ μεγέθει τῶν
πραγμάτων συνεπαιρόμενος· ἡμεῖς δὲ κατὰ τοὺς γηραιοὺς τῶν
ἵππων ἔξω τοῦ σταδίου τῆς ὑποθέσεως μένοντες τὸ οὖς μόνον ταῖς
ἐπὶ σοὶ τῶν λόγων ἁμίλλαις διαναστήσομεν, εἴ πού τις καὶ μέχρις
ἡμῶν φθάσειεν ἦχος σφοδρῷ τε καὶ συντεταμένῳ τῷ ἅλματι
διὰ τῶν σῶν θαυμάτων τὸν λόγον ἐλαύνων. ἐπεὶ δὲ συμβαίνει,
κἂν ὑπὸ γήρως ἔξω μένῃ τῶν ἀγώνων ὁ ἵππος, πολλάκις αὐτὸν
τῷ κτύπῳ τῶν κατακροαινόντων εἰς προθυμίαν διεγειρόμενον
τήν τε κεφαλὴν ἀνέχειν καὶ ὁρᾶν ἐναγώνιον πνέειν τε θυμῶδες
καὶ ὑποκινεῖν τοὺς πόδας κοινῇ, πυκνῶς τῷ ἐδάφει τὰς ὁπλὰς
GNO 68 ἐπαράσσοντα, ᾧ προθυμία μόνη πρὸς τοὺς ἀγῶνάς ἐστιν, ἡ δὲ |
τοῦ τρέχειν δύναμις προανηλώθη τῷ χρόνῳ· τὸν αὐτὸν τρόπον καὶ
ὁ ἡμέτερος λόγος ἐξαγώνιος μένων διὰ τὸ γῆρας καὶ παραχωρῶν
τοῦ σταδίου τοῖς ἀκμαίοις κατὰ τὴν παίδευσιν μόνην σοι δείκνυσι
τὴν προθυμίαν τοῦ ἐθέλειν ἂν καὶ ἐπὶ σοῦ ἀγωνίσασθαι, εἴπερ ἡβῴη
κατὰ τοὺς νῦν τοῖς λόγοις ἀκμάζοντας. ὅση δέ μοι τῆς προθυμίας
ἐστὶν ἡ ἐπίδειξις, οὐκ ἐν τῷ διηγήσασθαί τι τῶν σῶν. τούτου γὰρ
μόγις ἂν καὶ ὁ σφριγῶν τε καὶ συντεταμένος τύχοι λόγος, ὡς μὴ

To Hierius
On Infants Taken Away before Their Time
(*De infantibus praemature abreptis*)

1 All learned scholars and professional writers, my excellent friend, will try to display their powers of speech for you, attempting to run about the broad field of your wonderful achievements as in a kind of stadium. Indeed, any noble and abundant argument, when proposed by a skilled speaker, can, in a way, be put into words more powerfully still when it is elevated by the importance of the subject treated. But we, like aging horses who remain outside the stadium of the argument,[3] will only perk up our ears at the competition of ideas you propose, if some chance echo reaches us, too, driving on the chariots of words in intense and powerful leaps through your great achievements. And when that happens, even if a horse stays apart from the races because of age, he is often aroused by the thunder of hooves to lift up his head and look about competitively, to pant in a spirited way and stamp his feet in time with the rest, striking the ground hard with his hooves: all that is left in him is eagerness for the contest, while the power of running has been worn away by time! In the same way, although our literary skill remains outside of the competition because of our age, and we yield our place in the stadium to those in the prime of their erudition, nevertheless our skill eagerly wishes it could go and compete before you, to see if it is still as vigorous as they are, at the peak of their literary ability.

2 All this may explain my own eagerness, but says nothing about what you have achieved. Even an abundant and well-organized style

[3]Throughout the treatise, Gregory modestly claims to be too old to respond with real style to the challenge of his subject.

πολὺ κατόπιν τῆς ἀξίας ἀπολειφθῆναι, ὁ τὴν ἀμήχανον ταύτην ἁρμονίαν τοῦ ἤθους διερμηνεύων ἐκ τῶν ἐναντίων συγκεκραμένην πως. καθάπερ γὰρ ταῖς τῶν βλεφάρων προβολαῖς τὸ τῶν ἀκτίνων ἄκρατον ἡ φύσις ὑποσκιάζουσα κεκραμένον προσάγει τὸ φέγγος τοῖς ὄμμασιν, ὡς ἂν προσηνὴς ὁ ἥλιος γένοιτο πρὸς τὴν ἐκ τῶν βλεφαρίδων σκιὰν συμμέτρως τῇ χρείᾳ κατακιρνάμενος· οὕτως τὸ σεμνόν τε καὶ μεγαλοφυὲς τοῦ ἤθους τῇ ἐμμέτρῳ ταπεινοφροσύνῃ
PG 164 καταμιγνύμενον οὐκ ἀποστρέφει τὰς | ὄψεις τῶν προσορώντων, ἀλλὰ δι' ἡδονῆς βλέπειν παρασκευάζει, ὡς μήτε τῆς σεμνότητος τὴν μαρμαρυγὴν ἀμαυροῦσθαι μήτε διὰ ταπεινότητος καταφρονεῖσθαι τὸ ἐνδιάθετον, ἀλλὰ κατὰ τὸ ἴσον ἐν ἑκατέρῳ θεωρεῖσθαι τὸ ἕτερον, ἔν τε τῷ ὑψηλῷ τὴν κοινότητα καὶ ἐν τῷ ταπεινῷ τὸ ἔμπαλιν τὴν σεμνότητα. ἄλλος ταῦτα διεξερχέσθω καὶ τὸ πολυόμματον τῆς ψυχῆς ἀνυμνείτω, ὡς ἰσάριθμοι ταῖς θριξὶ τάχα τῆς κεφαλῆς οἱ τῆς ψυχῆς ὀφθαλμοί, πανταχόθεν ἐπ' ἴσης ὀξύ τε καὶ ἀπλανὲς δεδορκότες, ὥστε πόρρωθέν τε προϊδεῖν καὶ μὴ ἀγνοεῖν ἐκ
GNO 69 τοῦ | σύνεγγυς μηδὲ τὴν πεῖραν ἀναμένειν τοῦ λυσιτελοῦντος διδάσκαλον, ἀλλὰ τὸ μὲν τοῖς τῶν ἐλπίδων ὀφθαλμοῖς προορᾶν, τὸ δὲ θεωρεῖν διὰ τῆς μνήμης, ἄλλο δὲ κατὰ τὸ ἐνεστὼς ἐν κύκλῳ περιαθρεῖν, πάντα δὲ κατὰ ταὐτὸν ἐνεργεῖν ἀσυγχύτως πάσαις ταῖς τοιαύταις ἐνεργείαις τὸν νοῦν καταλλήλως ἐπιμερίζοντα. τόν τε σεμνὸν τῆς πενίας πλοῦτον θαυμαζέτω πάλιν ἐκεῖνος, εἴ τις ἔστιν ἐν τῷ καθ' ἡμᾶς βίῳ εἰδὼς τὸ τοιοῦτον ἐν ἐπαίνῳ ποιεῖσθαι καὶ θαύματι. τάχα δὲ εἰ καὶ μὴ πρότερον ἦν, ἀλλὰ νῦν διὰ σὲ καὶ πενίας ἀνθήσει πόθος καὶ πρὸ τῶν πολυταλάντων τοῦ Κροίσου πλίνθων ἡ σὴ λιτότης μακαρισθήσεται. τίνα γὰρ μακαριστὸν οὕτως ἀπέδειξε γῆ τε καὶ θάλασσα, ταῖς ἰδίαις ἑκατέρα προσόδοις δεξιουμένη, ὡς τὸν σὸν βίον ἡ πρὸς τὴν ὑλικὴν περιουσίαν ἀποδιάθεσις; ὡς γὰρ οἱ τοῦ σιδήρου τὸν ἰὸν ἀποξέοντες στιλπνὸν αὐτὸν καὶ ἀργυροειδῆ

could hardly achieve this, in a way that avoids remaining well below the standard, when interpreting the incredible harmony of your personality, which is an unusual blend of very different elements. For just as nature has shaded our eyes from the unmitigated rays of the sun by the awnings of eyelids, and makes its light available to our eyes in filtered form, so that the sun might become gentler to us, mingled with the shade of the eyelids in a way suited to our needs; so the noble greatness of your personality, mingled with moderation and humility, does not turn away the gaze of those who see you, but moves them to look at you with pleasure. In this way, the brilliance of your moral substance is not clouded over, nor will your inner disposition be regarded with contempt because of its humility; each is seen equally in the other: your common touch in your exalted manner, but also your nobility in your modesty.

Someone else should explain all this, and sing the praises of your broadly perceptive mind—should tell us that the eyes of your soul are as numerous as the hairs on your head, gazing out sharply and steadily on all sides, able to see far ahead but also not to miss what is up close; that you do not wait for experience to teach you of what is profitable, but look forward with the eyes of hope; contemplating [the past] by memory, gazing around at the circle of what exists at the present moment, and putting everything into use at once by distributing the mind's activity to all these operations without confusing the matter.[4] Let someone else, too, admire the exalted richness of your poverty, if anyone in our profession knows how to depict this in words of praise and admiration. Even if no one could have done this before, still now, because of you, a longing for voluntary poverty may perhaps flourish, and your simplicity of life may be seen as more blessed than the heavy ingots of Croesus. Have land and sea ever marked anyone out as so blessed, hailing him with their own proper riches, as the renunciation of material excess has shown your life to be? For just as those who scrape the rust off iron make it gleam like

[4]Gregory seems to ascribe to Hierius here the classic qualities of a good institutional leader.

κατεργάζονται, οὕτως σοὶ φανοτέρα γέγονεν ἡ τοῦ βίου ἀκτὶς ἀεὶ δι' ἐπιμελείας τοῦ ἰοῦ τῶν χρημάτων καθαιρομένη. καὶ ταῦτα παρείσθω τοῖς εἰπεῖν δυναμένοις καὶ ὅτι καλῶς ἐπίστασαι, ἐν τίσιν ἐστὶ τὸ λαβεῖν τοῦ καθαρεῦσαι λήμματος ἐνδοξότερον· δὸς γάρ μοι μετὰ παρρησίας εἰπεῖν, ὅτι οὐ πάντων ὑπερορᾷς τῶν λημμάτων, ἀλλ' ὧν οὔπω τις ἅψασθαι τῶν προλαβόντων δεδύνηται, μόνος περιεδράξω διπλῇ τῇ χειρί· ἀντὶ γὰρ ἐσθῆτός τινος ἢ χρημάτων ἢ ἀνδραπόδων αὐτὰς τῶν ἀνθρώπων τὰς ψυχὰς λαβὼν ἔχεις τῷ θησαυρῷ τῆς ἀγάπης ἐναποθέμενος. |

GNO 70 Ταῦτα λογογράφοι καὶ σοφισταὶ διεξίτωσαν, οἷς κόσμος καλῶς τὰ τοιαῦτα γράφειν, ὁ δὲ γηραιὸς ἡμῶν λόγος τοσοῦτον ἑαυτὸν ὑποκινείτω, ὅσον βάδην ἐπεξελθεῖν τῷ προτεθέντι ἡμῖν παρὰ τῆς σῆς σοφίας προβλήματι, τί χρὴ γινώσκειν περὶ τῶν πρὸ ὥρας ἀναρπαζομένων, ἐφ' ὧν μικροῦ δεῖν ἡ γένεσις τῷ θανάτῳ συνάπτεται· ἃ καὶ ὁ σοφὸς ἐν τοῖς ἔξω Πλάτων πολλὰ ἐκ προσώπου τοῦ ἀναβεβιωκότος περὶ τῶν ἐκεῖθεν δικαστηρίων φιλοσοφήσας ἀφῆκεν ἀπόρρητα, ὡς κρείττονα ὄντα δηλαδὴ ἢ ὥστε ὑπὸ λογισμὸν ἀνθρώπων ἐλθεῖν. εἰ μὲν οὖν τι τοιοῦτον ἐν τοῖς ἐξητασμένοις ἐστίν, ὡς λύειν τὰς τοῦ προβλήματος ἀμφιβολίας, δέξῃ δηλαδὴ τὸν εὑρεθέντα λόγον, εἰ δὲ μή, συγγνώσῃ πάντως τῷ γήρᾳ, μόνην τὴν προθυμίαν ἡμῶν εἰς τὸ παρασχεῖν τί σοι τῶν
PG 165 κεχαρισμένων | ἀποδεξάμενος. καὶ γὰρ τὸν Ξέρξην, ἐκεῖνον τὸν πᾶσαν τὴν ὑφ' ἡλίῳ μικροῦ δεῖν ἓν στρατόπεδον ποιησάμενον καὶ πᾶσαν ἑαυτῷ συγκινοῦντα τὴν οἰκουμένην, ὅτε κατὰ τῶν Ἑλλήνων ἐστράτευσε, μεθ' ἡδονῆς δέξασθαί φησιν ὁ λόγος πένητός τινος δῶρον. ὕδωρ δὲ τὸ ξένιον ἦν καὶ τοῦτο οὐκ ἐν κεράμῳ φερόμενον, ἀλλ' ἐν τῷ κοίλῳ τῆς τῶν χειρῶν παλάμης περιεχόμενον. οὕτως οὖν καὶ σὺ κατὰ τὴν προσοῦσάν σοι μεγαλοφυΐαν μιμήσῃ πάντως

---

[5]Gregory seems to imply here that the profit Hierius has personally derived from his role of leadership is above all the affection of his subjects.

[6]This seems to refer especially to the so-called "myth of Er" in *Republic* 10 (614b ff.).

silver, so the ray of your life's light always gleams brighter, because of your care to cleanse it of the corrosion of money. I will leave it, too, to those powerful in speech to show how well you understand in what ways having is more glorious than simply purifying oneself of possessions; just allow me to say out loud that you have not despised *all* possessions, but those that none of your predecessors has been able to grasp, you alone have seized with both hands: instead of clothing or money or slaves, you have laid hold of human souls, storing them away in the treasury of love.[5]

3 Let scholars and writers elaborate these themes who can compose such things elegantly and with ease; but let our own aging power of speech stir itself up only to take a step or two toward the theme proposed to us by your own wisdom: how we should think about those who have been taken away from life before their proper time, for whom birth is almost simultaneous with death. That secular wise man Plato left us, in his philosophical writings, a good deal of material about the judgments in the next life, through the mouth of one who had been raised from the dead;[6] but he left other things out of the discussion, presumably because they are too important to be subjected simply to human reason. If there is some contribution on this in our own investigations here, capable of helping solve the ambiguities of our problem, by all means take hold of the argument we have put together; but if not, at least forgive an old man, simply accepting the gift of our eagerness to offer you something that might please you. The story goes, after all, that Xerxes—that ruler who almost succeeded in making every region under the sun into a single armed camp, and who stirred up the whole world to be on his side—when he was invading Greece, was delighted to receive the gift of a poor man. The gift was water, and this not carried in a ceramic vessel, but held in the cupped palms of the man's hands.[7] So, too, may you imitate that great man in the nobility that

[7]This anecdote is reported by Plutarch, *Apophthegmata* 172 B; *Life of Artaxerxes* 1013 BC, and by Aelian, *Variae Historiae* 1.32.

ἐκεῖνον, ᾧ δῶρον ἐγένετο ἡ προαίρεσις, εἴπερ ἡμῶν βραχύ τε καὶ ὑδατῶδες εὑρεθείη τὸ δῶρον. |

GNO 71 Ὥσπερ ἐπὶ τῶν οὐρανίων θαυμάτων ὁρᾷ μὲν ἐπ᾽ ἴσης τὰ
φαινόμενα κάλλη κἂν πεπαιδευμένος κἂν ἰδιώτης τύχῃ τις ὢν
ὁ πρὸς τὸν οὐρανὸν ἀναβλέπων, διανοεῖται δὲ τὰ περὶ αὐτῶν
οὐχ ὁμοίως ὅ τε ἀπὸ φιλοσοφίας ὁρμώμενος καὶ ὁ μόναις ταῖς
αἰσθήσεσι τὸ φαινόμενον ἐπιτρέπων (οὗτος μὲν γὰρ ἢ ταῖς ἀκτῖσιν
ἥδεται τοῦ ἡλίου ἢ τὸ κάλλος τῶν ἄστρων θαύματος ἄξιον κρίνει ἢ
τὸν ἀριθμὸν τοῦ σεληναίου δρόμου ἐπὶ τοῦ μηνὸς παρετήρησεν, ὁ
δὲ διορατικὸς τὴν ψυχὴν καὶ διὰ παιδεύσεως πρὸς τὴν κατανόησιν
τῶν οὐρανίων κεκαθαρμένος, καταλιπὼν ταῦτα δι᾽ ὧν εὐφραίνεται
τῶν ἀλογωτέρων ἡ αἴσθησις, πρὸς τὴν τοῦ παντὸς ἁρμονίαν βλέπει
καὶ ἐκ τῆς ἐγκυκλίου κινήσεως τὴν ἐκ τῶν ἐναντίων εὐαρμοστίαν
ἐπισκοπεῖ· πῶς τῇ ἀπλανεῖ περιφορᾷ οἱ ἐντὸς κύκλοι πρὸς τὸ
ἔμπαλιν ἀνελίσσονται, πῶς τὰ ἐν αὐτοῖς θεωρούμενα τῶν ἄστρων
πολυειδῶς σχηματίζεται, ἐν προσεγγισμοῖς τε καὶ ἀποστάσεσι καὶ
ὑποδρομαῖς τε καὶ ἐκλείψεσι καὶ ταῖς ἐπὶ τὰ πλάγια παραδρομαῖς
τὴν ἀδιάλειπτον ἐκείνην ἁρμονίαν ἀεὶ κατὰ τὰ αὐτὰ καὶ ὡσαύτως
ἐξεργαζόμενα· οἷς οὐδὲ τοῦ βραχυτάτου τῶν ἄστρων ἡ θέσις
ἀθεώρητος περιορᾶται, ἀλλὰ πάντα τὴν ἴσην παρέχει φροντίδα
τοῖς διὰ τῆς σοφίας ἐπὶ τὰ ἄνω τὸν νοῦν μετοικίσασι)· τὸν αὐτὸν
τρόπον καὶ σύ, ὦ τιμία μοι κεφαλή, τὴν ἐν τοῖς οὖσι τοῦ θεοῦ
οἰκονομίαν βλέπων, ἀφεὶς ἐκεῖνα περὶ ἃ τῶν πολλῶν ἄσχολός ἐστιν
ἡ διάνοια (πλοῦτον λέγω καὶ τῦφον καὶ δόξης ἐπιθυμίαν κενῆς,
ἅπερ ἄντικρυς ἀκτίνων δίκην περιαστράπτοντα τοὺς ἀλογωτέρους
GNO 72 ἐκπλήττειν εἴωθεν), οὐδὲ τὰ δοκοῦντα | μικρότερα τῶν ἐν τοῖς
οὖσι θεωρουμένων ἀνεξέταστα καταλείπεις ἀνερευνῶν τε καὶ
διασκοπούμενος τὴν ἀνωμαλίαν τῆς ἀνθρωπίνης ζωῆς, οὐ μόνον
τὴν κατὰ πλοῦτον καὶ πενίαν θεωρουμένην ἢ τὰς κατὰ τὰ ἀξιώματα

is yours; all we have to offer is our affection, even if you find this gift of ours small and watery!

4 In the case of the wonders of the heavens, everyone who gazes up at the sky sees the beauty revealed there the same way, whether he is educated or not; but the one who sets out from natural philosophy and the one who considers simply what appears to our senses will understand them very differently. For the latter will either take delight in the sun's rays or will think the beauty of the stars something wonderful, or will measure out the number of the moon's movements month by month; but the one who is clear-sighted in soul, and whose education has purified him to have a real understanding of the heavens, will move beyond the things that delight the senses of less intellectual people. Instead, he will gaze on the harmony of the whole, and investigate the balance of opposites rooted in the circular movement of the universe: how the inner circles are twisted in the opposite direction to what constantly revolves; how what we see in them of the stars are gathered into different patterns, working out that unceasing harmony, always in the same way: by coming closer and moving farther apart, moving under each other, being eclipsed, and moving on the slant. To such people the position of even the tiniest of stars does not go unobserved; all claim equal importance with those who have directed their minds upward through wisdom.

In the same way, dear friend, when you, too, consider God's way of acting in the midst of created things, you let those things pass that are so engaging to the minds of most people: I mean wealth and blustering pride and the yearning for empty glory, which usually shine out like rays and dazzle the less reasonable; but you do not leave unexamined what seem to be the small details of the life of creatures, but investigate and weigh carefully the unevenness of human life.[8] I do not simply mean inequalities in wealth and poverty,

[8]Origen, too, in his *On First Principles* 2.9, gives serious attention to the differences in situation and opportunity among human beings, as a question that can be raised about God's justice in managing the universe. Origen's solution is to suggest,

καὶ τὰ γένη διαφοράς (οἶδας γὰρ ἀντ' οὐδενὸς εἶναι ταῦτα οἷς τὸ
εἶναι οὐ καθ' ὑπόστασιν οἰκείαν ἐστίν, ἀλλ' ἐν τῇ ματαίᾳ ὑπολήψει
τῶν τοῖς μὴ οὖσιν ὡς ὑφεστῶσι προσκεχηνότων· εἰ γοῦν τις
ἀφέλοιτο τοῦ λαμπρυνομένου τῇ δόξῃ τῶν εἰς αὐτὸν βλεπόντων
τὴν οἴησιν, οὐδὲν ὑπολειφθήσεται τῷ μεγαλοφρονοῦντι ἐπὶ τῷ
διακένῳ φυσήματι, κἂν πᾶσα τῶν χρημάτων ἡ ὕλη παρ' αὐτῷ
κατορωρυγμένη τύχῃ), ἀλλά σοι διὰ φροντίδος ἐστὶ γνῶναι τά
τε ἄλλα τῆς θείας οἰκονομίας, πρὸς ὅ τι τῶν γινομένων ἕκαστον
PG 168 βλέπει, καὶ τίνος χάριν τῷ | μὲν εἰς γῆρας μακρὸν παρατείνεται ἡ
ζωή, ὁ δὲ τοσοῦτον μετέχει τοῦ ζῆν, ὅσον δι' ἀναπνοῆς τὸν ἀέρα
σπάσαι καὶ εὐθὺς καταλῆξαι τοῦ βίου. εἰ γὰρ οὐδὲν ἀθεεὶ τῶν ἐν
τῷ κόσμῳ γινομένων ἐστί, πάντα δὲ τῆς θείας ἐξῆπται βουλήσεως,
σοφὸν δὲ καὶ προνοητικὸν τὸ θεῖον, πάντως τις ἔπεστι καὶ τούτοις
λόγος, τῆς σοφίας ἅμα τοῦ θεοῦ καὶ τῆς προνοητικῆς ἐπιμελείας τὰ
γνωρίσματα φέρων· τὸ γὰρ εἰκῇ τι καὶ ἀλόγως γινόμενον οὐκ ἂν
ἔργον εἴη θεοῦ· θεοῦ γὰρ ἴδιον, καθώς φησιν ἡ γραφή, τὸ Πάντα ἐν
GNO 73 σοφίᾳ ποιεῖν. τί οὖν τὸ σοφὸν ἐν ἐκείνῳ; παρῆλθε διὰ | γεννήσεως
εἰς τὸν βίον ὁ ἄνθρωπος, ἔσπασε τὸν ἀέρα, ἀπὸ οἰμωγῆς τοῦ ζῆν
ἤρξατο, ἐλειτούργησε τῇ φύσει τὸ δάκρυον, ἀπήρξατο τῷ βίῳ
τῶν θρήνων, πρίν τινος μετασχεῖν τῶν κατὰ τὸν βίον ἡδέων· πρὶν
τονωθῆναι τὴν αἴσθησιν, ἔτι λελυμένος τὰς τῶν μελῶν ἁρμονίας,
ἁπαλός τε καὶ διακεχυμένος καὶ ἀδιάρθρωτος, καὶ τὸ ὅλον εἰπεῖν
πρὶν γενέσθαι ἄνθρωπος (εἴπερ ἀνθρώπου ἴδιον ἡ λογικὴ χάρις
ἐστίν, ὁ δὲ οὔπω ἐν ἑαυτῷ τὸν λόγον ἐχώρησεν), οὗτος ὁ μηδὲν
πλέον ἔχων τοῦ ἔτι ἐν τῇ μητρῴᾳ νηδύϊ συνεχομένου πλὴν τὸ

---

at least as a hypothesis, that these inequalities are due to different moral choices made by created intelligences in a pre-corporeal existence, and are part of a longer-term strategy on God's part to put souls in a situation that will lead to their voluntary conversion and rehabilitation.

or differences in rank and ancestry. (For you know that these things are worth nothing, since they do not exist with a substance of their own, but simply in the foolish suppositions of those who gape after non-existent things as if they were substantial; but if one were to remove the opinion of onlookers from what seems to be so splendid, there would be nothing left for the person who sets such great store by what is a totally empty breath, even if all the material wealth that exists were gathered in his possession.) But you, by your practical reflection, have the ability to recognize all the aspects of the divine governance of things—the goal toward which everything that happens is directed—and the reason why one person's life is extended to old age, while another shares life only long enough to draw a breath and then immediately leaves the world of the living. For if nothing in the world of created things happens apart from God, but all is linked with the divine will, and if what is divine is also wise and provident, surely there is some reason for these things to happen, too, which will mark them with the signs of God's wisdom and provident care. For what occurs by chance and without explanation would not be a work of God; it is proper to God, as Scripture says, to have "made all things in wisdom" (Ps 103.24).

5 Where, then, is the wisdom in this?[9] A human being comes into the world of the living by the process of birth, draws a breath of air, begins life with a wail, pays nature the ritual gesture of a tear, offers life the sacrifice of lament, all before sharing in any of life's pleasures, before the senses are fully tuned, when the coordination of the limbs is still disordered, still tender and diffuse and physically undefined—in a word, before becoming *human* (if indeed graceful order is proper to being human, and this person has not yet begun to display the order of reason in himself); he possesses no more than had already come

[9]Here, in sections 5 and 6, Gregory comes to the heart of the problem proposed for his consideration: the phenomenon of infant mortality, whether accidental or caused by human intervention. How can a just and powerful God, whom we expect to judge the dead on how they have lived, allow infants to die before they are able to make responsible moral decisions? What fate in the afterlife may we expect for them?

ἐν ἀέρι γενέσθαι ἐν τούτῳ τῆς ἡλικίας ὢν διὰ θανάτου λύεται ἢ ἐκτεθεὶς ἢ καταπνιγεὶς ἢ κατὰ τὸ αὐτόματον δι᾿ ἀρρωστίας τοῦ ζῆν παυσάμενος· τί χρὴ περὶ αὐτοῦ ἐννοεῖν; πῶς περὶ τῶν οὕτω τετελευτηκότων ἔχειν; ὄψεται ἆρα κἀκείνη ἡ ψυχὴ τὸν κριτήν; παραστήσεται μετὰ τῶν ἄλλων τῷ βήματι; ὑφέξει τῶν βεβιωμένων τὴν κρίσιν; λήψεται τὴν κατ᾿ ἀξίαν ἀντίδοσιν ἢ πυρὶ καθαιρομένη κατὰ τὰς τοῦ εὐαγγελίου φωνὰς ἢ τῇ δρόσῳ τῆς εὐλογίας ἐναναψύχουσα; |

GNO 74 Ἀλλ᾿ οὐκ οἶδα, ὅπως χρὴ ταῦτα περὶ τῆς τοιαύτης ἐννοῆσαι
ψυχῆς· τὸ γὰρ τῆς ἀντιδόσεως ὄνομα τὸ χρῆναί τι πάντως
προπαρασχεθῆναι σημαίνει, τοῦ δὲ μὴ βεβιωκότος ὅλως ἡ ὕλη
τοῦ τι παρασχεῖν προαφῄρηται· ἐφ᾿ ὧν δὲ δόσις οὐκ ἔστιν, οὐδὲ
PG 169 ἀντίδοσις κυρίως | ὀνομασθήσεται. μὴ οὔσης δὲ τῆς ἀντιδόσεως,
οὔτε ἀγαθόν ἐστιν οὔτε κακὸν τὸ κατ᾿ ἐλπίδα προκείμενον· τὸ
γὰρ ὄνομα τοῦτο τῶν καθ᾿ ἑκάτερον νοουμένων τὴν ἀμοιβὴν
ἐπαγγέλλεται· τὸ δὲ μήτε ἐν ἀγαθῷ μήτε ἐν κακῷ εὑρισκόμενον
ἐν οὐδενὶ πάντως ἐστίν· ἄμεσος γὰρ ἡ τῆς τοιαύτης ἀντιθέσεως
ἐναντιότης, ἡ τοῦ ἀγαθοῦ καὶ τοῦ κακοῦ λέγω, ὧν οὐθέτερον
ἔσται τῷ μὴ θατέρου κατάρξαντι. τὸ οὖν ἐν μηδενὶ ὂν οὐδ᾿ ἂν εἶναί
τις εἴποι ὅλως. εἰ δέ τις τὸ τοιοῦτον καὶ εἶναι λέγοι καὶ ἐν ἀγαθοῖς
εἶναι, διδόντος, οὐκ ἀποδιδόντος τοῦ θεοῦ τὰ ἀγαθὰ τοῖς τοιούτοις,
ποίαν λέγει τῆς ἀποκληρώσεως ταύτης αἰτίαν; ποῦ τὸ δίκαιον

together in his mother's womb, except for being out in the air. Suppose that in this stage of growth, he is dissolved by death—either by being exposed or strangled, or else through illness without human agency—and ceases to live. What should we think about such a person? What should be our attitude toward those who meet their end in this way? Will such a soul gaze on our Judge? Will it stand, with all its fellows, before the judgment seat? Will it undergo the judgment that will be passed on all who have lived? Will it receive a just recompense, either being purified in fire, according to the teachings of the gospel, or being blessed with a drop of refreshing dew?[10]

I really do not know how one must think about the case of such a soul. For the word "recompense" [lit. "giving back"] means, surely, that something must have been done [by the subject] beforehand; but if someone has not had any life at all, the standard for providing some recompense is removed. If nothing has been "given" [by a person], there is no way to talk properly about [God's] "giving back." But if there will not be a recompense, nothing, either good or bad, lies in the future for a person to hope for. This word, after all, is applied to the process of paying back for what is understood [to have been given] on both sides; but surely what is neither found on the good side [of our account-book] nor on the bad is nowhere! The opposition of an antithesis such as this—I mean, of good and bad—has no halfway position; neither will it be found in one who has taken no steps in either direction. One might say, then, that what exists as neither good nor evil does not exist at all.

6 But if someone should say that a person like this both exists and will be numbered among the good, because God provides good things to such people as gifts rather than as rewards, what would he argue are the grounds for such good fortune?[11] What justice would

[10]See Luke 16.24, where the soul of the rich man in hades asks for such a drop to be given him by the soul of Lazarus.

[11]Here Gregory turns to take up the question of whether it would be just for God to bring newborn children who die directly into the state of beatitude, without their having performed any deeds to deserve it.

συναποδείξει τῷ λόγῳ; πῶς δὲ ταῖς εὐαγγελικαῖς φωναῖς σύμφωνον δείξει τὸ νόημα; ἐκεῖ συναλλαγματικήν τινα τῆς βασιλείας τὴν ἐμπορίαν τοῖς ἀξιουμένοις προσγίνεσθαι λέγει· ἐπειδὴ γὰρ τὸ καὶ τό, φησί, πεποιήκατε, τὴν βασιλείαν ἀντιλαβεῖν ἐστε δίκαιοι. ἐνταῦθα δὲ μηδεμιᾶς μήτε πράξεως μήτε προαιρέσεως ὑπούσης, τίνα καιρὸν ἔχει καὶ τούτοις παρὰ τοῦ θεοῦ γίνεσθαι λέγειν τὸ ἐξ ἀμοιβῆς ἐλπιζόμενον; εἰ δέ τις ἀβασανίστως τὸν τοιοῦτον δέξεται
GNO 75 λόγον, ὡς πάντως ἐν | ἀγαθοῖς ἐσομένου τοῦ παρελθόντος οὕτως ἐπὶ τὸν βίον, ἐκ τούτου μακαριστότερον ἀναφανήσεται τῆς ζωῆς τὸ μὴ μετέχειν ζωῆς, εἴπερ ἐκείνῳ μὲν ἀναμφίβολος ἡ τῶν ἀγαθῶν μετουσία, κἂν βαρβάρων τύχῃ γονέων καὶ μὴ νενομισμένῳ κυηθῇ γάμῳ, τῷ δὲ βεβιωκότι τὸν χωρητόν τε καὶ νόμιμον τῇ φύσει χρόνον πάντως ἢ πλέον ἢ ἔλαττον ὁ τῆς κακίας μολυσμὸς τῇ ζωῇ καταμίγνυται, ἤ, εἰ μέλλοι παντελῶς τῆς πρὸς τὸ κακὸν κοινωνίας ἐκτὸς εἶναι, πολλῶν αὐτῷ δεῖ ἱδρώτων πρὸς αὐτὸ τοῦτο καὶ πόνων· οὐ γὰρ ἀκμητὶ κατορθοῦται τοῖς μετιοῦσιν ἡ ἀρετὴ οὐδὲ ἄπονός ἐστι τοῖς ἀνθρώποις ἡ τῶν καθ' ἡδονὴν ἀλλοτρίωσις· ὥστε ἑνὶ τῶν ἀνιαρῶν ἐξ ἀμφοτέρων συνενεχθῆναι δεῖν πάντως τὸν μετασχόντα τοῦ χρονιωτέρου βίου, ἢ νῦν τῷ ἐπιπόνῳ τῆς ἀρετῆς ἐναθλοῦντα ἢ τότε διὰ τὴν ἐν κακίᾳ ζωὴν τῇ ἀντιδόσει τῶν ἀλγεινῶν ὀδυνώμενον· ἐπὶ δὲ τῶν ἀώρων τοιοῦτόν ἐστιν οὐδέν, ἀλλ' εὐθὺς ἡ ἀγαθὴ λῆξις τοὺς ἐν ἀωρίᾳ μεταστάντας ἐκδέχεται, εἴπερ ἀληθεύει τῶν οὕτως ὑπειληφότων ὁ λόγος. οὐκοῦν ἐκ τοῦ ἀκολούθου καὶ τοῦ λόγου προτιμοτέρα δειχθήσεται ἡ ἀλογία καὶ ἡ ἀρετὴ οὐδενὸς ἀξία διὰ τούτων ἀναφανήσεται· εἰ γὰρ μηδεμία γέγονε ζημία πρὸς τὴν τῶν ἀγαθῶν μετουσίαν τῷ μὴ μετασχόντι τῆς ἀρετῆς, μάταιον ἂν εἴη τὸ περὶ ταύτην πονεῖν καὶ ἀνόνητον, τῆς ἀλόγου καταστάσεως ἐν τῇ τοῦ θεοῦ κρίσει προτερευούσης.

he point to as part of such an argument? How will he show this thought to correspond to the gospel's promises? For there it says that the Kingdom is promised as a kind of contractual recompense to the deserving: when you have done this and that, Scripture says, you are judged worthy to receive the Kingdom. But here, where neither action nor choice is present, what point can there be in saying that what is hoped for in this exchange will come to these people, too, from God? And if one accepts this kind of suggestion without further examination—that a person who has come into life in this way will surely be counted among the good—then never having shared in life will be shown, on these grounds, to be more blessed than living, since a share in good things will unquestionably be granted to such a person, even if he has pagan parents and is conceived in an unlawful marriage; but for one who has lived out the time allotted and sanctioned by nature, surely the stain of evil will be mingled into his or her life to a greater or lesser extent—or else, if one is to remain completely free from sharing in evil, one will need to work toward this with much exertion and labor. Virtue, after all, is not acquired effortlessly by those who pursue it, nor can humans distance themselves from pleasures without working to do so. So that the person who participates in temporal life must surely deal with one of two challenging realities: either now to be involved in the laborious struggle to acquire virtue, or in the next life to suffer a painful retribution for living in vice. But with those who die before their time, nothing of either sort happens, but immediately the lot of the good will embrace those who make this premature transition—if, that is, the argument of those who assume this is true. As a consequence, irrationality will be shown more valuable than reason, and virtue will be shown by these people to be of little value. For if there is no disadvantage with respect to sharing in good things for one who has no share in virtue, to labor in acquiring it would be vain and foolish, and the state of one who lacks reason would be given first place in the divine judgment.

Ταῦτα σὺ πάντα καὶ τὰ τοιαῦτα διανοούμενος ἐξετάσαι τὸν περὶ τούτου λόγον διεκελεύσω, ὡς ἂν ἡμῖν διὰ τῆς ἀκολούθου
GNO 76 | ζητήσεως ἐπί τινος βεβαίου νοήματος ἡ περὶ αὐτοῦ ἱδρυθείη διάνοια. ἐγὼ δὲ πρὸς τὸ δυσθεώρητον τοῦ προτεθέντος ἡμῖν
PG 172 σκέμματος βλέπων ἁρμόζειν μὲν οἶμαι καὶ τὴν τοῦ ἀπο|στόλου φωνὴν τῷ παρόντι λόγῳ, ἣν ἐπὶ τῶν ἀνεφίκτων ἐκεῖνος πεποίηται λέγων Ὦ βάθος πλούτου καὶ σοφίας καὶ γνώσεως θεοῦ· ὡς ἀνεξερεύνητα τὰ κρίματα αὐτοῦ καὶ ἀνεξιχνίαστοι αἱ ὁδοὶ αὐτοῦ. τίς γὰρ ἔγνω νοῦν κυρίου; ἐπεὶ δὲ πάλιν ὁ ἀπόστολος ἴδιον τοῦ πνευματικοῦ φησι τὸ ἀνακρίνειν τὰ πάντα καὶ ἀποδέχεται τοὺς παρὰ τῆς θείας χάριτος πλουτισθέντας Ἐν παντὶ λόγῳ καὶ πάσῃ γνώσει, καλῶς ἔχειν φημὶ μὴ κατολιγωρῆσαι τῆς δυνατῆς ἐξετάσεως μηδὲ περιιδεῖν τὸ ζητούμενον ἐν τούτοις ἀνερεύνητόν τε καὶ ἀθεώρητον, ὡς ἂν μὴ καθ᾽ ὁμοιότητα τῆς τοῦ προβλήματος ὑποθέσεως καὶ ὁ περὶ αὐτοῦ λόγος ἀτελὴς ἀφανισθείη καὶ ἄωρος, καθάπερ τι νήπιον τῶν ἀρτιτόκων πρὶν εἰς φῶς προελθεῖν καὶ ἁδρυνθῆναι, οἷόν τινι θανάτῳ τῇ ῥαθυμίᾳ τῶν πρὸς τὴν ζήτησιν τῆς ἀληθείας ἀτονούντων διαφθειρόμενος.

Φημὶ τοίνυν καλῶς ἔχειν μὴ ῥητορικῶς τε καὶ ἀγωνιστικῶς εὐθὺς κατὰ στόμα πρὸς τὰς ἀντιθέσεις συμπλέκεσθαι, ἀλλά τινα τάξιν ἐπιθέντας τῷ λόγῳ δι᾽ ἀκολούθου προάγειν τὴν περὶ τοῦ προβλήματος θεωρίαν. τίς οὖν ἡ τάξις; τὸ γνῶναι πρῶτον ὅθεν ἡ ἀνθρωπίνη φύσις καὶ ὅτου χάριν ἦλθεν εἰς γένεσιν· εἰ γὰρ
GNO 77 τούτων μὴ διαμάρτοιμεν, οὐδὲ τῆς προκειμένης ἡμῖν θεωρίας ἡμαρτηκότες ἐσόμεθα. τὸ μὲν οὖν ἐκ θεοῦ πᾶν, ὅ τί πέρ ἐστι μετ᾽ αὐτὸν ἐν τοῖς οὖσιν | νοούμενόν τε καὶ ὁρώμενον, τὸ εἶναι ἔχειν περιττὸν ἂν εἴη λόγῳ κατασκευάζεσθαι, οὐδενός, οἶμαι, τῶν ὁπωσοῦν ἐπεσκεμμένων τὴν τῶν ὄντων ἀλήθειαν πρὸς τὴν

7 You have thought about all of this and the other issues implied, and have urged us to examine what can reasonably be said about this, so that our understanding of it might be established on some solid ideas by our discussion of its consequences. But as I consider the opacity of the speculation you have set out for us, I think the phrase of the Apostle, which he uttered about what is unattainable to us, seems also to fit our present subject: "O the depth of the riches and wisdom and knowledge of God! How unsearchable are his judgments, how untraceable his ways! 'For who has known the mind of the Lord?'" (Rom 11.33–34, quoting Is 40.13) But since the Apostle further says that it is proper to the spiritual person to judge all things (see 1 Cor 2.14–15), and recognizes those enriched by divine grace "in all speech and in all knowledge" (1 Cor 1.5), I insist that the right course is not simply to rule out of the field of possible thought what you have asked about this, as being beyond investigation or speculation, or to overlook it, lest, like the subject of our question, our argument about this should vanish before coming to full ripeness—still immature, like some newborn infant who has not yet come into the light and into full development, doomed to a kind of death by the laziness of those too weak to investigate the truth.

8 I say, then, that the best approach would not be to get involved immediately in face-to-face rhetorical and competitive oral debate,[12] but to impose a certain order on our argument, and to let the consideration of our problem develop step by step. What order am I thinking of? To try to understand, first of all, what is the source of human nature and why it has come into existence—for if we do not make a mistake on this, we also will not end up missing the point in the consideration before us. That everything has its being from God—everything whatever that is understood or seen to exist beside him—would be unnecessary to try to prove by reasoning; no one, I think, who has in any way examined the truth of creatures would

[12]Gregory seems here to be pointedly wresting the subject at hand from the arena of rhetorical competition, and to give it a more serious theological context.

τοιαύτην ὑπόληψιν ἐνισταμένου· ὁμολογεῖται γὰρ παρὰ πάντων
μιᾶς αἰτίας ἐξῆφθαι τὸ πᾶν καὶ οὐδὲν τῶν ὄντων αὐτὸ ἐξ ἑαυτοῦ
τὸ εἶναι ἔχειν οὐδὲ ἑαυτοῦ εἶναι ἀρχὴν καὶ αἰτίαν, ἀλλὰ μίαν μὲν
φύσιν εἶναι ἄκτιστον καὶ ἀΐδιον, ἀεὶ κατὰ τὰ αὐτὰ καὶ ὡσαύτως
ἔχουσαν, παντὸς διαστηματικοῦ νοήματος ὑπερκειμένην, ἀναυξῆ
τινα καὶ ἀμείωτον καὶ παντὸς ὅρου ἐπέκεινα θεωρουμένην, ἧς
ἔργον καὶ χρόνος καὶ τόπος καὶ τὰ ἐν τούτοις πάντα καὶ εἴ τι πρὸ
τούτων καταλαμβάνει ἡ ἔννοια νοητόν τε καὶ ὑπερκόσμιον. ἓν δὲ
τῶν γεγονότων καὶ τὴν ἀνθρωπίνην φύσιν εἶναί φαμεν, λόγῳ τινὶ
τῆς θεοπνεύστου διδασκαλίας ὁδηγῷ πρὸς τοῦτο συγχρώμενοι,
ὅς φησι πάντων παρὰ τοῦ θεοῦ παραχθέντων εἰς γένεσιν καὶ τὸν
ἄνθρωπον ἐπὶ τῆς γῆς ἀναδειχθῆναι ἐξ ἑτερογενῶν συγκεκραμένον
τὴν φύσιν, τῆς θείας τε καὶ νοερᾶς οὐσίας πρὸς τὴν ἀφ᾽ ἑκάστου τῶν
στοιχείων αὐτῷ συνερανισθεῖσαν μοῖραν καταμιχθείσης, γενέσθαι
δὲ τοῦτον παρὰ τοῦ πεποιηκότος, ἐφ᾽ ᾧτε εἶναι τῆς θείας τε καὶ
ὑπερκειμένης δυνάμεως ἔμψυχόν τι ὁμοίωμα. βέλτιον δ᾽ ἂν εἴη καὶ
αὐτὴν παραθέσθαι τὴν λέξιν ἔχουσαν οὕτως· Καὶ ἐποίησε, φησίν, ὁ
θεὸς τὸν ἄνθρωπον· κατ᾽ εἰκόνα θεοῦ ἐποίησεν αὐτόν. τὴν δὲ αἰτίαν
GNO 78 τῆς τοῦ ζῴου τούτου | κατασκευῆς τῶν πρὸ ἡμῶν τινες ταύτην
ἀποδεδώκασιν, ὅτι διχῇ διῃρημένης τῆς κτίσεως πάσης, καθὼς
φησιν ὁ ἀπόστολος, εἰς τὸ ὁρατόν τε καὶ ἀόρατον (σημαίνεται δὲ
PG 173 διὰ μὲν τοῦ ἀοράτου τὸ νοητὸν καὶ ἀσώμα|τον, διὰ δὲ τοῦ ὁρατοῦ
τὸ αἰσθητόν τε καὶ σωματῶδες)· εἰς δύο τοίνυν ταῦτα διῃρημένων
πάντων τῶν ὄντων (εἴς τε τὸ αἰσθητόν, λέγω, καὶ εἰς τὸ κατ᾽
ἔννοιαν θεωρούμενον) καὶ τῆς μὲν ἀγγελικῆς τε καὶ ἀσωμάτου
φύσεως, ἥτις τῶν ἀοράτων ἐστίν, ἐν τοῖς ὑπερκοσμίοις τε καὶ
ὑπερουρανίοις διαιτωμένης διὰ τὸ κατάλληλον εἶναι τῇ φύσει τὸ

---

[13]Gregory is apparently referring here to the Platonic forms, as well as perhaps to bodiless intelligences such as angels.

[14]See also Gregory's treatise *De hominis opificio* 5; *On the Soul and the Resurrection* (PG 46:26A ln. 6–29A ln. 5).

[15]Gregory seems here not to be referring to any particular earlier Christian source, but to be drawing in a general way on Genesis 1.26–30, and on those earlier

contest this assumption. For the universe is confessed by everyone to depend on one cause, and no being has its existence from itself or is its own source and cause; [we recognize] that there is one uncreated, eternal nature, which always remains the same and unchanging, above every notion of extension, a being that neither grows nor diminishes, and is thought of as beyond every definition; time and space and all that is in them are his work, and also whatever intelligible, super-worldly reality the mind understands to come before them.[13] And we say, too, that human nature is one of the things that has come to be, making use of a passage in the tradition of inspired teaching as our guide toward this; it says that of all the things that have been brought into existence by God, the human person has been revealed on earth to have a nature mixed from various elements, with the divine and intelligible substance being mingled with what is gathered together with it from each of the elements, and that this has been brought about by the creator so that there might be some living likeness of the divine power that is above all things.[14] It might be better to produce the passage that reads as follows: "And God created the human person," it says; "in the image of God he created him" (Gen 1.27).[15]

9 And some of those who have gone before us have identified the cause for the creation of this living being. All creation is divided in two parts—as the Apostle says, "visible and invisible" ([Col 1.16] and by "invisible" the intelligible and incorporeal is meant, by "visible" the perceptible and corporeal)—with all beings distinguished into these two [realms] (I mean the perceptible and that which is contemplated by the understanding). The angelic and bodiless nature—which is the nature of the unseen—dwells above the world and above the heavens, because the place where one dwells

commentators who saw in the formation of the human being, as the last work in God's "week" of creation, a confirmation of the human person's role as the "bond" (συνδεσμός, *syndesmos*) uniting all God had previously made. See Philo, *De opificio mundi* 23.27; Clement of Alexandria, *Protrepticus* 10 (PG 8:212C–213C); Nemesius of Emesa, *De natura hominis* 1 (ed. M. Morani [Leipzig: Teubner 1987], 4.24—5.8).

ἐνδιαίτημα (ἥ τε γὰρ νοερὰ φύσις λεπτή τις καὶ καθαρὰ καὶ ἀβαρὴς καὶ εὐκίνητος τό τε οὐράνιον σῶμα λεπτόν τε καὶ κοῦφον καὶ ἀεικίνητον), τῆς δὲ γῆς ὃ δὴ τῶν αἰσθητῶν ἐστιν ἔσχατον, οἰκείως τε καὶ καταλλήλως πρὸς τὴν τῶν νοητῶν ἐν αὐτῇ διαγωγὴν οὐκ ἐχούσης (τίς γὰρ ἂν γένοιτο τοῦ ἀνωφεροῦς τε καὶ κούφου πρὸς τὸ βαρύ τε καὶ ἐμβριθὲς κοινωνία;), ὡς ἂν μὴ τελείως ἄμοιρός τε καὶ ἀπόκληρος ἡ γῆ τῆς νοερᾶς τε καὶ ἀσωμάτου διαγωγῆς εἴη, τούτου χάριν προμηθείᾳ κρείττονι τὴν ἀνθρωπίνην συστῆναι γένεσιν, τῇ νοερᾷ τε καὶ θείᾳ τῆς ψυχῆς οὐσίᾳ τῆς γηΐνης μοίρας περιπλασθείσης, ὡς ἂν τῇ πρὸς τὸ ἐμβριθές τε καὶ σωματῶδες συμφυΐᾳ καταλλήλως ἡ ψυχὴ τῷ στοιχείῳ τῆς γῆς ἐμβιοτεύοι ἐχούσης τι πρὸς τὴν τῆς σαρκὸς οὐσίαν συγγενὲς καὶ ὁμόφυλον. σκοπὸς δὲ τῶν γινομένων ἐστὶ τὸ ἐν πάσῃ τῇ κτίσει διὰ τῆς νοερᾶς φύσεως τὴν τοῦ παντὸς ὑπερκειμένην δοξάζεσθαι δύναμιν, τῶν τε ἐπουρανίων καὶ τῶν ἐπιχθονίων διὰ τῆς αὐτῆς ἐνεργείας (λέγω δὲ
GNO 79 διὰ τοῦ πρὸς τὸν | θεὸν βλέπειν) ἀλλήλοις πρὸς τὸν αὐτὸν σκοπὸν συναπτομένων. ἡ δὲ τοῦ βλέπειν πρὸς τὸν θεὸν ἐνέργεια οὐδὲν ἄλλο ἐστὶν ἢ ζωὴ τῇ νοερᾷ φύσει ἐοικυῖά τε καὶ κατάλληλος. ὥσπερ γὰρ τὰ σώματα γήϊνα ὄντα ταῖς γηΐναις διακρατεῖται τροφαῖς καί τι σωματῶδες ζωῆς εἶδος ἐν τούτοις καταλαμβάνομεν, ὁμοίως ἐν ἀλόγοις τε καὶ λογικοῖς ἐνεργούμενον· οὕτως εἶναί τινα χρὴ καὶ νοητὴν ζωὴν ὑποτίθεσθαι, δι᾽ ἧς ἐν τῷ ὄντι συντηρεῖται ἡ φύσις. εἰ δὲ ἡ τῆς σαρκὸς τροφή, ἐπίρρυτός τις οὖσα καὶ ἀπορρέουσα, δι᾽ αὐτῆς τῆς παρόδου δύναμίν τινα ζωτικὴν ἐναποτίθεται οἷς ἂν ἐγγένηται, πόσῳ μᾶλλον ἡ μετουσία τοῦ ὄντως ὄντος, τοῦ ἀεὶ μένοντος καὶ πάντοτε ὡσαύτως ἔχοντος, ἐν τῷ εἶναι φυλάσσει τὸν μετασχόντα. εἰ οὖν αὕτη ἐστὶν ἡ οἰκεία τε καὶ κατάλληλος τῇ νοερᾷ φύσει ζωή, τὸ τοῦ θεοῦ μετέχειν, οὐκ ἂν διὰ τῶν ἐναντίων γένοιτο ἡ μετουσία, εἰ μὴ τρόπον τινὰ συγγενὲς εἴη τῷ ὀρεγομένῳ τὸ μετεχόμενον. ὡς γὰρ ὀφθαλμῷ γίνεται τῆς αὐγῆς ἡ ἀπόλαυσις τῷ φυσικὴν αὐγὴν ἐν ἑαυτῷ πρὸς τὴν τοῦ ὁμογενοῦς ἀντίληψιν

corresponds to one's nature (for an intellectual nature is something fine and pure and weightless and easily moved, and the heavenly body is finc and airy and always moving); but the earth, which is the ultimate boundary of visible things, quite appropriately does not contain in itself the dwelling-place of the intelligibles (for what would light, upwardly mobile things have in common with what is heavy and weighed down?). But so that the earth might not be completely separate, without any share in the intelligible and incorporeal realm, for this reason—by the good action of Providence—human nature came into existence: a share of the earthy was formed around the intelligible and godlike substance of the soul, so that the soul, by a natural union with a heavy body, might be organically one with the element of earth, which has something generically and specifically in common with the substance of flesh. The purpose of these events is that the power superior to the universe might be glorified in all creation by intelligible nature, with what is heavenly and what is earthly being united to each other by the same activity and toward the same end—I mean by the activity of looking at God. But "looking at" God is nothing else but life resembling and befitting an intellectual nature. For as bodies, being earthy, are supported by earthly nourishment, and we recognize some form of bodily life in them, which is operative the same way both in irrational and rational beings, so we must suppose there is some kind of life in intelligent creatures by which their nature is maintained in being.

But if the nourishment of the flesh, which is something unstable and fleeting, instills a kind of life-giving power to those into whom it enters, simply by passing through, how much more will a share in what truly is, what always remains and is the same at every moment, preserve in being the one who shares in it. If, then, this is the proper and appropriate life for the intellectual nature, to share in God, participation would not take place between opposites, unless in some way what is shared were related to the one who hungers for it. For just as, in the eye, the engagement with a ray of light comes about through its having a natural ray in itself to correspond to the

ἔχειν καὶ οὔτε δάκτυλος οὔτε ἄλλο τι τῶν μελῶν τοῦ σώματος
ἐνεργεῖ τὴν ὅρασιν διὰ τὸ μηδεμίαν ἐκ φύσεως αὐγὴν ἐν ἄλλῳ
τινὶ τῶν μελῶν κατεσκευάσθαι, οὕτως ἀνάγκη πᾶσα καὶ ἐπὶ τῆς
τοῦ θεοῦ μετουσίας εἶναί τι συγγενὲς πρὸς τὸ μετεχόμενον ἐν τῇ
PG 176 φύσει τοῦ | ἀπολαύοντος. διὰ τοῦτό φησιν ἡ γραφὴ Κατ᾽ εἰκόνα
θεοῦ γεγενῆσθαι τὸν ἄνθρωπον, ὡς ἄν, οἶμαι, τῷ ὁμοίῳ βλέποι
GNO 80 τὸ ὅμοιον. τὸ δὲ | βλέπειν τὸν θεόν ἐστιν ἡ ζωὴ τῆς ψυχῆς, καθὼς
ἐν τοῖς φθάσασιν εἴρηται. ἐπεὶ δέ πως ἡ τοῦ ἀληθῶς ἀγαθοῦ
ἄγνοια καθάπερ τις ὀμίχλη τῷ διορατικῷ τῆς ψυχῆς ἐπεσκότισεν,
παχυνθεῖσα δὲ ἡ ὀμίχλη νέφος ἐγένετο, ὥστε διὰ τοῦ βάθους τῆς
ἀγνοίας τὴν ἀκτῖνα τῆς ἀληθείας μὴ διαδύεσθαι, ἀναγκαίως τῷ
χωρισμῷ τοῦ φωτὸς καὶ ἡ ζωὴ αὐτῆς συνεξέλιπεν· εἴρηται γὰρ τὴν
ἀληθῆ ζωὴν τῆς ψυχῆς ἐν τῇ μετουσίᾳ τοῦ ἀγαθοῦ ἐνεργεῖσθαι,
τῆς δὲ ἀγνοίας πρὸς τὴν θείαν κατανόησιν ἐμποδιζούσης ἐκπεσεῖν
τῆς ζωῆς τὴν ψυχὴν τὴν τοῦ θεοῦ μὴ μετέχουσαν.

Μηδεὶς δὲ γενεαλογεῖν ἡμᾶς ἀναγκαζέτω τὴν ἄγνοιαν, πόθεν αὕτη λέγων καὶ ἀπὸ τίνος, ἀλλ᾽ ἐξ αὐτῆς νοείτω τῆς τοῦ ὀνόματος σημασίας, ὅτι ἡ γνῶσις καὶ ἡ ἄγνοια τὸ πρός τί πως ἔχειν τὴν ψυχὴν ἐνδείκνυται. οὐδὲν δὲ τῶν πρός τι νοουμένων τε καὶ λεγομένων οὐσίαν παρίστησιν· ἄλλος γὰρ ὁ τοῦ πρός τι καὶ ἕτερος ὁ τῆς οὐσίας λόγος. εἰ οὖν ἡ γνῶσις οὐσία οὐκ ἔστιν, ἀλλὰ περί τι τῆς διανοίας ἐνέργεια, πολὺ μᾶλλον ἡ ἄγνοια πόρρω τοῦ κατ᾽ οὐσίαν εἶναι ὡμολόγηται. τὸ δὲ μὴ κατ᾽ οὐσίαν ὂν οὐδὲ ἔστιν ὅλως. μάταιον τοίνυν ἂν εἴη περὶ τοῦ μὴ ὄντος τὸ ὅθεν ἐστὶ περιεργάζεσθαι.

Ἐπειδὴ τοίνυν ζωὴν μὲν ψυχῆς τὴν τοῦ θεοῦ μετουσίαν ὁ λόγος εἶναί φησι, γνῶσις δὲ κατὰ τὸ ἐγχωροῦν ἐστιν ἡ μετουσία,

ray that is like it, and neither the finger nor any other organ of the body can set vision in motion, because no naturally-generated ray is produced in any other limb, so it must be true that, also for our sharing in God, there is some kinship in the nature of the one who enjoys it, leading to the sharing. So Scripture says, "In the image of God" the human being came to be (Gen 1.27)—so that the human, I imagine, might look on his like by means of likeness. But looking on God is the life of the soul, as we have said previously. And since, somehow, ignorance of what is truly good overshadows like a mist the soul's ability to see—and in us a mist that has grown dense is a fog, such that the ray of truth cannot penetrate down through the depth of its ignorance—necessarily life departs from the soul along with its separation from the light. For we have already said that the true life of the soul is realized in its participation in the Good; but if ignorance stands in the way of divine knowledge, then the soul, by not participating in God, departs from life.

10 And let no one feel compelled to trace out for us the family tree of ignorance, telling us where it comes from and what its source is; but let each of us recognize, from the very meaning of the word, that "knowing" and "unknowing" reveal a relative disposition of the soul. Nothing that is thought of and described in the category of relation presents a substance to us; for the category of relationship is one thing, that of substance another.[16] But if knowledge is not a substance, but rather an activity concerned with some aspect of thinking, all the more can we agree that ignorance is far from what exists as substance. And what does not exist as substance does not exist at all. It would be a waste of time, then, to concern ourselves about the origins of what does not exist.

Since, then, our reason tells us that the life of the soul is participation in God, and to participate is to know as far as possible, but

[16]Gregory's discussion here alludes to the longer treatment in chapter 7 of Aristotle's *Categories*, where the philosopher goes to some lengths to prove his assertion that, taken in itself, "no substance [οὐσία, *ousia*] is relative [πρός τι, *pros ti*]." See Aristotle, *Categories* 8a14–b24.

ἡ δὲ ἄγνοια οὐχί τινός ἐστιν ὕπαρξις, ἀλλὰ τῆς κατὰ τὴν γνῶσιν
ἐνεργείας ἀναίρεσις, τῷ δὲ μὴ ἐνεργεῖσθαι τοῦ θεοῦ τὴν μετουσίαν
ἡ τῆς ζωῆς ἀλλοτρίωσις ἀναγκαίως ἐπηκολούθησεν (τοῦτο δ' ἂν
GNO 81 εἴη τῶν κακῶν τὸ ἔσχατον) | ἀκολούθως ὁ παντὸς ἀγαθοῦ ποιητὴς
τὴν τοῦ κακοῦ θεραπείαν ἐν ἡμῖν κατεργάζεται· ἀγαθὸν γὰρ ἡ
θεραπεία. τὸν δὲ τρόπον τῆς θεραπείας ἀγνοεῖ πάντως ὁ μὴ πρὸς
τὸ εὐαγγελικὸν βλέπων μυστήριον. κακοῦ τοίνυν ἀποδειχθέντος
τοῦ ἀλλοτριωθῆναι θεοῦ, ὅστις ἐστὶν ἡ ζωή, ἡ θεραπεία τοῦ
τοιούτου ἀρρωστήματος ἦν τὸ πάλιν οἰκειωθῆναι θεῷ καὶ ἐν
τῇ ζωῇ γενέσθαι. ταύτης οὖν τῆς ζωῆς κατ' ἐλπίδα προκειμένης
τῇ ἀνθρωπίνῃ φύσει, οὐκ ἔστιν εἰπεῖν κυρίως ἀντίδοσιν τῶν εὖ
βεβιωκότων γενέσθαι τὴν τῆς ζωῆς μετουσίαν καὶ τιμωρίαν τὸ
ἔμπαλιν· ἀλλ' ὅμοιόν ἐστι τῷ κατὰ τοὺς ὀφθαλμοὺς ὑποδείγματι
τὸ λεγόμενον· οὐδὲ γὰρ τῷ κεκαθαρμένῳ τὰς ὄψεις ἔπαθλόν
τί φαμεν εἶναι καὶ πρεσβεῖον τὴν τῶν ὁρατῶν κατανόησιν ἢ τῷ
νοσοῦντι τὸ ἔμπαλιν καταδίκην τινὰ καὶ τιμωρητικὴν ἀπόφασιν τὸ
μὴ μετέχειν τῆς ὁρατικῆς ἐνεργείας. ἀλλ' ὡς ἀναγκαίως ἕπεται τῷ
κατὰ φύσιν διακειμένῳ τὸ βλέπειν τῷ τε ἀπὸ πάθους παρενεχθέντι
τῆς φύσεως τὸ μὴ ἐνεργὸν ἔχειν τὴν ὅρασιν, τὸν αὐτὸν τρόπον
καὶ ἡ μακαρία ζωὴ συμφυής ἐστι καὶ οἰκεία τοῖς κεκαθαρμένοις
PG 177 τὰ | τῆς ψυχῆς αἰσθητήρια, ἐφ' ὧν δὲ καθάπερ τις λήμη τὸ κατὰ
τὴν ἄγνοιαν πάθος ἐμπόδιον πρὸς τὴν μετουσίαν τοῦ ἀληθινοῦ
φωτὸς γίνεται, ἀναγκαίως ἕπεται τὸ μὴ μετέχειν ἐκείνου, οὗ τὴν
μετουσίαν ζωὴν εἶναί φαμεν τοῦ μετέχοντος.

Τούτων τοίνυν οὕτως ἡμῖν διῃρημένων καιρὸς ἂν εἴη διεξετάσαι
τῷ λόγῳ τὸ προτεθὲν ἡμῖν πρόβλημα. τοιοῦτον δέ τι τὸ λεγόμενον
ἦν· εἰ κατὰ τὸ δίκαιον γίνεται τῶν ἀγαθῶν ἡ ἀντίδοσις, ἐν τίσιν
GNO 82 ἔσται ὁ ἐν νηπίῳ τελευτήσας τὸν βίον μήτε | ἀγαθόν τι μήτε κακὸν
ἐν τῇ ζωῇ ταύτῃ καταβαλόμενος, ὥστε διὰ τούτων γενέσθαι
αὐτῷ τὴν κατ' ἀξίαν ἀντίδοσιν; ᾧ πρὸς τὴν ἀκολουθίαν τῶν

ignorance is not the existence of something but the absence of the activity of knowing, and if an alienation from life necessarily follows from the non-realization of our participation in God (and this would be the ultimate evil!), it is clear, in consequence, that the creator of every good thing works in us the healing of evil—for healing is a good. But surely anyone who does not consider the gospel mystery will be unaware of how this healing takes place. If evil, then, is shown to be our alienation from God, who is our life, the healing of this malady would be to come to belong to God once again, and to be situated in life. Since, then, such a renewal of life is set before human nature by way of hope, one cannot precisely say that a participation in life is a reward for those who have lived well, and that the opposite is a punishment. What we must say, rather, is like the example of what happens with our eyes. For we do not say that the recognition of visible objects is a reward for someone with clear eyes, a kind of trophy; nor do we say, by contrast, that not sharing in the activity of seeing is a kind of punishment for one who is handicapped, or a vindictive deprivation. But just as seeing is the necessary consequence of our natural disposition, and not having an active sense of sight follows for the person prevented by disease from using his natural abilities, in the same way the life of blessedness is natural and proper for those whose soul's senses are pure, but for those in whom the pathology of ignorance, like a kind of eye-disease, becomes an obstacle to sharing in the true light, the necessary result is that they will not share in that blessing, whose sharing we say means life for the participant.

11 Since we have made these clarifying distinctions, it is time now for us to examine, in our argument, the problem set before us. It was expressed more or less like this: if the reward of blessedness is given according to the measure of justice, what will the situation be for the one whose life ended when he was an infant, without having established a record for either good or ill in this life, so that he might receive a fitting recompense because of it? If we look at

ἐξητασμένων ὁρῶντες ἀποκρινούμεθα, ὅτι τὸ προσδοκώμενον ἀγαθὸν οἰκεῖον μέν ἐστι κατὰ φύσιν τῷ ἀνθρωπίνῳ γένει, λέγεται δὲ κατά τινα διάνοιαν τὸ αὐτὸ καὶ ἀντίδοσις. τῷ δὲ αὐτῷ ὑποδείγματι πάλιν τὸ νόημα τοῦτο σαφηνισθήσεται· δύο γάρ τινες ὑποκείσθωσαν τῷ λόγῳ ἀρρωστήματί τινι κατὰ τὰς ὄψεις συνενεχθέντες. τούτων δὲ ὁ μὲν σπουδαιότερον ἑαυτὸν ἐπιδιδότω τῇ θεραπείᾳ, πάντα ὑπομένων τὰ παρὰ τῆς ἰατρικῆς προσαγόμενα, κἂν ἐπίπονα ᾖ· ὁ δὲ πρὸς λουτρά τε καὶ οἰνοφλυγίας ἀκρατέστερον διακείσθω, μηδεμίαν τοῦ ἰατρεύοντος συμβουλὴν πρὸς τὴν τῶν ὀφθαλμῶν ὑγίειαν παραδεξάμενος. φαμὲν τοίνυν πρὸς τὸ πέρας ἑκατέρου βλέποντες ἀξίως ἀντιλαβεῖν ἑκάτερον τῆς προαιρέσεως αὐτοῦ τοὺς καρπούς, τὸν μὲν τὴν στέρησιν τοῦ φωτός, τὸν δὲ τὴν ἀπόλαυσιν. τὸ γὰρ ἀναγκαίως ἑπόμενον ἀντίδοσιν ἐκ καταχρήσεως ὀνομάζομεν. ταῦτα καὶ ἐπὶ τῶν κατὰ τὸ νήπιον ζητουμένων ἔστιν εἰπεῖν, ὅτι ἡ τῆς ζωῆς ἐκείνης ἀπόλαυσις οἰκεία μέν ἐστι τῇ ἀνθρωπίνῃ φύσει, τῆς δὲ κατὰ τὴν ἄγνοιαν νόσου πάντων σχεδὸν τῶν ἐν τῇ σαρκὶ ζώντων ἐπικρατούσης, ὁ μὲν ταῖς καθηκούσαις θεραπείαις ἑαυτὸν ἐκκαθάρας καὶ οἷόν τινα λήμην τοῦ διορατικοῦ τῆς ψυχῆς ἀποκλύσας τὴν ἄγνοιαν ἄξιον τῆς σπουδῆς ἔχει τὸ κέρδος ἐν τῇ ζωῇ τῇ κατὰ φύσιν γενόμενος, ὁ δὲ τὰ διὰ τῆς ἀρετῆς φεύγων καθάρσια καὶ δυσίατον ἑαυτῷ διὰ τῶν ἀπατηλῶν ἡδονῶν κατασκευάζων τῆς ἀγνοίας τὴν νόσον, παρὰ φύσιν διατεθεὶς ἠλλοτρίωται τοῦ κατὰ φύσιν καὶ ἀμέτοχος γίνεται τῆς οἰκείας ἡμῖν καὶ καταλλήλου ζωῆς· τὸ δὲ ἀπειρόκακον
GNO 83 νήπιον, μηδεμιᾶς νόσου | τῶν τῆς ψυχῆς ὀμμάτων πρὸς τὴν τοῦ φωτὸς μετουσίαν ἐπιπροσθούσης, ἐν τῷ κατὰ φύσιν γίνεται μὴ δεόμενον τῆς ἐκ τοῦ καθαρθῆναι ὑγιείας, ὅτι μηδὲ τὴν ἀρχὴν τὴν νόσον τῇ ψυχῇ παρεδέξατο. καί μοι δοκεῖ διά τινος ἀναλογίας οἰκείως ἔχειν ὁ παρὼν τοῦ βίου τρόπος τῇ προσδοκωμένῃ ζωῇ.

the consequences of what we have investigated, we will answer that the blessing we expect is, in one sense, naturally proper to the human race, but that it can also, by a certain way of understanding, be seen as a recompense. This idea will become clear by means of the example we have just used. Let us suppose that two people are afflicted by some weakness in the eyes. One of them commits himself more eagerly to undergo treatment, and endures everything inflicted on him by the medical art, even if it is unpleasant; the other, let us suppose, involves himself uncontrollably in going to the baths and in drunkenness, without accepting at all the doctor's advice for the health of his eyes. We say, then, when we look to each one's end, that each justly reaped the fruits of his choice: the one by being deprived of the light, the other by enjoying it. For what necessarily follows we customarily call a requital. And we can say this about those we are considering in their state of infancy: the enjoyment of the next life is proper to human nature, and since the disease of ignorance afflicts practically all who live in the flesh, one person cures himself by using the appropriate remedies, and by purging out ignorance from the soul's eyes like a kind of bleary film, and so receives a worthy reward for his care and comes to share in the life that befits his nature. But another flees from the cleansing medications of virtue, and through deceptive pleasures makes the disease of ignorance hard to cure, in his case; so, being oriented away from nature, such a person is alienated from what is in accord with nature, and comes to be without a share in the life that is proper and fitting for us. The infant, however, who has no experience of evil, no illness blocking the eyes of his soul from sharing in the light, comes to be in the state that befits nature without needing health to be produced through a cure, because he had never contracted an illness in his soul to begin with.[17]

12 The way we presently live, too, seems to me to have a certain analogical resemblance to the life we hope for. Just as our first age,

[17]The notion of an inherited share in humanity's propensity to sin—what in later theology is referred to as the state of "original sin"—is more clearly developed in the Western theological tradition than in that of the Eastern Fathers.

PG 180 καθάπερ γὰρ θηλῇ καὶ γάλακτι ἡ πρώτη τῶν νηπίων | ἡλικία τιθηνουμένη ἐκτρέφεται, εἶτα διαδέχεται ταύτην κατάλληλος ἑτέρα τῷ ὑποκειμένῳ τροφή, οἰκείως τε καὶ ἐπιτηδείως πρὸς τὸ τρεφόμενον ἔχουσα, ἕως ἂν ἐπὶ τὸ τέλειον φθάσῃ· οὕτως οἶμαι καὶ τὴν ψυχὴν διὰ τῶν ἀεὶ καταλλήλων αὐτῇ τάξει τινὶ καὶ ἀκολουθίᾳ μετέχειν τῆς κατὰ φύσιν ζωῆς, ὡς χωρεῖ καὶ δύναται τῶν ἐν τῇ μακαριότητι προκειμένων μεταλαμβάνουσα, καθὼς καὶ παρὰ τοῦ Παύλου τὸ τοιοῦτον ἐμάθομεν, ἄλλως τρέφοντος τὸν ἤδη διὰ τῆς ἀρετῆς αὐξηθέντα καὶ ἑτέρως τὸν νήπιον καὶ ἀτελέστερον· πρὸς μὲν γὰρ τοὺς τοιούτους φησίν, ὅτι Γάλα ὑμᾶς ἐπότισα, οὐ βρῶμα· οὔπω γὰρ ἠδύνασθε· πρὸς δὲ τοὺς πεπληρωκότας τὸ μέτρον τῆς νοητῆς ἡλικίας Τελείων δέ ἐστι, φησίν, ἡ στερεὰ τροφή, τῶν διὰ τὴν ἕξιν τὰ αἰσθητήρια γεγυμνασμένα ἐχόντων. Καθάπερ τοίνυν οὐκ ἔστιν ἐν τοῖς ὁμοίοις εἰπεῖν εἶναι τὸν ἄνδρα τε καὶ τὸ νήπιον,
GNO 84 κἂν μηδεμία νόσος ἑκατέρῳ τούτων προσάπτηται | (πῶς γὰρ ἂν ἐν τῷ ἴσῳ τῆς τρυφῆς γένοιντο οἱ τῶν αὐτῶν μὴ μετέχοντες;), ἀλλὰ τὸ μὲν μὴ κακοῦσθαι νόσῳ τινὶ καὶ ἐπὶ τούτου καὶ ἐπ᾽ ἐκείνου λέγεται παραπλησίως, ἕως ἂν ἔξω πάθους ἑκάτερος ᾖ, τῶν δὲ κατὰ τρυφὴν ἡ ἀπόλαυσις οὐκέτι ὁμοίως παρὰ τῶν αὐτῶν ἐνεργεῖται (τῷ μὲν γὰρ ὑπάρχει καὶ διὰ λόγων εὐφραίνεσθαι καὶ πραγμάτων ἐπιστατεῖν καὶ εὐδοκίμως ἀρχὰς μετιέναι καὶ ταῖς τῶν δεομένων εὐεργεσίαις λαμπρύνεσθαι γαμετῇ τε συνοικεῖν, ἂν οὕτω τύχῃ καταθυμία, καὶ οἴκου ἄρχειν καὶ ὅσα μετὰ τούτων ἐστὶν ἡδέα παρὰ τὸν βίον εὑρεῖν· ἀκροάματά τε καὶ θεάματα, θῆραι καὶ λουτρὰ καὶ γυμνάσια καὶ συμποτικαὶ θυμηδίαι καὶ εἴ τι τοιοῦτον ἕτερον· τῷ δὲ νηπίῳ ἡ τρυφὴ τὸ γάλα ἐστὶ καὶ ἡ τῆς τιθήνης ἀγκάλη καὶ ἠρεμαία κίνησις τὸν ὕπνον ἐφελκομένη τε καὶ ἡδύνουσα·τὴν γὰρ ὑπὲρ τοῦτο εὐφροσύνην τὸ ἀτελὲς τῆς ἡλικίας χωρῆσαι φύσιν οὐκ ἔχει)· τὸν αὐτὸν τρόπον οἱ διὰ τῆς ἀρετῆς ἐν τῷ τῇδε βίῳ τὰς ψυχὰς

[18]Ancient Greek and Roman society tended to assume that talented people should show their personal gifts in an appropriately grand lifestyle and by an appropriately high degree of self-esteem and reputation; see Aristotle's classic discussion of "magnificence" (μεγαλοπρέπεια, *megaloprepeia*) and "magnanimity" (μεγαλοψυχία,

as infants, is sustained and nourished by the breast and by milk, but then a materially different form of nourishment succeeds it, in a way fitting and appropriate for the one being nourished, until our growth comes to fulfillment; so, I think, the soul, too, by the means proper to it, comes, by a certain order and sequence, to share in its natural life, participating according to its capacity and ability in the things that ultimately await us in the state of blessedness. We have learned this from Paul, that the one who is already grown up through virtue is nourished one way, and the infant and immature in another. For he says to the latter, "I gave you milk to drink, not solid food; for you were not yet able to digest that" (1 Cor 3.2). But to those who had completed the measure of the age of reason, he says, "Solid food is for the fully grown, who possess senses trained through practice" (Heb 5.14). So one cannot say that the grown adult and the baby are in the same situation, even if no disease attacks either of them—for how could those who do not share in the same things find themselves in an equal state of bliss?—but rather we say that not being laid low by a disease applies to the one and the other in the same way, while each is being healed from suffering; but the enjoyment of delight is not yet realized in an equal way through the same things. For it is usual for the one to delight in conversation, in taking charge of practical affairs, in discharging a public office in an illustrious way, in distinguishing himself by his benefactions to those in need, in living with his spouse (if he should find one of the same mind), in ruling his household, and in other pleasant aspects of life one can imagine besides these—concerts and spectacles and hunts and the baths and the gymnasium and drinking parties and other things of the same kind.[18] But for the infant, delight is found in milk, in his nurse's arms, in the gentle motion that induces sleep and makes it sweet; for someone still immature in age does not have the natural ability to find joy in things beyond these. In the same way, those who

megalopsychia) in *Nicomachean Ethics* 4.3–4 (1123b–1125b25). Gregory is also doubtless alluding to the pleasures Hierius rightfully enjoys as a successful, morally upright adult.

θρέψαντες καί, καθώς φησιν ὁ ἀπόστολος, καταγυμνάσαντες
ἑαυτῶν τὰ νοητὰ αἰσθητήρια, εἰ πρὸς τὴν ἀσώματον ἐκείνην
μετοικισθεῖεν ζωήν, πρὸς λόγον τῆς ἐνυπαρχούσης αὐτοῖς ἕξεώς
τε καὶ δυνάμεως τῆς θείας τρυφῆς μεταλήψονται, ἢ πλείονος ἢ
ἐλάττονος κατὰ τὴν παροῦσαν ἑκάστου δύναμιν τῶν προκειμένων
μετέχοντες· ἡ δὲ ἄγευστος τῆς ἀρετῆς ψυχὴ τῶν μὲν ἐκ πονηρίας
κακῶν, ἅτε μηδὲ τὴν ἀρχὴν συνενεχθεῖσα τῇ τῆς κακίας νόσῳ,
GNO 85 διαμένει | ἀμέτοχος, τῆς δὲ ζωῆς ἐκείνης, ἣν θεοῦ γνῶσίν τε καὶ
μετουσίαν ὁ πρὸ τούτων λόγος ὡρίσατο, τοσοῦτον μετέχει παρὰ
τὴν πρώτην, ὅσον χωρεῖ τὸ τρεφόμενον, ἕως ἂν καθάπερ τινὶ
τροφῇ καταλλήλῳ τῇ θεωρίᾳ τοῦ ὄντος ἐναδρυνθεῖσα χωρητικὴ
τοῦ πλείονος γένηται, ἐν δαψιλείᾳ τοῦ ὄντος κατ᾽ ἐξουσίαν
μετέχουσα.

Πρὸς ταῦτα βλέποντες ἔξω μὲν τῶν ἐκ πονηρίας κακῶν ὁμοίως
PG 181 εἶναί φαμεν τὴν ψυχὴν τοῦ τε διὰ | πάσης ἀρετῆς ἥκοντος καὶ
τοῦ μηδὲ ὅλως μετεσχηκότος τοῦ βίου· οὐ μὴν ἐν τῷ ὁμοίῳ τὴν
ἑκατέρου τούτων διαγωγὴν ἐννοοῦμεν. ὁ μὲν γὰρ ἤκουσε, καθὼς ὁ
προφήτης φησί, τῶν οὐρανίων διηγημάτων, δι᾽ ὧν ἡ δόξα τοῦ θεοῦ
καταγγέλλεται, καὶ διὰ τῆς κτίσεως πρὸς τὴν κατανόησιν ὡδηγήθη
τοῦ δεσπότου τῆς κτίσεως καὶ διδασκάλῳ τῆς ὄντως σοφίας
ἐχρήσατο τῇ ἐν τοῖς οὖσι θεωρουμένῃ σοφίᾳ τό τε τοῦ φωτὸς
τούτου κάλλος κατανοήσας ἀναλογικῶς τὸ τοῦ ἀληθινοῦ φωτὸς
κάλλος ἐνόησε καὶ ἐν τῷ παγίῳ τῆς γῆς τὸ τοῦ πεποιηκότος αὐτὴν
ἀμετάθετον ἐπαιδεύθη καὶ τὸ ἀμέτρητον τοῦ οὐρανίου μεγέθους
κατανοήσας πρὸς τὸ ἄπειρόν τε καὶ ἀόριστον τῆς ἐμπεριεχούσης
τὸ πᾶν δυνάμεως ὡδηγήθη τάς τε ἀκτῖνας ἰδὼν τοῦ ἡλίου ἐκ τῶν

have nurtured their souls by virtue during life here on earth, and who have, in the Apostle's words, "trained the senses" (Heb 5.14) of their own minds, when they come to share in that life that is free of the body, will participate in heavenly delight to the measure of the habits and powers they have acquired, sharing to a greater or lesser degree in what lies before them according to the ability each one has. But the soul that has not tasted virtue, on the other hand, remains without a share in the evil effects of wickedness, insofar as it has not been caught up in the disease of vice at all; yet it shares beyond the beginning stage[19] in this [human] life—which our discussion before has defined as knowledge of God and participation in him—only to the degree that the nursing infant can receive it, until eventually, made inwardly mature by a nourishment appropriate to contemplation, it comes to be able to receive more, and shares as much as it can in the rich abundance of what is real.[20]

13 With all this in view, we say that the soul of a person who has progressed through all the stages of virtue, and that of the one who has had as yet no share of human life at all, are equally free from the evil effects resulting from wickedness; still, we do not consider the course of each of their lives to be on the same level. For the one has heard, as the Prophet says, what "the heavens are telling" as they proclaim "the glory of God" (Ps 18.1), and through creation is led along the path of recognizing the Lord of creation;[21] he has made use of the wisdom recognized in things to teach him true wisdom, and by understanding the beauty of this light in an analogical way has come to know the beauty of "the true light" (Jn 1.9). In the solidity of the earth, he has been instructed on the unshakeable firmness of its creator, and by recognizing the immeasurable size of the heavenly realm has been led toward the limitless and infinite greatness of the power that surrounds all things. In seeing the rays of the sun coming

[19]Greek: παρὰ τὴν πρώτην (*para tēn prōtēn).*

[20]Here Gregory alludes, as he does in many other texts, to his conviction that the souls of the dead continue to grow in their ability to participate in God.

[21]Cf. Rom 1.20–21; Wis 13.5.

τοσούτων ὑψωμάτων μέχρις ἡμῶν διηκούσας τὸ μὴ ἀτονεῖν τὰς προνοητικὰς τοῦ θεοῦ ἐνεργείας πρὸς ἕκαστον ἡμῶν ἀπὸ τοῦ τῆς θεότητος ὕψους κατιέναι διὰ τῶν φαινομένων ἐπίστευσεν. εἰ γὰρ εἷς ὢν ὁ φωστὴρ κοινῇ τε τὸ ὑποκείμενον ἅπαν τῇ φωτιστικῇ δυνάμει καταλαμβάνει καὶ πᾶσι τοῖς μετέχουσιν ἑαυτὸν ἐπινέμων ὅλος ἑκάστῳ καὶ ἀδιαίρετος πάρεστι, πόσῳ μᾶλλον ὁ τοῦ φωστῆρος δημιουργὸς καὶ Πάντα ἐν πᾶσι γίνεται, καθώς φησιν ὁ
GNO 86 | ἀπόστολος, καὶ ἑκάστῳ πάρεστι τοσοῦτον ἑαυτὸν διδούς, ὅσον τὸ ὑποκείμενον δέχεται. ἀλλὰ καὶ στάχυν τις ἰδὼν ἐπὶ γῆς καὶ τὴν ἐκ φυτοῦ βλάστην καὶ βότρυν ὥριμον καὶ τὸ τῆς ὀπώρας κάλλος ἢ ἐν καρποῖς ἢ ἐν ἄνθεσι καὶ τὴν αὐτόματον πόαν καὶ ὄρος ἐπὶ τὸ αἰθέριον ὕψος ἀπὸ τῆς ἄκρας ἀνατεινόμενον καὶ τὰς ἐν ὑπωρείαις πηγάς, μαζῶν δίκην ἐκ τῶν λαγόνων τοῦ ὄρους ἐπιρρεούσας, ποταμούς τε διὰ τῶν κοίλων ῥέοντας καὶ θάλασσαν ὑποδεχομένην τὰ πανταχόθεν ῥεύματα καὶ ἐν τῷ μέτρῳ μένουσαν κύματά τε τοῖς αἰγιαλοῖς ὁριζόμενα καὶ οὐκ ἐπεξιοῦσαν ὑπὲρ τοὺς τεταγμένους ὅρους κατὰ τῆς ἠπείρου τὴν θάλασσαν· ὁ ταῦτα καὶ τὰ τοιαῦτα βλέπων πῶς οὐκ ἂν τὰ πάντα διαλάβοι τῷ λόγῳ, δι᾽ ὧν γίνεται τοῖς θεολογοῦσιν ἡ διδασκαλία τοῦ ὄντος, οὐ μικρὰν ἑαυτῷ δύναμιν πρὸς τὴν μετουσίαν τῆς τρυφῆς ἐκείνης παρασκευάσας τῷ εἶναι παρ᾽ αὐτῷ τὰ νοήματα, δι᾽ ὧν ὁδηγεῖται πρὸς ἀρετὴν ἡ διάνοια, γεωμετρίαν τε καὶ ἀστρονομίαν καὶ τὴν διὰ τοῦ ἀριθμοῦ κατανόησιν τῆς ἀληθείας πᾶσάν τε μέθοδον ἀποδεικτικὴν τῶν ἀγνοουμένων καὶ βεβαιωτικὴν τῶν κατειλημμένων καὶ πρό γε τούτων τὴν τῆς θεοπνεύστου γραφῆς φιλοσοφίαν, τελείαν ἐπάγουσαν κάθαρσιν τοῖς δι᾽ αὐτῆς τὰ θεῖα πεπαιδευμένοις μυστήρια; ὁ δὲ μηδενὸς τούτων ἐν γνώσει γενόμενος μηδὲ χειραγωγηθεὶς διὰ τοῦ κόσμου

down to us from such heights, he has come to believe that the providential activities of God are not too weak to come down to each of us through events of the sense-world, from the height of the Divinity. For if the heavenly light, which is single, comprehends all that lies beneath it with its light-giving power, and in giving itself to all who share it is present as one undivided whole to each of them, how much more will the creator of the light also become "all things to all" (1 Cor 15.28), as the Apostle says, and be present to each of them, giving so much of himself as the creature beneath him will receive.

But if someone sees an ear of corn on the earth, and the shoot of a plant and the ripe grape, and the beauty of late summer—either in its fruits or its flowers—and the grass that grows on its own, and a mountain reaching up from its peak toward the heights of the sky, and the springs in the foothills, gushing out from the hollows of the mountain as from breasts, and rivers flowing through the valleys, and the sea receiving the water that flows from all directions and still remaining within its measure, and the waves bound by the shores, and the sea not going beyond its appointed limits on the seashore: if one looks on these things and others like them, how could he not grasp in his reason all the things by which those who write of God are taught about being? This offers him no small ability to participate in that delightful state, in which he possesses those thoughts by which critical reason is guided toward virtue—geometry and astronomy and the ability to grasp the whole of truth in numerical form, and a method for demonstrating what is not known and of confirming the things we understand, and before all of this the wise way of life[22] taught in the inspired Scripture, which brings perfect purification to those instructed by it in the divine Mysteries.

But the person who has not come to know any of these things, who has not been led through the world toward the recognition of

[22]Literally, "the philosophy" (φιλοσοφία), which refers not so much to a particular intellectual discipline as to a form of life spent in seeking wisdom, and in leading others to seek it. Gregory is reflecting, in this passage, on the conception of continuing philosophical and dialectical instruction and self-discipline practiced generally by ancient philosophers since Socrates.

πρὸς τὴν τῶν ὑπερκοσμίων ἀγαθῶν κατανόησιν, ἁπαλός τις
GNO 87 καὶ ἀγύμναστος καὶ ἀτριβὴς | τὴν διάνοιαν παρελθὼν τὸν βίον,
ἐκεῖνος οὐκ ἂν ἐν τοῖς αὐτοῖς εἴη, ἐν οἷς ὁ λόγος τὸν προλαβόντα
PG 184 ἀπέδειξεν, ὡς μηκέτι διὰ τοῦτο μακαρι|στότερον ἀποδείκνυσθαι
κατὰ τὴν προενεχθεῖσαν ἡμῖν ἀντίθεσιν τὸν μὴ μετασχόντα τοῦ
βίου τοῦ μετασχόντος καλῶς. τοῦ μὲν γὰρ κακίᾳ συνεζηκότος
οὐ μόνον ὁ ἀπειρόκακος ἂν εἴη μακαριστότερος, ἀλλὰ τάχα καὶ
ὁ μηδὲ τὴν ἀρχὴν παρελθὼν εἰς τὸν βίον· τοιοῦτον γὰρ καὶ περὶ
τοῦ Ἰούδα διὰ τῆς εὐαγγελικῆς φωνῆς ἐδιδάχθημεν, ὅτι ἐπὶ τῶν
τοιούτων κρεῖττον τοῦ κατὰ κακίαν ὑφεστῶτός ἐστι τὸ παντελῶς
ἀνυπόστατον· τῷ μὲν γὰρ διὰ τὸ βάθος τῆς ἐμφυείσης κακίας εἰς
ἄπειρον παρατείνεται ἡ διὰ τῆς καθάρσεως κόλασις, τοῦ δὲ μὴ
ὄντος πῶς ἂν ὀδύνη καθάψαιτο; εἰ δέ τις πρὸς τὸν κατ᾽ ἀρετὴν
βίον κρίνοι τὸν νηπιώδη καὶ ἄωρον, ὄντως ἄωρος ὁ τοιοῦτός ἐστι
τοιαύτῃ κρίσει περὶ τῶν ὄντων χρώμενος.

Ἐρωτᾷς οὖν, ὅτου χάριν ἐν τούτῳ τῆς ἡλικίας τις ὢν τῆς ζωῆς
ὑπεξάγεται, τί διὰ τούτου τῆς θείας σοφίας προμηθουμένης. ἀλλ᾽
εἰ μὲν περὶ τούτων λέγοις, ὅσα τῆς παρανόμου κυήσεως ἔλεγχος
γίνεται καὶ διὰ τοῦτο παρὰ τῶν γεννησαμένων ἐξαφανίζεται,
οὐκ εἰκότως ἂν τῶν τῆς κακίας ἔργων τὸν θεὸν ἀπαιτοίης τὸν
λόγον, τὸν τὰ μὴ καλῶς ἐπὶ τούτῳ γεγενημένα εἰς κρίσιν ἄγοντα·
εἰ δέ τις καὶ ἀνατρεφομένων τῶν γεννητόρων καὶ δι᾽ ἐπιμελείας
θεραπευόντων καὶ δι᾽ εὐχῆς σπουδαζόντων ὅμως οὐ μετέχει τοῦ
βίου, κατακρατοῦντος μέχρι θανάτου τοῦ ἀρρωστήματος (ὃ μόνον
GNO 88 τῆς αἰτίας ἀναμφιβόλως ἐστίν), ταῦτα περὶ τῶν | τοιούτων εἰκάζομεν,
ὅτι τελείας ἐστὶ προνοίας οὐ μόνον γεγονότα θεραπεύειν τὰ πάθη,

[23]Gregory here recognizes both the fact and the sinful character of the deliberate abortion of unborn children, as well as the more widespread ancient practice of killing newborns. The killing or abandonment of unwanted newborn infants was a fairly widespread practice in antiquity, according to a number of pagan, biblical, and

the good things above the world, who goes through life as someone undeveloped, untrained, inexperienced in reasoning—he would not be in the same situation in which our argument has just shown the person we have spoken of to be. As a result, the one who has not had any share in life cannot any longer be thought more blessed, according to the contrast developed earlier, than someone will be who has shared in it well. For in that case, not only would the person who has no experience of vice be more blessed than one who has lived immersed in wickedness, but perhaps even one who has not entered on the normal course of living at all. We learn this kind of thing, after all, from the words of the Gospel about Judas: that for people like him, not to exist at all is better than existing in wickedness (see Mt 26.24; Mk 14.21); for purgative punishment will be extended indefinitely for such a person, due to the depth of wickedness that has come to be part of him—but how can pain take hold of one who has never lived? Yet if one judges the life of the infant who dies before his time as comparable to a life lived in virtue—the one who makes such a judgment about reality is truly immature!

14 You ask, then, what the reason is for which someone at such an age is removed from life—what the divine Wisdom has in mind to achieve through this. Now if you are speaking of those infants who provide the evidence of an illegitimate sexual act, and for that reason are done away with by their parents, you would not be right to hold God accountable for the deeds of human sinfulness, since in fact he will bring to judgment things done to such a child in a wicked way.[23] But if, despite the nurturing care of parents and their attempts to look after and heal the infant, and despite their earnest prayers for the child, nevertheless it does not live, but its illness dominates and leads to death—and if this is death's unmistakable cause—we offer the suggestion, for such cases, that it belongs to God's perfect providence not only to heal the illnesses that may occur in us, but

early Christian sources. For a useful, brief survey, see Michael J. Gorman, *Abortion in the Early Church: Christian, Jewish and Pagan Attitudes in the Greco-Roman World* (New York: Paulist Press, 1982).

ἀλλ’ ὅπως ἂν μηδὲ τὴν ἀρχήν τις τοῖς ἀπηγορευμένοις ἐγγένοιτο
προνοεῖν. τὸν γὰρ ἐγνωκότα ἐπ’ ἴσης τῷ παρεληλυθότι τὸ μέλλον
ἐπικωλύειν εἰκὸς τὴν ἐπὶ τὸ τέλειον τῆς ζωῆς τοῦ νηπίου πρόοδον,
ὡς ἂν μὴ τῇ προγνωστικῇ δυνάμει τὸ κατανοηθὲν κακὸν ἐπὶ τοῦ
μέλλοντος οὕτως βιώσεσθαι τελειωθείη καὶ γένηται τῷ τοιαύτῃ
προαιρέσει συζήσεσθαι μέλλοντι ὕλη κακίας ὁ βίος. ὑποδείγματι δέ
τινι ῥᾴδιον ἂν εἴη παραστῆσαι τὸ νόημα· ἔστω γὰρ καθ’ ὑπόθεσιν
παντοδαπή τις εὐωχία προκειμένη τῷ συμποσίῳ, ἐπιστατείτω δέ
τις τοιοῦτος τῶν δαιτυμόνων, οἷος ἀκριβῶς εἰδέναι τὰ τῆς ἑκάστου
φύσεως ἰδιώματα καὶ τί μὲν κατάλληλον τῇ τοιαύτῃ κράσει, τί
δὲ ἐπιβλαβὲς καὶ ἀνοίκειον· προσκείσθω δὲ τούτῳ καὶ αὐθεντική
τις ἐξουσία τοῦ κατὰ τὸ ἴδιον βούλημα τὸν μέν τινα μετέχειν τῶν
προκειμένων ἐᾶν, τὸν δὲ ἀποτρέπειν, καὶ πάντα ποιεῖν, ὡς ἂν
κατὰ τὴν ἑαυτοῦ κρᾶσιν ἕκαστος τῶν καταλλήλων προσάπτοιτο,
ἵνα μήτε ὁ νοσώδης ἐπιτριβείη, προσθεὶς ὕλην διὰ τῶν ἐδωδίμων
τῇ νόσῳ, μήτε ὁ εὐρωστότερος κάμοι, εἰς πληθωρικὴν ἀηδίαν
ἐκπίπτων τῇ ἀκαταλλήλῳ τροφῇ. ἐν τούτοις εἰ μεσοῦντος τοῦ
συμποσίου τις τῶν τῇ οἰνοφλυγίᾳ προσκειμένων ἐξάγεται ἢ ἐν
ἀρχῇ ὢν τῆς μέθης ἢ μέχρι τέλους παραμένει τῷ δείπνῳ, ταῦτα τοῦ
GNO 89 ἐπιστάτου | οἰκονομοῦντος, ὡς ἂν εὐσχημονοίη διαρκῶς ἡ τράπεζα
τῶν ἐκ πληθώρας καὶ μέθης καὶ παραφορᾶς κακῶν καθαρεύουσα.
ὥσπερ οὖν ὁ τῆς τῶν ἡδυσμάτων κνίσης ἀποσπώμενος οὐκ ἐν
PG 185 ἡδονῇ | ποιεῖται τῶν καταθυμίων τὴν στέρησιν, ἀλλ’ ἀκρισίαν τινὰ
τοῦ ἐπιστατοῦντος καταγινώσκει, ὡς φθόνῳ τινὶ καὶ οὐ προνοίᾳ
τῶν προκειμένων ἀπείργοντος, εἰ δὲ πρὸς τοὺς ἔτι ἀσχημονοῦντας
τῇ παρατάσει τῆς μέθης βλέποι ἐν ἐμέτοις καὶ καρηβαρίαις καὶ τῷ

[24]Cf. Wis 4.11, for a similar idea.

[25]In the ancient world, wine tended to be heavy and strong, and was generally diluted with water before drinking, usually in a ratio of one part wine to three or

also to contrive in advance a way for someone not to get involved at all in actions that are forbidden. For it is reasonable that the one who knows what will come, just as well as he knows what has happened in the past, should prevent the progress of the infant toward the completion of his life, so that the evil that God recognizes, by his power of foreknowledge, in the future of one who will live in this way, might not come about,[24] and so that the person's life might not become the raw material of evil, because he was going to live it out in accordance with bad choices.

15 It would be easy to illustrate the idea by an example. Let us suppose that all sorts of sumptuous provisions have been prepared for a banquet, and one of the banqueters will preside who knows precisely the personal characteristics of each guest, and what is suitable in a certain blend of drink, as well as what is harmful and unsuitable.[25] And let us suppose that he also genuinely possesses the power to let one guest participate as much as he will in what is provided, and to turn another away, so that each of them consumes what is appropriate for him from the menu the host has prepared—in such a way that neither the sick person is made worse by exacerbating his illness with food and drink, nor the healthy guest gets sick by feeling the discomfort of over-consuming what is inappropriate for him. With all these guests, deciding whether one of those at the table is to be led out in the middle of the banquet because he is drunk, or at the start of the drinking, or may remain at the banquet right to the end—all of this is managed by the president, so that the table might remain continually well-ordered, free of the evil effects of excessive eating and drinking and bad behavior. But just as the person distracted by the odor of delicious foods will not be pleased by being deprived of what he craves, but writes this off as some form of bad judgment on the president's part—preventing him from participating out of bad-will of some sort, not by his care for the guests at the table—yet

four parts water. The person who presided at a banquet was not simply a master of ceremonies, but seems to have had a good deal of discretion in regulating the strength of the drink and the pace of the drinking.

παραφθέγγεσθαί τι τῶν οὐ δεόντων, χάριν ὁμολογεῖ τῷ πρὸ τοῦ τοιούτου πάθους τῆς ἀμέτρου πλησμονῆς αὐτὸν ἀποστήσαντι· εἰ δὴ νενόηται ἡμῖν τὸ ὑπόδειγμα, ῥᾴδιον ἂν εἴη προσαγαγεῖν τὸ ἐν τούτῳ καταληφθὲν ἡμῖν θεώρημα τῷ προκειμένῳ νοήματι. τί γὰρ τὸ προκείμενον ἦν; ὅτου χάριν ὁ θεός, πολλῆς οὔσης τοῖς πατράσι σπουδῆς φυλαχθῆναι ἑαυτοῖς τὸν τοῦ βίου διάδοχον, ἄωρον πολλάκις ἐν τῷ ἀτελεῖ τῆς ἡλικίας ἐᾷ τὸ τεχθὲν ἀναρπάζεσθαι; πρὸς οὓς ἐροῦμεν τὸ συμποτικὸν ἐκεῖνο ὑπόδειγμα, ὅτι τῆς τοῦ βίου τραπέζης πολλήν τε καὶ παντοδαπὴν τῶν ἐδωδίμων τὴν παρασκευὴν ἐχούσης (νόει δέ μοι κατὰ τὴν ὀψαρτυτικὴν ἐμπειρίαν μὴ πάντα τῷ τῆς ἡδονῆς μέλιτι τὰ τοῦ βίου καταγλυκαίνεσθαι, ἀλλ᾽ ἔστιν ὅπου καὶ τοῖς αὐστηροτέροις τῶν συμπτωμάτων τὴν ζωὴν ἐπαρτύεσθαι, οἷα δὴ φιλοτεχνοῦσιν οἱ τῶν περὶ γαστέρα καὶ θοίνην ἡδονῶν τεχνῖται τοῖς δριμυτέροις ἢ ἁλμῶσιν ἢ παραστύφουσιν τὰς ὀρέξεις τῶν δαιτυμόνων ἀναρριπίζοντες)· ἐπεὶ οὖν οὐ διὰ πάντων ἐστὶ τῶν πραγμάτων μελιηδὴς ὁ βίος, ἀλλ᾽ ἔστιν ἐν οἷς ἅλμη τὸ ὄψον ἐστὶν ἢ στῦψις [ἢ] ὀξώδης, ἢ δηκτική
GNO 90 τις καὶ | δριμεῖα ποιότης ἐντριβεῖσα τοῖς πράγμασι δύσληπτον ποιεῖ τὴν καρυκείαν τοῦ βίου, πλήρεις δὲ οἱ τῆς ἀπάτης κρατῆρες παντοδαποῦ κράματος, ὧν οἱ μὲν τὸ φυσῶδες πάθος διὰ τοῦ τύφου τῆς ἀπάτης τοῖς ἐμπιοῦσιν ἐποίησαν, οἱ δὲ εἰς παραφορὰν τοὺς ἐμπιόντας ἐξεκαλέσαντο, ἄλλοις δὲ τῶν πονηρῶς κτηθέντων τὸν ἔμετον διὰ τῆς αἰσχρᾶς ἀποτίσεως ἀνεκίνησαν· ὡς ἂν οὖν μὴ ἐπιχρονίζοι τῇ τοιαύτῃ τῆς τραπέζης παρασκευῇ ὁ μὴ δεόντως τῷ συμποσίῳ χρησάμενος, θᾶττον ὑπεξάγεται τοῦ τῶν δαιτυμόνων πληρώματος, κερδαίνων τὸ μὴ ἐν ἐκείνοις γενέσθαι, ὧν ἡ ἀμετρία τῆς ἀπολαύσεως τοῖς λαιμαργοῦσι πρόξενος γίνεται. τοῦτό ἐστιν ὅ φημι τελείας εἶναι προνοίας κατόρθωμα, τὸ μὴ μόνον συστάντα

if he sees someone, among those badly affected by the length of the party, vomiting or heavy-headed or saying something inappropriate, he will express his thanks to the one who kept him from unlimited excess before he experienced such a situation himself.

If, then, we have grasped the example, it would be easy to apply the principle we recognize in it to the thought at hand. What was our subject? It was why God, when parents are deeply concerned that a successor in their living line be preserved for them, often allows the newborn child to be taken away prematurely, with his normal life-span still incomplete. In reply, we have offered this example: that since the table of life holds a wide and varied array of edible things—think, I ask you, in terms of your own experience with food—not all the details of life are sweetened with the honey of pleasure; in fact, there are times when life is flavored with somewhat harsh events, just as artists of the pleasures of eating and feasting sometimes like to rekindle the appetites of their diners with sharp or salty or astringent flavors.[26] Since, then, life is not consistently sweet to our taste, but at times offers us something salty or provides some strongly astringent food to eat, or if some acid or bitter flavoring, sprinkled into things, makes the artful cuisine of life's diet hard to perceive; and since life's treacherous punchbowls are filled with every kind of concoction, some of which cause gastric distress in those who drink, by their fog of deception, while others invite drinkers to lose mental focus, others induce them to vomit forth what they have over-indulged in, by a kind of shameful retribution; therefore, so that the one who takes part in the banquet in an unseemly way might not stay too long at a table so prepared, he is quickly ushered out of the dining room, drawing a benefit for himself by not being part of a company for whom immoderate consumption only encourages gluttony.[27] This is, in my view, the real proof of a perfect providence: not simply to heal passions when they have come into existence, but even to keep

[26]To make sense of this sentence, I have punctuated it somewhat differently than the editors of the Greek text have done.

[27]Literally, "becomes the patron of gluttons."

θεραπεύειν τὰ πάθη, ἀλλὰ καὶ κωλύειν πρὸ τῆς συστάσεως. ὃ δὴ καὶ περὶ τοῦ θανάτου τῶν ἀρτιτόκων ὑπενοήσαμεν, ὅτι ὁ λόγῳ τὰ πάντα ποιῶν ὑπὸ φιλανθρωπίας ἀφαιρεῖται τῆς κακίας τὴν ὕλην μὴ διδοὺς καιρὸν τῇ προαιρέσει τῇ διὰ τῆς προγνωστικῆς δυνάμεως γνωρισθείσῃ διὰ τῶν ἔργων ἐν κακίας ἐξοχῇ δειχθῆναι οἵα ἐστίν, ὅταν πρὸς τὸ κακὸν τὴν ὁρμὴν ἔχοι.

Πολλάκις δὲ τὴν σεσοφισμένην τῆς φιλαργυρίας ἀνάγκην διὰ τῶν τοιούτων ἐλέγχει ὁ συνιστῶν τὸ τοῦ βίου συμπόσιον, ὡς ἄν, οἶμαι, γυμνὸν τῶν εὐπροσώπων προκαλυμμάτων τὸ τῆς φιλαργυρίας ἀρρώστημα φαίνοιτο μηδενὶ παραπετάσματι
GNO c91 πεπλανημένῳ συσκιαζόμενον. φασὶ γὰρ οἱ πολλοὶ διὰ τοῦτο | ταῖς
τοῦ πλείονος ἐπιθυμίαις ἐπιπλατύνεσθαι, ὡς ἂν πλουσιωτέρους τοὺς ἐξ αὐτῶν γεγονότας ποιήσαιεν· ὧν ἐλέγχει τὴν νόσον ἰδίαν οὖσαν, οὐκ ἐξ ἀνάγκης ἐγγινομένην ἡ ἀπροφάσιστος τῶν ἀτέκνων πλεονεξία· πολλοὶ γὰρ οὔτε ἔχοντες διαδοχὴν ἐπὶ πολλοῖς οἷς ἐμόχθησαν οὔτε ἐν ἐλπίσι τοῦ σχεῖν ὄντες ἀντὶ μυρίων τέκνων πολλὰς ἐπιθυμίας ἐν ἑαυτοῖς παιδοτροφοῦσιν, οὐκ ἔχοντες ποῦ
PG 188 τὴν ἀνάγ|κην τῆς ἀρρωστίας ταύτης ἐπανενέγκωσιν.

Εἰ δέ τινες κακῶς ἐπιδημοῦντες τῷ βίῳ, τυραννικοί τε καὶ πικροὶ τὴν προαίρεσιν, πάσαις ἀκολασίαις δεδουλωμένοι, θυμῷ παραπλῆγες, φειδόμενοι τῶν ἀνηκέστων κακῶν οὐδενός, λῃσταὶ καὶ ἀνδροφόνοι καὶ πατρίδων προδόται ἢ εἴ τι τούτων ἐστὶν ἐναγέστερον οἷον πατροφόνοι τε καὶ μητρολῷαι καὶ παιδοκτόνοι καὶ ταῖς παρανόμοις μίξεσιν ἐπιλυσσῶντες, εἰ τοιοῦτοί τινες ὄντες ἐν τῇ κακίᾳ ταύτῃ γηράσκουσιν, πῶς ἐρεῖ τις συμβαίνειν ταῦτα τοῖς προεξητασμένοις; εἰ γὰρ τὸ πρὸ ὥρας ἀνάρπαστον, ὡς ἂν μὴ εἰς τέλος κατὰ τὸ ὑπόδειγμα τοῦ συμποσίου τοῖς πάθεσι τῆς ζωῆς ταύτης ἐλλαιμαργήσειεν, προνοητικῶς ὑπεξάγεται τοῦ βιωτικοῦ συμποσίου, τίνος χάριν ὁ τοιοῦτος μέχρι γήρως ἐμπαροινεῖ τῷ συμποσίῳ, πονηρὰν ἑαυτῷ τε καὶ τοῖς συμπόταις τὴν τῶν κακῶν ἑωλοκρασίαν ἐπισκεδάζων; πρὸς οὓς ἐροῦμεν μηδὲν ἔλαττον καὶ

them from being formed. And we suggest this in the case of the death of new-born children: that he who, by his Word, creates all things, kindly takes away the material for doing evil, giving no occasion for the choices that, through the power of foreknowledge, he knows will be revealed in action to be what they will be—supremely bad!—when the person comes to experience the urge toward vice.

16 Often, too, the President of life's banquet challenges the subtly-contrived "necessity" of greed through actions like this, so that—as I see it—the sickness of greed might appear stripped of its specious coverings, no longer shadowed by any misleading veil. For many people say they have become stronger in their desire for greater wealth for just one reason: to enrich their descendants. But the inexplicable greed of the childless reveals that this is personal disorder, not rooted in any necessity. After all, many who do not have any heirs for whom to work so hard, who may not even possess the hope of having them, produce, in place of many children, a tribe of selfish desires within themselves, and have no cause to which they can attribute this sickness as something necessary.

But if there are some people who settle into a pattern of vice in their lives—becoming domineering and quarrelsome by choice, enslaved to all kinds of undisciplined habits, paralyzed with rage, refraining from no form of incurable evil, thieves and murderers and betrayers of their country, or suffering from any condition still more accursed, being patricides or matricides or killers of children, madly lusting for immoral sexual unions—if they are this kind of person and grow older in such vice, someone might ask how this all squares with what we have discussed before. For if the child snatched away before its time is providentially led out of life's banquet, so that it might not—as in a long night's drinking—become swamped by the passions of an existence like this, what would be the reason for another person of this kind to remain until maturity, getting drunk at the party, spilling the wicked dregs of his vices all over himself and his fellow guests? In their case, we would answer that the provident

ἐπὶ τούτων τὴν προνοητικὴν τοῦ θεοῦ οἰκονομίαν διαφαίνεσθαι·
τὸ μὲν γὰρ δύνασθαι καὶ τὸν πρὸς τοῦτο τὸ μέτρον τῆς πονηρίας
ἐλάσαντα χρόνων τισὶ μακρῶν περιόδοις διὰ τῆς αἰωνίας
GNO 92 | καθάρσεως πάλιν ἀποδοῦναι τῷ τῶν σῳζομένων πληρώματι
παντὶ πρόδηλον πάντως τῷ πρὸς τὴν θείαν δύναμιν βλέποντι.
τίς γὰρ οὕτως τῆς θείας φύσεως ἀνεπίσκεπτος, ὡς τὰ ἄλλα τοῦ
θεοῦ βλέπων, ὅσα τῷ ὑπερέχοντι τῆς δυνάμεως ἐν μόνῃ τῇ τοῦ
θελήματος ὁρμῇ κατειργάσατο, περὶ τοῦτο μόνον ἀτονεῖν αὐτὸν
οἴεσθαι; εἰ γάρ τις ἀνθρωπικῶς ἐξετάζειν ἐθέλοι, δυσκολώτερον
εὑρεθήσεται τὸν οὐρανὸν καὶ τὴν γῆν καὶ πάντα τὸν ἐν τούτοις
κόσμον μὴ ὄντα παραγαγεῖν εἰς τὸ εἶναι ἢ διὰ κακίας πλανηθεῖσαν
ψυχὴν πάλιν ἐπαναγαγεῖν [αὐτὴν] πρὸς τὴν κατὰ φύσιν ζωήν,
ὥστε τὸ φιλάνθρωπον θέλημα οὐδὲ ἐπὶ τούτων ἀργὸν ἂν εἴη. τὸ δὲ
διαρκὲς τῆς ἐν κακίᾳ τούτῳ ζωῆς οὐ θεόθεν τὰς ἀφορμὰς ἔχει· τοῦ
μὲν γὰρ ζῆν τὴν δύναμιν παρὰ τοῦ τὴν ζωὴν πεποιηκότος ἐδέξατο,
τοῦ δὲ κακῶς ζῆν ἡ οἰκεία καθηγεῖται προαίρεσις, ἧς μὴ πρὸς
τοῦτο τὴν ῥοπὴν ἐχούσης οὐδ᾽ ἂν ἦν ὅλως ἐν κακίᾳ ὁ ἄνθρωπος.
κακὸν γὰρ κατ᾽ οἰκείαν ὑπόστασιν οὐδέν, μὴ ἐν τῇ προαιρέσει τοῦ
κακῶς βιοῦντος δημιουργούμενον. εἰ οὖν τῆς συνισταμένης ἔν τινι
κακίας ὁ θεὸς ἀναίτιος, οὐκέτι ἂν εὐλόγως εἰς ἐκεῖνον ἀναφέροιτο
τῆς ἐν κακίᾳ τούτων ζωῆς ἡ αἰτία.

Ἀλλὰ διὰ τί, πάντως ἐρεῖς, τὸν μὲν προνοητικῶς ὑπεξάγει
τοῦ βίου πρὶν τελειωθῆναι διὰ τοῦ κακοῦ τὴν προαίρεσιν, τὸν |
GNO 93 δὲ καταλείπει γενέσθαι τοιοῦτον, ὡς ἄμεινον αὐτῷ εἶναι τὸ μὴ
γενέσθαι ὅλως; πρὸς δὲ τοῦτο τοιοῦτόν τινα τοῖς εὐγνωμονεστέροις
ἀποδώσομεν λόγον, ὅτι πολλάκις ἡ ζωὴ τῶν εὖ βεβιωκότων καὶ
τοῖς ἐξ αὐτῶν αἰτία τοῦ βελτίονος γίνεται. καὶ μυρίαι τούτων ἐκ

care of God shines through equally on them. On the one hand, surely, it will be perfectly clear to anyone who has thought about God's power that God can restore to the full number of those who are saved, through the long passage of time, even the person who has reached this measure of wickedness, through ceaseless purification. For who is so unfamiliar with the divine nature that he can look on the other actions of God, which he accomplishes in the abundance of his power simply by an act of his will, yet thinks God is powerless concerning this alone? If one wanted to consider the matter in a human way, one might agree that it would be a greater sign of ill will to bring into existence heaven and earth and the whole world that includes them, when they had not existed before, than to restore again to its natural life the soul that has gone astray through evil, so that even in this case his beneficent will might not be frustrated. On the other hand, such a person's continuing in a life of vice does not take its original impulse from God. For he received the power to live from the one who has created life, but it is his own choice that has guided him toward living wickedly; and if this power of choice were not inclined in this direction, the human person would not live in wickedness at all.[28] For nothing is evil in its own substance, unless it has been so shaped by the faculty of choice of the one who lives wickedly. If, then, God is not responsible for the vice that comes to exist in a person, the blame for the lives of those who live in vice cannot reasonably be attributed to him.

17 But why, you will surely ask, does God providentially remove one person from life before his character is deformed by evil, but allow another to develop in that way, when it would be better for him not to exist at all? Our response to this, for those disposed to give us a favorable hearing, would be something like this: often the life of those who have lived well is the cause of something better, even for

[28]Gregory here suggests—in a way somewhat resembling the Western notion of an "original sin" or inherited impulse toward sinful choices—that the human will, as we experience it, is habitually inclined to choose what is evil, but that this is the effect of our history of misusing our freedom, not a result of God's creation.

τῆς θεοπνεύστου γραφῆς αἱ μαρτυρίαι, δι᾽ ὧν σαφῶς διδασκόμεθα τῆς παρὰ τοῦ θεοῦ γενομένης τοῖς ἀξίοις κηδεμονίας καὶ τοὺς ἐξ αὐτῶν συμμετέχειν. ἀγαθὸν δ᾽ ἂν εἴη κεφάλαιον καὶ τὸ ἐμποδὼν τινι πρὸς κακίαν γενέσθαι τῷ μέλλοντι πάντως κατ᾽ ἐκείνην βιώσεσθαι. ἐπεὶ δὲ τῶν ἀδήλων ὁ λόγος ἐνταῦθα καταστοχάζεται, πάντως οὐδεὶς αἰτιάσεται πολλαχῇ τοῦ στοχασμοῦ τὴν διάνοιαν ἄγοντος. οὐ μόνον γὰρ τοῖς καθηγουμένοις τοῦ γένους εἴποι τις ἂν τὸν θεὸν χαριζόμενον ὑπεξάγειν τῆς κακῆς ζωῆς τὸν κατ᾽ αὐτὴν βιωσόμενον, ἀλλ᾽ εἰ καὶ μηδὲν εἴη τοιοῦτον ἐπὶ τῶν πρὸ ὥρας ἀναρπαζομένων, οὐδὲν ἀπεικὸς οἴεσθαι τὸ χαλεπώτερον ἂν ἐκείνους ἀντιλαμβάνεσθαι τοῦ κατὰ κακίαν βίου ἢ τούτων ἕκαστον τῶν ἐπὶ πονηρίᾳ γνωρισθέντων παρὰ τὸν βίον. τὸ γὰρ μηδὲν ἀθεεὶ γίνεσθαι διὰ πολλῶν ἐπεγνώκαμεν, τὸ δ᾽ αὖ πάλιν μὴ τυχαῖά τε καὶ ἄλογα εἶναι τὰ θεόθεν οἰκονομούμενα πᾶς ἂν ὁμολογήσειεν, εἰδὼς ὅτι ὁ θεὸς λόγος ἐστὶ καὶ σοφία καὶ πᾶσα ἀρετὴ καὶ ἀλήθεια, οὐδὲν δὲ τοῦ λόγου ἄλογον οὐδὲ τοῦ σοφοῦ τι ἄσοφον, οὐδ᾽ ἂν ἡ ἀρετή τε καὶ ἡ ἀλήθεια τὸ μὴ ἐνάρετόν τε καὶ ἔξω τοῦ ἀληθοῦς καταδέξαιτο.

Εἴτε οὖν κατὰ τὰς εἰρημένας αἰτίας ἄωροί τινες ἀναρπάζονται
GNO 94 εἴτε τι καὶ ἕτερον παρὰ τὰ εἰρημένα ἐστί, τὸ πάντως ἐπὶ | σκοπῷ
τῷ βελτίονι ταῦτα γίνεσθαι συνομολογεῖσθαι προσήκει. οἶδα δέ
τινα καὶ λόγον ἕτερον παρὰ τῆς τοῦ ἀποστόλου σοφίας μαθών,
PG 189 δι᾽ ὅν τινες τῶν κατὰ κακίαν ὑπερβαλ|λόντων κατὰ τὴν ἑαυτῶν
προαίρεσιν ζῆσαι ἀφείθησαν· γυμνάσας γὰρ ἐπὶ πλέον τὴν τοιαύτην διάνοιαν ἐν τῷ πρὸς Ῥωμαίους λόγῳ καὶ ἀνθυπενεγκὼν ἑαυτῷ τὸ ἐκ τοῦ ἀκολούθου ἀντιτιθέμενον, τὸ μὴ ἂν εὐλόγως ἐν αἰτίᾳ τὸν κακὸν ἔτι γενέσθαι, εἴπερ θεόθεν ἔχει τὸ κακὸς εἶναι, μὴ ἂν γενόμενος πάντως, εἴπερ ἀβούλητον ἦν τῷ ἐπικρατοῦντι τῶν ὄντων, οὕτως ἀπαντᾷ τῷ λόγῳ διὰ βαθυτέρας τινὸς θεωρίας τὴν

their descendants. There are many texts witnessing to these things in the inspired Scripture, through which we are clearly instructed that descendants also share in the loving care God shows toward the worthy; a good argument [for death], on the other hand, is that it can act for someone as an obstacle to vice, if the person seems clearly bound to live in that way. And since our discussion here is indulging in guesswork about what is unclear, surely no one should be blamed if guessing often guides our understanding. For not only in the case of the founders of a family could one say that God has acted graciously in removing from an evil life one who was going live that way; but even if nothing of this kind [i.e., an evil life] is true for those who are taken away before their time, it is not unreasonable to think that they might have engaged themselves in a life of vice in some still more damaging way than each of those who have been notorious for wickedness while they lived. We have come to be convinced, over and over, that nothing happens without God; everyone would agree, moreover, that nothing in God's plan is fortuitous or unreasonable, since we know that God is Reason and Wisdom and all Virtue and Truth. No part of Reason is irrational, no part of Wisdom is foolish; nor could Virtue and Truth ever admit of what is not virtuous, or what is alien to truth.

18 Whether, then, some people are snatched away while still immature for the reasons we have explained, or whether there is another reason also, beyond what we have mentioned, it is right for us to agree, surely, that these things happen for the best. And I know another reason, from investigating the wisdom of the Apostle, why some of those who outdo the rest in vice have been allowed to live on in their preferred way of life. For, developing this line of thought at some length in his letter to the Romans, and answering for himself the implied opposing opinion—that the evil person can never rightly be held to blame, if he receives from God his evil ways, and surely would never have come to live this way if it were against the will of him who rules over all things—[Paul] replies to the argument as

ἀνθυποφορὰν ὑπεκλύων· φησὶ γὰρ τὸν θεὸν ἑκάστῳ τὸ κατ᾽ ἀξίαν νέμοντα ἔστιν ὅπου καὶ τῇ κακίᾳ διδόναι χώραν ἐπὶ σκοπῷ τῷ βελτίονι· τούτου γὰρ ἕνεκεν ἐᾶσαι γενέσθαι καὶ τοιοῦτον γενέσθαι τὸν Αἰγύπτιον τύραννον, ὡς ἂν τῇ ἐκείνου πληγῇ ὁ Ἰσραὴλ παιδευθείη, ὁ πολὺς ἐκεῖνος λαὸς καὶ πᾶσαν τὴν ἐξ ἀριθμοῦ περίληψιν διαβαίνων. ἴσως γὰρ τῆς θείας δυνάμεως διὰ πάντων γνωριζομένης καὶ πρὸς τὸ εὐεργετεῖν τοὺς ἀξίους ἱκανῶς ἐχούσης καὶ πρὸς τὴν κόλασιν τῆς κακίας οὐκ ἀτονούσης, ἐπεὶ δὲ πάντως ἐχρῆν ἀποικισθῆναι τῆς Αἰγύπτου τὸν λαὸν ἐκεῖνον, ὡς ἂν μή τις αὐτοῖς γένοιτο τῶν Αἰγυπτίων κακῶν κατὰ τὴν τοῦ βίου πλάνην κοινωνία, τούτου χάριν ὁ θεομάχος ἐκεῖνος, ὁ ἐπὶ παντὶ κακῷ |
GNO 95 ὀνομαστὸς Φαραὼ τῇ ζωῇ τῶν εὐεργετουμένων συνανέσχεν τε καὶ συνήκμασεν, ὡς ἂν τῆς διπλῆς τοῦ θεοῦ ἐνεργείας ἐφ᾽ ἑκατέρων μεριζομένης ἀξίως τῶν δύο λάβῃ τὴν γνῶσιν ὁ Ἰσραήλ, τὸ μὲν κρεῖττον ἐφ᾽ ἑαυτοῦ διδασκόμενος, τὸ δὲ σκυθρωπότερον ἐπὶ τῶν διὰ κακίαν μαστιγουμένων ὁρῶν, ὡς τῷ ὑπερβάλλοντι τῆς σοφίας εἰδότος τοῦ θεοῦ καὶ τὸ κακὸν ἐπὶ τῇ τοῦ ἀγαθοῦ συνεργίᾳ μεταχειρίζεσθαι. χρεία γὰρ τῷ τεχνίτῃ (εἰ χρὴ τὸν ἀποστολικὸν λόγον καὶ διὰ τῶν ἡμετέρων λόγων βεβαιωθῆναι), χρεία τοίνυν τῷ διὰ τῆς τέχνης πρός τι τῶν βιωφελῶν ἐργαλείων τυποῦντι τὸν σίδηρον οὐ μόνον τοῦ εὐκόλως τῇ τέχνῃ εἴκοντος ἔκ τινος φυσικῆς ἁπαλότητος, ἀλλὰ κἂν λίαν ἀντίτυπος ὁ σίδηρος ᾖ, κἂν μὴ ῥᾳδίως διὰ πυρὸς ἐκμαλάσσηται καὶ πρὸς τὸ σκεῦος τῶν ἀναγκαίων τοῦ βίου τυπωθῆναι τῷ ἀνυπείκτῳ τε καὶ στερρῷ μὴ οἷός τε ᾖ, καὶ τούτου ἡ τέχνη ἐπιζητεῖ τὴν συνεργίαν· ἄκμονι γὰρ χρήσεται τῷ τοιούτῳ, ὡς ταῖς ἐπὶ τούτου πληγαῖς τὸν εὐεργῆ τε καὶ ἁπαλὸν πρός τι τῶν χρησίμων ἀποτυποῦσθαι.

follows, undermining it by deeper reflection: he says that while God gives back to each person according to what they deserve, there are times when he gives room to vice, with an eye to better things; and for this reason he allowed the Egyptian tyrant to exist, and to exist in the way he did, so that Israel—that great people, exceeding all our ability to count them—might be trained by his punishing blows.[29]

For we might say that God's power is always recognized to be both able to benefit the worthy in an appropriate way, and not lacking in the strength to punish vice; still, when it was necessary to cause his people to leave their dwelling in Egypt, so that they might not share in Egypt's vices by a deviant way of life—for this reason, that enemy of God, Pharaoh, who was infamous for every kind of evil, flourished and came to maturity at the same time as that blessed people. The purpose was that Israel might come to knowledge of God's twofold activity, equitably divided between both peoples: it was taught that better fortune would be its own lot, but saw a severe fate come to those who were punished for evil-doing, since God, in the superabundance of his wisdom, knows how to steer even evil to benefit the good. It is helpful for the craftsman—if we are permitted to confirm the Apostle's argument also through arguments of our own—it is helpful, let us say, for [the blacksmith] who is pounding iron in order to make some tool that is useful for life, not simply to work with what easily yields to his craftsmanship, through some natural softness it possesses. Even if the iron is very resistant to being shaped, even if it is not easily softened in the fire and seems, in its resistance and hardness, incapable of being forged into a tool for the necessities of life—even this the blacksmith's art seeks to make co-operative. For he will use a piece of iron like this as an anvil, so that more workable, softer material might be shaped into something useful by hammer-blows against it.[30]

[29]Here Gregory is reflecting on Paul's treatment of God's "hardening of Pharaoh's heart," as suggested in Exodus 8.19 and in Romans 9.14–18. This problematic passage was also discussed at length by Origen in *On First Principles* 3.1.11–12; cf. *Homilies on Exodus* 3.3; 4.8.

[30]For this same example, developed at greater length, see *On the Dead* 18.

Ἀλλ᾽ ἐρεῖ τις, ὅτι οὐ πάντες παρὰ τὸν βίον τοῦτον τῆς ἑαυτῶν μοχθηρίας ἀπέλαυσαν· οὐδὲ γὰρ οἱ κατ᾽ ἀρετὴν βιοτεύοντες ἐν τῇ ζωῇ ταύτῃ τῶν τῆς ἀρετῆς ἱδρώτων ἀπώναντο· τί οὖν, φησί, τούτων εἶναι τὸ χρήσιμον ἐπὶ τῶν ἐν κακίᾳ ἀτιμωρήτως βεβιωκότων; παραθήσομαί σοι καὶ πρὸς τοῦτο λόγον τῶν ἀνθρωπίνων λογισμῶν ὑψηλότερον· φησὶ γάρ που τῆς ἑαυτοῦ προφητείας ὁ μέγας Δαβὶδ μέρος τι τοῖς ἐναρέτοις εὐφροσύνης καὶ τὸ τοιοῦτον εἶναι, ὅταν ἀντιπαραθεωρῶσι τοῖς οἰκείοις ἀγαθοῖς τὴν τῶν
GNO 96 κατακρίτων | ἀπώλειαν· Εὐφρανθήσεται, γάρ φησι, δίκαιος, ὅταν
PG 192 ἴδῃ ἐκδίκησιν ἀσεβοῦς· τὰς χεῖρας αὐτοῦ νίψεται ἐν | τῷ αἵματι τοῦ
ἁμαρτωλοῦ· οὐχ ὡς ἐπιχαίρων ταῖς τῶν ἀνιωμένων ὀδύναις, ἀλλ᾽ ὡς τότε μάλιστα γνωρίζων τὸ ἐξ ἀρετῆς τοῖς ἀξίοις παραγινόμενον. σημαίνει γὰρ διὰ τῶν εἰρημένων, ὅτι προσθήκη τῆς εὐφροσύνης καὶ ἐπίτασις τοῖς ἐναρέτοις γίνεται ἡ τῶν ἐναντίων ἀντιπαράθεσις· τὸ γὰρ εἰπεῖν, ὅτι Τὰς χεῖρας ἐν τῷ αἵματι τοῦ ἁμαρτωλοῦ νίπτεται, τοιαύτην παρίστησι τὴν διάνοιαν, ὅτι τὸ καθαιρόμενον αὐτοῦ τῆς κατὰ τὴν ζωὴν ἐνεργείας ἐν τῇ ἀπωλείᾳ τῶν ἁμαρτωλῶν διαδείκνυται· ἡ γὰρ τοῦ νίψασθαι λέξις καθαρότητος ἔμφασιν διερμηνεύει, ἐν αἵματι δὲ οὐχὶ νίπτεταί τις ἀλλὰ μολύνεται, ὥστε διὰ τούτου δῆλον γενέσθαι, ὅτι ἡ τῶν σκυθρωποτέρων ἀντιπαράθεσις τὴν τῆς ἀρετῆς μακαριότητα δείκνυσιν.

Συναπτέον τοίνυν ἐπὶ κεφαλαίῳ τὸν λόγον, ὡς ἂν εὐμνημόνευτα γένοιτο τὰ ἐξητασμένα νοήματα. ἡ γὰρ ἄωρος τελευτὴ τῶν νηπίων οὔτε ἐν ἀλγεινοῖς εἶναι τὸν οὕτω τοῦ ζῆν παυσάμενον νοεῖν ὑποτίθεται οὔτε κατὰ τὸ ἴσον τοῖς διὰ πάσης ἀρετῆς κατὰ τὸν τῇδε βίον κεκαθαρμένοις γίνεται, προμηθείᾳ κρείττονι τοῦ θεοῦ τὴν τῶν κακῶν ἀμετρίαν κωλύοντος ἐπὶ τῶν μελλόντων οὕτω βιώσεσθαι. τὸ δὲ ἐπιβιῶναί τινας τῶν κακῶν οὐκ ἀνατρέπει τὴν

19 But someone will observe that not everyone manages to drive out their own evil inclinations in the course of this life. Not even those who make the effort to live according to virtue succeed in profiting, during this life, from the hard effort virtue demands. What, they ask, does one derive as benefit from these efforts, when compared with those who have lived in vice without undergoing any retribution? In response to this, too, I will propose to you an argument that reaches above human calculation. For the great David says, somewhere in his prophetic writings, that a part of the joy experienced by the virtuous is simply this: to contemplate, alongside their own blessings, the downfall of the damned. "The righteous shall be glad," he says, "when he sees punishment of the impious; he shall wash his hands in the blood of the sinner" (Ps 57.10). It is not that he rejoices in the sufferings of those who are in distress, but that he comes to recognize most fully, through them, the reward of virtue that will come to the worthy. For he indicates by what he says that the contrasting state of those living in an opposite way will be an addition to, and an extension of, the happiness of the virtuous. For to say, "He will wash his hands in the blood of the sinner," suggests this meaning: that what has been purified in a person's own activity during life is made thoroughly clear by the destruction of sinners. For the term "wash" suggests the meaning of purity; but one surely does not wash in blood, but rather is stained by it. By this it is clear that the opposite condition of those in distress reveals the blessedness of virtue.

20 We must now bring our argument together in a brief summary, so that the ideas we have examined can be easily committed to memory. The untimely end of infants does not suggest that the one who thus ceases to live is in a state of suffering, but he also does not come to live in an equal state with those who have been purified during this life by acquiring every kind of virtue.[31] By his superior foreknowledge, God forecloses the indiscipline of vice from those

[31]Gregory assumes that purification during this present life is precisely the laborious acquisition of virtues, which involves also the gradual elimination of the habits that point us toward wrongdoing.

ἀποδοθεῖσαν διάνοιαν· τῇ γὰρ πρὸς τοὺς γεννησαμένους χάριτι τὸ κακὸν ἐπ᾽ ἐκείνων ἐνεποδίσθη· οἷς δὲ οὐκ ἦν τις ἐκ γονέων πρὸς τὸν θεὸν παρρησία οὐδὲ τοῖς ἐξ ἐκείνων τὸ τοιοῦτον ἔτι τῆς εὐεργεσίας εἶδος συμπαρεπέμφθη· ἢ πολλῷ χαλεπώτερος τῶν ἐπὶ κακίᾳ γνωρίμων ὁ κωλυθεὶς διὰ τοῦ θανάτου γενέσθαι κακὸς ἐφάνη ἄν, εἴπερ ἀκώλυτον ἔσχε τὴν πονηρίαν, ἢ εἴ τινες καὶ εἰς τὸ
GNO 97 ἀκρότατον | τῆς πονηρίας μέτρον προεληλύθασιν, ἡ ἀποστολικὴ θεωρία παραμυθεῖται τὸ ζήτημα, ὡς εἰδότος τοῦ πάντα ἐν σοφίᾳ ποιοῦντος καὶ διὰ τοῦ κακοῦ τι τῶν ἀγαθῶν κατεργάσασθαι. εἰ δέ τις καὶ ἐν πονηρίᾳ τὸ ἄκρον ἔχει καὶ ἐπ᾽ οὐδενὶ χρησίμῳ κατὰ τὸ ῥηθὲν ἡμῖν ὑπόδειγμα παρὰ τῆς τοῦ θεοῦ τέχνης κατεχαλκεύθη, τοῦτο προσθήκη τῆς εὐφροσύνης τῶν εὖ βεβιωκότων γίνεται, καθὼς ἡ προφητεία νοεῖν ὑποτίθεται, ὅπερ οὐ μικρὸν ἐν ἀγαθοῖς ἄν τις λογίσαιτο οὐδὲ τῆς τοῦ θεοῦ προμηθείας ἀνάξιον.

who will be inclined to live in this way. And that some wicked people survive does not refute this line of thought we have just offered. For out of graciousness toward their parents, the evil[32] has been checked in their case. But for those who have not received from their parents such a familiar relationship with God, and to whom, as their descendants, not even a form of beneficence such as this is accorded, then either the one prevented by death from becoming an evil person would have turned out much worse than those recognized as living in vice, if he held to his wickedness unchecked; or else, if some still have advanced to the very peak of wickedness, the Apostle's consideration raises the question whether he who has created all things in his Wisdom knows how to achieve some form of good, even through an evil person.[33] But if someone has reached the summit of wickedness and has not been re-forged in any beneficial way by the art of God—to return to the image we have articulated—this very fact will become an addition to the happiness of those who have lived well, as the Prophet leads us to think;[34] and one might consider this no small blessing, not unworthy of God's provident care.

[32]The evil, presumably, that such infants would have done if allowed to live.
[33]See Rom 9.14–18.
[34]I.e., the speaker in Ps 57.10.

On the “Final Subjection” of Christ
(*In illud: Tunc et ipse filius*)

A Note on the Text

This detailed essay—apparently addressed to a single correspondent (see section 18), like many of Gregory’s smaller theological works—is essentially a careful exegesis of a difficult and theologically challenging passage in Paul: 1 Corinthians 15.24–28. It is both an example of Gregory’s clear Christological and Trinitarian interpretation of Scripture, and a ringing affirmation of his hope that all creation, united to the incarnate Son, will eventually share in life and salvation. The date of the work, like that of many of Gregory’s treatises, is completely open to conjecture. Daniélou places it after 385, and thus among Gregory’s late works; J. Kenneth Downing, the editor of the critical text, suggests 383, because of verbal reminiscences he sees between it and the *Refutatio confessionis Eunomii*, which was composed in that year. See Maraval, “Chronology of Works,” *Brill Dictionary*, 155; see also the articles of Hübner and Lienhard cited above, p. 12 n. 8.

The Greek text translated here is the critical edition by J. Kenneth Downing, in *Gregorii Nysseni Opera* [GNO] III/2 (Leiden: Brill, 1987), 3–28. The standard earlier edition appeared in PG 44:1303–1326. For convenience in reference, I have numbered the sections of the text myself.

GNO III/2:3
PG 44:1304

ΓΡΗΓΟΡΙΟΥ ΕΠΙΣΚΟΠΟΥ ΝΥΣΣΗΣ ΕΙΣ ΤΟ ΤΟΤΕ ΚΑΙ ΑΥΤΟΣ Ο ΥΙΟΣ ΥΠΟΤΑΓΗΣΕΤΑΙ ΤΩΙ ΥΠΟΤΑΞΑΝΤΙ ΑΥΤΩΙ ΤΑ ΠΑΝΤΑ

Πάντα μὲν τὰ λόγια τοῦ κυρίου λόγιά ἐστιν ἁγνά τε καὶ καθαρά, καθώς φησιν ὁ προφήτης, ὅταν, καθ' ὁμοιότητα τῆς περὶ τὸν ἄργυρον ἐν πυρὶ γινομένης καθάρσεως, πάσης αἱρετικῆς ὑπολήψεως ἐκκεκαθαρμένος ὁ νοῦς τῶν λογίων τὴν οἰκείαν ἔχῃ καὶ κατὰ φύσιν τῆς ἀληθείας αὐγήν. πρὸ πάντων δὲ οἶμαι δεῖν τοῖς τοῦ ἁγίου Παύλου δόγμασι πᾶσαν προσμαρτυρεῖν λαμπηδόνα καὶ καθαριότητα, διότι ἐν τῷ παραδείσῳ μυηθεὶς τῶν ἀπορρήτων τὴν γνῶσιν καὶ λαλοῦντα ἔχων ἐν ἑαυτῷ τὸν Χριστὸν τοιαῦτα ἐφθέγγετο οἷα εἰκὸς τὸν ἐκ τοῦ τοιούτου διδασκαλείου πεπαιδευμένον φθέγγεσθαι ὑπὸ καθηγεμόνι τε καὶ διδασκάλῳ τῷ Λόγῳ. |

GNO 4 Ἐπειδὴ δὲ οἱ πονηροὶ κάπηλοι ἀδόκιμον ἐπιχειροῦσι ποιεῖν τὸ θεῖον ἀργύριον, τῇ μίξει τῶν αἱρετικῶν τε καὶ κιβδήλων νοημάτων ἀμαυροῦντες τοῦ Λόγου τὴν λαμπηδόνα, καὶ τὰ μυστηριώδη τοῦ ἀποστόλου νοήματα, ἢ μὴ συνιέντες ἢ κακούργως πρὸς τὸ δοκοῦν ἐκλαμβάνοντες, εἰς συνηγορίαν τῆς κακίας αὐτῶν ἐπισύρονται, λέγοντες πρὸς καθαίρεσιν τῆς τοῦ μονογενοῦς θεοῦ δόξης τὸν ἀποστολικὸν αὐτοῖς συμβάλλεσθαι λόγον ὅς φησιν ὅτι Τότε ὑποταγήσεται ὁ υἱὸς τῷ ὑποτάξαντι αὐτῷ τὰ πάντα, ὡς δουλικήν τινα ταπεινότητα τῆς τοιαύτης λέξεως ἐμφαινούσης· τούτου χάριν ἀναγκαῖον ἐφάνη δι' ἐπιμελείας ἐξετάσαι τὸν περὶ τούτου λόγον,

On the Text, "Then the Son himself will be made subject to the One who has subjected all things to him" (1 Cor 15.28) [=On the Final Subjection of Christ] (*In illud: Tunc et ipse filius*)

1 All "the words of the Lord are pure and holy words" as the Prophet says (Ps 11.6), when the mind—as in the purification that happens to silver in fire—is purged of all heretical understanding, and grasps the proper, natural brightness of truth. Before praising anyone else in this way, I believe we should affirm all the brilliance and purity that inheres in the teachings of St Paul, because, mystically initiated into a knowledge of unspeakable things in paradise,[1] and having Christ speaking within himself, he spoke things that it seems proper only for one tutored in such a school to utter, under the guidance and teaching of the Word.

But since wicked merchants try to make God's silver into something cheap, lessening the brilliance of the Word by mixing in heretical, counterfeit ideas, and either do not understand the secret, holy themes of the Apostle, or else interpret them with evil intent, in a sense against their apparent meaning; since they drag the texts in to support their own wickedness—arguing that the Apostle's words agree with them in destroying the glory of God's Only-begotten, when he writes, "Then the Son will be subject to the one who has subjected all things to him" (1 Cor 15.28), as if this saying reveals some slave-like humility; for this reason, it seems necessary to examine

[1]See 2 Cor 12.4.

ὥστε δεῖξαι καθαρὸν ὡς ἀληθῶς τὸ ἀποστολικὸν ἀργύριον πάσης
ῥυπαρᾶς τε καὶ αἱρετικῆς ἐννοίας κεχωρισμένον καὶ ἀνεπίμικτον.

Ἔγνωμεν τοίνυν ἐν τῇ χρήσει τῆς ἁγίας γραφῆς πολύσημον
οὖσαν τὴν τοιαύτην φωνὴν καὶ οὐ τοῖς αὐτοῖς ἀεὶ ἐφαρμοζομένην
νοήμασιν, ἀλλὰ νῦν μὲν τοῦτο σημαίνουσαν πάλιν δὲ ἕτερον
PG 1305 ἐνδεικνυμένην, οἷον· Οἱ δοῦλοι, | φησί, τοῖς ἰδίοις δεσπόταις
ὑποτασσέσθωσαν· καὶ περὶ τῆς ἀλόγου φύσεως, ὅτι τῷ ἀνθρώπῳ
ὑποτέτακται ὑπὸ τοῦ θεοῦ, ὡς ὁ προφήτης λέγει· Πάντα ὑπέταξας
ὑποκάτω τῶν ποδῶν αὐτοῦ· καὶ περὶ τῶν διὰ πολέμου κεχειρωμένων
GNO 5 φησίν· Ὑπέταξε | λαοὺς ἡμῖν καὶ ἔθνη ὑπὸ τοὺς πόδας ἡμῶν· τῶν
τε αὖ δι᾽ ἐπιγνώσεως σῳζομένων ἐπιμνησθεὶς ὡς ἐκ προσώπου τοῦ
θεοῦ λέγει τὸ Ἐμοὶ ἀλλόφυλοι ὑπετάγησαν. ᾧ δοκεῖ πως οἰκεῖον
εἶναι τὸ ἐξητασμένον ἡμῖν ἐν τῷ πρώτῳ καὶ ἑξηκοστῷ ψαλμῷ διὰ
τοῦ Οὐχὶ τῷ θεῷ ὑποταγήσεται ἡ ψυχή μου· ἐπὶ πᾶσι δὲ τούτοις
ἐκεῖνο τὸ παρὰ τῶν ἐχθρῶν ἡμῖν προφερόμενον ἐκ τῆς πρὸς
Κορινθίους ἐπιστολῆς, ὅτι Τότε αὐτὸς ὁ υἱὸς ὑποταγήσεται τῷ
ὑποτάξαντι αὐτῷ τὰ πάντα.

Ἐπειδὴ τοίνυν ἐπὶ πολλὰ νοήματα φέρεται τῆς φωνῆς ταύτης ἡ σημασία, καλῶς ἂν ἔχοι ἕκαστον τούτων ἐφ᾽ ἑαυτοῦ διελομένους ἐπιγνῶναι πρὸς ποῖον τῆς ὑποταγῆς σημαινόμενον ἡ τοῦ ἀποστόλου ῥῆσις οἰκείως ἔχει. φαμὲν τοίνυν ὅτι ἐπὶ τῶν μὲν διὰ πολέμου τῇ τῶν κεκρατηκότων δυναστείᾳ κεχειρωμένων τὸ ἀκουσίως τε καὶ κατηναγκασμένως ὑποκύψαι τοῖς νενικηκόσι τὸ τῆς ὑποταγῆς ἐνδείκνυται σημαινόμενον· εἰ γάρ τις τοῖς αἰχμαλώτοις προσγένηται δύναμις, ἐλπίδα τοῦ ὑπερσχήσειν τῶν κεκρατηκότων ὑποδεικνῦσα, πάλιν ἑαυτοὺς ἀντεγείρουσι τοῖς κρατήσασιν, ὕβριν καὶ ὄνειδος τὸ τοῖς ἐχθροῖς ὑποτετάχθαι κρίνοντες. τὰ δὲ ἄλογα
τοῖς λογικοῖς εἰσι ὑποχείρια καθ᾽ ἕτερον τρόπον, τῷ ἐλλιπῶς
GNO 6 ἔχειν τὴν φύσιν αὐτοῖς τοῦ | μεγίστου τῶν ἀγαθῶν, τουτέστι τοῦ
λόγου, ὡς ἀνάγκην εἶναι τῷ πλεονεκτοῦντι κατὰ τὴν εὐκληρίαν τῆς φύσεως ὑποτετάχθαι τὸ ἐλαττούμενον. οἱ δὲ ἐν τῷ ζυγῷ τῆς δουλείας διὰ νομίμου τινὸς ἀκολουθίας κεκρατημένοι, κἂν ἐν τῇ φύσει τὸ ὁμότιμον ἔχωσιν, ἀλλ᾽ οὖν πρὸς τὸν νόμον ἀντισχεῖν οὐ

this text about Christ carefully, so as to show that the Apostle's silver is uncontaminated, free of any filthy heretical notions.

2 We know, after all, that in a passage of Holy Scripture a phrase such as this can have many meanings, and does not always represent the same concepts, but now means this, now signifies that. For instance, it says, "Let slaves be subject to their own masters" (Tit 2.9); and of irrational nature it says it was subjected to man by God, since the Prophet writes "You put all things in subjection under his feet" (Ps 8.6); and about those defeated in war, Scripture says, "You have subjected peoples under us, and the nations under our feet" (Ps 46.3); and recalling those saved through deeper knowledge, it says—as if from God's own lips—"the foreigners have been subjected unto me" (Ps 59.8). What we have investigated concerning Psalm 61 seems to be close to this, as well, because of the phrase, "Shall not my soul be subject to God?" (Ps 61.1) And in addition to all these, we have this interpretation of this text offered us by our opponents from the Letter to the Corinthians, "Then the Son himself will be subjected to the one who has subjected all things to him."

3 Since, then, the meaning of this phrase suggests to us many ways of understanding it, it would be good to distinguish each of them for itself, so that we might learn to which meaning of *subjection* the Apostle's saying is properly related. So we say that the term "subjection" refers to the unwilling and forcible bowing before their conquerors of those defeated in war by a mightier power; for if the captives should acquire any power that shows them a hope of overthrowing their conquerors, they will rise up against their masters, considering it an insult and a disgrace to be subject to their enemy. But irrational creatures are subject to rational ones in a different way, because their nature is deficient in the greatest of goods—that is, reason—so that necessarily the being that has less, in terms of nature's blessings, will be subject to the one who has more. And those who are bound under the yoke of slavery by some legal argument—even though they are of equal value by nature—since they cannot hold

δυνάμενοι, δέχονται τῶν ὑποχειρίων τὴν τάξιν τῷ ἀπαραιτήτῳ τῆς ἀνάγκης πρὸς τὴν ὑποταγὴν ἐναγόμενοι. τῆς δὲ πρὸς τὸν θεὸν γινομένης ἡμῖν ὑποταγῆς ὁ σκοπός ἐστιν ἡ σωτηρία, καθὼς παρὰ τῆς προφητείας ἐμάθομεν ἥ φησι· Τῷ θεῷ ὑποτάγηθι ἡ ψυχή μου· παρ᾽ αὐτῷ γὰρ τὸ σωτήριόν μου.

Ὅταν τοίνυν προφέρηται παρὰ τῶν ἐναντίων ἡμῖν ἡ τοῦ ἀποστόλου φωνὴ ἡ τὸν υἱὸν ὑποταγήσεσθαι τῷ πατρὶ λέγουσα, ἀκόλουθον ἂν εἴη κατὰ τὴν διεσταλμένην τῆς τοιαύτης φωνῆς σημασίαν ἐρωτᾶν αὐτοὺς πρὸς ποῖον σημαινόμενον τῆς ὑποταγῆς ὁρῶντες ταύτην ἐφαρμόζειν οἴονται δεῖν τῷ μονογενεῖ θεῷ τὴν φωνήν. ἀλλὰ δῆλον ὅτι κατ᾽ οὐδένα τρόπον τῶν εἰρημένων τοῦ υἱοῦ τὴν ὑποταγὴν ἐροῦσι νοεῖν· οὔτε γὰρ ἐχθρὸς ὢν διὰ πολέμου γέγονεν ὑποχείριος, ὥστε πάλιν αὐτῷ τὴν κατὰ τοῦ κρατοῦντος ἐπανάστασιν δι᾽ ἐλπίδος τε καὶ σπουδῆς εἶναι· οὔτε ὡς ἕν τι τῶν ἀλόγων ὁ Λόγος διὰ τῆς τοῦ ἀγαθοῦ ἐλλείψεως ἀναγκαίαν ἐν τῇ φύσει τὴν ὑποταγὴν ἔχει, ὡς πρόβατα καὶ κτήνη καὶ βόες πρὸς τὸν ἄνθρωπον ἔχουσιν· ἀλλὰ μὴν οὐδὲ καθ᾽ ὁμοιότητα τῶν ἀργυρωνήτων ἢ οἰκογενῶν ἀνδραπόδων νόμῳ δεδουλωμένος
PG 1308 ἀναμένει δι᾽ εὐνοίας ἢ χάριτος | τοῦ ζυγοῦ ποτε γενέσθαι τῆς |
GNO 7 δουλείας ἐλεύθερος· ἀλλ᾽ οὐδὲ κατὰ τὸν τῆς σωτηρίας σκοπὸν
εἴποι τις ἂν τὸν μονογενῆ θεὸν τῷ πατρὶ ὑποτάσσεσθαι, ὡς διὰ τούτου καθ᾽ ὁμοιότητα τῶν ἀνθρώπων τὴν σωτηρίαν ἑαυτῷ παρὰ τοῦ θεοῦ πραγματεύεσθαι. ἐπὶ μὲν γὰρ τῆς τρεπτῆς φύσεως τῆς διὰ μετουσίας ἐν τῷ ἀγαθῷ γινομένης ἀναγκαία ἐστὶν ἡ πρὸς θεὸν ὑποταγὴ διὰ τὸ ἐκεῖθεν γίνεσθαι τῶν ἀγαθῶν ἡμῖν τὴν κοινωνίαν·

---

[2]Here and in a number of other passages in his works, Gregory suggests that all humans are naturally equal, and that slavery—though legally practiced throughout the ancient world—is inherently unnatural. See the more explicit discussion in his *Homily 4 on Ecclesiastes* (GNO V:336.10–338.22).

[3]Literally "the Only-begotten God." In this work, Gregory favors this phrase for the Son, generally avoiding the word Υἱός (*Huios*). See n. 5 below.

[4]Since *Logos* in Greek means (among other things) "reason," it is understood that God's Logos cannot act "irrationally."

[5]John's Gospel characteristically refers to God the Son in this way—see, e.g., Jn 1.18 (var.).

[6]Gregory proceeds here to argue for his first, essentially Christological and

out against the law, still accept a subject's status, being forced by merciless necessity into subjection.[2] But the purpose of our own subjection to God, when that happens, is salvation, as we learn from the prophecy which says, "O my soul, be subject to God, for of him is my salvation" (Ps 61.5, 1).

So when the Apostle's saying that the Son will be "subject to" the Father is brought up by our opponents, it would be appropriate to ask them, in light of the meanings of this term that we have mentioned, what understanding of "subjection" they have in view when they suggest that the word should be applied to the only Son of God.[3] Clearly they will answer that they do not understand the subjection of the Son in any of the ways we have mentioned. For he was not, like an enemy, made subject because of war, so that he would cherish a hope and an eagerness to rise up at a later time against the one who had conquered him. Nor does the Logos, like some irrational creature,[4] evince a necessary subjection by nature, due to a lack of some good quality, as sheep and livestock and cows do in relation to the human person. Nor, like those sold or born into slavery, does he anticipate someday being freed from the yoke of slavery through benevolence or grace. Nor could one even say that the Only-begotten God[5] is subjected to the Father in order to reach the goal of salvation [himself], in such a way that his salvation is worked out for him by God through this, in the same way it is for human beings.[6] For in the case of a changeable nature, which comes into existence by participation in the Good, subjection to God is necessary, because from him comes our share in good things. But in the changeless and unalterable Power,[7]

theological point: that 1 Corinthians 15.28 may not be understood in a subordinationist sense, as a number of the opponents of Nicaea had done, and as was even implied in the modalist theology of Marcellus of Ancyra. See Marcellus, Fragments 41 and 116, in *Eusebius: Gegen Marcell*, ed. E. Klostermann and G. C. Hansen (Berlin: Akademie Verlag, 1972), 192 and 209. Gregory presupposes here the equality of Father and Son—and also, as he will argue in section 14 below, of the Holy Spirit—in all the attributes and activities proper to God.

[7]Here Gregory seems to be referring to the divine nature or essence, fully possessed by the Son, who is "true God from true God," according to the Nicene profession of faith.

ἐν δὲ τῇ ἀτρέπτῳ καὶ ἀναλλοιώτῳ δυνάμει ἡ ὑποταγὴ χώραν οὐκ ἔχει ἐν ᾗ πᾶν ἀγαθὸν ὄνομά τε καὶ νόημα θεωρεῖται, τὸ ἀΐδιον, τὸ ἄφθαρτον, τὸ μακάριον, τὸ ἀεὶ ὡσαύτως ἔχον, τὸ μήτε κρεῖττον μήτε χεῖρον γενέσθαι δυνάμενον· οὔτε γὰρ προσθήκην ἐν τῷ ἀγαθῷ ἐπιδέχεται οὔτε τὴν πρὸς τὸ χεῖρον ῥοπήν· ὃ <γὰρ> τοῖς ἄλλοις πηγάζει τὴν σωτηρίαν, οὐκ αὐτὸ τοῦ σῴζοντος ἐνδεῶς ἔχει.

Ποῖον τοίνυν εὐλόγως φήσουσιν ἐπ' αὐτοῦ κυρίως νοεῖν τὸ τῆς ὑποταγῆς σημαινόμενον; ηὑρέθη γὰρ τὰ ἐξητασμένα πάντα μακρὰν ἀπέχοντα τοῦ κυρίως ἐπὶ τοῦ μονογενοῦς θεοῦ καὶ νοεῖσθαι καὶ λέγεσθαι. εἰ δὲ χρὴ κἀκεῖνο τὸ τῆς ὑποταγῆς εἶδος προσθεῖναι ὅ φησι τὸ κατὰ Λουκᾶν εὐαγγέλιον ὅτι Ἦν ὑποτασσόμενος τοῖς γονεῦσιν εἰς δωδέκατον προελθὼν ἔτος ὁ κύριος, οὐδὲ ἐκεῖνο ἁρμόζοι ἂν ἐπὶ τοῦ προαιωνίου τε καὶ ἀληθινοῦ <υἱοῦ> πρὸς τὸν ἀληθινὸν ἑαυτοῦ πατέρα λέγεσθαι. ἐκεῖ μὲν γὰρ ὁ πεπειραμένος κατὰ πάντα καθ' ὁμοιότητα χωρὶς ἁμαρτίας ἐδέξατο καὶ διὰ
GNO 8 τῶν ἡλικιῶν προελθεῖν τῆς | φύσεως ἡμῶν, καὶ ὥσπερ παιδίον γενόμενος τὴν βρεφικὴν τροφὴν προσήκατο, βούτυρον καὶ μέλι φαγών, οὕτω καὶ εἰς μειράκιον προελθὼν τὸ κατάλληλόν τε καὶ πρέπον τῇ τοιαύτῃ ἡλικίᾳ οὐ παρῃτήσατο, τύπος εὐταξίας τῷ βίῳ γενόμενος. ἐπειδὴ γὰρ ἐπὶ τῶν ἄλλων ἀνθρώπων ἀτελὴς ἐν τοῖς τοιούτοις ἐστὶν ἡ διάνοια καὶ χρεία τῇ νεότητι τῆς διὰ τῶν τελειοτέρων πρὸς τὸ κρεῖττον γινομένης χειραγωγίας, τούτου χάριν ὁ δωδεκαέτης τῇ μητρὶ ὑποτάσσεται, ἵνα δείξῃ ὅτι τὸ διὰ προκοπῆς τελειούμενον πρὶν εἰς τὸ τέλειον φθάσαι καλῶς τὴν ὑποταγὴν ὡς χειραγωγὸν πρὸς τὸ ἀγαθὸν καταδέχεται. ὁ δὲ ἀεὶ τέλειος ὢν ἐν παντὶ ἀγαθῷ καὶ μήτε προκοπὴν μήτε μείωσιν

---

[8]Gregory here echoes the terminology and ideas of the Nicene Creed. The actual word "Son" here is not in the manuscripts of the text, but has been supplied in a suggestion of Werner Jaeger.

[9]Gregory seems to be echoing, in different terms, Irenaeus' characteristic idea

subjection has no place. In it, every good word and thought can be contemplated: it is eternal, incorruptible, blessed, ever remaining the same, able neither to become better or worse; it does not admit of any addition in goodness, nor any impulse toward what is less good. Indeed, then, it is the fount of salvation for other beings, but does not itself stand in any need of a savior.

4 How, then, people reasonably ask, should we rightly understand what the term "subjection" means when it is applied to him [i.e., Christ]? For all the meanings we have investigated have been found to be far distant from what can properly be thought and said of the Only-begotten God. And if we must add to them the form of subjection that the Gospel of Luke speaks of, that the Lord, when he reached the age of twelve, "was subject to his parents" (Lk 2.51)—not even that would be fitting to say about the one who was true Son before all ages, in relation to his true Father.[8] For in that case [i.e., that of Luke 2], he who was "tested in every way as we are, apart from sin" (Heb 4.15) allowed himself to go forward through all the natural stages of our life,[9] and just as, becoming a child, he accepted an infant's food, "eating butter and honey" (Is 7.15),[10] so when he grew to be a teenager he did not refuse what was appropriate and proper for that age, becoming the standard of good order for [all of] human life. For since the critical reason, in other humans, is not yet fully developed in people of this age, and youth needs the kind of guidance toward the right thing that is given by elders, for this reason the twelve-year-old [Jesus] was "subject to" his mother, that he might show that what grows toward perfection gradually, before it reaches full perfection, rightly takes on a state of subjection as a guide toward what is good.

But those who want to explain everything without due circumspection cannot tell us why the one who exists eternally in perfect possession of every good thing, who cannot experience either

that the incarnate Son "recapitulates" or sums up in himself all the perfections God intends the human creature to attain.

[10]Butter and honey seem to have been the ancient Jewish version of baby food.

δυνάμενος ἐφ' ἑαυτοῦ καταδέξασθαι διὰ τὸ ἀπροσδεὲς τῆς φύσεως αὐτοῦ καὶ ἀμείωτον, ὑπὲρ τίνος ὑποτάσσεται οὐκ ἂν εἰπεῖν ἔχοιεν οἱ πάντα λέγοντες ἀπερισκέπτως. ὅτι γὰρ διὰ σαρκὸς τῇ ἀνθρωπίνῃ συναναστρεφόμενος φύσει ἐν τῇ παιδικῇ ἡλικίᾳ ἐνομοθέτει, δι' ὧν ἐποίει, τὴν ὑποταγὴν τῇ νεότητι, δῆλόν ἐστιν ἐκ τοῦ πρὸς τὸ τέλειον τῆς ἡλικίας αὐτὸν προελθόντα μηκέτι πρὸς τὴν τῆς μητρὸς ἐξουσίαν βλέπειν. προτρεπομένης γὰρ αὐτὸν ἐκείνης ἐν Κανὰ τῆς Γαλιλαίας δεῖξαι τὴν δύναμιν ἐν τῷ λείποντι τῇ πανδαισίᾳ τῶν γάμων καὶ τὴν τοῦ οἴνου χρείαν τῇ εὐωχίᾳ χαρίσασθαι, τὴν μὲν χάριν τοῖς δεομένοις παρασχεῖν οὐκ ἠρνήσατο, τὴν δὲ μητρῴαν συμβουλὴν ὡς οὐκέτι κατὰ καιρὸν αὐτῷ προσαγομένην ἀπεποιήσατο εἰπών· Τί ἐμοὶ καὶ σοί, γύναι; μὴ καὶ ταύτης μου τῆς ἡλικίας ἐπιστατεῖν ἐθέλεις; Οὔπω ἥκει μου ἡ ὥρα ἡ τὸ αὐτοκρατὲς παρεχομένη τῇ ἡλικίᾳ καὶ αὐτεξούσιον; |

GNO 9 Εἰ οὖν ἐν τῇ διὰ | σαρκὸς ζωῇ τὸ καθῆκον τῆς ἡλικίας μέτρον
PG 1309 τὴν τῆς γεννησαμένης ὑποταγὴν ἀποσείεται, τίνα χώραν ἔχει ἡ ὑποταγὴ ἐπὶ τοῦ δεσπόζοντος ἐν τῇ δυναστείᾳ αὐτοῦ τοῦ αἰῶνος οὐκ ἄν τις εἰπεῖν ἔχοι. ἴδιον γὰρ τῆς θείας καὶ μακαρίας ἐστὶ ζωῆς τὸ πάντοτε ἐν τῷ αὐτῷ διαμένειν καὶ τὴν ἐξ ἀλλοιώσεως μεταβολὴν μὴ προσίεσθαι. ἐπεὶ οὖν ὁ ἐν ἀρχῇ ὢν Λόγος, ὁ μονογενὴς θεός, ἀλλότριός ἐστι προκοπῆς πάσης καὶ ἀλλοιώσεως, πῶς ὃ νῦν οὐκ ἔστι μετὰ ταῦτα γίνεται; οὐ γὰρ ὡς ἀεὶ ὑποτεταγμένου τοῦ υἱοῦ φησιν ὁ ἀπόστολος, ἀλλ' ὡς πρὸς τῷ τέλει τῆς τοῦ παντὸς συμπληρώσεως μέλλοντος ὑποτάσσεσθαι. καίτοι εἰ καλὸν ἡ ὑποταγὴ καὶ ἄξιον περὶ θεοῦ λέγεσθαι, πῶς νῦν ἄπεστι τοῦ θεοῦ τὸ καλόν; ἐπίσης γὰρ πάντως ἀμφοτέροις καλὸν τῷ τε ὑποτασσομένῳ υἱῷ καὶ τῷ τὴν ὑποταγὴν τοῦ υἱοῦ δεχομένῳ πατρί. λείπει τοίνυν ἐν τῷ παρόντι καὶ τῷ πατρὶ καὶ τῷ υἱῷ τὸ τοιοῦτον καλόν, καὶ ὃ μὴ ἔσχεν πρὸ τῶν αἰώνων μήτε ὁ πατὴρ μήτε ὁ υἱός, τοῦτο ἐπὶ

---

[11]Gregory takes this puzzling exchange between Jesus and his mother in a different sense from that given by most modern commentators. He does, however, read Jesus' second phrase as a question: "Has not my hour come?" For an evaluation of this interpretation as a genuine possibility, see Albert Vanhoye, "Interrogation johannique et exégèse de Cana (Jn 2.4)," *Biblica* 55 (1974): 157–67. Vanhoye points to other modern

advancement or diminishment in himself—since his nature is incapable of increase and decrease—should experience subjection. For it is clear that he who associated himself with human nature, through his flesh, in his childhood legislated subjection for the young by his actions; yet still, when he advanced to full maturity, he no longer looked to his mother's authority. So when she urged him, at Cana in Galilee, to show his power as the wedding celebration had run out of supplies, and to supply graciously the needed wine for the feast, he did not refuse to bestow this favor on those who needed it; but he rejected his mother's urging, as no longer offered to him at the right time, saying, "What is this to me and to you, woman?" (Jn 2.4)[11]—Surely you do not want to give me orders, even at my age? "Has not my hour come"—the hour conferring on my age self-sufficiency and independence?

5 If, then, an appropriate sense of his age in life eventually freed [Jesus] from subjection to his mother during his fleshly life, no one will be able to explain what place there will be, in his "Lordship over the ages" (1 Tim 1.17), for subjection in him as one who rules. For it is characteristic of the blessed life of God always to remain as it is, and not to admit of the transformation that comes from change. Since, then, the Word who "was in the beginning" (Jn 1.1), the "Only-begotten God" (Jn 1.18) is far removed from any progress or change, how will he afterward become what he now is not? For the Apostle is not speaking as if the Son is always subject, but says he "*will* be subject" at the end, in the final fulfillment of all things.

If subjection is a good thing, on the other hand, and worthy to be ascribed to God, how is this good thing now *not* present in God? For surely it must be equally good, both for the Son who is subject and for the Father who receives the Son's subjection. This good thing, then, must be lacking to both Father and Son at the present time; so

biblical interpreters who have also considered reading the text as a question; among the works of patristic exegetes, this passage of Gregory is the only extant Greek work to do so, but Vanhoye also refers to the Arabic version of Tatian's *Diatesseron*, and to various passages in Ephrem (see p. 159 n.1).

συμπληρώσει τῶν χρόνων καὶ τῷ πατρὶ καὶ τῷ υἱῷ προσγενήσεται,
τοῦ μὲν ὑπομένοντος τὴν ὑποταγὴν τοῦ δὲ προσθήκην τινὰ καὶ
ἐπαύξησιν τῆς ἑαυτοῦ δόξης διὰ τούτου λαμβάνοντος ἣν ἐν τῷ
παρόντι τέως οὐκ ἔχει. ποῦ τοίνυν ἐν τούτῳ τὸ ἀναλλοίωτον;
τὸ γὰρ μετὰ ταῦτά τι γινόμενον νῦν δὲ μὴ ὂν ἴδιον τῆς τρεπτῆς
ἐστι φύσεως. εἴτε οὖν καλὸν ἡ ὑποταγή, καὶ νῦν εἶναι προσήκει
πιστεύειν τῷ θεῷ τὸ καλόν· εἴτε ἀνάξιον ἐπὶ τοῦ θεοῦ τὸ τοιοῦτον,
GNO 10 οὔτε νῦν οὔτε ἄλλοτε· | ἀλλὰ μήν φησιν ὁ ἀπόστολος τότε
ὑποταγήσεσθαι τῷ θεῷ καὶ πατρὶ τὸν υἱόν, οὐχὶ νῦν ὑποτετάχθαι·
ἄρα πρὸς ἄλλον τινὰ σκοπὸν βλέπει ὁ λόγος καὶ πόρρω τῆς τῶν
αἱρετικῶν κακονοίας ἐστὶ τὸ τοῦ ὀνόματος σημαινόμενον.

Τίς οὖν ὁ λόγος; τάχα διὰ τῆς συμφράσεως τῶν <ἐν> τῷ μέρει
τούτῳ συγγεγραμμένων μᾶλλον ἄν τις κατίδοι τὸ νόημα. ἐπειδὴ
γὰρ ἀγωνιστικὸν πρὸς τοὺς Κορινθίους ἐνεστήσατο λόγον, οἳ τὴν
μὲν εἰς τὸν κύριον παρεδέξαντο πίστιν τὸ δὲ περὶ τῆς ἀναστάσεως
τῶν ἀνθρώπων δόγμα μῦθον ᾠήθησαν λέγοντες· Πῶς ἐγείρονται
οἱ νεκροὶ καὶ ποίῳ σώματι ἔρχονται, οἷς πολυτρόπως καὶ πολυειδῶς
μετὰ τὸν θάνατον εἰς ἀφανισμὸν περιῆλθε τὰ σώματα, ἢ διὰ σήψεως
ἢ διὰ τῶν σαρκοβόρων ἑρπετῶν νηκτῶν πετεινῶν τετραπόδων
ἀναλωθέντα; διὰ τοῦτο πολλοὺς αὐτοῖς παρέθετο λογισμούς,
πείθων μὴ τῇ ἑαυτῶν δυνάμει τὴν τοῦ θεοῦ παρεικάζειν μήθ᾽ ὅσον
ἀνθρώπῳ ἀμήχανον καὶ ἐπὶ θεοῦ τὸ ἴσον οἴεσθαι, ἀλλ᾽ ἐκ τῶν
γνωρίμων ἡμῖν ὑποδειγμάτων τὸ μεγαλεῖον τῆς θείας ἐξουσίας
ἀναλογίζεσθαι· καὶ οὕτω προτίθησιν αὐτοῖς τὴν περὶ τὰ σώματα
τῶν σπερμάτων θαυματουργίαν τῶν ἀεὶ καινοτομουμένων ὑπὸ
τῆς θείας δυνάμεως καὶ <δείκνυσιν> ὡς οὐκ ἠτόνησεν ἡ τοῦ θεοῦ
σοφία μυρία σωμάτων εἴδη κατὰ τὸ πᾶν ἐξευρεῖν, λογικῶν ἀλόγων
GNO 11 ἐναερίων χερσαίων καὶ τῶν | κατ᾽ οὐρανὸν ἡμῖν προφαινομένων,
τοῦ τε ἡλίου καὶ τῶν λοιπῶν ἀστέρων, ὧν ἕκαστον <τῇ> θείᾳ

what neither Father nor Son had before the ages, will be added to both Father and Son in the fullness of time—the one undergoing subjection, the other receiving through it some addition to, and increase of, his own glory, which at present, for a time, he does not possess. Where is changelessness in all of this? For something that will happen in the future, but presently does not exist, is proper to changeable nature. If, then, subjection is a good thing, it is right for us to believe that this good belongs to God even now; but if such a thing is unworthy in God, [it will belong to him] neither now nor at any other time! Yet the Apostle says, "*then* will the Son be subject to his God and Father," not that he is *now* subject. So the text must have another purpose in view, and the meaning of the saying is far removed from the misconception of the heretics.

6 What, then, is the explanation? Perhaps one might grasp the thought better through the context of what is actually written in this passage. For since [Paul] had stirred up a controversy with the Corinthians, who had accepted faith in the Lord but thought the teaching about human resurrection to be a myth, saying, "How shall the dead be raised? In what sort of body will they return?" (1 Cor 15.35)—for bodies after death pass out of our view in many ways, and through many stages: either through corruption or by being eaten by carnivorous creatures, consumed by snakes or fish or winged raptors or four-footed animals—for this reason, he [Paul] offers the Corinthians many arguments, urging them not to compare God's power to their own, nor to think that whatever is impossible to a human is equally so for God, but rather to imagine the great abundance of God's power from parallels familiar to us. So he proposes to them, from the realm of bodies, the miraculous vitality of seeds, which are always being brought to life again by the divine power; and he shows that God's wisdom does not lack the power to devise countless forms of body all the time: for rational creatures, irrational ones, creatures in the air, creatures on land, as well as for those that appear to us in the heavens, the sun, and the other

δυνάμει γενόμενον τοῦ καὶ κατὰ τὴν ἀνάστασιν μὴ ἂν ἀπορῆσαι
PG 1312 τὸν θεὸν τῶν ἡμετέρων σωμάτων ** ἡμᾶς | ἀπόδειξις γίνεται. εἰ γὰρ τὰ ὄντα πάντα οὐκ ἔκ τινος ὑποκειμένης ὕλης πρὸς τὸ φαινόμενον μετεσκευάσθη ἀλλὰ τὸ θεῖον θέλημα ὕλη καὶ οὐσία τῶν δημιουργημάτων ἐγένετο, πολὺ μᾶλλον δυνατὸν εἶναι κατασκευάζει τὸ ἤδη ὂν εἰς τὸ ἴδιον σχῆμα πάλιν ἐπαναχθῆναι ἢ τὸ ἐξ ἀρχῆς μὴ ὂν εἰς ὑπόστασίν τε καὶ οὐσίαν ἐλθεῖν.

Δείξας τοίνυν ἐν τοῖς πρὸς αὐτοὺς λόγοις ὅτι, τοῦ πρώτου ἀνθρώπου εἰς γῆν διὰ τῆς ἁμαρτίας ἀναλυθέντος καὶ διὰ τοῦτο χοϊκοῦ κληθέντος, ἀκόλουθον ἦν κατ᾽ ἐκεῖνον καὶ τοὺς ἐξ ἐκείνου γενέσθαι πάντας χοϊκοὺς καὶ θνητοὺς τοὺς ἐκ τοῦ τοιούτου φύντας, ἀναγκαίως ἐπήγαγεν καὶ τὴν δευτέραν ἀκολουθίαν δι᾽ ἧς ἀναστοιχειοῦται πάλιν ἐκ τοῦ θνητοῦ πρὸς ἀθανασίαν ὁ ἄνθρωπος, ὁμοιοτρόπως λέγων τὸ ἀγαθὸν ἐγγεγενῆσθαι τῇ φύσει ἐξ ἑνὸς εἰς πάντας χεόμενον, ὥσπερ καὶ τὸ κακὸν δι᾽ ἑνὸς εἰς πλῆθος ἐχέθη τῇ διαδοχῇ τῶν ἐπιγινομένων συμπλατυνόμενον. τούτοις δὲ κέχρηται τοῖς ῥήμασι τὸ περὶ τούτου δόγμα κατασκευάζων Ὁ πρῶτος, |
GNO 12 φησίν, ἄνθρωπος ἐκ γῆς χοϊκός· ὁ δεύτερος ἐξ οὐρανοῦ· οἷος ὁ χοϊκὸς τοιοῦτοι καὶ οἱ χοϊκοί, καὶ οἷος ὁ ἐπουράνιος τοιοῦτοι καὶ

[12]Gregory seems to share here the common opinion of Greek natural philosophers that the celestial bodies, which move in predictable patterns, were living beings, whose bodies were formed of an ethereal and durable substance. For the history of this notion, see Alan B. Scott, *Origen and the Life of the Stars: The History of an Idea* (Oxford: Oxford University Press, 1991). See also 1 Cor 15.38–41.

[13]The words in italics here translate a conjectural supplement to the text in the manuscripts, suggested by the most recent editor, J. Kenneth Downing. As it stands, the text in the manuscripts seems to be missing an explicit mention of Gregory's (and Paul's) point: that God does have the power to raise decomposed bodies to new life.

[14]One can see here Gregory's tendency toward idealism.

[15]Gregory's rhetorical construction is a little complicated here, but his point is clear enough: restoring decomposed bodies to life is, if one thinks about it, less of a

stars.[12] Each of these transformations, occurring by divine power, serves as proof that God does not lack power to *gather together the seeds* of our own bodies in the resurrection *and raise them to life.*[13] For if all that exists was not simply transformed from some underlying matter into its visible form, but God's will became both the matter and the actual substance of what is created,[14] this makes it all the more possible that what has once existed should be restored again to its proper shape—[more likely] than that what in the beginning did not exist should come to exist concretely as a substance.[15]

[Paul] has shown, then, in his words to them, that since the first man was dissolved into earth because of sin, and for this reason came to be called "the man of earth," it was an appropriate consequence, in his view, that all those who were descended from him should be earthly and mortal, since they are sprung from such a person. But he [Paul] necessarily adds the second consequence as well: the human person will be assembled all over again, transformed from mortal to immortal, because—Paul says—goodness is now born into our nature, poured out from one into all, in the same way as once evil was poured out through one man into the whole race, spreading out by the succession of the generations. He uses these words, in fact, when he develops his teaching about this: "The first man," he says, "is earthy, from the earth; the second is from heaven. As the man from earth is, so also are the earthy ones; and as the Heavenly Man is, so are the heavenly ones. And just as we have borne the image of

challenge to human faith than creating them from nothing. This is a point already familiar from the apologetic tradition: see Athenagoras, *On the Resurrection* 9; Irenaeus, *Against Heresies* 5.3; Tertullian, *Apology* 48; Hippolytus, *Against Plato, on the Cause of the Universe* (PG 10:800 A12—B9); Gregory of Nyssa, *On the Soul and the Resurrection* (PPS 12:69–75); John Chrysostom, *Homilies on the Rich Man and Lazarus* (PPS 9); see also Cyril of Jerusalem, *Cat.* 18.3, 9; Ambrose, *On the Death of Satyrus* 2.60–64. Gregory is, in general, opposed to the Aristotelian and Neoplatonic notion of an unformed "prime matter," devoid of any qualities, which—in much of the Greek philosophical tradition—underlies all identifiable substances as the passive recipient of substantial form; see Richard Sorabji, *Matter, Space and Motion: Theories in Antiquity and Their Sequel* (Ithaca: Cornell University Press, 1988), 52–55. For Gregory, the reality of each thing is simply due to its intelligible form.

οἱ ἐπουράνιοι· καὶ καθὼς ἐφορέσαμεν τὴν εἰκόνα τοῦ χοϊκοῦ, οὕτω φορέσομεν καὶ τὴν εἰκόνα τοῦ ἐπουρανίου.

Τούτοις τοίνυν καὶ τοῖς τοιούτοις λογισμοῖς κρατύνας τὸν περὶ τῆς ἀναστάσεως λόγον καὶ διὰ πολλῶν ἑτέρων τοὺς αἱρετικοὺς τοῖς συλλογισμοῖς συμποδίσας ἐν οἷς ἀπεδείκνυεν τὸν ἀπιστοῦντα τῇ τῶν ἀνθρώπων ἀναστάσει μηδὲ τοῦ Χριστοῦ προσδέχεσθαι τὴν ἀνάστασιν, διὰ τῆς τῶν συνημμένων ἀλλήλοις πλοκῆς κατεσκεύασε τὸ ἐν τοῖς συμπεράσμασιν ἄφυκτον λέγων ὅτι Εἰ ἀνάστασις νεκρῶν οὐκ ἔστιν, οὐδὲ Χριστὸς ἐγήγερται· εἰ δὲ Χριστὸς οὐκ ἐγήγερται, ματαία καὶ ἡ εἰς αὐτὸν πίστις ἐστίν. τῆς γὰρ προτάσεως ἀληθοῦς οὔσης ὅτι Χριστὸς ἐκ νεκρῶν ἐγήγερται, καὶ τὸ συνημμένον τούτῳ πάντως ἀληθὲς εἶναι χρή· τὸ νεκρῶν εἶναι ἀνάστασιν· τῇ γὰρ μερικῇ ἀποδείξει καὶ τὸ καθόλου συναποδείκνυται. καὶ τὸ ἔμπαλιν, εἴ τις τὸ καθόλου ψεῦδος εἶναι λέγοι· τὸ νεκρῶν εἶναι ἀνάστασιν, οὐδὲ τὸ ἐπὶ μέρους πάντως ἀληθὲς εὑρεθήσεται· τὸ τὸν Χριστὸν ἐκ νεκρῶν ἐγηγέρθαι· εἰ γὰρ καθόλου ἀδύνατον, οὐδὲ <ἕν> τινι
GNO 13 δυνατόν | ἐστι πάντως. ἀλλὰ μὴν τοῦτο τοῖς παραδεξαμένοις τὸν Λόγον πιστόν ἐστι καὶ ἀναντίρρητον ὅτι Χριστὸς ἐγήγερται ἐκ νεκρῶν· ἀναγκαίως ἐν τῇ μερικῇ τῆς ἀναστάσεως τοῦ Χριστοῦ πίστει καὶ ἡ καθόλου τὸ πιστὸν ἕξει.

Οὕτω τοίνυν αὐτοὺς συλλογιστικῶς πρὸς τὴν παραδοχὴν τοῦ δόγματος συναναγκάσας ἐκ τοῦ εἰπεῖν ὅτι Εἰ μή ἐστιν (τὸ γὰρ καθόλου μὴ ὂν οὐδὲ ἔν τινι δυνατὸν εἶναι· εἰ δὲ τοῦτον ἐγηγέρθαι πιστεύομεν, τῆς καθόλου τῶν ἀνθρώπων ἀναστάσεως ἡ περὶ τούτου πίστις ἀπόδειξις γίνεται) καὶ προσθεὶς ἐκεῖνο τῷ λόγῳ ᾧ πᾶσα ἡ περὶ τοῦ δόγματος τούτου κατασκευὴ συμπεραίνεται τὸ Ὥσπερ ἐν τῷ Ἀδὰμ πάντες ἀποθνῄσκουσιν οὕτως καὶ ἐν τῷ Χριστῷ πάντες ζωοποιηθήσονται, σαφῶς ἐκκαλύπτει τὸ περὶ τούτου μυστήριον πρὸς ὅ τι βλέπει, ἐν τοῖς ἐφεξῆς διά τινος ἀναγκαίας ἀκολουθίας πρὸς τὸ πέρας τῶν ἐλπιζομένων διευθύνων τὸν λόγον. |

the earthly man, so also we shall bear the likeness of the Heavenly Man" (1 Cor 15.47–49).

7 With this argument, then, and arguments like it, he reinforces his words about the resurrection. And through many other arguments he ties the heretics up in syllogisms, in which he proves that the person who does not believe in the resurrection of humanity also will not be able to accept the resurrection of Christ. Through the interweaving of these themes into unity with each other, he proves that what stands as the conclusion is inescapable: namely, that "If there is no resurrection of the dead, then Christ has not been raised; and if Christ is not raised, faith in him is also vain" (1 Cor 15.13, 17). For if the first premise is true—that Christ is risen from the dead—then surely that which is implied along with it—that there *is* a resurrection of the dead—must be true as well; in the proof of the specific assertion, the universal truth is proved with it. And the opposite also holds: if someone should argue that the universal statement, "there is a resurrection of the dead," is a lie, then surely the specific statement, "Christ has been raised from the dead," will be found not to be true. For if something is impossible in general, surely it will not be possible in particular cases. But for those who have accepted the Word [of the gospel], this is credible, even irrefutable: that Christ has been raised from the dead; necessarily, then, in our specific faith in Christ's resurrection, the general expectation will find its warrant also.

In this way, compelling them by syllogisms to accept the teaching, simply by saying, "If this is not true . . ." (for what is not true generally, is not possible in individual cases; but if we believe this individual was raised, belief about him comes to be a proof of the resurrection of humanity in general), and connecting this to the saying by which the whole argument concerning this teaching is brought to a conclusion—"As in Adam all die, so also in Christ will all be brought to life" (1 Cor 15.22)—Paul clearly reveals the Mystery toward which he is looking; and in what follows, he continues his argument, by a kind of necessary chain of consequences, toward the final goal of what we hope for.

PG 1313 Ὁ δὲ σκοπὸς τῶν λεγομένων οὗτός ἐστιν. ἐκθήσομαι δὲ πρότερον τῇ ἐμαυτοῦ λέξει τὴν διάνοιαν τῶν γεγραμμένων, εἶθ' οὕτω παραθήσω τοῦ ἀποστόλου τὸν λόγον τὸν τῇ παρ' ἡμῶν προεκτεθείσῃ διανοίᾳ ἐφαρμοζόμενον.

Τίς οὖν ὁ τοῦ λόγου ἐστὶ σκοπὸς ὃν δογματίζει ἐν ἐκείνῳ τῷ
μέρει ὁ θεῖος ἀπόστολος; ὅτι ποτὲ πρὸς τὸ μὴ ὂν ἡ τοῦ κακοῦ φύσις
GNO 14 μεταχωρήσει, παντελῶς ἐξαφανισθεῖσα τοῦ ὄν|τος, καὶ πᾶσαν
λογικὴν φύσιν ἡ θεία τε καὶ ἀκήρατος ἀγαθότης ἐν ἑαυτῇ περιέξει,
μηδενὸς τῶν παρὰ τοῦ θεοῦ γεγονότων τῆς βασιλείας τοῦ θεοῦ
ἀποπίπτοντος, ὅταν πάσης τῆς ἐμμιχθείσης τοῖς οὖσι κακίας
οἷόν τινος ὕλης κιβδήλου διὰ τῆς τοῦ καθαρσίου πυρὸς χωνείας
ἀναλωθείσης, τοιοῦτον γένηται πᾶν ὃ παρὰ τοῦ θεοῦ ἔσχε τὴν
γένεσιν, οἷον ἐξ ἀρχῆς ἦν ὅτε οὔπω τὴν κακίαν ἐδέξατο. τοῦτο δὲ
γίνεσθαι λέγει οὕτως· ἐγένετο, φησίν, ἐν τῇ θνητῇ τε καὶ ἐπικήρῳ
τῶν ἀνθρώπων φύσει ἡ καθαρὰ καὶ ἀκήρατος τοῦ μονογενοῦς
θεότης. ἐκ πάσης δὲ τῆς ἀνθρωπίνης φύσεως ᾗ κατεμίχθη τὸ θεῖον,
οἷον ἀπαρχή τις τοῦ κοινοῦ φυράματος, ὁ κατὰ Χριστὸν ἄνθρωπος
ὑπέστη δι' οὗ προσεφύη τῇ θεότητι πᾶν τὸ ἀνθρώπινον. ἐπειδὴ
τοίνυν ἐν ἐκείνῳ πᾶσα κακίας φύσις ἐξηφανίσθη Ὃς ἁμαρτίαν
οὐκ ἐποίησεν, καθώς φησιν ὁ προφήτης, οὐδὲ εὑρέθη δόλος ἐν τῷ
στόματι αὐτοῦ, συνηφανίσθη δὲ μετὰ τῆς ἁμαρτίας ἐν τῷ αὐτῷ
καὶ ὁ ἐπακολουθῶν αὐτῇ θάνατος (οὐ γάρ ἐστιν ἄλλη θανάτου
γένεσις πλὴν ἁμαρτία), ἀρχὴν ἔλαβεν ἀπ' ἐκείνου ὅ τε τῆς κακίας
GNO 15 ἀφανισμὸς καὶ ἡ τοῦ θανάτου κατάλυσις. εἶτα ὥσπερ | τις τάξις
ἐπετέθη διά τινος ἀκολουθίας τῷ γινομένῳ. τὸ γὰρ ἀεὶ κατὰ τὴν τοῦ
ἀγαθοῦ ὑπόβασιν μᾶλλον ἀφεστὼς τοῦ πρώτου ἢ προσεχέστερον

8 The direction of my own argument is this: I shall begin by proposing what the Scriptures here mean, in my own reading of them; then I will lay out the argument of the Apostle [in the text we are discussing], as it corresponds to the meaning we have proposed.

What, then, is the heart of the doctrine that the divine Apostle is teaching us in this passage? It is that at some point the nature of evil will be transformed into non-existence, completely made to disappear from reality, and pure divine goodness will contain all rational nature within itself; nothing of all that has come into being from God will fall outside the boundaries of God's Kingdom, but when all the evil that has been mingled with existing things is consumed, like some material impurity, by the melting-process of purifying fire, everything will become just as it was when it had its origin from God—as it was when it had not yet come to share in evil.

9 He says it will happen this way. The pure and immortal divinity of the only Son has come to live in the midst of mortal human nature, bound up with death. From the whole of human nature, into which the divine was mingled, the man identified as the Christ[16] has come into existence, as a kind of first-fruit of the mixture that will include us all; through Christ, all that is human has been joined to the divinity, since the entire nature of evil has been annihilated in this man, "who committed no sin," as the Prophet says, "nor was deceit found in his mouth" (Is 53.9).[17] And along with sin, death, which accompanies it, has also disappeared in the same person (for there is no other starting-point for death but sin). So evil has begun to disappear, death to be destroyed, with him as the starting point; and then a sort of succession has been extended within what is created, in a kind of ordered series. For just as the good declines, and each thing constantly is found to be more distant from, rather than closer to,

[16]Greek: ὁ κατὰ Χριστὸν ἄνθρωπος (*ho kata Christon anthrōpos*)—literally, "the man according to Christ," "the man associated with Christ," perhaps even "the Christly man."

[17]The LXX text of Isaiah, however, has ἀνομίαν (*anomian*) rather than ἁμαρτίαν (*hamartian*).

εὑρισκόμενον, ὅπως ἂν ἀξίας τε καὶ δυνάμεως ἕκαστον ἔχῃ,
οὕτως ἐπακολουθεῖ τῷ προάγοντι· ὥστε μετὰ τὸν ἐν τῷ Χριστῷ
ἄνθρωπον ὃς ἐγένετο ἀπαρχὴ τῆς φύσεως ἡμῶν δεξάμενος ἐν
ἑαυτῷ τὴν θεότητα, ὃς καὶ Ἀπαρχὴ τῶν κεκοιμημένων ἐγένετο
καὶ Πρωτότοκος ἐκ τῶν νεκρῶν Λύσας τὰς ὠδῖνας τοῦ θανάτου·
μετὰ τοῦτον τοίνυν τὸν ἄνθρωπον, τὸν καθόλου τῆς ἁμαρτίας
κεχωρισμένον καὶ καταργήσαντα ἐν ἑαυτῷ τοῦ θανάτου τὸ κράτος
καὶ πᾶσαν αὐτοῦ ἀρχήν τε καὶ ἐξουσίαν καὶ δύναμιν καταλύσαντα,
εἴ τις κατὰ τὸν Παῦλον εὑρεθείη, τὸν ὡς ἦν δυνατὸν μιμητὴν τοῦ
Χριστοῦ γενόμενον ἐν τῇ τοῦ κακοῦ ἀλλοτριώσει, ὁ τοιοῦτος τῇ
ἀπαρχῇ κατόπιν ἀκολουθήσει ἐν τῷ τῆς παρουσίας καιρῷ· καὶ
πάλιν τούτῳ, λέγω δὲ καθ᾽ ὑπόθεσιν, ὁ Τιμόθεος, ἂν οὕτω τύχῃ,
ὁ καθὼς οἷός τε ἦν μιμησάμενος ἐν ἑαυτῷ τὸν διδάσκαλον, ἤ τις
τοιοῦτος ἕτερος· καὶ οὕτω καθεξῆς ὅσοι διὰ τῆς κατ᾽ ὀλίγον τοῦ
ἀγαθοῦ ὑφέσεως τῶν ἀεὶ προλαμβανόντων κατόπιν εὑρίσκονται,
ἕως ἂν εἰς ἐκείνους ἡ ἀκολουθία τῶν ἑπομένων φθάσῃ ἐν οἷς
τοῦ κακοῦ πλεονάζοντος ἐλάττων ἡ τοῦ κρείττονος εὑρίσκεται
μοῖρα· κατὰ τὴν αὐτὴν ἀναλογίαν παρὰ τῶν ἐν κακίᾳ τὸ ἔλαττον
GNO 16 ἐχόντων τῆς | ἀκολουθίας ἐπὶ τοὺς προέχοντας ἐν τῷ κακῷ τὴν
PG 1316 τάξιν τῶν πρὸς τὸ κρεῖτ|τον ἀναλυόντων ποιούσης, ἕως ἂν ἐπὶ
τὸ ἀκρότατον τοῦ κακοῦ πέρας ἡ τοῦ ἀγαθοῦ πρόοδος φθάσῃ
τὴν κακίαν ἐξαφανίζουσα. ὅπερ δὴ τέλος τῆς ἐλπίδος ἐστίν, ὡς
μηδὲν ὑπεναντίον τῷ ἀγαθῷ περιλειφθῆναι, ἀλλὰ διὰ πάντων
τὴν θείαν ζωὴν διεξελθοῦσαν ἐξαφανίσαι καθόλου ἐκ τῶν ὄντων
τὸν θάνατον, προαναιρεθείσης αὐτοῦ τῆς ἁμαρτίας ἀφ᾽ ἧς, καθὼς
εἴρηται, τὴν βασιλείαν κατὰ τῶν ἀνθρώπων ὁ θάνατος ἔσχεν.

its original state, so each must follow in the steps of what precedes it in order to have some share [again] in its dignity and power. As a result, after the human component of Christ—who was the first-fruit of our nature, and possessed the godhead in himself, becoming "the first-fruit of those who have fallen asleep" (1 Cor 15.20) and "the first-born of the dead" (Col 1.18), having "eased the birth pangs of death" (Acts 2.24)[18]—after this man, then, who was completely separate from sin and who destroyed in himself the strength of death[19] and "annihilated all its rule and authority and power" (1 Cor 15.24), if one is found to be like Paul, who became, as far as he could, Christ's imitator in distancing himself from evil: such a person will follow behind the "first-fruits," at the time of Christ's second coming. So again Timothy, to take another example, or some other like him, followed *his* teacher, imitating him as far as possible in his own life; and so, too, [will come] in due order those who are found to be always following behind others who surpass them, because of a slight deficiency in goodness, until the sequence of successors comes down to people in whom the share of what is good is found to be less than that of growing evil. Then, in the same measure, among those who have a lesser share of evil, a consistent ordering will continue to form, in comparison to those who outdo them in evil—an ordering of those being drawn back toward what is better—until the point where the progress of the Good reaches out to the farthest limit of evil. And surely this is the goal of our hope: the point where nothing opposed to the Good is left, but divine life penetrates all things, and completely puts an end to death within creation, with sin first to be removed from it—since it was from sin, as we have said, that death first established its reign among human beings.[20]

[18]The phrase, "the birth pangs of death," is already familiar in the Old Testament; see 2 Sam 22.6; Ps 17.4; Ps 114.3.

[19]See Heb 2.14, and cf. 2 Tim 1.10.

[20]The thought in the preceding paragraph is somewhat obscure, and the style cumbersome; but Gregory is clearly trying to follow Paul's thought in presenting

Πάσης τοίνυν πονηρᾶς ἐξουσίας τε καὶ ἀρχῆς ἐν ἡμῖν καταλυθείσης καὶ μηκέτι μηδενὸς πάθους τῆς φύσεως ἡμῶν κυριεύοντος, ἀνάγκη πᾶσα μηδενὸς κατακρατοῦντος ἑτέρου πάντα ὑποταγῆναι τῇ ἐπὶ πάντων ἀρχῇ. θεοῦ δὲ ὑποταγή ἐστιν ἡ παντελὴς τοῦ κακοῦ ἀλλοτρίωσις. ὅταν οὖν κατὰ μίμησιν τῆς ἀπαρχῆς ἔξω τοῦ κακοῦ πάντες γενώμεθα, τότε ὅλον τὸ φύραμα τῆς φύσεως τῇ ἀπαρχῇ συμμιχθὲν καὶ ἓν κατὰ τὸ συνεχὲς σῶμα γενόμενον τοῦ ἀγαθοῦ μόνου τὴν ἡγεμονίαν ἐφ' ἑαυτοῦ δέξεται, καὶ οὕτω παντὸς τοῦ τῆς φύσεως ἡμῶν σώματος πρὸς τὴν θείαν τε καὶ ἀκήρατον φύσιν ἀνακραθέντος ἐκείνη ἡ τοῦ υἱοῦ λεγομένη ὑποταγὴ δι' ἡμῶν γίνεται, τῆς ἐν τῷ σώματι αὐτοῦ κατορθωθείσης ὑποταγῆς εἰς αὐτὸν ἀναφερομένης τὸν ἐν ἡμῖν τὴν χάριν τῆς ὑποταγῆς ἐνεργήσαντα.

Ἡ μὲν οὖν διάνοια τῶν ὑπὸ τοῦ μεγάλου Παύλου δογματισθέντων ἐστίν, ὥς γε ὑπειλήφαμεν, αὕτη. καιρὸς δ' ἂν εἴη
GNO 17 καὶ αὐτὰ παραθέσθαι τοῦ ἀποστόλου τὰ ῥήματα ἔχοντα | οὕτως· Ὥσπερ γὰρ ἐν τῷ Ἀδὰμ πάντες ἀποθνήσκουσιν, οὕτως καὶ ἐν τῷ Χριστῷ πάντες ζωοποιηθήσονται· ἕκαστος δὲ ἐν τῷ ἰδίῳ τάγματι· ἀπαρχὴ Χριστός, ἔπειτα οἱ τοῦ Χριστοῦ ἐν τῇ παρουσίᾳ αὐτοῦ, εἶτα τὸ τέλος, ὅταν παραδιδῷ τὴν βασιλείαν τῷ θεῷ καὶ πατρί, ὅταν καταργήσῃ πᾶσαν ἀρχὴν καὶ ἐξουσίαν καὶ δύναμιν. δεῖ γὰρ αὐτὸν βασιλεύειν ἕως ἂν θῇ τοὺς ἐχθροὺς ὑπὸ τοὺς πόδας αὐτοῦ. ἔσχατος ἐχθρὸς καταργεῖται ὁ θάνατος· πάντα γὰρ ὑπέταξεν ὑπὸ τοὺς πόδας αὐτοῦ. ὅταν δὲ εἴπῃ ὅτι πάντα ὑπέταξεν, δῆλον ὅτι

Christ as the inaugurator and model of a gradual, ordered restoration of humanity to embody the original image of God, in which we were created, and suggesting that there will be a gradual elimination of moral and physical evil, through the proclamation of the victory God has accomplished in the incarnation of the Word and in Christ's resurrection from the dead. Gregory emphasizes understanding and imitation, aimed at growth in virtue and the consequent acquisition of indestructible life, as keys to our sharing in Christ's process of transformation, and he clearly suggests that the salvation of intelligent creatures will be universal, since evil is always of only limited reality. For Gregory's understanding of the sinless person of Christ as the cause and mode of human transformation to a life of moral virtue and physical immortality, see my articles, "Divine Transcendence and Human Transformation: Gregory of Nyssa's Anti-Apollinarian Christology," *Studia Patristica* 32 (1997): 87–95; reprinted in

10 When every wicked power and rule in us has been destroyed,[21] and no passion rules over our nature any longer, it is clearly necessary that with no external force dominating us, all will be subject to the power that rules all things. But submission to God is the utter removal of evil. When, then, all of us come to be outside the realm of evil, in imitation of our "first-fruit," then the whole mix that is nature, blended in with the first-fruit and becoming one body in its solidarity, will receive within itself the rule of the Good alone;[22] so, with the whole body of our nature mingled with the divine, immortal nature, that subjection here ascribed to the Son will become reality through us, as subjection is brought to fulfillment in his Body and is referred to him, who works in us the grace of submission.

11 This, then, is the meaning of what is taught by the great Paul, as we have understood it. Now it is time to expound the very words of the Apostle, which read as follows: "For as in Adam all die, so also in Christ all shall be made to live. But each in his proper order: Christ the first-fruit, then those who are Christ's at his second coming; and then will be the completion, when he hands over royal power to God his Father, [and] when he reduces to nothing all rule and authority and power; for he must reign until he puts all his enemies under his feet. And the last enemy that will be destroyed is death: for he has 'put all things in subjection under his feet' (Ps 8.6). But when it says that he [i.e., God] has 'subjected all things,' it is clear that this does not include the one who subjected all things to him. And when he

Modern Theology 18 (2002): 497–506; also in Sarah Coakley, ed., *Re-Thinking Gregory of Nyssa* (Oxford: Blackwell, 2003), 67–76; and "'Heavenly Man' and 'Eternal Christ': Apollinarius and Gregory of Nyssa on the Personal Identity of the Savior," *Journal of Early Christian Studies* 10 (2002): 469–88.

[21]Rom 5.4, 21.

[22]As in a number of his anti-Apollinarian works on the constitution of Christ, Gregory here relies heavily on the Pauline image of Christ as the "first-fruit" of a harvest of saved humanity (see 1 Cor 15.23), and also on the Gospel parable of a small amount of yeast, gradually leavening a whole "mass" of mixed dough. In the humanity of the incarnate Word, Gregory frequently insists, we see gradually revealed both the godlike virtue and the God-given victory over sickness and death that are central to human salvation.

ἐκτὸς τοῦ ὑποτάξαντος αὐτῷ τὰ πάντα. ὅταν δὲ ὑποτάξῃ αὐτῷ τὰ πάντα, τότε καὶ αὐτὸς ὑποταγήσεται τῷ ὑποτάξαντι αὐτῷ τὰ πάντα, ἵνα ᾖ ὁ θεὸς τὰ πάντα ἐν πᾶσιν.

Σαφῶς γὰρ ἐν τῷ τελευταίῳ τῶν εἰρημένων τὸ τῆς κακίας ἀνύπαρκτον τῷ λόγῳ παρίστησιν ἐν τῷ εἰπεῖν ἐν πᾶσι γίνεσθαι τὸν θεὸν πάντα ἑκάστῳ γινόμενον. δῆλον γὰρ ὅτι τότε ἀληθὲς ἔσται τὸ ἐν πᾶσι τὸν θεὸν εἶναι, ὅταν μηδὲν κακὸν ἐνθεωρῆται τοῖς οὖσιν. οὐ γὰρ δὴ καὶ ἐν κακῷ τὸν θεὸν εἰκός ἐστι γίνεσθαι. ὥστε ἢ οὐκ ἐν πᾶσιν ἔσται ὅταν ὑπολειφθῇ τι κακὸν ἐν τοῖς οὖσιν ἤ, εἰ ἀληθῶς ἐν πᾶσι χρὴ πιστεύειν αὐτὸν εἶναι, τὸ μηδὲν κακὸν εἶναι τῇ περὶ τούτου πίστει συναποδείκνυται. οὐ γάρ ἐστι δυνατὸν ἐν κακῷ τὸν θεὸν γενέσθαι. |

GNO 18 Τὸ δὲ πάντα γίνεσθαι τὸν θεὸν <ἐν πᾶσι> τοῖς οὖσι τὸ ἁπλοῦν
καὶ μονοειδὲς τῆς ἐλπιζομένης ἡμῖν ζωῆς ὑποδείκνυσι. τὸ γὰρ
μηκέτι διὰ πολλῶν καὶ ποικίλων καθ᾽ ὁμοιότητα τοῦ νῦν βίου τὴν
ζωὴν ἡμῖν συνερανίζεσθαι τῷ λόγῳ τοῦτο παρίστησιν τὸ πάντα
ἡμῖν τὸν θεὸν γίνεσθαι ὅσα τῇ ζωῇ ταύτῃ ἀναγκαῖα δοκεῖ, διά
τινος ἀναλογίας ἑκάστου μεταλαμβανομένου πρὸς τὸ θειότερον·
PG 1317 ὥστε καὶ βρῶσιν | εἶναι τὸν θεὸν ἡμῖν, ὡς εἰκὸς βρωθῆναι θεόν,
καὶ πόσιν, ὡσαύτως ἔνδυμά τε καὶ σκέπην ἀέρα τόπον πλοῦτον ἀπόλαυσιν κάλλος ὑγίειαν ἰσχὺν φρόνησιν δόξαν μακαριότητα καὶ πᾶν ὅσον ἐν τῇ ἀγαθῇ κρίνεται μοίρᾳ οὗ ἐπιδεὴς ἡ φύσις ἐστί, πρὸς τὸ θεοπρεπὲς ἀναγομένης τῆς σημασίας τῶν εἰρημένων· ὡς διὰ τούτου μαθεῖν ὅτι ὁ ἐν τῷ θεῷ γενόμενος πάντα ἔχει ἐν τῷ ἐκεῖνον ἔχειν. οὐδὲν δὲ ἕτερόν ἐστι τὸ ἔχειν τὸν θεὸν ἢ τὸ ἑνωθῆναι θεῷ. οὐκ ἂν δέ τις ἄλλως ἑνωθείη μὴ σύσσωμος αὐτῷ γενόμενος, καθὼς ὀνομάζει ὁ Παῦλος· οἱ γὰρ πάντες τῷ ἑνὶ σώματι τοῦ Χριστοῦ συναπτόμενοι διὰ τῆς μετουσίας ἓν αὐτοῦ γινόμεθα σῶμα.

[God] has subjected all things to him, then he himself [i.e., Christ] will be subjected to the one who has subjected all things to him, so that God will be all in all things" (1 Cor 15.22–28).[23]

Clearly, in the final phrase of the passage, Paul presents the insubstantial character of evil in his very words, by saying that God will be "in all things," having become everything to each [creature]. For obviously it will then be true that "God is in all things," when no evil is to be seen in the things that are. For surely it is not likely that God will be also "in" what is evil! So that either he will *not* be in all things, if some trace of evil remains in what exists; or, if one must believe that he truly *will* be in all things, then it is also proved at the same time, by our faith concerning this, that there will be nothing evil left. For it is not possible that God should come to be in evil.

12 But that God will "be all in all things" also reveals the simple, uniform character of the life we hope for. For that it will no longer be maintained in us in the same way as life now is, through many sources of various kinds, the passage proves by saying that "God will be all" for us—he will be all that seems necessary for a life such as ours. So we must interpret each detail in a more divine direction, by a kind of analogy: so that God will be our food, in the way it is appropriate for God to be "eaten," and our drink, just as he will be our clothing and our shelter, our air, our location, our wealth, our refreshment, our beauty, our health, our strength, our prudence, our glory, our blessedness, and every need of nature that is judged to be part of the good life—as the meaning of what is said points us upward toward an interpretation that befits God. As a result, we learn by this that the one who comes to be in God has everything, simply by having him. And "having" God is nothing else than being united with God; but one cannot be united with him in any way except by becoming "one Body" with him, as Paul explains: "For all of us who are joined to the one Body of Christ become his one Body by participation in it" (1 Cor 10.17).

[23]Here, for the first time in the essay, Gregory gives the text of the whole passage he is analyzing.

Ὅταν οὖν διὰ πάντων ἔλθῃ τὸ ἀγαθόν, τότε ὅλον αὐτοῦ
τὸ σῶμα ὑποταγήσεται τῇ ζωοποιῷ ἐξουσίᾳ, καὶ οὕτως ἡ τοῦ
σώματος τούτου ὑποταγὴ αὐτοῦ λέγεται εἶναι τοῦ υἱοῦ ὑποταγὴ
τοῦ ἀνακεκραμένου πρὸς τὸ ἴδιον σῶμα, ὅπερ ἐστὶν ἡ ἐκκλησία,
καθώς φησι πρὸς τοὺς Κολοσσαεῖς ὁ ἀπόστολος, οὑτωσὶ λέγων
GNO 19 τῷ ῥήματι· Νῦν χαίρω ἐν τοῖς παθήμασί μου | καὶ ἀνταναπληρῶ
τὰ ὑστερήματα τῶν ὑπὲρ Χριστοῦ θλίψεων ἐν τῇ σαρκί μου ὑπὲρ
τοῦ σώματος αὐτοῦ, ὅ ἐστιν ἡ ἐκκλησία, ἧς ἐγενόμην διάκονος
κατὰ τὴν οἰκονομίαν. καὶ πρὸς τὴν Κορινθίων ἐκκλησίαν φησίν·
Ὑμεῖς ἐστε σῶμα Χριστοῦ καὶ μέλη ἐκ μέρους. σαφέστερον δὲ
τοῖς Ἐφεσίοις τὸ περὶ τούτου παρατίθεται δόγμα δι᾽ ὧν φησιν ὅτι
Ἀληθεύοντες δὲ ἐν ἀγάπῃ αὐξήσωμεν εἰς αὐτὸν τὰ πάντα ὅς ἐστιν
ἡ κεφαλή, ὁ Χριστός, ἐξ οὗ πᾶν τὸ σῶμα συναρμολογούμενον καὶ
συμβιβαζόμενον διὰ πάσης ἁφῆς <τῆς> ἐπιχορηγίας κατ᾽ ἐνέργειαν
ἐν μέτρῳ ἑνὸς ἑκάστου μέρους τὴν αὔξησιν τοῦ σώματος ποιεῖται
εἰς οἰκοδομὴν ἑαυτοῦ ἐν ἀγάπῃ· ὡς διὰ τῶν ἀεὶ προστιθεμένων
τῇ πίστει ἑαυτὸν τοῦ Χριστοῦ οἰκοδομοῦντος. ὃς τότε παύσεται
ἑαυτὸν οἰκοδομῶν ὅταν εἰς τὸ ἴδιον μέτρον φθάσῃ ἡ τοῦ σώματος
αὐτοῦ αὔξησίς τε καὶ τελείωσις, καὶ μηκέτι λίπῃ τῷ σώματι τὸ
δι᾽ οἰκοδομῆς προστιθέμενον, πάντων ἐποικοδομηθέντων ἐπὶ τῷ
θεμελίῳ τῶν προφητῶν τε καὶ ἀποστόλων καὶ προσθεμένων τῇ
πίστει, ὅταν, καθώς φησιν ὁ ἀπόστολος, Καταντήσωμεν οἱ πάντες
εἰς τὴν ἑνότητα τῆς πίστεως καὶ τῆς ἐπιγνώσεως τοῦ υἱοῦ τοῦ
θεοῦ εἰς ἄνδρα τέλειον, εἰς μέτρον ἡλικίας τοῦ πληρώματος τοῦ
Χριστοῦ.

Εἰ τοίνυν κεφαλὴ ὢν αὐτὸς τὸ ἐφεξῆς αὐτοῦ σῶμα οἰκοδομεῖ
διὰ τῶν ἀεὶ προστιθεμένων συναρμολογῶν καὶ συμβιβάζων τοὺς
πάντας εἰς ἃ πέφυκεν ἕκαστος κατὰ τὸ μέτρον τῆς ἐνεργείας,
GNO 20 ὥστε ἢ χεῖρα ἢ ὀφθαλμὸν ἢ πόδα ἢ ἀκοὴν ἢ | ἄλλο τι γενέσθαι
τῶν συμπληρούντων τὸ σῶμα κατὰ τὴν ἀναλογίαν τῆς ἑκάστου

When, then, the Good comes to be identified with all things,[24] then the whole Body of it will be subjected to the life-giving Power; and so the subjection of this Body will be said to be the subjection of the Son himself, who is identified with his own Body, which is the Church, as the Apostle writes to the Colossians. He says literally this: "Now I rejoice in my sufferings, and in my flesh I fill up what is lacking in sufferings on Christ's behalf, for the sake of his Body, which is the Church—of which I have become a servant, in God's plan" (Col 1.24–25). And to the Church of the Corinthians he says: "You are the Body of Christ, and individually his members" (1 Cor 12.27). And he proposes this teaching more clearly still to the Ephesians, by saying, "Speaking the truth in love, let us in every way grow together into him, who is the head: [so] Christ—from whom the whole Body grows together and is unified in every joint by sharing in his active generosity, to the measure of which each of us is capable, makes possible growth together into his dwelling place in love" (Eph 4.15–16). Christ is the one who builds himself, by means of those who are constantly being added to the community of faith.[25] And he will only then cease building himself, when the growth and perfecting of his Body comes to its proper measure, and nothing remains to be added to that Body by the builder, but all have been "built on the foundation of prophets and Apostles" (Eph 2.20) and added to the community of faith—when, as the Apostle says, "We all attain to the unity of faith and of knowledge of the Son of God, to perfect manhood, to the measure of the maturity of the fullness of Christ" (Eph 4.13).

13 If, then, Christ himself, being the head, builds up his own well-structured Body through those who are constantly being added, fitting it together and unifying all of its members in the role each has been given, according to the measure of his active gift[26]—so that one becomes a hand or an eye or a foot or ear or some other part of

[24]Literally: "when the Good has proceeded through all things."
[25]Literally, "to the faith."
[26]See Eph 4.16.

πίστεως, ταῦτα δὲ ποιῶν ἑαυτὸν οἰκοδομεῖ, καθὼς εἴρηται, δῆλον ἂν εἴη διὰ τούτων ὅτι ἐν πᾶσι γινόμενος εἰς ἑαυτὸν δέχεται πάντας τοὺς ἑνουμένους αὐτῷ διὰ τῆς κοινωνίας τοῦ σώματος, καὶ μέλη τοῦ ἰδίου σώματος ποιεῖται τοὺς πάντας, ὥστε εἶναι Πολλὰ μὲν μέλη ἓν δὲ σῶμα.

Ὁ τοίνυν πρὸς ἑαυτὸν ἡμᾶς ἑνώσας καὶ ἡμῖν ἑνωθεὶς καὶ
PG 1320 διὰ πάντων ἓν πρὸς | ἡμᾶς γενόμενος τὰ ἡμέτερα οἰκειοῦται πάντα. κεφάλαιον δὲ τῶν ἡμετέρων ἀγαθῶν ἡ πρὸς τὸ θεῖόν ἐστιν ὑποταγή, ὅταν ὁμόφωνος πᾶσα ἡ κτίσις γένηται πρὸς ἑαυτὴν καὶ Πᾶν αὐτῷ γόνυ κάμψῃ ἐπουρανίων καὶ ἐπιγείων καὶ καταχθονίων καὶ πᾶσα γλῶσσα ἐξομολογήσηται ὅτι κύριος Ἰησοῦς Χριστός. Τότε πάσης τῆς κτίσεως ἓν σῶμα γενομένης καὶ πάντων διὰ τῆς ὑπακοῆς μετ᾽ ἀλλήλων ἐν αὐτῷ συμφυέντων, τὴν τοῦ ἰδίου σώματος πρὸς τὸν πατέρα ὑποταγὴν εἰς ἑαυτὸν ἀναφέρει.

Μηδεὶς δὲ ξενιζέσθω τῷ λεγομένῳ. καὶ γὰρ καὶ ἡμεῖς τὸ διὰ τοῦ σώματος ἡμῶν γινόμενον κατά τινα συνήθειαν τῇ ψυχῇ λογιζόμεθα, ὡς ὁ διαλεγόμενος ἐκεῖνος τῇ ἰδίᾳ ψυχῇ ἐπὶ τῇ εὐφορίᾳ τῆς χώρας, ὅτι Φάγε καὶ πίε καὶ εὐφραίνου, τὴν τῆς σαρκὸς πλησμονὴν εἰς τὴν ψυχὴν ἀναφέρει. οὕτω κἀκεῖ ἡ τοῦ ἐκκλησιαστικοῦ σώματος ὑποταγὴ ἀναφέρεται εἰς τὸν ἐνοικοῦντα τῷ σώματι.

GNO 21 Καὶ ἐπειδὴ πᾶν τὸ γενόμενον ἐν αὐτῷ σῴζεται, ἡ δὲ | σωτηρία διὰ τῆς ὑποταγῆς ἑρμηνεύεται, καθὼς ἡ ψαλμῳδία νοεῖν ὑποτίθεται, ἀκολούθως τὸ μηδὲν ἔξω τῶν σῳζομένων εἶναι πιστεύειν ἐν τῷ μέρει τούτῳ τοῦ ἀποστόλου μανθάνομεν. τοῦτο δὲ τῇ τοῦ θανάτου καθαιρέσει καὶ τῇ τοῦ υἱοῦ ὑποταγῇ διασημαίνει ὁ λόγος, διότι

---

[27]Gregory's reference here to the sharing (κοινωνία, *koinōnia*) of members in the body of Christ seems to have a eucharistic meaning.

[28]Paul's reference to the "subjection" of the Son to the Father at the end of the ages, in other words, is read here by Gregory as meaning that all creatures will be subject to Christ and united to him as members of his Body; Christ, as eternal Son,

what makes up the Body, in a way corresponding to each person's faith—and by doing this [Christ] builds up himself, as we have said, it should be clear through these images that by coming to be *in all*, he receives all *into himself*, united to him by sharing in his Body; and he makes all into members of his own Body, so that there are "many members, but one Body" (1 Cor 12.20).[27]

The one, then, who has united all of us to himself, and who is both united to us and has become one with us all in his relationship to us, makes everything that is ours his own. And the chief of all the blessings he bestows on us will be submission to God, when all creation comes to be in harmony with itself, and "Every knee will bend to him, of those in heaven and on earth and under the earth, and every tongue will confess that Jesus Christ is Lord" (Phil 2.10–11). Then, when all creation has become one body, and all have come together with each other in him by their obedience, he will offer to the Father the obedience of his own Body to himself.[28]

Let no one be put off by what we say. For we, too, by a kind of habit of speech, attribute what is experienced through our body to our soul—as that fellow [in the Gospel], in a sense of contentment with his situation, and saying to his own soul, "Eat and drink and enjoy yourself," refers the satisfaction of the flesh to his soul (Lk 12.19). So in this passage, the submission of the Body of the Church is referred to him who dwells in the Body.

And since the whole realm of becoming[29] will be saved in him, but salvation is signified by subjection, as the Psalms suggest,[30] we consequently have learned to believe that according to this passage of the Apostle, too, there will nothing outside the realm of what is saved. The Scripture makes this very clear in speaking both of the abolition of death[31] and the subjection of the Son, because these

will then in turn offer this universal subjection of his own Body to the Father, as part of his own filial unity with him.

[29]I.e., everything created.

[30]See above, section 2, where Gregory cites Psalms 59.8 and 61.1 as instances in which salvation is spoken of as subjection to God.

[31]See 1 Cor 15.26.

συμβαίνει ταῦτα πρὸς ἄλληλα, τό τε μὴ εἶναί ποτε τὸν θάνατον καὶ τὸ πάντας ἐν ζωῇ γενέσθαι· ζωὴ δὲ ὁ κύριος, δι᾽ οὗ γίνεται, κατὰ τὸν ἀποστολικὸν λόγον, παντὶ τῷ σώματι αὐτοῦ ἡ προσαγωγὴ πρὸς τὸν πατέρα,

Ὅταν παραδιδῷ τὴν βασιλείαν ἡμῶν τῷ θεῷ καὶ πατρί. σῶμα δὲ αὐτοῦ, καθὼς εἴρηται πολλάκις, πᾶσα ἡ ἀνθρωπίνη φύσις ᾗ κατεμίχθη.

Δι᾽ αὐτὸ δὲ τοῦτο τὸ νόημα καὶ Μεσίτης θεοῦ καὶ ἀνθρώπων ὠνομάσθη παρὰ τοῦ Παύλου ὁ κύριος. ὁ γὰρ ἐν τῷ πατρὶ ὢν καὶ ἐν ἀνθρώποις γενόμενος ἐν τούτῳ πληροῖ τὴν μεσιτείαν ἐν τῷ ἑαυτῷ πάντας ἑνῶσαι καὶ δι᾽ ἑαυτοῦ τῷ πατρί, καθώς φησιν ἐν τῷ εὐαγγελίῳ ὁ κύριος, πρὸς τὸν πατέρα τὸν λόγον ποιούμενος· Ἵνα πάντες ἓν ὦσι καθὼς σύ, πάτερ, ἐν ἐμοὶ κἀγὼ ἐν σοί, ἵνα οὕτω κἀκεῖνοι ἐν ἡμῖν ἓν ὦσιν. σαφῶς γὰρ τοῦτο παρίστησιν ὅτι ἑαυτῷ ἡμᾶς ἑνώσας ὁ ἐν τῷ πατρὶ ὢν δι᾽ ἑαυτοῦ τὴν πρὸς τὸν πατέρα συνάφειαν ἡμῶν ἀπεργάζεται.

Ἀλλὰ καὶ τὰ ἐφεξῆς τοῦ εὐαγγελίου συνᾴδει τοῖς εἰρημένοις· Τὴν
GNO 22 δόξαν ἣν δέδωκάς μοι δέδωκα αὐτοῖς· δόξαν | γὰρ ἐνταῦθα λέγειν αὐτὸν οἶμαι τὸ πνεῦμα τὸ ἅγιον ὃ ἔδωκε τοῖς μαθηταῖς διὰ τοῦ προσφυσήματος. οὐ γὰρ ἔστιν ἄλλως ἑνωθῆναι τοὺς ἀπ᾽ ἀλλήλων διεστηκότας μὴ τῇ ἑνότητι τοῦ πνεύματος συμφυομένους· Εἰ γάρ τις πνεῦμα Χριστοῦ οὐκ ἔχει, οὗτος οὐκ ἔστιν αὐτοῦ. τὸ δὲ πνεῦμα ἡ δόξα ἐστί, καθώς φησιν ἑτέρωθι πρὸς τὸν πατέρα· Δόξασόν με τῇ δόξῃ ᾗ εἶχον ἀπ᾽ ἀρχῆς παρὰ σοὶ πρὸ τοῦ τὸν κόσμον εἶναι. ὁ γὰρ θεὸς Λόγος ὁ πρὸ τοῦ κόσμου ἔχων τὴν τοῦ πατρὸς δόξαν, ἐπειδὴ ἐπ᾽ ἐσχάτων τῶν ἡμερῶν σὰρξ ἐγένετο, ἔδει [δὲ] καὶ τὴν

correspond to each other: that there will be no more death, and that all things will come to be in life. But the Lord is life, and through him access to the Father will be realized for his whole Body, according to the Apostle's words, "when he hands over his kingly power" over us "to God his Father" (1 Cor 15.24).[32] And his Body, as we have often said, is the whole of human nature, into which he has been mingled.

14 For this very consideration, too, the Lord is called by Paul "the Mediator of God and humanity" (1 Tim 2.5). For he who exists in the Father, and has come to be among human beings, fulfills the act of mediation in this very event: in unifying all to himself and through himself to the Father, as the Lord says in the Gospel, when addressing the Father, "That all may be one as you, Father, are in me and I in you, so that thus they, too, may be one in us" (Jn 17.21). For he makes this point clearly: that having united us to himself, the one who is in the Father has brought to fulfillment, through himself, our unity with the Father.

But what follows in the Gospel also agrees with what we have been saying: "The glory that you have given to me I have given to them" (Jn 17.22). For I think "glory" here means the Holy Spirit himself, which [Jesus] gave to the disciples by breathing on them.[33] For it is not possible for those who greatly differ from one another to be made one, except by growing together in the unity of the Spirit. "For if one does not have the Spirit of Christ, he does not belong to him" (Rom 8.9).[34] But the Spirit *is* glory, as [Jesus] says to his Father in another place: "Glorify me with the glory that I had with you from the beginning, before the world came to be" (Jn 17.5). For when God the Word, who possessed the Father's glory before there was a world, became flesh in the last days, the flesh, too, by mingling with the

[32]Gregory, of course, has added ἡμῶν (*hēmōn*)—"over us"—to the Pauline discussion of Christ's kingly power here.

[33]See Jn 20.22.

[34]Gregory seems to be thinking here first of the unification of alienated humans with *Christ* by the Spirit, which makes possible their unity with one another.

σάρκα διὰ τῆς πρὸς τὸν Λόγον ἀνακράσεως ἐκεῖνο γενέσθαι ὅπερ ὁ Λόγος ἐστίν· γίνεται δὲ ἐκ τοῦ ἐκεῖνο λαβεῖν ὃ πρὸ τοῦ κόσμου εἶχεν ὁ Λόγος· τοῦτο δὲ ἦν τὸ πνεῦμα τὸ ἅγιον· οὐδὲν γὰρ ἄλλο
PG 1321 προαιώνιον πλὴν πατρὸς καὶ υἱοῦ καὶ ἁγίου πνεύματος. διὰ | τοῦτο
καὶ ἐνταῦθά φησιν ὅτι Τὴν δόξαν ἣν δέδωκάς μοι δέδωκα αὐτοῖς, ἵνα δι' αὐτῆς ἐμοὶ ἑνωθῶσιν καὶ δι' ἐμοῦ σοί.

Ἴδωμεν δὲ καὶ τὰ ἐφεξῆς ἐν τῷ εὐαγγελίῳ προσκείμενα· Ἵνα ὦσιν ἓν καθὼς ἡμεῖς ἕν ἐσμεν· σὺ ἐν ἐμοὶ κἀγὼ ἐν αὐτοῖς· ὅτι ἐγὼ καὶ σὺ ἕν ἐσμεν· ἵνα ὦσι τετελειωμένοι εἰς τὸ ἕν. ταῦτα γὰρ οὐδεμιᾶς ἐπεξηγήσεως οἶμαι χρῄζειν πρὸς τὸ συναρμοσθῆναι τῷ προκειμένῳ νοήματι, αὐτῆς φανερῶς τῆς λέξεως τὸ περὶ τούτων δόγμα ἐκτιθεμένης.Ἵνα ὦσιν ἓν καθὼς ἡμεῖς ἕν ἐσμεν· οὐ γάρ ἐστι
GNO 23 δυνατὸν ἄλλως τοὺς | πάντας ἓν γενέσθαι Καθὼς ἡμεῖς ἐσμεν ἕν,
εἰ μὴ πάντων τῶν ἀπ' ἀλλήλων αὐτοὺς διαμεριζόντων χωρισθέντες ἑνωθεῖεν ἡμῖν οἵτινές ἐσμεν ἕν,Ἵνα ὦσιν ἓν καθὼς ἡμεῖς ἐσμεν ἕν. τοῦτο δὲ πῶς γίνεται; ὅτι Ἐγὼ ἐν αὐτοῖς. οὐ γάρ ἐστι δυνατὸν ἐμὲ γενέσθαι μόνον ἐν αὐτοῖς, ἀλλὰ πάντως καὶ σέ, ἐπειδὴ Ἐγὼ καὶ σὺ ἕν ἐσμεν. καὶ οὕτω γενήσονται Τετελειωμένοι εἰς τὸ ἓν οἱ ἐν ἡμῖν τελειωθέντες· ἡμεῖς γὰρ τὸ ἕν.

Τὴν δὲ τοιαύτην χάριν φανερώτερον διασημαίνει τῷ ἐφεξῆς λόγῳ οὕτως εἰπὼν ὅτι Ἠγάπησας αὐτοὺς καθὼς ἐμὲ ἠγάπησας. εἰ γὰρ ὁ πατὴρ ἀγαπᾷ τὸν υἱόν, ἐν δὲ τῷ υἱῷ πάντες γινόμεθα οἱ διὰ τῆς εἰς αὐτὸν πίστεως σῶμα αὐτοῦ γινόμενοι, ἀκολούθως ὁ τὸν υἱὸν ἑαυτοῦ ἀγαπῶν ἀγαπᾷ καὶ τοῦ υἱοῦ τὸ σῶμα ὡς αὐτὸν τὸν υἱόν· ἡμεῖς δὲ τὸ σῶμα. οὐκοῦν φανερὸν διὰ τῶν εἰρημένων γέγονε τὸ ἀποστολικὸν νόημα, ὅτι πάσης ἀνθρωπίνης φύσεως τὴν γινομένην τοῦ ὄντος ἐπίγνωσίν τε καὶ σωτηρίαν ἡ τοῦ υἱοῦ πρὸς τὸν πατέρα ὑποταγὴ διασημαίνει.

Word, had to become that which the Word is; and it becomes this by receiving that which the Word had before the world existed—and this was the Holy Spirit. For there was nothing else before the ages except Father and Son and Holy Spirit! That is the reason he says also here, "The glory that you have given to me I have given to them" (Jn 17.22), that through it they may be unified with me, and through me with you.

15 Let us consider, too, the passage that follows in the Gospel, "That they may be one just as we are one: you in me and I in them"—for I and you are one reality—"that they may be perfected into one" (Jn 17.21, 23).[35] For I think this needs no additional explanation to be seen as fitting together with the thought before us, since the very wording itself lays out its teaching on all of this clearly. "That they may be one just as we are one": for it is not possible for all people to become one "as we are one" any other way, unless, being separated from all those things that divide them from each other, they become one with us, who are truly one—"so that they may be one, just as we are one." And how will this come about? Because "I will be in them." For it is not possible simply for me alone to be in them; surely you must be in them, too, since "I and you are one" (Jn 10.30). So, too, those who will be perfected in us will be "perfected as one;" for *we* are one!

He indicates this grace even more clearly in the next verse, saying, "You have loved them as you have loved me" (Jn 17.23). For if the Father loves the Son, and if all of us, who through faith in him have become his Body, have come to be *in* the Son, it follows that he who loves his own Son also loves his Son's Body, as he loves the Son himself. But we are that Body. Thus the Apostle's thought, too, becomes clear through what is said [here]: that the subjection of the Son to the Father signifies the intuitive knowledge of reality and the salvation that has come to be a reality in all human nature.

[35]Gregory here develops his interpretation of Scripture's promise of universal salvation through unity with Christ and the whole Trinity, in a kind of running paraphrase of John 17 that interweaves and slightly expands a number of phrases and verses in the text.

Σαφέστερος δὲ γένοιτ᾽ ἂν ἡμῖν ὁ λόγος καὶ ἐξ ἑτέρων τινῶν
ἀποστολικῶν νοημάτων ἐξ ὧν ἑνὸς ἐπιμνησθήσομαι μόνου, τὰς
πολλὰς τῶν μαρτυριῶν, εὐλαβείᾳ τοῦ μὴ εἰς πλῆθος ἐκτεῖναι τὸν
λόγον, παραιτησάμενος. φησὶ γάρ που τῶν ἑαυτοῦ λόγων ὁ Παῦλος
GNO 24 ὅτι Χριστῷ συνεσταύρωμαι· ζῶ δὲ | οὐκέτι ἐγώ, ζῇ δὲ ἐν ἐμοὶ
Χριστός. οὐκοῦν εἰ μηκέτι ὁ Παῦλος ζῇ ὁ τῷ κόσμῳ σταυρωθείς,
ἀλλ᾽ ὁ Χριστὸς ἐν αὐτῷ ζῇ, πᾶν τὸ παρὰ τοῦ Παύλου γινόμενόν τε
καὶ λεγόμενον εἰκότως εἰς τὸν ἐν αὐτῷ ζῶντα Χριστὸν ἀναφέρεται.
καὶ γὰρ τὰ ῥήματα τοῦ Παύλου παρὰ τοῦ Χριστοῦ λαλεῖσθαί
φησιν ὁ εἰπών·Ἢ δοκιμὴν ζητεῖτε τοῦ ἐν ἐμοὶ λαλοῦντος Χριστοῦ;
καὶ τὰ εὐαγγελικὰ κατορθώματα οὐκ αὐτοῦ φησιν εἶναι ἀλλὰ τῇ
χάριτι τοῦ Χριστοῦ τῇ οἰκούσῃ ἐν αὐτῷ ἀνατίθησιν. εἰ τοίνυν ὁ ἐν
αὐτῷ ζῶν Χριστὸς ἐνεργεῖν τε καὶ φθέγγεσθαι τὰ ἐκείνου κατὰ τὸ
ἀκόλουθον λέγεται, πάντων δὲ ἀποστὰς ὁ Παῦλος τῶν πρότερον
ἐπικρατούντων, ὅτε ἦν βλάσφημος καὶ διώκτης καὶ ὑβριστής, πρὸς
μόνον τὸ ἀληθινὸν ἀγαθὸν βλέπει καὶ τούτῳ ἑαυτὸν ποιεῖ εὐπειθῆ
καὶ ὑπήκοον, ἄρα καὶ ἡ ὑποταγὴ τοῦ Παύλου ἡ πρὸς τὸν θεὸν
γενομένη εἰς τὸν ἐν αὐτῷ ζῶντα τὴν ἀναφορὰν ἔχει ὃς καὶ λαλεῖ ἐν
τῷ Παύλῳ τὰ ἀγαθὰ καὶ ἐργάζεται. ἀγαθῶν δὲ πάντων κεφάλαιον
ἡ πρὸς τὸν θεόν ἐστιν ὑποταγή.

Ὃ δὲ ἐπὶ τοῦ ἑνὸς εὗρεν ὁ λόγος, τοῦτο καὶ πάσῃ τῇ κτίσει
PG 1324 τῶν ἀνθρώπων εὐλόγως ἐφαρμοσθήσεται, ὅταν, κα|θώς φησιν ὁ
κύριος, ἐν παντὶ τῷ κόσμῳ τὸ εὐαγγέλιον γένηται. Πάντων γὰρ
ἀποθεμένων τὸν παλαιὸν ἄνθρωπον σὺν ταῖς πράξεσι καὶ ταῖς
ἐπιθυμίαις αὐτοῦ καὶ δεξαμένων ἐν αὐτοῖς τὸν κύριον, ἀναγκαίως
GNO 25 ὁ ἐν αὐτοῖς ζῶν ἐνεργεῖ τὰ ἀγαθὰ τὰ παρ᾽ ἐκείνων | γινόμενα. τὸ
δὲ ἀκρότατον τῶν ἀγαθῶν πάντων ἡ σωτηρία ἡ διὰ τῆς τοῦ κακοῦ
ἀλλοτριώσεως ἡμῖν γινομένη· ἀλλὰ μὴν οὐκ ἔστιν ἄλλως τοῦ
κακοῦ χωρισθῆναι μὴ τῷ θεῷ διὰ τῆς ὑποταγῆς ἀνακραθέντας·
ἄρα καὶ αὐτὴ ἡ πρὸς τὸν θεὸν ὑποταγὴ εἰς τὸν ἐν ἡμῖν ζῶντα τὴν

16 The argument might become clearer for us on the basis of several other of the Apostle's thoughts, of which I will recall only one, passing over most of these testimonies out of concern not to make our discourse too long. Paul says, in one of his other writings, "I am crucified along with Christ; and I live—no longer I, but Christ lives in me" (Gal 2.19–20). If Paul, then no longer lives—he who is "crucified to the world" (Gal 6.14)—but Christ lives in him, then everything that is done and said by Paul is properly referred to Christ, who lives in him. So, for example, he says the words of Paul are being spoken by Christ, saying: "Do you seek a proof that Christ is the one speaking in me?" (2 Cor 13.3) And he says that the commands of the gospel are not his own,[36] but he refers them to the grace of Christ dwelling in him. If, then, Christ, living in him, is said to be at work, and accordingly to be speaking his own words in him, and if Paul distances himself from the things that had previously dominated him, when he was a blasphemer and a persecutor and a man of pride,[37] but he is looking only toward the true Good and is making himself obedient to this, subject to this—then surely the submission to God that has taken place in Paul refers to the one who "lives in him," who also speaks and works what is good in Paul. And the chief source of all good things is submission to God.

And what has been found to hold for one individual, Scripture very properly will apply to the whole of human creation, when, as the Lord says, "the gospel will come to be preached in the whole world" (Mt 24.14). And when all have "put off the old man with his practices and his desires" (Col 3.9; Eph 4.22), and have received the Lord in themselves, necessarily the one who lives in them will accomplish the good things that come about by their efforts. And the chief of all good things is salvation, which comes about in us by our distancing ourselves from evil; but surely it is impossible to be separated from evil in any other way than by being mingled with God through subjection. But clearly also, this subjection to God refers to the one who

[36]See 1 Cor 7.10–11.
[37]See 1 Cor 15.9; Gal 1.13.

ἀναφορὰν ἔχει. Εἴ τι, γάρ, καλόν, αὐτοῦ καὶ εἴ τι ἀγαθόν, παρ' αὐτοῦ, φησί τις τῶν προφητῶν. ἐπεὶ οὖν καλόν τε καὶ ἀγαθὸν ἡ ὑποταγὴ ἀνεδείχθη ἐκείνου, καὶ τούτου τὸ ἀγαθὸν πάντως παρ' οὗ παντὸς ἀγαθοῦ φύσις, ὡς ὁ τοῦ προφήτου λόγος.

Μηδεὶς δὲ πρὸς τὴν κοινὴν κατάχρησιν τοῦ τῆς ὑποταγῆς ὀνόματος βλέπων ἀθετείτω τὸ ὄνομα. οἶδε γὰρ ἡ σοφία τοῦ μεγάλου Παύλου πρὸς τὸ δοκοῦν κεχρῆσθαι κατ' ἐξουσίαν τοῖς ῥήμασι, καὶ τῷ ἰδίῳ τῆς διανοίας εἱρμῷ προσαρμόζειν τὰς τῶν ῥημάτων ἐμφάσεις, κἂν πρὸς ἄλλας τινὰς ἐννοίας ἡ συνήθεια τὴν κατάχρησιν τῶν λέξεων φέρῃ. ἐπεὶ πόθεν εἴληπται αὐτῷ ἡ τοῦ Ἐκένωσεν ἑαυτὸν χρῆσις, καὶ Τὸ καύχημά μου οὐδεὶς κενώσει, καὶ τὸ Κεκένωται ἡ πίστις, καὶ Ἵνα μὴ κενωθῇ ὁ σταυρὸς τοῦ Χριστοῦ; ἐκ ποίας ταῦτα χρήσεως εἰς τὸν ἑαυτοῦ παρεδέξατο λόγον; τίς δὲ κρινεῖ αὐτὸν εἰπόντα ὅτι Ὁμειρόμενοι ὑμῶν, δι' ἧς λέξεως τὴν ἀγαπητικὴν ἐνδείκνυται σχέσιν; πόθεν δὲ τὸ ἀνυπερήφανον τῆς ἀγάπης διὰ τῆς τοῦ μὴ περπερεύεσθαι λέξεως ἐνεδείξατο; ἡ δὲ ἐριστικὴ καὶ ἀμυντικὴ φιλονεικία, πῶς τῷ τῆς ἐριθείας παρ' αὐτοῦ
GNO 26 σημαίνεται ῥήματι, φανεροῦ πᾶσιν ὄντος ὅτι ἐκ | τῆς ἐριουργίας ἡ ἔριθος ἐκ<τὸς> τῆς γραφῆς ὀνομάζεται καὶ τὴν περὶ τὰ ἔρια σπουδὴν τῷ ὀνόματι τῆς ἐριθείας σημαίνειν εἰώθαμεν; ἀλλ' ὅμως χαίρειν ἐάσας ὁ Παῦλος τὰς ἐτυμολογίας τὰς ψυχρὰς δι' ὧν βούλεται λέξεων ὃ βούλεται παρίστησι νόημα. καὶ γὰρ καὶ ἄλλα

[38]Zech 9.17 (LXX). Gregory is taking this quotation from the Septuagint of Zechariah—which is, in any case, somewhat different in sense from the Hebrew text—out of its context, where, in an oracle of the eschatological salvation promised by God, the text says, "If there is anything fine of his [i.e., God's], anything good from him, there will be grain for the young men and gladsome wine for the young women."

[39]Gregory now turns to Paul's sometimes creative use of the Greek language as background for his interpretation of what Paul means by "subjection" (ὑποταγή,

lives within us. "For if there is anything fine, it is his, and if there is anything good, it is from him," one of the prophets says (Zech 9.17).[38] Since, then, submission to him has been shown to be fine and good, then surely this good is his, from whom the nature of all good comes, as the prophet's word tells us.

17 And no one, thinking of the normal meaning of the word "subjection," should reject the word [as it is used here]. For in his wisdom, the great Paul was capable of using words as he chose, in contrast to their seeming meaning, and to fit the meaning of his phrases to the particular sequence of his thought, even if custom should point the significance of his language in the direction of other meanings.[39] Where, for instance, does he take his usage of "empty" from, in "He emptied himself" (Phil 2.7), and in "No one will make empty my boast" (1 Cor 9.15), and "Faith is empty" (Rom 4.14), and "In order that the cross of Christ not be made empty [of meaning]" (1 Cor 1.17)? From what kind of idiomatic usage did he take these into his own vocabulary? Who will judge him negatively for saying "We long for you" (1 Thess 2.8)—a phrase meant to indicate a loving relationship? How does he come to indicate the humility of love by saying, "it does not brag" (1 Cor 13.4)?[40] And as for quarrelsome and defensive competitiveness, how does this come to be signified in his writings by the expression "partisan efforts" (ἐριθεία, *eritheia*),[41] when everybody knows that outside Scripture the word "efforts" is taken from the weaver's trade, and we normally signify the labor of weaving wool by this word? Nevertheless, Paul does not concern himself much for frigid etymologies, but presents the thought he wants to communicate through the expressions he chooses to use. And

hypotagē). Perhaps more than Gregory realizes, Paul's use of Greek terms is biblical and Semitic.

[40]Greek: οὐ περπερεύεται (*ou perpereuetai*). This is another rare verbal form in Greek, based on the equally rare noun πέρπερος (*perperos*), "braggart."

[41]Greek: ἐριθεία (*eritheia*). As Gregory observes, this word, which appears twice in the New Testament in the sense of "competitiveness," normally simply means "hard work," "committed effort" in Greek, and is apparently derived from the terminology of weaving.

πολλὰ τοῖς ἀκριβῶς ἐξετάζουσιν εὑρεθείη ἂν ἐν τοῖς λόγοις τοῦ ἀποστόλου μὴ δουλεύοντα τῇ χρήσει τῆς συνηθείας, ἀλλὰ κατά τινα ἰδιότροπον ἔννοιαν ἐπ' ἐξουσίας παρ' αὐτοῦ προφερόμενα μηδὲν ἐπιστρεφομένου πρὸς τὴν συνήθειαν.

Οὕτω τοίνυν καὶ ἐνταῦθα τὸ τῆς ὑποταγῆς σημαινόμενον ἄλλο τι παρὰ τὰς κοινὰς ἐννοίας ὑπὸ τοῦ Παύλου νενόηται. ἀπόδειξις δὲ τοῦ λόγου ὅτι οὐδὲ ἡ ἐν τῷ μέρει τούτῳ τῶν παρ' αὐτοῦ μνημονευθέντων ἐχθρῶν ὑποταγὴ τὸ κατηναγκασμένον τε καὶ ἀκούσιον ἔχει, καθὼς ἂν εἴποιεν οἱ τῇ συνηθείᾳ δουλεύοντες, ἀλλὰ σαφῶς ἐπ' αὐτῶν ἡ σωτηρία τῷ ὀνόματι τῆς ὑποταγῆς ἑρμηνεύεται· τεκμήριον δὲ τὸ διεστάλθαι κατὰ τὸ μέρος τοῦτο ὑπὸ τοῦ Παύλου τὸ τῆς ἔχθρας ὄνομα εἰς διπλῆν σημασίαν· τῶν γὰρ ἐχθρῶν, τοὺς μὲν ὑποταγήσεσθαι λέγει, τοὺς δὲ καταργηθήσεσθαι. καταργεῖται μὲν οὖν ὁ τῇ φύσει ἐχθρός, τουτέστι ὁ θάνατος, καὶ
PG 1325 ἡ περὶ αὐτὸν τῆς ἁμαρτίας ἀρχή τε | καὶ ἐξουσία καὶ δύναμις. ὑποταγήσονται δὲ οἱ καθ' ἕτερον λόγον ἐχθροὶ τοῦ θεοῦ λεγόμενοι,
GNO 27 οἱ ἀπὸ τῆς | βασιλείας πρὸς τὴν ἁμαρτίαν αὐτομολήσαντες, ὧν καὶ ἐν τῷ πρὸς Ῥωμαίους μέμνηται λόγῳ εἰπὼν ὅτι Εἰ γὰρ ἐχθροὶ ὄντες κατηλλάγημεν τῷ θεῷ· τὴν γὰρ ἐνταῦθα ὑποταγὴν ἐκεῖ καταλλαγὴν ὀνομάζει, ἓν νόημα δι' ἑκατέρου τῶν ὀνομάτων ἐνδειξάμενος τὴν σωτηρίαν. ὧς γὰρ ἐκ τῆς ὑποταγῆς τὸ σωθῆναι προσγίνεται, οὕτω καὶ ἐν ἑτέρῳ φησὶν ὅτι Καταλλαγέντες σωθησόμεθα ἐν τῇ ζωῇ αὐτοῦ. τοὺς μὲν οὖν τοιούτους ἐχθροὺς ὑποτάσσεσθαι λέγει τῷ θεῷ καὶ πατρί, τὸν δὲ θάνατον καὶ τὴν περὶ αὐτὸν ἀρχὴν μηκέτι ἔσεσθαι. τοῦτο γὰρ ἐνδείκνυται ἡ τοῦ καταργηθήσεσθαι λέξις· ὡς διὰ τούτου γενέσθαι δῆλον ὅτι τῶν μὲν κακῶν ἡ δυναστεία εἰς τὸ παντελὲς ἐξαργηθήσεται. οἱ δὲ διὰ τῆς παρακοῆς ἐχθροὶ τοῦ θεοῦ κληθέντες, οὗτοι διὰ τῆς ὑποταγῆς φίλοι τοῦ κυρίου γενήσονται, ὅταν πεισθῶσι τῷ λέγοντι ὅτι Ὑπὲρ Χριστοῦ πρεσβεύομεν, ὡς τοῦ θεοῦ παρακαλοῦντος δι' ἡμῶν· δεόμεθα ὑπὲρ Χριστοῦ, καταλλάγητε τῷ θεῷ, καὶ κατὰ τὴν γενομένην ἐν τῷ εὐαγγελίῳ

indeed, many other examples could be found in the writings of the Apostle by careful researchers, which are not enslaved to customary usage, but are uttered by him authoritatively, with an idiosyncratic meaning, without his paying much regard to convention.

So, then, also in this case the language of "subjection" is understood by Paul as signifying something else than its common set of meanings. Proof of this point is that not even the "subjection" of the "enemies" he refers to in this passage has anything constrained or unwilling implied in it, as the slaves of customary meaning might argue, but clearly *salvation* for these enemies, too, is what is signified by the term "subjection." The evidence is the fact that, in this passage, the term "enemy" is distinguished by Paul into two senses; he speaks of some enemies being "made subject," and of others being annihilated. On the one hand, the enemy of human nature—that is, death—will be abolished, along with the cause and power and force that surrounds it, which is sin. But others also will be "subjected," who are called God's enemies in a different sense: those who have deserted from his kingdom to commit themselves to sin, whom he refers to in his Letter to the Romans when he says, "If, when we were enemies, we were reconciled to God" (Rom 5.10). For what he calls here "subjection" he there names "reconciliation," signifying by both terms the one idea, which is salvation. For as salvation is the final result of subjection, so in the other passage [in Romans] he says, "Being reconciled, we will be saved through his life" (Rom 5.10). Enemies of this kind he says, in one place, will be "subjected" to God the Father, and death and the domination it brings will cease to be. For this is what the term "will be annihilated" (1 Cor 15.26) signifies—so that from this it will become clear that domination by evil will completely lose its force. And those who are called "enemies of God" because of their disobedience will become friends of the Lord through subjection [to him], when they believe the word of the one who proclaims, "We are ambassadors for Christ, as if God were pleading through us, 'We beg on Christ's behalf, be reconciled with God!'" (2 Cor 5.20) And as is promised in the Gospel, those

ὑπόσχεσιν οὐκέτι ἐν τοῖς δούλοις ὑπὸ τοῦ κυρίου ἀλλ' ἐν τοῖς φίλοις καταλλαγέντες ἀριθμηθήσονται.

Τὸ δὲ Δεῖ γὰρ αὐτὸν βασιλεύειν, ἕως ἂν θῇ τοὺς ἐχθροὺς ὑπὸ τοὺς πόδας αὐτοῦ, εὐσεβῶς, ὡς οἶμαι, παραδεξόμεθα τὸ ἀριστεύειν αὐτὸν διὰ τοῦ βασιλεύειν νοήσαντες. τότε γὰρ παύεται τῆς ἀριστείας ὁ δυνατὸς ἐν πολέμῳ, ὅταν ἀφανισθῇ πᾶν τὸ τῷ ἀγαθῷ ἀντικείμενον, ὅταν πᾶσαν τὴν ἑαυτοῦ βασιλείαν συναγαγὼν προσαγάγῃ τῷ θεῷ καὶ πατρί, πρὸς ἑαυτὸν ἑνώσας
GNO 28 τὰ πάντα. τὸ γὰρ παραδοῦναι αὐτὸν τῷ πατρὶ | τὴν βασιλείαν ταὐτόν ἐστι κατὰ τὴν διάνοιαν τῷ προσαγαγεῖν τοὺς πάντας τῷ θεῷ, δι' οὗ ἔχομεν τὴν προσαγωγὴν ἐν ἑνὶ πνεύματι πρὸς τὸν πατέρα. πάντων τοίνυν τῶν ποτε ἐχθρῶν ὑποπόδιον τῶν ποδῶν τοῦ θεοῦ γενομένων ἐν τῷ δέξασθαι τὸ θεῖον ἴχνος ἐν ἑαυτοῖς, καὶ τοῦ θανάτου καταργηθέντος (μὴ γὰρ ὄντων τῶν ἀποθνῃσκόντων οὐδὲ ὁ θάνατος ἔσται πάντως), τότε ἐν τῇ πάντων ἡμῶν ὑποταγῇ, ἥτις οὐχὶ δουλικὴ νοεῖται ταπεινότης ἀλλὰ βασιλεία καὶ ἀφθαρσία καὶ μακαριότης, ὁ ἐν ἡμῖν ζῶν ὑποταγήσεσθαι τῷ θεῷ παρὰ τοῦ Παύλου λέγεται, ὁ τὸ ἀγαθὸν ἡμῶν δι' ἑαυτοῦ τελειῶν καὶ ποιῶν ἑαυτῷ ἐν ἡμῖν τὸ εὐάρεστον.

Ταῦτα κατὰ τὸ μέτρον τῆς διανοίας ἡμῶν ἐκ τῆς μεγάλης τοῦ Παύλου σοφίας, ὅσον ἐχωροῦμεν, ἐν τῷ μέρει τούτῳ κατενοήσαμεν, δεῖξαι βουλόμενοι τὸ μὴ ἐπεσκέφθαι τοὺς τῶν αἱρετικῶν δογμάτων προστάτας τὸν τοῦ ἀποστόλου σκοπὸν πρὸς ὃν βλέπων τὸν παρόντα λόγον πεποίηται. εἰ μὲν οὖν αὐτάρκης σοι γέγονεν ἡ ἐπὶ τῷ ζητήματι τούτῳ πληροφορία διὰ τῶν εἰρημένων, εἰς τὸν θεὸν ἀνακτέον τὴν χάριν· εἰ δέ τι καὶ λείπειν σοι φαίνοιτο, δεξόμεθα ἐν προθυμίᾳ τὴν τοῦ λείποντος ἀναπλήρωσιν, εἴπερ ἡμῖν παρὰ σοῦ τε γνωρισθείη διά τοῦ γράμματος καὶ παρὰ τοῦ ἁγίου πνεύματος φανερωθείη διὰ τῶν εὐχῶν ἡμῶν ἡ τῶν κρυφίων φανέρωσις.

---

[42]Jn 15.14–15.

[43]Gregory may be referring here to the "seal" or mark of baptism.

[44]Here, at the conclusion of his essay, Gregory for the first time addresses the unnamed recipient directly. Significantly, he speaks to him or her in the second per-

reconciled by the Lord will no longer be counted among his servants, but among his friends.[42]

18 And we will be reverently taking the phrase, "He must reign until he puts his enemies under his feet" (1 Cor 15.25), I think, if we understand that by "reign" here Paul means "be dominant." For the one who is "mighty in battle" (Ps 23.8) will cease from his domination when all that opposes the Good vanishes, when he gathers all his Kingdom together and presents it to God his Father, after uniting all things to himself. For his "handing the Kingdom over to the Father" means the same thing as leading all people to God: "through him we have access in one Spirit to the Father" (Eph 2.18). When all, then, who were formerly enemies have become "footstools of God's feet" (see Ps 109.1) by receiving in themselves God's footprint,[43] and when death is annihilated (for if those destined for death no longer exist, surely death will no longer exist, either), then in the subjection of us all—which is no longer understood as servile humility, but royal rule and incorruptibility and blessedness—the one who lives in us will be, in Paul's words, "subject to God," bringing our good to perfection through himself, and creating what is well pleasing to himself in us.

This is what we have come to understand in this passage of the great Paul's wisdom, as far as we are able, according to the limits of our intelligence. We have intended to show that the purveyors of heretical teaching have not had the intention of the Apostle in view, which he was aiming at when he wrote the present text. If you[44] have found convincing reassurance on the subject of our investigation through what we have said, thanks are due to God; but if something seems to you to be missing, we will eagerly receive suggestions to fill out what is lacking—in the hope that the revelation of hidden mysteries might be extended to us: by you in writing, and by the Holy Spirit through our prayers.

son singular, suggesting that the work, like a number of his more specialized theological treatises, was originally intended for one correspondent, rather than delivered as an address to a more general audience.

An Oration on the Holy Pascha
(*In sanctum Pascha III*)

A Note on the Text

Five homilies connected with the feast of Easter are attributed to Gregory; this one is usually published as Homily 3. Of the other four, the "first"—sometimes called *De tridui spatio*—is a discourse dealing with the question of how to understand Jesus' time in the tomb as genuinely constituting "three days," and the short "fourth" homily is usually taken to be the concluding section of that same discourse. What appears as Gregory's "second" Paschal homily in the PG is in fact Severus of Antioch's Homily 77; and the "fifth" is now thought to be a work of the "other Cappadocian," Amphilochius of Iconium, who was Gregory Nazianzen's cousin. Thus only this present work appears to be a genuine Paschal homily by Gregory of Nyssa. Daniélou and Bernardi date it as delivered on Easter Sunday (April 21), 379; Misago suggests a date of about 382 (see Maraval, "Chronology of Works," *The Brill Dictionary of Gregory of Nyssa,* 162).

The Greek text I have translated here is edited critically by Ernst Gebhardt, in *Gregorii Nysseni Opera* IX [= Sermones, Pars I] (Leiden: Brill, 1967), 245–70. It was translated into English previously by Stuart G. Hall, in *The Easter Sermons of Gregory of Nyssa*, Patristic Monograph Series 9 (Winchendon, MA: Philadelphia Patristic Foundation, 1981), 5–23. I have added section numbers to this translation, for convenience in reference.

GNO IX:245 PG 46:652

ΓΡΗΓΟΡΙΟΥ ΕΠΙΣΚΟΠΟΥ ΝΥΣΣΗΣ ΛΟΓΟΣ ΕΙΣ ΤΟ ΑΓΙΟΝ ΠΑΣΧΑ

Οἱ πένητες τῶν ἀνθρώπων φιλέορτοι δὲ καὶ προθύμῳ τῇ ψυχῇ καὶ
γαύρῳ τῷ σχήματι τὰς πανηγύρεις κατασπαζόμενοι, κἂν οἴκοθεν
ἑαυτοῖς μὴ ἐπαρκῶσιν εἰς τὴν σπουδαζομένην φαιδρότητα, παρὰ
τῶν οἰκείων καὶ γνωρίμων πᾶσαν πολυτέλειαν συνερανιζόμενοι
ἀνενδεεῖς ἑαυτοὺς εἰς τὴν προκειμένην χρείαν παρασκευάζουσιν.
ὅπερ δοκῶ μοι πρὸς τὴν παροῦσαν ἡμέραν πάσχειν ἐγώ· οὐδὲν
PG 653 γὰρ ἔχων μεγαλοπρεπὲς ἐν ταῖς | προκειμέναις εὐφημίαις παρ᾽
ἐμαυτοῦ συντελεῖν πρὸς τὴν ἱερὰν ᾠδήν, ἣν ἀρτίως ᾔσαμεν,
καταφεύξομαι. ἐκεῖθεν δὲ ταῖς ἀφορμαῖς χρησάμενος ἀποτίσω τὸ
χρέος τῇ γραφικῇ λέξει προσυφήνας καὶ τὰ ἐμά, εἴ τινα ἄρα καὶ
τυγχάνει παρὰ τῷ πένητι δούλῳ τῆς εἰς τὸν δεσπότην εὐχαριστίας
ἐγκώμια. ἔλεγε τοίνυν ἀρτίως ὁ Δαβὶδ καὶ ἡμεῖς μετ᾽ ἐκείνου·
Αἰνεῖτε τὸν κύριον πάντα τὰ ἔθνη, ἐπαινέσατε αὐτὸν πάντες
οἱ λαοί. πάντα τὸν ἐξ Ἀδὰμ ἄνθρωπον πρὸς τὸν ὕμνον καλεῖ
GNO 146 μηδένα | καταλιμπάνων ἔξω τῆς κλήσεως, ἀλλὰ τοὺς ἑσπερίους,
τοὺς ἑῴους, τοὺς παρ᾽ ἑκάτερα, εἴ τις τῆς ἄρκτου γείτων καὶ
τῆς μεσημβρίας ἔνοικος, ὁμοῦ πάντας δημαγωγεῖ τῷ ψαλμῷ. καὶ
ἀλλαχοῦ μὲν ἀπὸ μέρους τισὶ τῶν ἀνθρώπων προσδιαλέγεται
ἢ τοὺς ὁσίους καλῶν ἢ τοὺς παῖδας πρὸς ὕμνον ἐγείρων, ἐπὶ δὲ
τοῦ παρόντος ἔθνη καὶ λαοὺς τῷ ψαλτηρίῳ συνάγει. ὅταν γὰρ
κατὰ τὸν ἀπόστολον παρέλθῃ τὸ σχῆμα τοῦ κόσμου τούτου,
βασιλεὺς δὲ καὶ θεὸς ἐπιφανῇ πᾶσιν Χριστὸς πᾶσαν ψυχὴν ἄπιστον
πληροφορήσας καὶ γλῶσσαν βλάσφημον χαλινώσας, στήσῃ

An Oration on the Holy Pascha
(*In sanctum Pascha III*)

1 The poor among us love festivals, and welcome solemn celebrations with eager souls and splendid costumes; even if privately they cannot afford the high style they are attempting to display, they collect whatever money they need by borrowing from family and friends, and put themselves in debt for the occasion at hand. I seem to be having the same experience with regard to this present day. For having nothing impressive of my own to contribute in this present oration, I will take refuge in the words of the sacred song we have just sung. Taking my start there, I plan to fulfill my obligation by weaving my own words into those of Scripture, hoping that there perhaps may be some words of praise in the heart of this poor servant that will express my thanks to the Lord. David, after all, has said, and we have just sung with him: "Praise the Lord, all you nations; praise him, all you peoples!" (Ps 116.1) He calls on every human being descended from Adam to join the hymn, and leaves no one out of his invitation. He calls those from the West, those from the East, those on all sides—any neighbor from the north, any resident from the south—and brings all of them together in the Psalm. In other passages, he will address some people separately, calling on the holy ones[1] or arousing children[2] to join the hymn; but in this present Psalm, he brings all "the nations and the peoples" together with his lyre.

For when, in the Apostle's words, "the shape of this world passes away" (1 Cor 7.31), and Christ appears as King and God of all, assuring every unbelieving soul and restraining every blasphemous

[1]Ps 149.1.
[2]Ps 8.2.

δὲ Ἑλλήνων τὴν ματαιότητα καὶ Ἰουδαίων τὴν πλάνην καὶ τῶν
αἱρέσεων τὴν ἀδάμαστον γλωσσαλγίαν, τότε δὴ, τότε πάντα τὰ
ἔθνη καὶ οἱ ἀπ᾽ αἰῶνος λαοὶ ὑποκύψαντες ἄμαχον τὴν προσκύνησιν
ἀναπέμψουσι καὶ θαυμαστή τις ἔσται συμφωνία δοξολογίας
τῶν μὲν ὁσίων συνήθως ὑμνούντων τῶν δὲ ἀσεβῶν ἐξ ἀνάγκης
ἱκετευόντων· καὶ τότε ἀληθῶς ὁ ἐπινίκιος ὕμνος συμφώνως παρὰ
πάντων ᾀσθήσεται καὶ τῶν κρατηθέντων καὶ τῶν νικησάντων·
τότε καὶ ὁ τῆς ταραχῆς ὑπαίτιος, ὁ τὴν τοῦ δεσπότου φαντασθεὶς
ἀξίαν μαστιγίας οἰκέτης ὀφθήσεται πᾶσι παρ᾽ ἀγγέλων πρὸς τὴν
τιμωρίαν συρόμενος καὶ πάντες οἱ τῆς ἐκείνου κακίας ὑπηρέται καὶ
συνεργοὶ ταῖς πρεπούσαις κολάσεσι καὶ δικαίαις ὑποβληθήσονται,
εἷς δὲ φανήσεται βασιλεὺς καὶ κριτὴς κοινὸς δεσπότης παρὰ
πάντων ὁμολογούμενος, ἡσυχία δὲ ἔσται κατεσταλμένη, ὥσπερ
ὅταν ἄρχοντος ἐπὶ βήματος καθημένου ὁ μὲν κήρυξ ὑποσημαίνῃ
τὴν σιωπήν, οἱ λαοὶ δὲ καὶ ὄψιν καὶ ἀκοὴν συντείναντες τὴν τῆς
GNO 247 δημηγορίας ἀκρόασιν | ἀναμένωσιν. διὰ τοῦτο Αἰνεῖτε τὸν κύριον
πάντα τὰ ἔθνη, ἐπαινέσατε αὐτὸν πάντες οἱ λαοί. αἰνέσατε ὡς
δυνατόν, ἐπαινέσατε ὡς φιλάνθρωπον, ὅτι πεσόντας καὶ νεκροὺς
ὄντας αὖθις ἐζωοποίησε καὶ τὸ πονέσαν σκεῦος ἀνενεώσατο πάλιν
καὶ τὴν ἐν τοῖς τάφοις τῶν λειψάνων ἀηδίαν εἰς ζῷον ἄφθαρτον
φιλανθρώπως ἐμόρφωσε καὶ ψυχὴν τὴν πρὸ [τεσσάρων] χιλιάδων
ἐτῶν καταλιποῦσαν τὸ σῶμα ὡς ἐκ μακρᾶς ἀποδημίας εἰς <τὴν>
ἰδίαν οἰκίαν ἐπανήγαγεν οὐδὲν ἀπὸ χρόνου καὶ λήθης ξενιζομένην
πρὸς τὸ ἴδιον ὄργανον, ἀλλὰ θᾶττον ἐπ᾽ αὐτὸ χωροῦσαν ἢ ὄρνις
ἐπὶ τὴν καλιὰν τὴν οἰκείαν καθίπταται.

PG 656 Εἴπωμεν γὰρ τὰ οἰκεῖα τῆς ἑορτῆς, ἵνα ἀκολούθως | καὶ
προσφυῶς τοῖς πράγμασιν ἑορτάσωμεν· τὸ γὰρ ἀνοίκειον καὶ
ἀλλότριον πρὸς τῷ μηδὲν ὠφελεῖν ἄτακτόν ἐστι καὶ ἀλλόκοτον
οὐκ ἐν τοῖς περὶ θρησκείας καὶ εὐσεβείας λόγοις μόνον, ἀλλὰ καὶ ἐπὶ

tongue; when he puts a stop to the foolishness of the Greeks, the deviant thinking of the Jews, and the irrepressible chatter of the heretical sects; then indeed, and only then, will all the nations and the peoples of ancient times bow low and offer up unchallenged adoration, and there will be a wondrous common hymn of praise, as the saints lift up their song with one heart, and even sinners will be forced to join them as suppliants. Then truly the hymn of victory will be sung in unison by all—by the conquered and the victors! Then even the one responsible for discord, who imagined the rank of lordship for himself, will be recognized by all as a slave who needs a whipping, dragged forward by the angels for punishment, and all his lackeys and the collaborators in his wickedness will be subjected to appropriate and just punishment. One will then appear as King and Judge, acknowledged in common by all as the Lord; and calm will settle on all, as when, with the ruler seated on his throne, the herald signals silence, and the people strain eyes and ears, ready to listen to his public address. Therefore, "Praise the Lord, all you nations; praise him, all you peoples!" (Ps 116.1) Sing out to him as powerful, sing out to him as loving, because when we were fallen and dead he brought us to life again; he has again renewed the worn-out vessel, and the corruption of bodies in the tombs he has generously transformed into incorruptible life; the soul that abandoned its body thousands of years[3] ago he has brought home, as from a long journey—not estranged at all, by time or forgetfulness, from its proper instrument, but rushing to it more quickly than a bird descends to its own nest.

2 Let us speak, then, of what is proper to this feast, so that we may celebrate in a way appropriate and suitable to the events. For what is inappropriate and foreign, in addition to being of no help to us, is out of order and absurd—not only in discourses dealing with religion and piety, but even on secular subjects that reflect the

[3]The Greek manuscripts have "forty thousand years," but Gebhardt, the editor, has omitted the word signifying the multiplier of four, because of a later, apparently parallel, reference in section 5 simply to "thousands of years."

τῶν ἔξωθεν καὶ τῆς τοῦ κόσμου σοφίας. τίς γὰρ οὕτως ἀνόητος καὶ ὑπεργέλοιος ῥήτωρ, ὡς κληθεὶς εἰς φαιδρότητα γάμου ἀποστῆναι μὲν τῶν ἁρμοδίων λόγων καὶ γλαφυρῶν συνευπαθούντων ταῖς τῆς πανηγύρεως χάρισι, γοερὰ δὲ μέλη θρηνεῖν καὶ τὰ ἐκ τραγῳδίας κακὰ τῶν παστάδων κατολοφύρεσθαι, ἢ τὸ ἔμπαλιν ἐπιταχθεὶς ἑνὶ τῶν τετελευτηκότων τὰ νενομισμένα τελεῖν ἐπιλαθέσθαι μὲν τοῦ πάθους, φαιδρύνεσθαι δὲ πρὸς τὸν κατηφείας γέμοντα σύλλογον; εἰ δὲ ἐν τοῖς ἐγκοσμίοις καλὸν ἡ τάξις καὶ ἐπιστήμη, πολλῷ δήπου πλέον ἐν τοῖς μεγάλοις καὶ οὐρανίοις ἁρμοδιώτερον.

GNO 248 Χριστὸς τοίνυν ἀνέστη σήμερον ὁ θεός, ὁ ἀπαθής, ὁ | ἀθάνατος (καὶ μικρὸν ἐπίσχες ὁ ἐθνικὸς παρεὶς τὸν προπετῆ γέλωτα, μέχρις ἂν πάντων ἀκούσῃς), οὐ πρὸς ἀνάγκην παθὼν οὐδὲ τὴν ἐξ οὐρανῶν κάθοδον βιασθεὶς οὐδὲ τὴν ἀνάστασιν ὡς ἀπροσδόκητον εὐεργεσίαν παρ᾽ ἐλπίδας εὑρών, ἀλλ᾽ εἰδὼς πάντων τῶν πραγμάτων τὸ τέλος καὶ οὕτω τὴν ἀρχὴν ποιησάμενος. ἔχων ἐν ὀφθαλμοῖς τῆς θεότητος τῶν προκειμένων τὴν γνῶσιν καὶ πρὶν ἐξ οὐρανῶν κατελθεῖν βλέπων καὶ τῶν ἐθνῶν τὴν ταραχὴν καὶ τοῦ Ἰσραὴλ τὴν σκληρότητα καὶ Πιλάτον προκαθήμενον καὶ Καϊάφαν ἑαυτῷ τὴν ἐσθῆτα περισπαράσσοντα καὶ τὸν στασιώδη δῆμον φλεγμαίνοντα καὶ Ἰούδαν προδιδόντα καὶ Πέτρον ὑπερμαχόμενον καὶ μετ᾽ ὀλίγον ἑαυτὸν τῇ ἀναστάσει εἰς δόξαν ἀφθαρσίας μεταμορφούμενον καὶ πᾶν τὸ μέλλον ἔχων ὑπογεγραμμένον τῇ γνώσει οὐκ ἀνεβάλετο τὴν εἰς τὸν ἄνθρωπον χάριν οὐδὲ ὑπερέθετο τὴν οἰκονομίαν, ἀλλ᾽ ὥσπερ οἱ τὸν ἀσθενῆ παρὰ χαράδρας συρόμενον βλέποντες εἰδότες, ὡς ἔστι καὶ τῷ βορβόρῳ τοῦ χειμάρρου ἐνειληθῆναι καὶ τῆς πληγῆς ἀνασχέσθαι τῶν λίθων τῶν συνωθουμένων παρὰ τοῦ ὕδατος, ὅμως διὰ τὸ συμπαθὲς τὸ περὶ τὸν κινδυνεύοντα οὐκ ὀκνοῦσι τὴν εἴσοδον, οὕτω καὶ ὁ φιλάνθρωπος ἡμῶν σωτὴρ ἐθελοντὴς ὑβριστικὰ καὶ ἄτιμα κατεδέξατο, ἵνα τὸν ἐξ ἀπάτης ἀπολλύμενον σώσῃ. κατῆλθεν εἰς τὸν βίον, ἐπειδὴ προῄδει καὶ τὴν ἄνοδον ἔνδοξον, ἀποθανεῖν τῷ ἀνθρωπίνῳ ἑαυτοῦ συνεχώρησεν,

world's wisdom. For what speaker is so stupid and awkward that, when he is invited to a splendid wedding, he distances himself from the elegant language that fittingly reflects the joys of the feast, and chants mournful melodies, darkening the bridal chamber with sad themes from tragedy? Or who, in contrast, when summoned to pay the respects owed to someone who has died, would forget all feeling and beam happily at the gathering as it groans in sadness? If a grasp of what is fitting is helpful in worldly events, surely it is all the more appropriate on great, heavenly subjects.

3 Christ, then, is risen today: God, free from suffering, deathless—Gentile stranger, restrain your impulsive laughter a little, until you hear all we have to say! He did not suffer out of necessity, nor was he forced to descend from heaven; nor did he receive the gift of resurrection as an unexpected blessing, contrary to all hope. He knew the outcome of all the events of his life, and so undertook them from the beginning. Having a vision of what lay before him in his divine sight—seeing, even before he came down from heaven, the "rage of the Gentiles"[4] and the hard-heartedness of Israel,[5] and Pilate on his seat, and Caiaphas tearing his robe, and the people inflamed with resentment, and Judas betraying him, and Peter overcome [by grief]; and seeing, a little later, himself transformed in the resurrection to incorruptible glory—having all that was to happen engraved on his mind, he did not defer the gift of grace to humanity, or delay the divine plan. But just as those who look at a weak person, swept away by a mountain stream, know that it is possible they may get stuck in the river's mud and take a beating from the rocks that are let loose by the water, will nevertheless, out of sympathy for the one in danger, not hesitate to jump in, so our loving Savior willingly accepted insults and dishonor so that he might save the one who was deceived into destruction. He came down to live with us, since he knew in advance that he would also ascend in glory; he accepted dying in his own humanity, since he knew in advance that he would

[4]See Ps 2.1.
[5]Cf. Mk 10.5.

ἐπειδὴ καὶ τὴν ἔγερσιν προεγίνωσκεν· οὐ γὰρ ὡς εἷς τῶν κοινῶν
ἀνθρώπων ῥιψοκινδύνως ἐτόλμα τῇ ἀδηλίᾳ τοῦ μέλλοντος
ἐπιτρέπων τὴν ἔκβασιν, ἀλλ᾽ ὡς θεὸς ᾠκονόμει τὸ προκείμενον ἐπὶ
ῥητῷ καὶ ἐγνωσμένῳ τῷ τέλει. |

GNO 249 Αὕτη τοίνυν ἡ ἡμέρα, ἣν ἐποίησεν ὁ κύριος, ἀγαλλιασώμεθα
καὶ εὐφρανθῶμεν ἐν αὐτῇ· μὴ μέθαις καὶ κώμοις, μὴ χοροῖς καὶ
παροινίαις, ἀλλὰ ταῖς θεοειδέσιν ἐννοίαις. Σήμερον ἅπασαν
τὴν οἰκουμένην ἔστιν ἰδεῖν ὡς μίαν οἰκίαν εἰς συμφωνίαν ἑνὸς
PG 657 | πράγματος συναχθεῖσαν καὶ παντὸς ἀμελήσασαν τοῦ κατὰ
συνήθειαν πράγματος, μετασκευασθεῖσαν δὲ ἑνὶ συνθήματι εἰς τὴν
σπουδὴν τῆς εὐχῆς. αἱ λεωφόροι τοὺς ὁδοιπόρους οὐκ ἔχουσιν,
ἡ θάλασσα σήμερον ναυτῶν καὶ πλωτήρων ἔρημος, ὁ γεωργὸς
τὴν σκαπάνην καὶ τὸ ἄροτρον ῥίψας εἰς τὸ τοῦ ἑορτάζοντος
σχῆμα ἐκαλλωπίσατο, αἱ καπηλεῖαι τῆς ἐμπορίας σχολάζουσιν,
αἱ ὀχλήσεις ἐλύθησαν ὡς χειμὼν ἐπιφανέντος ἔαρος, θόρυβοι καὶ
ταραχαὶ καὶ ζάλαι τοῦ βίου τῇ εἰρήνῃ τῆς ἑορτῆς ὑπεξέστησαν,
ὁ πένης ὡς πλούσιος καλλωπίζεται, ὁ πλούσιος τῆς συνηθείας
περιφανέστερος δείκνυται, ὁ πρεσβύτης ὡς νέος τρέχει πρὸς τὴν
μετουσίαν τῆς εὐφροσύνης, ὁ ἀσθενὴς καὶ τὴν νόσον βιάζεται,
τὸ παιδίον τῇ ἐξαλλαγῇ τῆς ἐσθῆτος αἰσθητῶς ἑορτάζει, ἐπειδὴ
νοητῶς οὐδέπω δύναται, ἡ παρθένος ὑπεργάνυται τὴν ψυχήν, ὅτι
τῆς ἰδίας ἐλπίδος λαμπρὰν καὶ οὕτω τιμωμένην τὴν ὑπόμνησιν
βλέπει, ἡ ἔγγαμος ὅλῳ τῷ πληρώματι τῆς οἰκίας ἑορτάζουσα
χαίρει· νῦν γὰρ αὐτῇ καὶ ὁ σύνοικος καὶ οἱ παῖδες καὶ οἱ οἰκέται
καὶ πάντες ἐφέστιοι ἀγάλλονται. καὶ ὥσπερ τὸ σμῆνος τῶν
μελισσῶν τὸ νέον καὶ ἀρτίτοκον πρῶτον τῆς καταδύσεως ἢ τῶν
καλαθίσκων πρὸς τὸν ἀέρα καὶ τὸ φῶς ἐξιπτάμενον ἄθρουν ὁμοῦ
GNO 250 καὶ συνημμένον | ἑνὶ κλάδῳ δένδρου προσπλάσσεται, οὕτως ἐπὶ
ταύτης τῆς ἑορτῆς ὁλόκληρα τὰ γένη πρὸς τὰς ἑστίας συντρέχει.

---

[6]Following other editors, Ernst Gebhardt suggests that "in a single task" may be an erroneous textual reading, perhaps for the original phrase, "in a single song." Werner Jaeger suggests "in a single chorus," Hadwig Hörner "in a single company."

[7]Gregory seems to be referring to the liturgical assembly, gathered for the Easter Eucharist. The congregation is a single household, gathered for a single festival,

also rise. For he did not, like some ordinary human daredevil, take a risk while ignorant of the future, simply trusting in the outcome; but as God, he managed the days ahead of him in light of an outcome that was already specified and known (see Heb 12.2).

4 "This," then, "is the day which the Lord has made; let us rejoice and be glad in it" (Ps 117.24)—"not in drinking and carousing, not in songs and drunken behavior" (Rom 13.13), but with godly thoughts. Today one can see the whole world as a single house, gathered harmoniously in a single task,[6] forgetful of all day-to-day business, transformed by a single profession of faith for the serious activity of prayer.[7] The highways have no travelers; the sea today is empty of sailors and passengers; the farmer, tossing aside his spade and plow, has put on joyous festal clothes, the stalls of the merchants are quiet; the crowds are melted away like winter at the approach of spring; the disturbances and troubles and squalls of daily life have given way to the peace of the feast; the poor man is decked out as if he were rich, the rich man appears more resplendent than usual; the old person runs to share in the joy as if he were a youth; the weak person struggles against his sickness; the child celebrates visibly just by changing costume, since he cannot yet do it with full understanding; the virgin exults deep in her soul, because she sees the memorial of her own hope so brilliantly honored; the married woman is eager to keep the feast with her full household, for now she, her spouse, her children, her household slaves, and her whole family rejoice together. As a newly-hatched swarm of bees, before seeking out a hole or a hive,[8] flies upward into the air and the light together, in a close-knit mass, and attaches itself to a single branch of a tree, so on this feast families cluster together at the hearth.

formed by the renewal of their single profession of faith, unified by shared liturgical prayer.

[8]The Greek word Gregory uses here, καλαθίσκος (*kalathiskos*), usually designates a kind of small basket, narrower at the bottom than at the top. Here it seems to refer to a humanly-made beehive (in German: *Bienenkorb*, "bee-basket")—but it is apparently, when used in this sense in Greek, a hapax legomenon.

καὶ ἀληθῶς τῇ μιμήσει πρὸς τὴν μέλλουσαν ἡμέραν ἡ παροῦσα
καλῶς ἀναφέρεται· ἀθροιστικαὶ γὰρ ἀνθρώπων ἀμφότεραι, ἐκείνη
τῶν καθόλου, αὕτη τῶν ἐπὶ μέρους. ἵνα δὲ τὸ ἀληθέστερον εἴπωμεν,
ὅσον εἰς φαιδρότητα φέρει καὶ εὐθυμίαν, αὕτη τῆς προσδοκωμένης
χαριεστέρα, ἐπειδὴ τότε μὲν ἐπάναγκες καὶ τοὺς ὀδυρομένους
ὁρᾶσθαι, ὧν αἱ ἁμαρτίαι ἀποκαλύπτονται, νῦν δὲ ἀνεπίδεκτος τῶν
σκυθρωπῶν ἐστιν ἡ εὐπάθεια· ὅ τε γὰρ δίκαιος εὐφραίνεται καὶ ὁ τὸ
συνειδὸς μὴ καθαρεύων ἀναμένει τὴν ἐκ τῆς μετανοίας διόρθωσιν
καὶ πᾶσα λύπη ἐπὶ τῆς παρούσης ἡμέρας κοιμίζεται, οὐδεὶς δὲ
οὕτω κατώδυνος, ὡς ἄνεσιν μὴ εὑρέσθαι τῇ μεγαλοπρεπείᾳ τῆς
ἑορτῆς. νῦν ὁ δεσμώτης λύεται, ὁ χρεώστης ἀφίεται, ὁ δοῦλος
ἐλευθεροῦται τῷ ἀγαθῷ καὶ φιλανθρώπῳ τῆς ἐκκλησίας κηρύγματι
οὐ ῥαπιζόμενος ἀσχημόνως κατὰ τῆς παρειᾶς καὶ πληγῇ τῆς
πληγῆς ἀφιέμενος οὐδὲ ὥσπερ ἐν πομπῇ τῷ δήμῳ δεικνύμενος
ἐφ᾽ ὑψηλῷ βήματι, ὕβριν δὲ ἔχων καὶ ἐρυθριασμὸν τὴν ἀρχὴν
τῆς ἐλευθερίας, ἀλλ᾽ οὕτω κοσμίως ἀφιέμενος ὡς γινώσκεται.
εὐεργετεῖται καὶ ὁ μένων ἐπὶ τῆς δουλείας ἔτι· εἰ γὰρ καὶ πολλὰ καὶ
βαρέα τὰ ἁμαρτήματα παραίτησιν ὑπερβαίνοντα καὶ συγγνώμην,
αἰδούμενος ὁ δεσπότης τὸ τῆς ἡμέρας γαληνὸν καὶ φιλάνθρωπον
δέχεται τὸν ἀπερριμμένον καὶ ἐν τοῖς ἀτίμοις ὁρώμενον ὡς ὁ
Φαραὼ τὸν οἰνοχόον ἐκ τοῦ δεσμωτηρίου· οἶδε γάρ, ὡς κατὰ τὴν
προθεσμίαν τῆς ἀναστάσεως, ἧς καθ᾽ ὁμοιότητα τὴν παροῦσαν
τιμῶμεν, χρῄζει καὶ αὐτὸς τῆς ἀνεξικακίας καὶ τῆς ἀγαθότητος
GNO 251 τοῦ δεσπότου καὶ δανείζων ἐνταῦθα τὸν ἔλεον προσδοκᾷ | τὴν
ἀπόδοσιν ἐν καιρῷ. ἠκούσατε οἱ δεσπόται, φυλάξατε τὸν λόγον ὡς
ἀγαθόν, μὴ διαβάλητέ με παρὰ τοῖς δούλοις ὡς ψευδῶς τὴν ἡμέραν
PG 660 ἐγκωμιάζοντα, ἀφέλετε τὴν | λύπην τῶν θλιβομένων ψυχῶν ὡς ὁ
κύριος τῶν σωμάτων τὴν νέκρωσιν, μεταμορφώσατε τοὺς ἀτίμους

[9] I.e., the day of final judgment, when Christ will come again in glory.

[10] Possibly: “freed with a kind of decorum that he [alone] realizes.” The sentence seems to refer to the fresh experience of baptism as liberation from sin on the part of the neophytes, and suggests, by contrast, that in Gregory’s time the civil manumission of slaves could often be carried out in a humiliating, even punitive way.

[11] I.e., one who is not yet baptized.

In truth, this present day points by anticipation to the day that is to come;[9] for both gather people together—that day all people at once, today people in smaller groups. And to say more truly what marks out its splendor and delight: this day is still more joyful than that day to come, since then, of necessity, mourners will also be seen, whose sins are revealed, but today our happiness has no share of lament. For the righteous person rejoices, and the one who has not yet purged his conscience awaits conversion and correction; every sorrow on this day is put to rest, but no one is so weighed down with affliction that he does not find relief in the splendor of the festival. Today the chained prisoner is released, the debtor forgiven, the slave set free by the gracious, loving proclamation of the Church—not slapped on the cheek in a demeaning way, nor released from a beating with a blow, nor made a public spectacle on a high platform, as in a parade, receiving insults and blushing in order to begin his life as a free man—but freed with the decorum that consists in being [personally] recognized.[10] Even the one who still remains enslaved[11] is blessed; for although his sins are many and weigh heavily, going beyond dismissal and forgiveness, the Lord respects the peaceful and loving character of the day, and receives the exile, the one regarded as having no rights, as Pharaoh recognized the wine-waiter from prison.[12] For he knows, as in the expectation of resurrection, which we celebrate in [sacramental] likeness on this present day, that he himself will experience the patience and kindness of the Master; and in showing mercy here in this life, he looks forward to the repayment of that loan at the proper time.

Listen to me, you masters: receive our message as good news; do not defame me among the slaves, as if I were praising this day falsely; dismiss the grief of oppressed souls, as the Lord will dismiss

[12]Gregory is alluding to a detail from the story of Joseph, in Genesis 40.20–22. The young Joseph, sold into slavery by his envious brothers, has arrived in Egypt and is working as a prison-guard, when his ability to interpret dreams helps him to foretell the fate of two fellow prisoners. One, a cupbearer to Pharaoh, after being restored to his position, remembers Joseph's abilities when Pharaoh has two disturbing dreams; this gives Joseph the chance to interpret the dreams of Pharaoh himself.

εἰς ἐπιτιμίαν, τοὺς θλιβομένους εἰς χαράν, τοὺς ἀπαρρησιάστους εἰς παρρησίαν, ἐξαγάγετε τῆς γωνίας τοὺς ῥιφέντας ὡς τάφων, ἐπανθησάτω τὸ τῆς ἑορτῆς κάλλος ὡς ἄνθος τοῖς πᾶσιν. εἰ γὰρ βασιλέως ἀνθρώπου γενέθλιος ἡμέρα ἀνοίγει δεσμωτήριον ἢ ἐπινίκιος ἑορτή, Χριστὸς ἀναστὰς οὐκ ἀφήσει τοὺς τεθλιμμένους; οἱ πτωχοὶ τὴν ὑμετέραν τροφὸν ἀσπάσασθε, οἱ διερρυηκότες καὶ λελωβημένοι τὰ σώματα τὴν ἰωμένην ὑμῶν τὰς συμφοράς· διὰ γὰρ τὴν ἀπὸ τῆς ἀναστάσεως ἐλπίδα καὶ ἀρετὴ σπουδάζεται καὶ κακία μισεῖται, ἐπεὶ ἀναστάσεως ἀνῃρημένης εἷς παρὰ πᾶσι κρατῶν εὑρεθήσεται λόγος· Φάγωμεν καὶ πίωμεν, αὔριον γὰρ ἀποθνῄσκομεν.

Πρὸς ταύτην βλέπων ὁ ἀπόστολος τὴν ἡμέραν τῆς ζωῆς τῆς ἐπικαίρου καταφρονεῖ, ἐπιθυμεῖ δὲ τῆς μελλούσης, ἐξευτελίζων δὲ τὰ ὁρώμενά φησιν· Εἰ ἐπὶ τῇ ζωῇ ταύτῃ ἠλπικότες ἐσμέν, ἐλεεινότεροι πάντων ἀνθρώπων ἐσμέν. διὰ ταύτην τὴν ἡμέραν κληρονόμοι θεοῦ ἄνθρωποι καὶ συγκληρονόμοι Χριστοῦ. διὰ ταύτην τὴν ἡμέραν, ὅπερ οἱ σαρκοβόροι ὄρνιθες ἔφαγον πρὸ χιλίων ἐνιαυτῶν μέρος τοῦ σώματος, εὑρεθήσεται μὴ λεῖπον, καὶ ὅπερ κήτη καὶ κύνες καὶ τὰ ἐνάλια ζῷα κατεβοσκήθησαν, ἐγειρομένῳ τῷ ἀνθρώπῳ συναναστήσεται, καὶ ὅπερ διέφλεξε πῦρ καὶ σκώληξ ἐν τάφοις κατεδαπάνησε καὶ ἁπλῶς πάντα τὰ σώματα, ὅσα μετὰ τὴν γένεσιν ἠφάνισεν ἡ φθορά, ἀνελλιπῆ καὶ
GNO 252 ἀκέραια ἀναδοθήσεται | ἐκ τῆς γῆς καί, ὡς Παῦλος διδάσκει, ἐν ῥιπῇ ὀφθαλμοῦ τελεσθήσεται ἡ ἀνάστασις (ῥιπὴ δὲ ὀφθαλμοῦ ἐπίμυσις βλεφάρων ἐστί)· καὶ τούτου τοῦ τάχους οὐκ ἂν ἕτερον

---

[13]Gregory is one of the few early Christian writers who unequivocally categorizes the legal status of slavery as unnatural in human society, a sign of our common inheritance of sin. See especially *Homily 4 on Ecclesiastes* (GNO V:336.10–338.22).

[14]Here Gregory echoes a theme that had been emphasized by Christian apologists since the second century: that if one concedes that God is the sole creator of the universe, with all its living inhabitants, there is nothing incredible in supposing that, by his creative power, he can restore again to the risen human body those parts that have been consumed by other creatures, or have simply decayed as part of the normal cycle of life. See, for instance, Athenagoras, *On the Resurrection* 4.9; Tertullian, *On*

the dying of our bodies; transform the dishonorable by leading them to a state of honor, the oppressed to joy, the voiceless to freedom of speech; lead them out from the corners where they have been tossed as from their tombs; let the beauty of this feast blossom like a flower upon us all.[13] For if the birthday or the victory celebration of a human king throws open the prison, will the risen Christ not release those who are oppressed? Poor people, welcome your nourishment—you who are wasted or deformed in body, welcome the day that heals you from your fate! For through the hope that comes from the resurrection, virtue will be cultivated seriously, vice detested; but if resurrection is ruled out, one motto will be found to be in force among us all: "Let us eat and drink, for tomorrow we die!" (1 Cor 15.32)

5 Looking toward this day, the Apostle plays down the importance of this present life, but desires the life to come. So, making light of the things we see, he says, "If we have placed our hope in this life, we are of all people the most to be pitied" (1 Cor 15.19). Because of this day, human beings are "heirs of God, and fellow heirs with Christ" (Rom 8.17). Because of this day, that part of the body that scavenging birds ate thousands of years ago will be found lacking nothing, and what sharks and dogs and sea-creatures have devoured will rise as part of the human person; what fire burned up and the worm in the graves consumed—quite simply, all of our bodies, whatever corruption has made to disappear since our birth—will be given back by the earth complete and intact.[14] As Paul said, the resurrection will be accomplished "in the twinkling of an eye" (1 Cor 15.52) (and the twinkling of an eye is just the blink of an eyelid—nothing is quicker

the Resurrection of the Flesh 11–13; Augustine, *On the City of God* 22.12–21, esp. 20; *Enchiridion* 23.88. And see Gregory of Nyssa's own treatment of the subject, in *On the Soul and the Resurrection* (GNO III/3:56.15–57.20; PG 46:77B8–80A12; *De hominis opificio* 27.5.2). In fact, Gregory's way here of imagining the reunion of the separated soul with the atoms of his or her body, scattered long before in death, resembles closely his treatment of this same eschatological process of restoration in *On the Soul and the Resurrection*; see especially there GNO III/3:30.18–31.15; 54.16–24; 62.5–16; PG 46:48A10–B10; 76A13–B6; 85A1–14.

ὀξύτερον γένοιτο. σὺ δὲ ἀνθρωπικῶς καὶ κατὰ τὴν δύναμιν τὴν
σαυτοῦ λογιζόμενος πόσα διαστήματα χρόνων διαγράφεις ἐν τῇ
ψυχῇ σου; πρῶτον, ἵνα τὰ διασαπέντα τῶν ὀστέων καὶ γεωθέντα
εἰς τὴν σκληρότητα καὶ λειότητα συμπαγῇ, ἑνωθέντα δὲ ἐκ τῆς
θρύψεως πάλιν εἰς ῥυθμὸν ἁρμονίας καὶ τὴν φυσικὴν συνέλθῃ
συνάφειαν· εἶτα ἐπινοεῖς τὴν τῶν σαρκῶν περίπλασιν καὶ νεύρων
ἀποτεταμένας συνδέσεις καὶ φλεβῶν καὶ ἀρτηριῶν λεπτοὺς
ὀχετοὺς ὑφηπλωμένους τῷ δέρματι, ψυχῶν δὲ ἀμύθητον καὶ
ἀναρίθμητον πλῆθος ἔκ τινων οἰκήσεων ἀπορρήτων κινούμενον,
γνωρίζουσαν δὲ ἑκάστην ὡς ἱμάτιον ἐξαίρετον τὸ ἴδιον σῶμα καὶ
τούτῳ πάλιν ἐνοικοῦσαν ὀξέως, ἀπλανῆ δὲ ἔχουσαν τὴν διάκρισιν
κατὰ πλήθους τοσούτου ὁμοφύλων πνευμάτων. ἐννόησον γὰρ τὰς
ἀπὸ Ἀδὰμ ψυχὰς καὶ τὰ ἀπ᾽ ἐκείνου σώματα πλῆθος τοσούτων
οἰκιῶν λυθεισῶν καὶ οἰκοδεσποτῶν ἐκ μακρᾶς τῆς ἀποδημίας
ὑποστρεφόντων, πάντα δὲ παραδόξως τελούμενα· οὔτε γὰρ ἡ οἰκία
ἀνακτιζομένη βραδύνει οὔτε ὁ ἔνοικος πλανᾶται καὶ θυραυλεῖ
PG 661 ζη|τῶν, ποῦ τὰ ἴδια καὶ ἐξαίρετα, εὐθὺς δὲ ἐπ᾽ αὐτὴν χωρεῖ ὡσεὶ
περιστερὰ πρὸς τὸν ἴδιον πύργον, κἂν πολλοὶ καὶ συνεχεῖς περὶ
τὸν αὐτὸν τόπον ὦσι δι᾽ ὁμοίων σχημάτων ἐκλάμποντες. πόθεν
πάλιν ἡ ἀνάμνησις καὶ ὁ ἀναλογισμὸς τοῦ προτέρου βίου καὶ
ἑκάστης πράξεως ἔννοια οὕτως ὀξέως συναπαρτιζομένη τῷ |
GNO 253 ζῴῳ πρὸ τοσούτων αἰώνων διαλυθέντι; καίτοιγε καὶ ἐξ ὕπνου
ἄνθρωπος ἀνεγερθεὶς βαρυτέρου ἐπ᾽ ὀλίγον ἀγνοεῖ, ὅστις ἐστὶ
καὶ ὅπου διάγει, καὶ τῶν συνήθων ἐπιλανθάνεται, μέχρις ἂν ἡ
ἐγρήγορσις τὴν νάρκην ἀποσκεδάσασα πάλιν τὸ μνημονικὸν καὶ
ἐνεργὲς ἀναζωπυρήσῃ.

Ταῦτα καὶ τὰ τοιαῦτα τοὺς λογισμοὺς τῶν πολλῶν ὑποτρέχοντα θαύματος ὑπερβάλλοντος πληροῖ τὴν διάνοιαν, συνεισάγει δὲ τὴν ἀπιστίαν τῷ θαύματι· ἐπειδὴ γὰρ ὁ νοῦς οὐχ εὑρίσκει τῶν ἀπορουμένων καὶ ζητουμένων τὴν λύσιν οὐδὲ δύναται τὴν ἑαυτοῦ

than this!). And when you calculate humanly, as far as your powers allow, how many separate moments can you distinguish here, in your soul? First, when the rotted fragments of bone that have turned to earth come together again into something hard and smooth, and once they are unified from their fragmentary state, they are to be joined again into a regular harmonic structure and a natural connection. Then imagine the weaving of flesh and the reconnection of detached tendons, and of the arteries and veins—that delicate plumbing-system spread under the skin; and imagine that untold, uncountable multitude of souls, set in motion from some unknown dwelling-places, each recognizing its own body as its proper garment and coming to dwell in it quickly once again, making use of an unwavering judgment amidst such a great multitude of similar spirits. Imagine for yourself the souls since Adam and the bodies descended from him: a multitude of so many destroyed homes, and of homeowners returning from faraway, all brought to completion mysteriously. The rebuilding of the house will not take long, nor will the owner wander around, camping in the open as he searches for where his own proper house is; but he will move toward it directly, like a dove to its own high nest, although there may be many close to each other in the same place, resplendent in similar shapes. And how, again, will there be a recollection and a reconsideration of one's former life, and an understanding of each action, sharply conformed to fit a life extinguished so many ages ago?[15] Yet surely a person awakening from a deep sleep is unaware for a moment of who he is and where he is going, and forgets his companions for a moment, until his waking state shakes off his sleepiness and warms to life again his powers of memory and action.

6 Such things, and others like them, reaching well beyond most people's powers of reasoning, fill our thoughts with [the image of] an overpowering miracle, but along with wonder it brings doubt. For when the mind cannot find the solution to the problems it is

[15]Gregory clearly assumes that the general resurrection of humanity will occur as the first stage in the process of God's judgment.

πολυπραγμοσύνην εὑρέσει καὶ καταλήψει προσαναπαῦσαι, χωρεῖ πρὸς ἀπιστίαν λοιπὸν ἐν τῇ ἀσθενείᾳ τῶν ἰδίων λογισμῶν ἐκβάλλων καὶ ἀθετῶν τὴν τῶν πραγμάτων ἀλήθειαν. μᾶλλον δὲ ἐπειδὴ ὁδῷ προβαίνων ὁ λόγος πρὸς τὸ συνεχῶς λαλούμενον ἀφίκετο ζήτημα καὶ τῆς παρούσης ἑορτῆς ἡ ὑπόθεσις οἰκεία καὶ συγγενής, φέρε μικρὸν εἰς ἀρχὴν πρέπουσαν ἀναγαγόντες τὸ προκείμενον πληροφορίαν ἐμποιῆσαι πειραθῶμεν τοῖς πρὸς τὰ φανερὰ κακῶς ἀμφιβάλλουσιν.

Ὁ τῶν ὅλων δημιουργὸς θελήσας κτίσαι τὸν ἄνθρωπον οὐχ ὡς εὐκαταφρόνητον ζῷον ἀλλ' ὡς τιμιώτερον πάντων εἰς τὸ εἶναι παρήγαγε καὶ τῆς ὑπ' οὐρανὸν κτίσεως ἀνέδειξε βασιλέα. τοῦτο δὲ προελόμενος καὶ τοιοῦτον ἀπαρτίσας σοφὸν καὶ θεοειδῆ καὶ πολλῇ κατακοσμήσας τῇ χάριτι ἆρα μετὰ γνώμης τοιαύτης εἰς τὸ εἶναι παρήγαγεν, ἵνα γεννηθεὶς φθαρῇ καὶ τελείαν ὑποστῇ τὴν ἀπώλειαν; ἀλλὰ μάταιος ὁ σκοπὸς καὶ σφόδρα γε ἀνάξιον τὴν τοιαύτην ἔννοιαν εἰς θεὸν ἀναφέρειν· παιδίοις γὰρ οὕτως ἀπεικάζεται |
GNO 254 οἰκοδομοῦσι σπουδῇ καὶ λύουσι ταχέως τὸ κατασκεύασμα πρὸς οὐδὲν πέρας εὔχρηστον τῆς διανοίας αὐτῶν καταληγούσης. πᾶν δὲ τοὐναντίον ἐδιδάχθημεν, ὅτι τὸν πρωτόπλαστον ἀθάνατον ἔκτισεν, ἐπισυμβάσης δὲ τῆς παραβάσεως καὶ τῆς ἁμαρτίας εἰς δίκην τοῦ πλημμελήματος τῆς ἀθανασίας ἐστέρησεν· εἶτα ἡ πηγὴ τῆς ἀγαθότητος ὑπερβλύζουσα τὴν φιλανθρωπίαν καὶ πρὸς τὸ ἔργον ἐπικλασθεῖσα τῶν ἰδίων χειρῶν σοφίᾳ καὶ ἐπιστήμῃ κατεκόσμησεν οὓς εἰς τὴν ἀρχαίαν [ἡμᾶς] εὐδόκησεν ἀνακαινίσαι κατάστασιν.

Ταῦτα καὶ ἀληθῆ τυγχάνει καὶ τῆς περὶ θεοῦ ὑπολήψεως ἄξια· προσμαρτυρεῖ γὰρ αὐτῷ μετὰ τῆς ἀγαθότητος καὶ τὴν δύναμιν. τὸ δὲ ἀπαθῶς ἔχειν καὶ σκληρῶς πρὸς τὰ ἀρχόμενά τε καὶ ποιμαινόμενα οὐδὲ ἀνθρώπων ἐστὶ χρηστῶν καὶ βελτίστων·
PG 664 οὕτως ὁ ποιμὴν βούλεται ἐρρῶσθαι τὸ ποίμνιον αὐτῷ καὶ | σχεδὸν

considering, and cannot put a stop to its own restless inquiry by the process of discovery and conceptualization, it moves, in consequence, toward unbelief, in the weakness of its own reasonings casting out and rejecting the truth of what actually has happened. Or rather, since our discourse, going forward on its way, has arrived at the question that is constantly on people's lips, and since the story of this present feast is a familiar and congenial one—come, let us briefly connect our subject with its own proper principles, and try to supply some satisfaction for those who are unfortunately still in doubt about what seems so obvious.

7 When the fashioner of all things wanted to create the human person, he brought him into being not as an animal easy to despise, but as one more honorable than all the others, and revealed him as king of all creation under heaven. Destining him in advance for this, and equipping him to be so wise and godlike, and arraying him with so much grace, would he have so carefully brought him into being in order to let him be destroyed after he was born, and undergo complete annihilation? Surely such a plan would be foolish, and to attribute such a purpose to God would be utterly unworthy; for he would thus be acting like children eagerly building something, and then quickly destroying what they had made, their plan ending in no useful result. We have been taught quite the opposite: that God created the first human being immortal, but when transgression and sin came about, as a just result of this error he deprived [the human person] of immortality. But then the spring of goodness overflowed with love for humanity; and moved with pity toward the work of his own hands, God adorned them with wisdom and knowledge, being pleased to bring them once again to their original state.

All of this, in fact, is true, and worthy of our conception of God. For it bears witness to his power, too, along with his goodness. To remain unmoved and harsh toward what one has begun and nurtured, after all, is not even proper to upright, respectable humans; so the shepherd wants his flock to flourish, almost to be immortal; the

ὑπάρχειν ἀθάνατον καὶ ὁ βουκόλος παντοδαπαῖς θεραπείαις αὔξει τὰς βοῦς καὶ τὰς αἶγας διδυμοτόκους ὑπάρχειν ὁ αἰπόλος εὔχεται καὶ πᾶς ἀγελάρχης ἁπλῶς διαμένειν αὐτῷ καὶ εὐθηνεῖσθαι ποθεῖ τὴν ἀγέλην πρός τι τέλος εὔχρηστον ἀφορῶν. τούτου δὲ οὕτως ἔχοντος καὶ ἐκ τῶν ἀρτίως ἡμῖν εἰρημένων δειχθέντος πρεπωδέστατον ὑπάρχειν τῷ δημιουργῷ καὶ τεχνίτῃ τοῦ γένους ἡμῶν ἀναπλάσαι τὸ φθαρὲν ποίημα πρόδηλον, ὡς οἱ τοῖς ἑξῆς ἀπειθοῦντες οὐκ ἄλλοθέν ποθεν ἀπομάχονται ἢ διὰ τὸ νομίζειν ἀδύνατον εἶναι τῷ θεῷ τὸ τεθνηκὸς καὶ διαλυθὲν ἀνεγεῖραι. νεκρῶν ἀληθῶς καὶ ἀναισθήτων τὸ φρόνημα τὸ ἀδύνατον καὶ ἀμήχανον ἐπὶ θεοῦ λογιζομένων καὶ τὰ τῆς ἰδίας ἀσθενείας ἐπὶ τὴν παντοδύναμον φερόντων μεγαλοπρέπειαν. ἵνα δὲ λόγοις
GNO 255 ἐλεγκτικοῖς τῆς ἀνοίας αὐτῶν | καθικώμεθα, ἐκ τῶν γεγονότων καὶ ὄντων ἀποδειχθήτω τὸ μέλλον καὶ ἀπιστούμενον· ἤκουσας, ὅτι ὁ χοῦς ἐπλάσθη καὶ ἐγένετο ἄνθρωπος, δίδαξον οὖν με, παρακαλῶ, ὁ πάντα ἀξιῶν τῇ σοφίᾳ τῇ ἑαυτοῦ περιδράσσεσθαι, πῶς ὁ λεπτὸς χοῦς ὁ ἐσκεδασμένος συνήχθη, πῶς ἡ γῆ σὰρξ ἐγένετο καὶ ἡ αὐτὴ ὕλη καὶ ὀστέα ἐποίησε καὶ δέρμα καὶ πιμελὴν καὶ τρίχας, πῶς μιᾶς οὔσης τῆς σαρκὸς διάφοροι αἱ ἰδέαι τῶν μελῶν καὶ αἱ ποιότητες καὶ ἁφαί, πῶς ὁ πνεύμων ἁπαλὸς τὴν ἁφήν, πελιδνὸς τὴν χρόαν, τὸ ἧπαρ στριφνὸν καὶ ἐρυθρόν, ἡ καρδία πεπιλημένη καὶ σκληρότατον μόριον ἐν σαρκί, ὁ σπλὴν ἀραιὸς καὶ μέλας, ὁ ἐπίπλους λευκὸς καὶ ὡς δίκτυον ἁλιευτικὸν συμπεπλεγμένος παρὰ τῆς φύσεως. σκεψώμεθα κἀκεῖνα, πῶς ἡ πρώτη γυνὴ ἀπὸ μικροῦ μέρους τῆς πλευρᾶς ὑπέστη ζῷον ὁλόκληρον ὅμοιον τῷ τελείῳ καὶ πρώτῳ καὶ τὸ μέρος πρὸς πάντα διήρκεσε καὶ τὸ ὀλίγον τὸ πᾶν συνεστήσατο· ἡ πλευρὰ ἐγένετο κεφαλή, χεῖρες καὶ πόδες, ἐγκάτων σκολιὰ καὶ ποικίλη διάπλασις, σὰρξ καὶ τρίχες, ὀφθαλμὸς καὶ ῥὶς καὶ στόμα καὶ πάντα ἁπλῶς, ἵνα μὴ μακρὰν ἀπαγάγω τὸν λόγον, πάντα θαυμαστὰ καὶ παράδοξα ἡμῖν τοῖς

cowherd uses all kinds of tactics to increase the number of his cows; the goatherd prays his goats will bear twins. Every herdsman longs, quite simply, that his herd will long remain with him and flourish, as he imagines a happy future. Since this is so, and since it is evident from what we have just said that it is most appropriate for the creator and fashioner of our race to form his corrupted creature again, it is perfectly clear that those who disbelieve the narrative that will follow reject it for no other reason than that they think it impossible for God to raise up what has died and is corrupted. But the thinking of those who reckon anything impossible or unachievable for God is itself truly something dead and unperceiving; they are ascribing features of their own weakness to the splendor that can do all things.

8 But that we might reach their stupidity with critical arguments, let what will be proposed, but what seems hard to believe, be demonstrated from what is already reality. You have heard that clay was shaped into what became a human person; teach me, then, I ask you—since you think you have grasped everything just by your own wisdom: how was light soil, which had been scattered around, clumped together? How did earth become flesh, and the same matter form bones and skin and hair? How, when there is one flesh, are there different types of body parts, with different qualities and feel—why is the lung soft to the touch but livid in color, the liver solid and red, the heart dense and the hardest part of the body, the spleen spongy and black, the ear white and naturally bent like a fish-hook?[16] And let us consider those other details: how was the first woman formed from a small piece of rib to become a complete living being, similar to the first, perfect one; how was the part sufficient to become everything, the small portion to bring about the whole? The rib became head, hands and feet, twisted inner organs of all kinds, flesh and hair, eye and nose and mouth: quite simply, everything, lest I make the account too long—all of this amazing and

[16]As in many passages in his works, Gregory seems eager here to demonstrate his knowledge of contemporary physiology and anatomy. He may have witnessed dissections at some stage in his education.

ὀλίγοις. πρόχειροι δὲ παρὰ θεῷ τῆς κατασκευῆς οἱ λόγοι καὶ λίαν
ὁμολογούμενοι· πῶς οὖν σωφρονεῖν δόξουσιν οἱ τὴν μὲν μίαν
πλευρὰν συγχωροῦντες γενέσθαι ἄνθρωπον, ἀπὸ δὲ ὁλοκλήρου
τῆς τοῦ ἀνθρώπου ὕλης ἀπιστοῦντες τὸν αὐτὸν ἀνακτίζεσθαι;
οὐκ ἔστιν, οὐκ ἔστιν ἐπινοίαις ἀνθρωπικαῖς θεοῦ πολυπραγμονεῖν
ἐνεργείας· εἰ γὰρ πάντα ἦν ἡμῖν καταληπτά, οὐκ ἂν κρείττων ἦν
ἡμῶν ὁ κρείττων. τί λέγω περὶ θεοῦ; οὐδὲ πρὸς τὰ ἄλογα τῶν
GNO 256 ζῴων ἐπί τινων δυνάμεων | σύγκρισίν τινα ἔχομεν, ἀλλὰ κἀκείνων
ἀπολειπόμεθα. αὐτίκα δρόμῳ μὲν ἡμᾶς ὑπερβάλλονται ἵπποι καὶ
κύνες καὶ ἄλλα πολλά, δυνάμει δὲ κάμηλοι καὶ ἡμίονοι, σημειώσει
δὲ ὁδῶν οἱ ὄνοι καὶ τὸ τῆς δορκάδος ὀξυωπὸν ἐν ἡμετέροις
PG 665 ὀφθαλμοῖς οὐχ εὑρίσκεται. | διὸ εὐγνωμόνων καὶ σωφρονούντων
ἐστὶ πιστεύειν τοῖς παρὰ τοῦ θεοῦ λεγομένοις, τοὺς δὲ τρόπους
καὶ τὰς αἰτίας τῶν ἐνεργειῶν ὡς ὑπερβαινούσας μὴ ἀπαιτεῖν, ἐπεὶ
λεχθήσεται ἑνὶ τῶν πολυπραγμόνων· δεῖξόν μοι τῷ λόγῳ σου τὴν
τῶν ὁρωμένων οὐσίωσιν, εἰπὲ ποίᾳ τέχνῃ τὴν πολύμορφον ταύτην
ἐργασίαν ἐδημιούργησεν. ἂν γὰρ ταῦτα ἐξεύρῃς, εἰκότως ἀμηχανεῖς
καὶ ἀσχάλλεις, διότι τὴν τῆς παλιγγενεσίας μετακόσμησιν ἀγνοεῖς
ὁ τῆς γενέσεως τὸν λόγον εἰδώς. εἰ δὲ ὄναρ σοι ἐκεῖνα καὶ φαντασία
καὶ πανταχόθεν ἡ ἐπίγνωσις ἄπορος, μὴ ἀγανάκτει, εἰ τὸν λόγον
τῆς κατασκευῆς ἀγνοῶν καὶ τὴν διόρθωσιν τοῦ φθαρέντος οὐ
συνορᾷς, ὁ αὐτὸς τεχνίτης ἐστὶ καὶ τῆς πρώτης κτίσεως καὶ τῆς
δευτέρας μετακοσμήσεως. οἶδεν ὅπως τὸ ἴδιον ἔργον διάλυσιν
ὑπομεῖναν συναρμόσει πάλιν εἰς τὴν ἀρχαίαν κατάστασιν. εἰ
σοφίας χρεία, ἡ πηγὴ τῆς σοφίας παρ᾽ ἐκείνῳ, εἰ δυνάμεως, οὐ
χρῄζει συνεργοῦ καὶ συλλήπτορος. οὗτός ἐστιν ὁ κατὰ τὴν φωνὴν

---

[17]The Greek text, as presented in Gebhardt's edition and in most manuscripts, says literally, "to us insignificant ones." A marginal gloss in one manuscript explains this, however, as "who are small and humble." Manuscript D, from the tenth century, reads λόγοις (*logois*) instead of ολίγοις (*oligois*). I have drawn on both readings.

puzzling, to our little minds![17] The works of creating come easily to God—everyone agrees on that. How, then, can those seem sober and wise who concede that one rib became a human person, but cannot believe that the same person can be re-created from a whole person's matter?

It is impossible—simply impossible—to probe the depths of God's actions with human ways of thinking. For if everything were within our intellectual grasp, the one who is greater would *not* be greater. And why do I simply mention God? Even with reference to some irrational animals, we stand to compare well with some of their powers, but fall far short of others. Horses and dogs and many other animals outrun us right from the start, camels and mules surpass us in their endurance, donkeys in their recognition of roads, and the gazelle's sharp vision has no rival in [the powers of] our own eyes. For that reason, it seems proper for well-intentioned, modest people to believe in what has been said by God, and not to demand explanations of the "how" and "why" of his activities, since that is above our understanding. For it will be said to each over-curious inquirer: show me by your reason how all you see was formed; tell me by what art [God] created this multiform masterpiece![18]

9 For even if you discover this, you will likely be confused and distressed, because although you may have an explanation for the creation of things, you do not understand the transformation that will occur in their being created anew. But if these things seem to you a dream and a fantasy, and full understanding is impossible for all kinds of reasons, do not complain if, being ignorant of the explanation of creation, you also do not grasp how what is corrupted will be restored. The same one is the craftsman both of the first creation and of the second re-creation. He knows how to form his own production, which has undergone destruction, once again into its original condition. If this calls for wisdom, the fountain of Wisdom is with him; if it calls for power, he is not lacking a collaborator to assist him.

[18]Gregory is apparently not citing Scripture directly here, but is alluding more generally to God's challenge to human curiosity, in passages like Job 38–39.

τοῦ σοφωτάτου προφήτου μετρήσας τῇ χειρὶ τὸ ὕδωρ καὶ τὸν μέγαν καὶ ἄπλετον οὐρανὸν σπιθαμῇ καὶ τὴν γῆν δρακί. θεώρησον εἰκόνας ἐναργεῖς σημασίας παρεχομένας τῆς ἀρρήτου δυνάμεως, ἀπόγνωσιν ἐμποιούσας τοῖς λογισμοῖς ἡμῶν τοῦ μηδὲν δύνασθαι ἄξιον τῆς τοῦ θεοῦ φύσεως φαντασθῆναι. παντοδύναμος καὶ ἔστι καὶ λέγεται (τάχα γὰρ οὐ ζυγομαχήσεις πρὸς τοῦτο, ἀλλὰ δώσεις ὡς
GNO 257 | συγκεχωρημένον κρατεῖν), τῷ δὲ πάντα δυναμένῳ οὐδὲν ἄπορον ἢ ἀμήχανον. ἔχεις πολλὰ τῆς πίστεως ἐνέχυρα ἀναγκαστικῶς σε συνελαύνοντα πρὸς τὸ συντίθεσθαι τοῖς παρ᾽ ἡμῶν λεγομένοις· πρῶτον μὲν πᾶσαν τὴν ποικίλην καὶ πολυσύνθετον κτίσιν βοῶσαν παντὸς κηρύγματος εὐσημότερον, ὅτι ὁ μέγας καὶ σοφὸς τεχνίτης ὁ πάντα τὰ βλεπόμενα τεχνησάμενος· πρὸς δὲ ταύτην προμηθὴς ὢν ὁ θεὸς καὶ τὰ τῶν ἀπίστων ψυχάρια πόρρωθεν καθορῶν ἔργῳ τὴν τῶν νεκρῶν ἔγερσιν ἐβεβαίωσεν πολλὰ σώματα τῶν τετελευτηκότων ψυχώσας. διὰ τοῦτο Λάζαρος τετραήμερος νεκρὸς τῆς θήκης ἐξήλατο καὶ τῆς χήρας ὁ μονογενὴς ἀπεδόθη τῇ μητρὶ ἐκ τῆς κλίνης καὶ τῆς ἐκφορᾶς πρὸς τοὺς ζῶντας ἀναλυθεὶς καὶ ἄλλοι μυρίοι, οὓς ἀπαριθμεῖσθαι νῦν ὀχληρόν. τί λέγω περὶ τοῦ θεοῦ καὶ σωτῆρος, ὁπότε, ἵνα ἐπὶ πλέον δυσωπηθῶσιν οἱ ἀμφιβάλλοντες, καὶ τοῖς δούλοις αὐτοῦ τοῖς ἀποστόλοις τὴν τοῦ ἐγείρειν νεκροὺς ἐχαρίσατο δύναμιν; ἔστιν οὖν ἡ ἀπόδειξις ἐναργής, καὶ διὰ τί οἱ φιλόνεικοι πράγματα ἡμῖν παρέχετε ὡς ἀναποδείκτων λόγων ἐξηγηταῖς; ὡς εἷς ἠγέρθη, οὕτω καὶ δέκα, ὡς οἱ δέκα καὶ τριακόσιοι, ὡς τριακόσιοι καὶ οἱ πολλοί· ὁ γὰρ ἑνὸς ἀνδριάντος τεχνίτης ἔσται ῥᾳδίως καὶ μυρίων δημιουργός. οὐκ εἴδετε τοὺς μηχανικούς, ὅπως τῶν μεγάλων καὶ ἐξαισίων οἰκοδομημάτων ἐν ὀλίγῳ κηρῷ τὰς

This is he who, in the words of the wise Prophet, "has measured the waters with his hand, and the great, empty heavens with his fingers' span, and the earth with the breadth of his palm" (Is 40.12, LXX). Reflect on the clear, meaningful images of his unspeakable power, inserting into your thoughts the clear warning that we cannot even imagine anything worthy of the nature of God. He is—and is said to be—almighty (perhaps you will not quarrel with this, but will grant that what you concede is true); nothing, then, is difficult or impossible for the one who can do all things. You have many testimonies of faith, which necessarily move you toward agreeing with what we have said. First of all, there is the whole of creation in its variety and its manifold connectedness, shouting out more clearly than any verbal proclamation that the great and wise craftsman is the one who has devised all that we can see. In addition, God, in his providence—seeing from afar the little souls of those who would not believe—confirmed in action the resurrection of the dead by raising to life again the bodies of many of those who had already died. So Lazarus came forth from the tomb on the fourth day after his death, and the only son of the widow was given back to his mother from his bier, released back to the living from his funeral procession—and countless others, whom it would be troublesome now to narrate in detail. But why am I speaking of our God and Savior, since—in order to cause yet more chagrin for those who contest this—he has bestowed the power to raise the dead even on his servants the apostles?[19]

10 This, then, is a clear proof. Why do you, in your desire to win arguments, keep raising issues as if we were expounding unproved stories? Just as one is risen, so there will be ten; and as ten, so three hundred; and as three hundred, so a great throng—for the sculptor of one image will easily be the craftsman of countless others. Don't you know that builders form in advance, in little pieces of wax, the shapes

[19]Gregory is alluding to miracles like that of Peter raising Tabitha (Acts 9.36–41), and perhaps to Paul's raising the young man Eutychus, who had fallen from an upper window and was presumed dead (Acts 20.7–12). Cf. Mt 10.8.

μορφὰς καὶ τοὺς τύπους προαναπλάττουσι καὶ ὁ ἐν τῷ μικρῷ λόγος
τὴν αὐτὴν ἔχει δύναμιν ἐν ταῖς πολλαῖς καὶ μεγάλαις κατασκευαῖς;
μέγας ὁ οὐρανός, τεχνικὸν τοῦ θεοῦ δημιούργημα· ἐπειδὴ δὲ
PG 668 λογικὸν ζῷον ὁ θεὸς τὸν ἄνθρωπον | ἐποίησεν, | ἵνα τῇ καταλήψει
GNO 258 τῶν ποιημάτων δοξάσῃ τὸν σοφὸν καὶ εὐμήχανον ποιητήν, ὄψει τὸ
τοῦ ἀστρονόμου σφαιρίον μικρὸν μέν, ἐν δὲ τῇ χειρὶ κινούμενον
τοῦ ἐπιστήμονος οὕτως ὡς <ὁ> οὐρανὸς παρὰ τοῦ θεοῦ. καὶ τὸ
ἐλάχιστον κατασκεύασμα τοῦ μεγάλου δημιουργήματος εἰκὼν
γίνεται καὶ ἐν τοῖς μικροῖς ὁ λόγος ἑρμηνεύει τὰ ὑπέρογκα καὶ
τὰ τὴν αἴσθησιν ἡμῶν ὑπερβαίνοντα. ταῦτα δὲ πρὸς τί διῆλθον;
ἵνα γινώσκῃς, ὅτι κἂν ἐρωτήσῃς με, πῶς ἔσται τῶν ἀπ' αἰῶνος
σωμάτων ἡ ἀνάστασις, ἀντακούσῃ ταχέως· πῶς ὁ τετραήμερος
ἠγέρθη Λάζαρος; πρόδηλον γὰρ ὡς τὴν ἐπὶ τῷ ἑνὶ πληροφορίαν
κἀν τοῖς πολλοῖς ὁμοίως ὁ σωφρονῶν παραδέξεται. θεὸν
ὑποτιθέμενος τὸν ποιοῦντα μηδὲν εἴπῃς ἀδύνατον μηδὲ τῇ σαυτοῦ
ἐννοίᾳ καταληπτὴν νομίσῃς τὴν τοῦ ἀκαταλήπτου σοφίαν· οὔτε
γὰρ ἐκείνῳ τι ἄπειρον καὶ σοὶ τὰ τοῦ ἀπείρου ἀνεξερεύνητα.

Ὀψόμεθα δὲ τοῦτον τὸν λόγον καλῶς, ἂν πρὸς τοῖς εἰρημένοις καὶ τὸν τρόπον τῆς γενέσεως ἡμῶν δοκιμάσωμεν, οὐ τὸν πρῶτον καὶ πρεσβύτατον ἐκεῖνον τὸν παρὰ θεοῦ, περὶ οὗ ἐν τοῖς ἔμπροσθεν εἴρηται, ἀλλὰ τὸν μέχρι νῦν ἀκολούθως παρὰ τῆς φύσεως ἐκτελούμενον· ἄπορος γὰρ οὗτος καὶ λογισμῷ ἀνθρωπίνῳ ἀπρόσιτος. πῶς γὰρ τὸ σπέρμα οὐσία οὖσα ὑγρὰ καὶ ἄπλαστος καὶ ἀνείδεος εἰς κεφαλὴν πήγνυται καὶ εἰς ἀντικνήμια καὶ πλευρὰς στερεοῦται καὶ ποιεῖ ἐγκέφαλον ἁπαλὸν καὶ μανὸν καὶ τὸ περιέχον αὐτὸν ὀστέον οὕτω σκληρὸν καὶ ἀντιτυπὲς καὶ τὴν ποικίλην τοῦ ζῴου κατασκευήν, ἵνα συντόμως εἴπω καὶ μὴ παρέλκω λεπτομερῶς ἐπεξιὼν τοῖς καθ' ἕκαστα; ὡς οὖν τὸ σπέρμα ὑπάρχον ἄμορφον ἐν

and figures of their large, impressive buildings and that the structure conceived on a small scale has the same application for a number of large constructions? The heavens are enormous—a creation of God's artistry. And since God has created the human person as a rational animal, so that by understanding [other] creatures he might glorify his wise and inventive creator, so the astronomer's model sphere may be a small thing in appearance, but when moved by the hand of a scientist, it behaves just as the heavens do when moved by God. Our smallest device can become an image of creation writ large, and by focusing on little things, reason interprets what is huge in bulk and far exceeds our perception. Why am I explaining this? So that you might realize that if you ask me how the resurrection of age-old bodies will happen, you will hear the quick reply: how was Lazarus raised on the fourth day? For clearly a wise person will recognize that as it was accomplished in the case of one, so also it will be in the many. When you recognize that God is creator, you will not call anything impossible, nor will you think that what is conceivable by your intellectual powers defines the wisdom of him who is beyond our understanding. Nothing is boundless to him, even those boundless things that for you are beyond investigation.

11 We will see this argument clearly, if, in addition to what we have said, we also consider the manner of our generation: not that first, eldest one brought about by God,[20] about which we have already spoken, but what has been achieved in accordance with nature since then, right up to the present. For this is a puzzle, resistant to human reasoning. How, after all, does human seed, which is a moist substance, without shape or form, become solidified as a head and take shape as shins and ribs? How does it form the soft, spreading brain tissue, and the skull that contains it, so bony and resistant, and all the varied construction of the living person—if I may speak summarily, and not go minutely through all the details? Just as the seed, then, which in the beginning is shapeless, is forged into a shape

[20]I.e., Adam.

ἀρχαῖς εἰς σχῆμα τυποῦται καὶ εἰς ὄγκους ἁδρύνεται τῇ ἀπορρήτῳ
GNO 259 τοῦ θεοῦ κατασκευαζόμενον τέχνῃ, οὕτως οὐδὲν ἀπεικός, | ἀλλὰ
καὶ πάνυ ἀκόλουθον, τὴν ἐν τοῖς τάφοις ὕλην τήν ποτε οὖσαν ἐν
εἴδει αὖθις εἰς τὴν παλαιὰν ἀνακαινισθῆναι διάπλασιν καὶ πάλιν
γενέσθαι τὸν χοῦν ἄνθρωπον, ὥσπερ δὴ καὶ τὸ πρῶτον ἐκεῖθεν
ἔσχε τὴν γένεσιν.

Συγχωρήσωμεν τῷ θεῷ δύνασθαι τοσοῦτον ὅσον ὁ κεραμεὺς
ἰσχύει. τί γὰρ οὗτος ποιεῖ, λογισώμεθα· πηλὸν λαβὼν ἄμορφον
εἰς σκεῦος εἰδοποιεῖ καὶ τοῦτο πρὸς τὴν ἀκτῖνα τὴν ἡλιακὴν
προθέμενος ξηραίνει καὶ στερεὸν ἀπεργάζεται, ἔστι δὲ ἀμφορίσκος
ἢ πίναξ ἢ πίθος τὸ πλαττόμενον· ἀλλ᾽ ἐμπεσόντος τινὸς ἀτάκτως
καὶ ἀνατρέψαντος συντρίβεται καταπεσὼν καὶ γίνεται ἀμόρφωτος
γῆ, ὁ δὲ τεχνίτης βουληθεὶς ὀξέως ἐπανορθοῖ τὸ συμβὰν καὶ
πάλιν πηλὸν σχηματίσας τῇ τέχνῃ οὐδὲν χεῖρον τοῦ ποτε ὄντος
ἀπεργάζεται τὸ σκεῦος. καὶ ὁ μὲν κεραμεὺς οὕτως μικρὸν τῆς
PG 669 τοῦ θεοῦ δυνάμεως κτίσμα, ὁ δὲ θεὸς ἀπιστεῖται ὑπ|ισχνούμενος
ἀνακαινίζειν τὸν τεθνηκότα. πολλῆς ταῦτα τῆς ἀνοίας ἐστίν.

Θεωρήσωμεν καὶ τὸ τοῦ σίτου ὑπόδειγμα, ᾧ Παῦλος ὁ
πάνσοφος παιδεύει τοὺς ἄφρονας λέγων· Ἄφρων σύ, ὃ σπείρεις,
<οὐ ζωοποιεῖται, ἐὰν μὴ ἀποθάνῃ, καὶ ὃ σπείρεις,> οὐ τὸ σῶμα
τὸ γενησόμενον σπείρεις, ἀλλὰ γυμνὸν κόκκον, εἰ τύχοι, σίτου
ἤ τινος τῶν λοιπῶν σπερμάτων, ὁ δὲ θεὸς δίδωσιν αὐτῷ σῶμα,
καθὼς ἠθέλησεν. ἀκριβῶς προσέχωμεν τῇ γενέσει τοῦ σίτου, καὶ
τάχα τὸν περὶ ἡμῶν λόγον διδαχθησόμεθα. ὁ σῖτος ῥίπτεται εἰς
τὴν γῆν, διασαπεὶς δὲ ἐν τῇ νοτίδι καί, ὡς ἂν εἴποι τις, τελευτήσας
ἀπολήγει εἴς τινα γαλακτώδη οὐσίαν, ἥτις παγεῖσα μικρὸν ὀξὺ
GNO 260 καὶ λευκὸν | γίνεται κέντρον, αὐξηθεῖσα δὲ ὅσον προκύψαι τῆς
γῆς ἐκ τοῦ λευκοῦ πρὸς τὸ ἠρέμα χλοαινόμενον μεταβάλλεται,
εἶτα γίνεται πόα καὶ κόμη τῶν βώλων, ἐφαπλωθεῖσα δὲ αὐτοῖς καὶ
σκεδασθεῖσα μετρίως πολυσχιδῆ κάτωθεν ὑποτρέφει τὴν ῥίζαν τῷ

[21]Gregory uses this same example in his *Catechetical Discourse* 8.3–7 (GNO III/4: 29.13—31.21; PPS 60:83–85), and in his *Funeral Oration for Pulcheria* 10. For the same image of the potter reshaping his broken clay pot, compare, e.g., Jer 18.1–6, Is 64.8, Rom 9.21–23, and Methodius, *On the Resurrection* 1.44.

and matures as bulky masses, wrought by the unspeakable craft of God, so it is not at all unlikely, but seems in fact fully consistent, that matter which once had a form but is now in the grave should again be renewed in its old structure, and that earth should again become a human being, just as the human had his origin from there.

Let us grant God the power to do as much as a potter can do! Reflect, then, on just what that potter does: he takes shapeless clay, forms it into a pot, and then sets this out in the rays of the sun to dry. So he succeeds in hardening it, and what is shaped is a little wine-jar, or a plate, or a large bowl. But if someone comes past carelessly and upsets it, it falls and is smashed, and again becomes shapeless mud; yet the craftsman, if he wishes, quickly picks up the smashed pot and once again shapes, by his art, something just as good as what once existed, and completes the vessel.[21] And the potter is only a small creation of divine power—yet we disbelieve God when he promises to raise the dead again! What great foolishness!

12 Let us consider also the example of grain, with which the all-wise Paul educates the ignorant, saying, "You foolish one, what you sow will not come to life, unless it dies. And what you sow is not the body that shall later come to be, but a bare grain, if you will, of wheat or some other seed, and God gives it a body as he chooses" (1 Cor 15.36–38).[22] Let us pay close attention to the germination of wheat, and perhaps we will learn the answer about ourselves. The grain of wheat is thrown into the ground, rots in the moisture, and ends (one might say) by becoming a kind of milky substance; but this, when it is implanted, soon becomes a sharp, white spur, then grows enough to emerge from the earth and is transformed from white to something faintly green; then it becomes a sprout, and takes form as foliage on the clods of earth; and as it widens on the earth and gradually spreads out, it builds up a mass of roots below, carefully preparing a support system below for the weight that is to come. And

[22]Gebhardt, the editor, has supplied the words of verse 36—"will not come to life, unless it dies. And what you sow"—which are missing from Gregory's text in the manuscripts.

μέλλοντι βάρει τὴν ὑποβάθραν προευτρεπίζουσα· καὶ ὥσπερ οἱ ἱστοὶ τῶν πλοίων πλείστοις πανταχόθεν διατείνονται κάλοις, ἵνα πάγιοι μένωσιν ἰσορρόποις ταῖς ὁλκαῖς ἀντισπώμενοι, οὕτως αἱ σχοινοειδεῖς ἀποφύσεις τῆς ῥίζης ἀντιλαβαὶ τῶν ἀσταχύων γίνονται καὶ ἐρείσματα. ἐπειδὰν δὲ εἰς κάλαμον ὁ σῖτος διαναστῇ καὶ πρὸς τὸ ὕψος ἐπείγηται, γόνασιν αὐτὸν καὶ κόμβοις ὁ θεὸς ὑπερείδει οἷον οἰκίαν τινὰ συνδέσμοις ἀσφαλιζόμενος διὰ τὴν προσδοκωμένην τῆς κόμης βαρύτητα. εἶτα τῆς ἰσχύος ἑτοιμασθείσης τὴν κάλυκα σχίσας προάγει τὸν ἄσταχυν. καὶ πάλιν ἐκεῖ θαύματα κρείττονα· στοιχηδὸν γὰρ ὁ σῖτος αὐτῷ περιφύεται καὶ τῶν κόκκων ἕκαστος ἐξαίρετον ἔχει τὴν ἀποθήκην καὶ τελευταῖοι προβέβληνται οἱ ἀνθέρικες ὀξεῖς καὶ λεπτοί, ὅπλα οἶμαι κατὰ τῶν σπερμολόγων ὀρνίθων, ἵνα ταῖς ἐκείνων ἀκμαῖς νυττόμενοι τῷ καρπῷ μὴ λυμαίνωνται. ὁρᾷς, ὅσην εἷς κόκκος διασαπεὶς θαυματουργίαν ἔχει καὶ μόνος πεσὼν μεθ' ὅσων ἐγείρεται· ἄνθρωπος δὲ οὐδὲν προσλαμβάνει πλέον, ὃ δὲ εἶχεν, ἀπολαμβάνει, καὶ διὰ τοῦτο τῆς γεωργίας τοῦ σίτου ὁ ἡμέτερος ἀνακαινισμὸς εὐκολώτερος ἀναφαίνεται.

Ἐντεῦθεν μετάβηθι πρὸς τὴν ἔννοιαν τῶν δένδρων, ὅπως ὁ
χειμὼν αὐτοῖς καθ' ἕκαστον ἔτος ἀντὶ θανάτου γίνεται· ἀπορρύεται
γὰρ ἡ ὀπώρα καὶ τὸ φύλλον πίπτει καὶ ξηρὰ μένει τὰ ξύλα πάσης
χάριτος ἐστερημένα. ἐπειδὰν δὲ τοῦ ἔαρος ὁ καιρὸς ἐπιλάβοι, ἄνθος
GNO 261 αὐτοῖς χαριέστατον ὑπερφύεται καὶ | μετὰ τὸ ἄνθος ἐπιγίνεται τῶν
φύλλων ἡ σκέπη καὶ τότε ὡς εὐειδὲς θέαμα ἀνθρώπων τε τὰς ὄψεις
ἐφέλκεται καὶ ὀρνίθων ᾠδικῶν ἐργαστήρια γίνεται τοῖς πετάλοις
ἐγκαθημένων καὶ θαυμαστή τις περὶ αὐτὰ χάρις ἐκλάμπει, ὥστε
πολλοὶ καὶ οἶκον ἀφῆκαν χρυσῷ κεκοσμημένον καὶ λίθῳ τῷ
Θεσσαλῷ καὶ Λάκωνι, τερπνὴν δὲ μᾶλλον ἑαυτοῖς ἔθεντο τὴν
ὑπὸ δένδρα διαγωγήν. διὸ καὶ ὁ πατριάρχης Ἀβραὰμ ὑπὸ δρυῒ τὴν
σκηνὴν ἐπήξατο οὐκ οἰκίας πάντως ἀπορῶν, ἀλλὰ τῇ σκέπῃ τῶν
κλάδων ἐπαγαλλόμενος. |

as the masts of boats are secured by many ropes from all sides, so that they remain upright as the boats strain against winds of equal force, so here the rope-like growths of the roots become buttresses and supports for the stalks. And when the wheat grows into a stalk and is pushed up to its proper height, God supports it with joints and wrappings—making a kind of solid house with these supports, because of what will become the heavy weight of the plant's crown. Then, with its strength now sufficient, it splits the pod and brings forth the ear. And there, again, still greater marvels take place: for the wheat grows on the ear in a row, and each of the grains has its own special chamber; on their tips sharp, light hairs are put forth, which I assume are defensive weapons against birds gathering seeds, so that when they are stabbed by these little blades they will avoid injuring the fruit. See what wonderful power a single decayed seed possesses; although it falls into the ground alone, with how many seeds it rises! A [risen] human being, on the other hand, does not gather anything more into himself, but only receives back what he had; in this way, our renewal is obviously easier than cultivating wheat!

13 Go on from there to consider trees: how winter, every year, acts in the place of death for them! Late summer fades, the leaves fall, and the branches remain dry, stripped of all their beauty. But when the moment of spring arrives, a lovely blanket of blossoms covers them, and after the blossoms comes the shade of leaves; this attracts the gaze of humans with its beautiful display, and becomes a building-site for birds' nests hidden among the leaves. A certain wonderful charm radiates around them, so that many will trade a house decked out with gold and marble from Thessaly and Laconia, to seek pleasure for themselves by spending their time under the trees. So the patriarch Abraham pitched his tent beneath an oak, surely not because he was homeless but because he delighted in its sheltering branches.[23]

[23]See Gen 18.1.

PG 672 Ὁδηγεῖ με πρὸς συγκατάθεσιν τοῦ προκειμένου λόγου καὶ τῶν ἑρπετῶν ἡ ζωή· νεκροῦται γὰρ ἐκείνων ὥρᾳ χειμῶνος ἡ ζώπυρος δύναμις καὶ τὸν χρόνον τῶν ἓξ μηνῶν ἐν τοῖς φωλεοῖς κατάκειται παντελῶς ἀκίνητα. ἐπειδὰν δὲ ὁ τεταγμένος ἔλθῃ καιρὸς καὶ βροντὴ κατηχήσῃ τοῦ κόσμου, ὥσπερ τι σύνθημα τῆς ζωῆς τὸν κτύπον δεχόμενα ὀξέως ἀναπηδᾷ καὶ διὰ μακροῦ τοῦ χρόνου ἐνεργεῖ τὰ συνήθη. τίς ὁ λόγος οὗτος; λεγέτω μοι ὁ τῶν πράξεων τοῦ θεοῦ βασανιστὴς καὶ ἐπιγνώμων καὶ διδασκέτω με, πῶς βροντῇ μὲν τοὺς ὄφεις διεγείρεσθαι συγχωρεῖ νεκροὺς ὑπάρχοντας, ἀνθρώπους δὲ οὐ δίδωσι ψυχοῦσθαι τῆς τοῦ θεοῦ σάλπιγγος ἐξ οὐρανῶν ἐπηχούσης, καθὼς ὁ θεῖος λόγος φησί· Σαλπίσει γὰρ καὶ οἱ νεκροὶ ἀναστήσονται· καὶ ἀλλαχοῦ πάλιν σαφέστερον· Καὶ ἀποστελεῖ τοὺς ἀγγέλους αὐτοῦ μετὰ σάλπιγγος φωνῆς μεγάλης καὶ ἐπισυνάξει τοὺς ἐκλεκτοὺς αὐτοῦ.

Μὴ τοίνυν ταῖς ἀλλοιώσεσι καὶ τοῖς ἀνακαινισμοῖς ἀπιστῶμεν·
GNO 262 καὶ γὰρ φυτῶν καὶ ζῴων διαφόρων ὁ βίος καὶ | αὐτῶν γε τῶν ἀνθρώπων ἡμᾶς ἐκπαιδεύει, ὡς οὐδὲν ἐν ταυτότητι τῶν ἐν φθορᾷ καὶ γενέσει, ἐν ἀλλοιώσει δὲ καὶ τροπῇ. καὶ πρῶτόν γε εἰ δοκεῖ τὴν ἐν ταῖς ἡλικίαις ἡμῶν μεταβολὴν καταμάθωμεν· τὸ παιδίον τὸ ὑπομάζιον οἷόν ἐστι γνωρίζομεν. ὀλίγου χρόνου παρελθόντος τὴν ἑρπυστικὴν λαμβάνει δύναμιν καὶ οὐδὲν διαφέρει τῶν μικρῶν σκυλάκων τέτρασιν ἐρειδόμενον βάσεσιν· περὶ τὸν τρίτον ἐνιαυτὸν ὄρθιον γίνεται καὶ φωνὴν ὑποτραυλιζομένην καὶ ψελλιζομένην προΐεται· εἶτα διαρθροῖ τὸν λόγον καὶ χαρίεν ἀποτελεῖται μειράκιον· ἀπ' ἐκείνης τῆς ἡλικίας πρὸς τὸν ἔφηβον καὶ νεανίσκον ἐκβαίνει· ἰούλου δὲ τὴν παρειὰν καλύψαντος γενειὰς λάσιος μετ' ὀλίγον καὶ ἄλλος ἐξ ἄλλου· εἶτα ἀνὴρ ἀκμάζων τραχὺς τληπαθής. ἐπειδὰν δὲ παρέλθωσι τέσσαρες δεκάδες ἐνιαυτῶν, ἀρχὴ τῆς ὑποστροφῆς καὶ πολιὰ ἠρέμα ὑπολευκαίνει τὴν κεφαλὴν καὶ ἡ ῥώμη πρὸς ἀσθένειαν

[24]Aristotle, in the *History of Animals*, tells of the effect of thunder on nesting birds (560a4) and on some kinds of fish (602b22), but does not recount this detail of thunder awaking snakes from hibernation; it is not clear what Gregory's source is for

Even the life of snakes leads me to extend the argument I have been making here. For their spark of life seems to die out in wintertime, and for a space of six months they lie completely motionless in their holes. But when the appointed time comes, and thunder echoes around their world,[24] they perceive the crash like some signal of life and quickly start up again, acting as they usually do for the long season ahead. What does this report signify? Let him tell me, who studies and discerns the actions of God; let him explain to me how he can agree that snakes in a lifeless state are raised up by thunder, yet will not concede that humans will be enlivened when God's trumpet echoes in the heavens, as Holy Scripture tells us: "For the trumpet shall sound, and the dead shall be raised" (1 Cor 15.52). And it says yet more clearly in another place: "And he will send his angels with the sound of a loud trumpet, and will gather his chosen ones together" (Mt 24.31).

14 Let us not refuse to believe, then, in the forms of change and renewal. The life of various plants and animals, after all, and even that of human beings themselves, teaches us that nothing that comes to be and passes away [always] remains just as it is, but is involved in transformation and change. First, then, if you will, let us consider the various changes that take place in our own life. We know what an infant at the breast is like. When a little time has passed, he acquires the ability to crawl, and is no different from a little puppy, moving on all fours. Around the age of two, he stands up straight and makes lisping, inarticulate sounds; then he develops articulate speech and achieves the state of a graceful child. From that age, he moves on to become a teenager and a youth; and after down has covered his cheeks, his face becomes bearded, little by little and step by step. Then, as a mature man, he is tough and enduring. But when forty years have come upon him, another change begins: the hair on his head gradually turns white, his strength declines toward weakness,

this piece of information. There is, however, a traditional Native American belief that snakes emerge from their winter sleep at the first clap of thunder in spring; this may be a conviction shared by many ancient cultures.

ἀποκλίνει καὶ παραγίνεται τελευταῖον τὸ γῆρας τέλειος ἀφανισμὸς
τῆς ἰσχύος, κλίνεται δὲ τὸ σῶμα καὶ κυρτοῦται πρὸς γῆν ὡς οἱ
ὑπερξηρανθέντες τῶν ἀσταχύων καὶ τὸ λεῖον ἀποτελεῖται ῥυσὸν
καὶ πάλιν βρέφος ὅ ποτε νεανίσκος καὶ ἀριστεὺς ψελλιζόμενος,
ἀνοηταίνων, ἐπὶ χειρῶν καὶ ποδῶν ὁμοίως ἕρπων ὡς πάλαι. ταῦτα
πάντα τί σοι δοκεῖ; οὐκ ἀλλοιώσεις; οὐ μεταβολαὶ πολύτροποι;
οὐ διάφοροι καινότητες τὸ θνητὸν ζῷον μεταμορφοῦσαι καὶ πρὸ
θανάτου; ὁ δὲ ὕπνος ἡμῶν καὶ ἡ ἐγρήγορσις πῶς οὐκ ἂν τῷ
σοφῷ γένοιτο διδασκάλιον τοῦ ζητουμένου; ὁ μὲν γὰρ εἰκών
ἐστι τοῦ θανάτου, ἡ δὲ τῆς ἀναστάσεως μίμημα. διὸ καί τινες
GNO 263 τῶν | ἔξωθεν σοφῶν ἀδελφὸν προσεῖπον τοῦ θανάτου τὸν ὕπνον
διὰ τὴν ὁμοιότητα τῶν ἀφ᾽ ἑκατέρου συμβαινόντων παθῶν·
PG 673 λήθη γὰρ ὁμοίως ἐπ᾽ ἀμφοτέρων καὶ ἄγνοια τῶν | παρελθόντων
καὶ τῶν μελλόντων καὶ τὸ σῶμα κεῖται ἀναίσθητον φίλον οὐκ
εἰδός, ἐχθρὸν οὐ γινῶσκον, τοὺς περιεστῶτας καὶ θεωροῦντας
μὴ βλέπον, παρειμένον νεκρόν, πάσης ἀμοιροῦν ἐνεργείας, οὐδὲν
διαφέρον τῶν ἀποκειμένων ἐν τάφοις καὶ θήκαις. οὕτω τοι συλᾷς
ὡς νεκρὸν εἰ θέλοις τὸν καθεύδοντα, κενοῖς τὴν οἰκίαν, δεσμὰ
προσάγεις καὶ οὐδεμία τῶν πραττομένων αἴσθησις ἐπιγίνεται·
ὀλίγον δὲ ὕστερον, ὅταν ἀνοχή τις καὶ λώφησις γένηται τοῦ
πάθους, ὥσπερ ἄρτι ζωοποιηθεὶς ὁ ἄνθρωπος διανίσταται κατὰ
μικρὸν εἰς συναίσθησιν ἑαυτοῦ καὶ τῶν πραγμάτων ἐρχόμενος
καὶ σχολῇ τὰς ἐνεργείας ἀναλαμβάνων καὶ οἷον ψυχούμενος τῇ
ζωπυρήσει τῆς ἐγρηγόρσεως. εἰ δὲ ὑφεστῶτος ἔτι τοῦ ζῴου καὶ
περιόντος τοσαῦται νύκτωρ καὶ μεθ᾽ ἡμέραν ἐκστάσεις ἀλλοιώσεις
μεταβολαὶ λῆθαι καὶ μνῆμαι τῷ βίῳ παραπεπήγασι, λίαν ἀνόητον

---

[25]Gregory presents here a version of the classical trope of the successive "ages of man," which goes back at least to the time of Solon in the early 6th century BC. The most famous English version of this ancient idea is that in Jacques' speech, beginning "All the world's a stage," in Shakespeare's *As You Like It*, Act II, Scene 7. For a summary

and in the end old age is accompanied by a complete vanishing of strength. The body becomes bent and stooped toward the ground, like a dried-out ear of corn; what was smooth becomes wrinkled, and the one who was formerly a heroic young man becomes an infant again—inarticulate, demented, moving on hands and feet as long before.[25]

15 What does all this seem to mean, in your opinion? Are these not changes? Not various forms of transformation? Don't these different new stages give new forms to the living mortal, even before death? And our sleep and our waking—how could they not be instructive for a wise person, on the subject we are discussing? The one is an image of death, after all, the other an imitation of resurrection. So some wise secular writers have addressed sleep as "the brother of death,"[26] because of the similar things we experience as a result of each: forgetfulness comes with each in the same way, and unawareness of past and future; the body, too, lies without perception, neither knowing friend nor recognizing enemy, not seeing those who stand around it gazing—a motionless corpse, not showing any signs of activity, not a bit different from those who lie in graves and sepulchers. So, if you wish, you can strip a sleeping person as if he were dead, ransack his house, bind him in chains, and he will show no awareness of what you are doing. But a little later, when there is some lessening or even an interruption of his condition, the person stands up as if just given a new life, little by little coming to be aware of himself and what is happening, slowly resuming his activities and reanimated, as it were, by the spark of waking life. And if, while a living person still exists and survives, so many changes, transformations and alterations, forgettings and rememberings, are recorded night and day in one's life, it is extremely silly and overly polemical

of classical reflection on this theme, and of its terminology, see R. Larry Overstreet, "The Greek Concept of the 'Seven Stages of Life' and its New Testament Significance," *Bulletin for Biblical Research* 19 (2009): 537–63.

[26]See Homer, *Iliad* 14.231; 16.672, 682; Hesiod, *Theogony* 212.

καὶ φιλόνεικον θεῷ μὴ πιστεύειν τὸν ἔσχατον ἀνακαινισμὸν ἐπαγγελλομένῳ τῷ καὶ τὴν πρώτην πλάσιν δημιουργήσαντι.

Ὃ δὲ μάλιστα φράττει τοὺς ἀντιλέγοντας καὶ ἀπιστεῖν παρασκευάζει, τοῦτο πρὸ πάντων ὡς οἶμαι τὸ νομίζειν ἀφανισμὸν παντελῆ γίνεσθαι τῶν σωμάτων. ἔχει δὲ οὐχ οὕτως· οὐ γὰρ τέλεον ἀφανίζεται, ἀλλὰ διαλύεται εἰς τὰ ἐξ ὧν συνετέθη καὶ ἔστιν ἐν ὕδατι καὶ ἀέρι καὶ γῇ καὶ πυρί. τῶν δὲ πρωτοτύπων στοιχείων μενόντων καὶ τῶν ἀπ᾽ ἐκείνων μετὰ τὴν διάλυσιν ἐκείνοις προσχωρησάντων ἐν τοῖς καθόλου σῴζεται καὶ τὰ μέρη. θεῷ δὲ μάλιστα μὲν εὔπορον
GNO 264 | ἐξ οὐκ ὄντων δημιουργεῖν (καὶ γὰρ οὕτως ἐν ἀρχαῖς ἔλαβε τὰ πάντα τὴν γένεσιν), τὸ δὲ ἐξ ἀρχῶν τῶν οὐσῶν γενεσιουργεῖν πολλῷ δήπου ῥᾷστον καὶ εὐκολώτατον. μὴ τοίνυν τὴν καλὴν ἐλπίδα τῶν ἀνθρώπων ἀνέλωμεν τὴν ἐπανόρθωσιν τῆς ἀσθενείας ἡμῶν καὶ τὴν δευτέραν ὡς ἂν εἴποι τις γένεσιν τὴν ἐλευθέραν θανάτου μηδὲ φιληδονίας ὑπερβολῇ τὴν ἀγαθὴν καὶ φιλάνθρωπον τοῦ θεοῦ ὑπόσχεσιν καθυβρίσωμεν· ἐμοὶ γὰρ δοκοῦσιν οἱ τῆς προκειμένης ὑποθέσεως ἐναντίοι ἄνδρες εἶναι κακίας ἑταῖροι καὶ ἀρετῆς ἐχθροί, λάγνοι καὶ πλεονέκται καὶ ἀκρατεῖς ὀφθαλμοῖς καὶ ἀκοῇ καὶ ὀσφρήσει καὶ πάσαις ταῖς αἰσθήσεσι ῥέουσαν ἐπ᾽ αὐτοῖς τὴν ἡδονὴν εἰσδεχόμενοι. ἐπειδὴ δὲ ὁ τῆς ἀναστάσεως λόγος προκειμένην ἔχει τὴν κρίσιν καὶ τῶν ἱερῶν βίβλων ἀκούουσι λεγουσῶν διαρρήδην, ὡς οὐκ ἀνεύθυνος ἡμῶν ὁ βίος (ἀλλ᾽ ὅταν πρὸς τὴν δευτέραν ἀνακαινισθῶμεν ζωήν, πάντες παραστησόμεθα τῷ βήματι τοῦ Χριστοῦ, ὡς ὑπ᾽ ἐκείνῳ κριτῇ τὰς πρὸς ἀξίαν ἀμοιβὰς τῶν βεβιωμένων κομίσασθαι), συνειδότες ἑαυτοῖς πράξεις αἰσχίστας πολλῶν ἀξίας τιμωριῶν μίσει τῆς κρίσεως ἀναιροῦσι καὶ τὴν ἀνάστασιν, ὥσπερ οἱ πονηροὶ τῶν δούλων οἱ τὴν οὐσίαν τοῦ κυρίου δαπανήσαντες, θανάτους δὲ τοῦ δεσπότου καὶ ἀπωλείας

not to believe God's promise of a final renewal, since he has brought about our first formation.

16 What especially blocks the thought of those who reject this promise, and leads them not to believe, is, I think, above all the thought that bodies disappear completely. But this is not what happens; for they do not vanish completely, but are broken up into the parts of which they are composed, and they continue to exist in the form of water and air and earth and fire. So, since the most basic elements remain, and things derived from them are restored to that form after bodies are broken up, the parts, too, are preserved in the universal matter. It is easy, at least for God, to create from nothing—for this is the way that all things came into being at the beginning; to realize their formation, then, from principles that already exist is surely easier by far, and ready to be realized. Therefore let us not destroy the good hope of humanity—the overcoming of our weakness, what one might call our second creation, free from death; and let us not, in our excessive fondness for earthly pleasure, make light of God's good and loving promise.

17 For those who oppose the proposal before us seem to me to be people who ally themselves with vice and are enemies of virtue: lecherous and greedy, undisciplined in eye and ear and smell and all the sense-organs, welcoming pleasure as it flows toward them. But since the word of the resurrection holds judgment up before them, and they hear the holy books saying expressly that our life will not go unexamined (but when we are raised up to our second life, we shall all stand before the judgment seat of Christ, so as to receive from him as judge the just recompense for the way we have lived),[27] then—aware in their own consciences of shameful actions, which are worthy of many punishments—through their dread of judgment they reject the resurrection as well, just like those wicked slaves who have wasted their master's wealth, contriving for themselves their master's death and their own destruction, and fashioning vain ideas

[27]Cf. 2 Cor 5.10.

ἑαυτοῖς ὑπογράφοντες καὶ πρὸς τὴν ἰδίαν ἐπιθυμίαν διακένους
PG 676 λογισμοὺς ἀναπλάσσοντες. | ἀλλ᾽ οὐδὲ εἷς οὕτω φρονήσει τῶν
σωφρονούντων· τί γὰρ ὄφελος δικαιοσύνης καὶ ἀληθείας καὶ
χρηστότητος καὶ παντὸς τοῦ καλοῦ, ὑπὲρ τίνος δὲ μοχθοῦσι καὶ
φιλοσοφοῦσιν ἄνθρωποι γαστρὸς ἡδονὴν δουλαγωγοῦντες καὶ
ἀγαπῶντες ἐγκράτειαν καὶ ὕπνου πρὸς ὀλίγον μεταλαγχάνοντες
καὶ παρατάττόμενοι πρὸς χειμῶνα καὶ πνῖγος, εἰ ἀνάστασις οὐκ
ἔστιν; εἴπωμεν πρὸς ταῦτα τὰ ῥήματα Παύλου· Φάγωμεν καὶ
GNO 265 πίωμεν, | αὔριον γὰρ ἀποθνῄσκομεν. εἰ ἀνάστασις οὐκ ἔστιν, ἀλλὰ
πέρας τοῦ βίου θάνατος, ἄνελέ μοι κατηγορίας καὶ ψόγους, δὸς
ἀκώλυτον τῷ ἀνδροφόνῳ τὴν ἐξουσίαν, ἄφες τὸν μοιχὸν μετὰ
παρρησίας ἐπιβουλεύειν τοῖς γάμοις, τρυφάτω κατὰ τῶν ἀλλοτρίων
ὁ πλεονέκτης, μηδεὶς ἐπικοπτέτω τὸν λοίδορον, ὀμνύτω συνεχῶς
ὁ ἐπίορκος, μένει γὰρ θάνατος καὶ τὸν εὔορκον, ψευδέσθω ἄλλος
ὅσα βούλεται, οὐδεὶς γὰρ τῆς ἀληθείας καρπός, μηδεὶς ἐλεείτω τὸν
πένητα, ἄμισθος γάρ ἐστιν ὁ ἔλεος. ταῦτα τὰ φρονήματα χείρονα
ποιεῖ τοῦ κατακλυσμοῦ σύγχυσιν καὶ πάντα μὲν ἐκβάλλει σώφρονα
λόγον, πᾶν δὲ νόημα μανικὸν καὶ λῃστρικὸν ἐπιθήγει· εἰ γὰρ
ἀνάστασις οὐκ ἔστιν, οὐδὲ κρίσις, εἰ δὲ κρίσις ἀνῄρηται, καὶ φόβος
θεοῦ συνεκβάλλεται· ὅπου δὲ φόβος οὐ σωφρονίζει, ἐκεῖ χορεύει
μετὰ τῆς ἁμαρτίας ὁ διάβολος. καὶ λίαν ἁρμοδίως πρὸς τοὺς
τοιούτους ὁ Δαβὶδ ἐκεῖνον ἀνέγραψε τὸν ψαλμόν· Εἶπεν ἄφρων
ἐν καρδίᾳ αὐτοῦ· οὐκ ἔστι θεός. διεφθάρησαν καὶ ἐβδελύχθησαν
ἐν ἐπιτηδεύμασιν. εἰ ἀνάστασις οὐκ ἔστι, μῦθος ὁ Λάζαρος καὶ ὁ
πλούσιος καὶ τὸ φρικῶδες χάσμα καὶ ἡ τοῦ πυρὸς ἄσχετος φλόγωσις
καὶ ἡ διακαὴς γλῶσσα καὶ ἡ ποθουμένη σταγὼν τοῦ ὕδατος καὶ ὁ
δάκτυλος τοῦ πτωχοῦ. πρόδηλον γάρ, ὅτι ταῦτα πάντα τὸ μέλλον
ἐξεικονίζει τῆς ἀναστάσεως· γλῶσσα γὰρ καὶ δάκτυλος οὐ τῆς

---

[28]Perhaps a loose reference to Jesus' parable of the "wicked husbandmen" (Mt 21.33–41).

[29]Gregory's word is "lead the philosophic life [φιλοσοφοῦσιν, *philosophousin*]."

[30]All of these are details from Jesus' parable of the rich man and the beggar Lazarus in Luke 16.19–31—a story that was regarded by many of the Fathers as a depiction

according to their own desires.[28] But surely no disciplined person will think this way. What advantage will there be, after all, in justice and truthfulness and generosity and every virtue? What reason will people have to labor and lead an ascetical life,[29] holding subordinate the pleasure of the belly and gladly practicing continence, indulging in sleep only for short periods, and living exposed to the winter and the stifling heat, if there is no resurrection? Let us say about these things the words of Paul: "Let us eat and drink, for tomorrow we die!" (1 Cor 15.32) If there is no resurrection, but death is the final limit of life, you can do away with accusations and censures! Give unhindered power to the murderer, let the adulterer plot to undermine marriages as much as he will, allow the greedy person to feast without limit on the property of others, let no one restrain the person who speaks abusively, let the perjurer swear false oaths constantly—for death awaits the one who swears truly, too! Let another lie as much as he will, for there is no fruit to be reaped from the truth! Let no one be merciful to the poor, for mercy is without its reward! Thoughts such as these will overwhelm us worse than a flood, and drive out every sober principle, intensifying every mad and criminal notion. For if there is no resurrection, there is no judgment; and if judgment is removed, fear of God will be eliminated with it. And where fear does not bring sobriety, there the devil dances with sin.

18 David most fittingly referred this Psalm-verse to people like this: "The fool has said in his heart, 'There is no God.' They are become corrupt and abominable in their ways" (Ps 13.1). If there is no resurrection, Lazarus and the Rich Man and the terrible "great gulf" are a myth, as is the unquenchable burning of the fire and the burning tongue and the longing for a drop of water and the beggar's finger.[30] For it is perfectly clear that all these things mirror for us what will come to reality in the resurrection: the tongue and the finger, after

of the fates that await saints and sinners after death. See, for instance, Tertullian, *On the Soul* 56, 58; Hippolytus, *Against Plato* (PG 10:797 A13–C7); Augustine, *Confessions* 9.3.6; *De Gen. ad litt.* 8.5; 12.33.63l; Paulinus of Nola, *Ep.* 23.1; Andrew of Caesarea, *Commentary on the Apocalypse* 68.12–5; 206.2–3).

ἀσωμάτου ψυχῆς μέλη νοεῖται, ἀλλὰ μέρη τοῦ σώματος. καὶ μηδεὶς
οἰέσθω ταῦτα ἤδη πεπρᾶχθαι, ἀλλὰ προαναφώνησιν εἶναι τοῦ
μέλλοντος· ἔσται δὲ τότε, ὅταν ἡ μετακόσμησις ψυχώσασα τοὺς
νεκροὺς πρὸς τὰς εὐθύνας ἕκαστον τῶν βεβιωμένων ἀναγάγῃ
σύνθετον ὄντα καθὼς πρότερον καὶ διὰ ψυχῆς καὶ σώματος
GNO 266 συνεστῶτα. ὁ δὲ | θεοφορούμενος Ἰεζεκιὴλ καὶ τῶν μεγάλων
ὀπτασιῶν θεωρὸς πρὸς ποίαν ἄρα διάνοιαν ὁδηγούμενος ἔβλεπε
τὸ μέγα καὶ ἀνηπλωμένον ἐκεῖνο πεδίον τὸ γέμον τῶν ἀνθρωπίνων
ὀστέων, καθ᾽ ὧν ἐκελεύετο προφητεύειν; καὶ σάρκες μὲν εὐθὺς
ἐκείνοις περιεφύοντο, τὰ δὲ λελυμένα καὶ ἀτάκτως διερριμμένα
εἰς τάξιν καὶ ἁρμονίαν ἀλλήλοις συνεκολλᾶτο. ἢ πρόδηλον, ὡς
διὰ τῶν τοιούτων λόγων τὴν τῆς σαρκὸς ταύτης ἀναβίωσιν ἡμῖν
ἱκανῶς ὑποδείκνυσιν; ἐμοὶ δὲ δοκοῦσιν οἱ πρὸς τοῦτον τὸν λόγον
ἐριστικῶς ἔχοντες οὐ δυσσεβεῖς μόνον ἀλλὰ καὶ παραπαίοντες
εἶναι· ἀνάστασις γὰρ καὶ ἀναβίωσις καὶ μετακόσμησις καὶ πάντα
τὰ τοιαῦτα ὀνόματα πρὸς τὸ σῶμα τὸ τῇ φθορᾷ ὑποκείμενον
τοῦ ἀκροωμένου φέρει τὴν ἔννοιαν. ὡς ἥ γε ψυχὴ αὐτὴ καθ᾽ |
PG 677 ἑαυτὴν ἐξεταζομένη οὔποτε ἀναστήσεται, ἐπειδὴ μήτε τελευτᾷ,
ἀλλ᾽ ἄφθαρτός ἐστι καὶ ἀνώλεθρος, ἀθάνατος δὲ ὑπάρχουσα
θνητὸν ἔχει τὸ κοινωνὸν τῶν πραγμάτων καὶ διὰ τοῦτο παρὰ
τῷ δικαίῳ κριτῇ ἐν τῷ καιρῷ τῶν εὐθυνῶν ἐνοικήσει πάλιν τῷ
συνεργῷ, ἵνα μετ᾽ ἐκείνου κοινὰς δέξηται τὰς κολάσεις ἢ τὰς τιμάς.
μᾶλλον δὲ ἵνα καὶ πλέον ἡμῖν ὁ λόγος ἀκολουθότερος γένηται,
οὕτω σκοπήσωμεν· τὸν ἄνθρωπον τί φαμεν; τὸ συναμφότερον ἢ
τὸ ἕτερον; ἀλλὰ πρόδηλον, ὡς ἡ συζυγία τῶν δύο χαρακτηρίζει τὸ
ζῷον· οὐ γὰρ προσῆκεν ἐν τοῖς ἀναμφισβητήτοις καὶ γνωρίμοις
παρέλκειν. τούτου δὲ οὕτως ἔχοντος κἀκεῖνο προσλογισώμεθα,
πότερον, ἃ πράττουσιν ἄνθρωποι οἷον μοιχείαν φόνον κλοπὴν καὶ
πᾶν εἴ τι τούτοις ἐχόμενον ἢ τοὐναντίον σωφροσύνην ἐγκράτειαν
καὶ πᾶσαν τὴν ἀντίθετον τῆς κακίας ἐνέργειαν, τῶν δύο φαμὲν

all, are not conceived of as limbs of the bodiless soul, but as parts of the body. And let no one think that these things have already happened; rather, they are a foretelling of what is to come. For it will come to pass then, when the reshaping of the world will give life to the dead, and will bring each person who has lived to judgment, in a composite state as before, formed again as one from soul and body.

To what understanding was that seer of great visions, the inspired Ezekiel, led, when he gazed on the great plain, laid open to view and full of human bones, to which he was commanded to prophesy?[31] Flesh suddenly grew around them, and parts that had been disjointed and scattered about in disorder were joined to each other in order and harmony. Is it not perfectly clear that by words like these he is suggesting to us clearly the revival of this flesh? Those who are opposed to this argument seem to me not only to be irreverent, but completely off the mark! For "resurrection" and "revival" and "transformation" and words such as these draw the understanding of the person who listens carefully toward the body that has undergone decay. Just as the soul, considered in and by itself, will never rise again, since it never dies, but is incorruptible and indestructible, so, being immortal, it has a mortal partner in its actions, and for this reason it will come to dwell again in its partner and appear before the just judge, in the time of retribution, so that, along with its partner, it might receive the same punishments or honors.

19 Or rather—that the argument might be still easier for us to follow—let us consider it this way: What do we say the human being is? Both [body and soul] together, or only one of them? It is clear, surely, that the joining of the two of them is characteristic of the living being—it makes no sense to spin out a discussion of what is undisputed and well known! And since this is so, let us consider another point in addition: shall we say of human acts such as adultery, murder, theft, and whatever is in that category—or, on the other hand, of sobriety, continence, and every activity opposed to vice—that they

[31] Ezek 37.1–14.

ὑπάρχειν ἀποτελέσματα, ἢ τῇ ψυχῇ μόνῃ τὰς πράξεις περιορίζομεν;
GNO 267 ἀλλὰ κἀν τούτῳ | πρόδηλος ἡ ἀλήθεια· οὐδαμοῦ γὰρ ἀποσχίζουσα
τοῦ σώματος ἡ ψυχὴ ἢ τὴν κλοπὴν ἐπιτηδεύει ἢ τὴν τοιχωρυχίαν
ἐργάζεται οὐδ' αὖ μόνη τῷ πεινῶντι ἄρτον δίδωσιν ἢ ποτίζει τὸν
διψῶντα ἢ πρὸς τὸ δεσμωτήριον ἀόκνως ἐπείγεται, ἵνα θεραπεύσῃ
τὸν δεσμωτηρίῳ κεκαμωμένον, ἀλλ' ἐπὶ πάσης πράξεως ἀλλήλοις
ἀμφότερα συνεφάπτεται καὶ συναποτελεῖ τὰ γινόμενα. πῶς τοίνυν
τούτων οὕτως ἐχόντων καὶ κρίσιν τῶν βεβιωμένων ἔσεσθαι
συγχωρῶν ἀποσπᾷς τοῦ ἑτέρου τὸ ἕτερον καὶ κοινῶν ὄν<των>
τῶν εἰργασμένων τῇ ψυχῇ μόνῃ περιορίζεις τὸ δικαστήριον; εἰ δέ
τις ἀκριβὴς γένοιτο δικαστὴς τῶν ἀνθρωπίνων πλημμελημάτων
καὶ σκοπήσειεν ἐπιμελῶς, πόθεν φύονται αἱ πρῶται τῆς ἁμαρτίας
αἰτίαι, τάχα πρῶτον ἀτακτοῦν ἐν τοῖς ἐγκλήμασιν εὑρήσει τὸ
σῶμα. ἠρεμούσης γὰρ πολλάκις τῆς ψυχῆς καὶ γαλήνην ἐχούσης
ἀτάραχον εἶδεν ὁ ὀφθαλμὸς ἐμπαθῶς, ἃ μὴ θεάσασθαι βέλτιον
ἦν, καὶ τῇ ψυχῇ παραπέμψας τὴν νόσον εἰς χειμῶνα καὶ κλύδωνα
τὴν ἡσυχίαν μετέβαλεν. ὁμοίως αἱ ἀκοαὶ ἀσχημόνων τινῶν ἢ
παροξυντικῶν ἐπακούσασαι λόγων οἷον διά τινων σωλήνων
ἑαυτῶν τὸν τῆς ταραχῆς ἢ τὸν τῆς ἀκοσμίας βόρβορον τοῖς
λογισμοῖς ἐπεισφέρουσιν. ἔστι δὲ ὅτε καὶ ἡ ῥὶς διὰ τῆς ὀσφρήσεως
καὶ τῶν ἀτμῶν μεγάλα τε καὶ ἀνήκεστα κακὰ † διατίθησι τὸν
ἔσωθεν ἄνθρωπον. οἴδασι δὲ καὶ αἱ χεῖρες διὰ τῆς ἐπαφῆς καρτερᾶς
ψυχῆς ἐκθηλύνειν στερρότητα. καί μοι κατὰ μικρὸν οὕτως ἐπιόντι
καὶ σκοπουμένῳ ὑπαίτιον εὑρίσκεται τῶν πολλῶν ἁμαρτιῶν τὸ
σωμάτιον.

Φέρει δὲ καὶ τοὺς ὑπὲρ ἀρετῆς πόνους καὶ τοῖς ἀγῶσιν |
GNO 268 ἐμμοχθεῖ τῶν καλῶν τεμνόμενον σιδήρῳ καὶ πυρὶ φλεγόμενον

---

[32]Reading κακωμένον (*kakōmenon*) for κεκαωμένον (*kekaōmenon*), "burned," which is the reading of the manuscripts and the editor Gebhardt here.

[33]Gregory reflects here the common view of Greek antiquity that the root of voluntary evil is the passions: disorder caused in the mind and will by our undisciplined sensual desires and drives. See also *On the Soul and the Resurrection* (GNO III/3:42–43; PG 46:61–64).

[34]Following Jaeger's conjecture that something has been left out of the manuscript, Gebhardt supplies a few words to fill out the sense.

are the achievements of both [parts], or do we define these actions as restricted to the soul by itself? Is not the truth obvious here, as well? For the soul is never separated from the body when it undertakes theft or carries out a burglary, nor is it, indeed, alone, when it gives bread to the hungry or drink to the thirsty, or when it makes eager haste to the prison to care for the one distressed[32] by imprisonment; but in every one of these acts, each part is united with the other and performs it jointly.

20 If this is how things are, then, and if you concede that there will be a judgment on the way we have lived our lives, how do you separate one aspect of us from the other? If our deeds have been done by both elements together, why do you limit the judgment to the soul alone? In fact, if someone wants to be an accurate judge of human failings, and examine carefully what the original sources of sin might be, perhaps he would find that the body was the first part to be undisciplined, in the ways charged. For often, when the soul is quiet and possessed of an undisturbed calm, the eye looks in a passionate way on something it would be better not to see, and by communicating the disease to the soul, transforms its peace into stormy waves.[33] So, too, the ears, by hearing unseemly or aggravating words, import the filth of disturbance or disorder into our thoughts as if they were sewers. At times even the nose, by the sense of smell and by our breathing, [works] great and incurable evils and puts our inner self into a state [of disorder].[34] The hands, too, can often soften the firmness of the soul's strength through the sense of touch. So, as I go over the senses in this way and consider them one by one, it seems to me, too, that our bodily component is to be held responsible for the majority of our sins.

But it [i.e., the body] also endures labors for the sake of virtue, and in the contest is cut by the harsh sword of evil people,[35] is

[35]Emending καλῶν (*kalōn*), in Gebhardt's text and the manuscripts, to κακῶν (*kakōn*), which in the context seems to give better sense. If one retains the standard reading, one would have to translate the phrase: "in the contests is cut by the hard-striking sword of good works," or "of good people."

καὶ ξαινόμενον μάστιξι καὶ βαρυνόμενον ἀργαλέοις δεσμοῖς καὶ
πᾶσαν ὑπομένον λώβην, ἵνα μὴ προδῷ τὴν ἱερὰν φιλοσοφίαν
ὥσπερ τινὰ πόλιν καλλίπυργον κεκυκλωμένην τῷ τῆς κακίας
PG 680 πολέμῳ. εἰ τοίνυν ἐν κατορθώμασι συμμοχθεῖ τῇ ψυχῇ καὶ | ἐν
ἁμαρτήμασιν οὐκ ἀπολιμπάνεται, πόθεν ὁρμώμενος μόνην τὴν
ἀσώματον ἐπὶ τὸ δικαστήριον ἄγεις; ἀλλ' οὐκ ἔστιν οὔτε δίκαιος
οὔτε σωφρονούντων ὁ λόγος. εἰ μόνη καὶ γυμνὴ διήμαρτε, μόνην
καὶ κόλασον, εἰ δὲ φανερὸν ἔχει τὸν συνεργόν, οὐκ ἀφήσει τοῦτον ὁ
κριτὴς δίκαιος ὤν. ἐγὼ δὲ καὶ τοῦτο τῆς γραφῆς ἀκούω λεγούσης,
ὅτι τοῖς κατεγνωσμένοις ἐπιτεθήσονται δίκαιαι τιμωρίαι πῦρ καὶ
σκότος καὶ σκώληξ· ἃ πάντα τῶν συνθέτων καὶ ὑλικῶν σωμάτων
κολάσεις εἰσίν, ψυχῆς δὲ καθ' ἑαυτὴν οὔποτ' ἂν ἅψαιτο πῦρ οὐδ'
ἂν σκότος αὐτὴν λυπήσειεν ἀμοιροῦσαν ὀφθαλμῶν καὶ τῶν
βλεπτικῶν ὀργάνων. τί δ' ἂν καὶ ὁ σκώληξ πράξειε σωμάτων
ὑπάρχων φθαρτικός, οὐ πνευμάτων; καὶ διὰ τοῦτο τοῖς ἀκολούθοις
τούτοις λογισμοῖς πανταχόθεν συνελαυνόμεθα πρὸς συγκατάθεσιν
τῆς ἐγέρσεως τῶν νεκρῶν, ἣν τοῖς καθήκουσι χρόνοις ἐκτελέσει ὁ
θεὸς ἔργοις βεβαιῶν τὰς ἰδίας ἐπαγγελίας.

Πιστεύσωμεν τοίνυν τῷ λέγοντι· Σαλπίσει γὰρ καὶ οἱ νεκροὶ
GNO 269 ἀναστήσονται, καὶ πάλιν· Ἔρχεται ὥρα, ἐν ᾗ πάντες | οἱ ἐν τοῖς
μνημείοις ἀκούσονται τῆς φωνῆς αὐτοῦ καὶ ἐκπορεύσονται οἱ τὰ
ἀγαθὰ ποιήσαντες εἰς ἀνάστασιν ζωῆς, οἱ δὲ τὰ φαῦλα πράξαντες εἰς
ἀνάστασιν κρίσεως. οὐ γὰρ ὑπισχνεῖται μόνον, ἀλλὰ καὶ τοῖς ἔργοις,
οἷς ἐκτελεῖ καθ' ἡμέραν, διδάσκει σαφῶς, ὥς ἐστι παντοδύναμος·
οὔτε γὰρ ἐν ἀρχῇ δημιουργῶν ἔκαμεν οὔτε μεταμορφῶν
ἀπορήσει σοφίας. τὰ παρόντα θεωρήσωμεν, καὶ τῷ μέλλοντι οὐκ
ἀπιστήσομεν· πάσης γὰρ ἐνεργείας τοῦ θεοῦ ἀκόλουθον ἐχούσης
τὴν ἔκπληξιν καὶ πολὺ τὸ θαῦμα καὶ ἄφραστον ὅταν τὰς τῶν
πατέρων καὶ προπάππων ὁμοιότητας κατίδωμεν μεταβαινούσας

burned in the fire and scourged by whips and fettered by burdensome chains, undergoing every sort of harm in order not to betray its sacred way of life, as if it were a well-fortified city holding out against the attacks of vice. If, then, in times of success it holds out with the soul in its labors, and does not abandon it by sinning, why are you eager to bring only the bodiless part of us before the judgment seat? This is not a fair argument, or one proper to sensible people! If it [i.e., the soul] has sinned by itself, nakedly, then punish it alone as well; but if it has an obvious accomplice, the just judge will not spare either of them. I hear this point, too, when Scripture says that just punishments will be inflicted on the condemned: fire and darkness and the worm.[36] All of these are punishments for composite [beings with] material bodies; but no fire could ever catch hold of a soul by itself, nor would darkness cause it pain if it had no eyes or visual organs. And what would the worm be doing, which exists to harm bodies, but not spirits? So we are driven on all sides, by arguments consistent with these, to affirm the resurrection of the dead, which in times to come God will bring to reality, confirming by deeds his own promises.

21 Let us believe, then, the one who says, "The trumpet shall sound, and the dead shall be raised" (1 Cor 15.52), and again, "The hour is coming, in which all who are in their tombs will hear his voice, and those who have done good works will come out to a resurrection of life, but those who have done evil deeds to a resurrection of judgment" (Jn 5.28–29). For [God] does not simply promise this, but clearly teaches, in the works he performs day after day, that he is all-powerful. For he did not grow tired when creating at the beginning, nor in the work of transformation will he be at a loss for wisdom. Let us consider the present, and we will not lack faith for the future. For if every action of God appropriately draws our amazement, and if we feel great and inexpressible wonder when we consider the likenesses of parents and great-grandparents passing down exactly into

[36]See, for instance, Mk 9.43, 48; Mt 5.22; 8.12; 18.8; 22.13.

ἀκριβῶς εἰς τὰς τῶν ἀπογόνων μορφὰς καὶ ἐκμαγεῖα γινομένους τοὺς παῖδας ἀπὸ τῶν προπατόρων, τότε δὴ τὴν πάνσοφον τέχνην τοῦ ἀριστοτέχνου θεοῦ καὶ σωτῆρος ὑπερεκπλήττομαι, πῶς τῶν μήτε ὄντων μήτε φαινομένων ἀρχετύπων αἱ μιμήσεις ἐν ἀπορρήτῳ μυστηρίῳ δημιουργοῦνται καὶ ἀναπλάσσονται ἄλλους τινὰς τοὺς τεθνεῶτας διὰ τῆς ἐνεργείας τῶν τύπων ἐγείρουσαι. Πολλάκις δὲ καὶ πολλῶν ὁμοῦ προσώπων τὰ ἰδιώματα ἐν ἑνὶ ἐξεικονίζεται σώματι· τοῦ πατρὸς ἡ ῥίς, τοῦ πάππου ὁ ὀφθαλμός, τοῦ θείου τὸ βάδισμα, τῆς μητρὸς τὸ φθέγμα, καὶ εἷς ἄνθρωπος θεωρεῖται καθάπερ τι φυτὸν πολλῶν δένδρων τὰς ἐπιβολὰς δεξάμενον καὶ μυρία καρποφοροῦν γένη τοῖς ὀπωρίζουσιν.

Ταῦτα πάντα θαυμαστὰ μὲν καὶ ὅπως γίνεται ἡμῖν ἀγνοούμενα,
πρόχειρα δὲ τῷ δημιουργῷ καὶ μετὰ πολλῆς ὡς ἴσμεν τῆς ῥᾳστώνης
ἐπιτελούμενα. ἄτοπον δὲ λίαν καὶ ἀμαθές, τὰ μὲν τῶν σαπέντων
καὶ φθαρέντων ἤδη σωμάτων γνωρίσματα ἐν τοῖς νῦν καθ' ἡμέραν
φυομένοις ἐγείρεσθαι καὶ τὰ ἀλλότρια μεταβαίνειν εἰς ἄλλους, τὰ
GNO 270 δὲ ἴδια καὶ ἐξαίρετα περὶ αὐτῶν τῶν ποτε κεκτημένων | ἀνανεοῦσθαι
καὶ ἀναβιώσκεσθαι μὴ συνομολογεῖν, ἀλλὰ τοὐναντίον ἀκυροῦν
καὶ διαμάχεσθαι καὶ μῦθον οὐ λόγον τὴν ἐπαγγελίαν νομίζειν
PG 681 τοῦ πᾶν τόδε τὸ ὁρώμενον συστησαμένου καὶ | κοσμήσαντος,
ὡς ἠθέλησεν. ἀλλ' ἡμεῖς γε πεπιστεύκαμεν τῇ ἀναστάσει δόξαν
ἀναπέμποντες τῷ πατρὶ καὶ τῷ υἱῷ καὶ τῷ ἁγίῳ πνεύματι νῦν καὶ
ἀεὶ καὶ εἰς τοὺς αἰῶνας τῶν αἰώνων, ἀμήν.

the forms of their descendants, and children coming into the world who are images of their ancestors, on that day I will be all the more astounded at the all-wise artistry of God, our great craftsman and savior, seeing how the representations of originals that do not now exist or appear will be created as part of this unspeakable mystery, and will shape others once again, raising the dead through the activity of their forms.[37] Often, too, the features of many faces at once are recaptured in a single body: the father's nose, the grandfather's eye, the uncle's gait, the mother's voice; yet one human being is contemplated there, like a plant that has received grafts from many trees, and that bears countless kinds of fruit for the harvesters.

All these things are marvels; we do not know how they come about, but they are everyday occurrences for the Creator, and are accomplished by him, as we know, with great ease. It would be completely nonsensical and stupid for the features of bodies already decayed and corrupted to be raised up among the living beings that we encounter every day, and for one person's characteristics to be passed on to others, yet not to admit that the particular, distinguishing characteristics marking those once created can themselves be renewed and raised again to life, but rather to dismiss and deny and consider an unreasonable myth the promise of the one who gave existence and order, as he wished, to all this world we see. We, however, have come to believe in the resurrection, giving glory to the Father and the Son and the Holy Spirit, now and always and to the ages of ages. Amen.

[37]The understanding of the future resurrection that Gregory suggests here seems to depend on a Platonic understanding of the continuity of individual souls, even after death, as forms of their bodies.

A Funeral Oration for Meletius, Bishop of Antioch

A Note on the Text

This oration was apparently written to be delivered at a funeral liturgy for Meletius, bishop of Antioch, who had been one of the leading promoters of the international synod of bishops that began in Constantinople in late May 381, and which is recognized as the Second Ecumenical Council. Meletius, a veteran of the theological and political conflicts and intrigues that had wrapped themselves around most of the eastern churches in the latter half of the fourth century, had urged the new emperor Theodosius—a soldier, a westerner, and a devout adherent to Nicene theology—after his accession in 379, to bring together a new council to confirm the Nicene position as the imperial norm of orthodox Christianity; Meletius himself was asked by Theodosius to preside at its sessions. During the first few weeks of the council, however, Meletius suddenly died, and Gregory of Nyssa, widely recognized as one of the most theologically astute, as well as one of the most classically eloquent bishops in attendance, was apparently one of those invited—perhaps by his family friend Gregory of Nazianzus, now Nicene bishop of Constantinople, who succeeded Meletius for a while as chairman of the council—to give a funeral oration. It was apparently delivered in the Church of the Holy Apostles, in the imperial capital, sometime in June 381—perhaps even at a ceremony sending Meletius' body back to Antioch for burial (see section 2). Its final paragraphs evoke the splendor of that solemn occasion.

For a discussion of Meletius' long and complex career as bishop, and of his significance for the Greek-speaking Church and its doctrine in the second half of the fourth century, see my article, "The Enigma of Meletius of Antioch," in Ronnie J. Rombs and Alexander Y. Hwang, eds, *Tradition and the Rule of Faith in the Early Church: Essays in Honor of Joseph T. Lienhard, SJ* (Washington: Catholic University of America Press, 2010), 128–50. The Greek text used for this translation of Gregory's oration is the critical text edited by Andreas Spira, in GNO IX:441–57. For ease in reference, I have added section numbers to this translation.

GNO IX:441
PG 46:852

ΓΡΗΓΟΡΙΟΥ ΕΠΙΣΚΟΠΟΥ ΝΥΣΣΗΣ ΕΠΙΤΑΦΙΟΣ ΕΙΣ ΜΕΛΕΤΙΟΝ ΕΠΙΣΚΟΠΟΝ ΑΝΤΙΟΧΕΙΑΣ

Ηὔξησεν ἡμῖν τὸν ἀριθμὸν τῶν ἀποστόλων ὁ νέος ἀπόστολος, ὁ συγκαταψηφισθεὶς μετὰ τῶν ἀποστόλων· εἵλκυσαν γὰρ οἱ ἅγιοι πρὸς ἑαυτοὺς τὸν ὁμότροπον, τὸν ἀθλητὴν οἱ ἀθληταί, τὸν στεφανίτην οἱ στεφανῖται, τὸν ἁγνὸν τῇ ψυχῇ οἱ καθαροὶ τῇ καρδίᾳ, τὸν κήρυκα τοῦ λόγου οἱ ὑπηρέται τοῦ λόγου. ἀλλὰ μακαριστὸς μὲν ὁ πατὴρ ἡμῶν τῆς τε ἀποστολικῆς συσκηνίας καὶ τῆς πρὸς τὸν Χριστὸν ἀναλύσεως, ἐλεεινοὶ δὲ ἡμεῖς· οὐ γὰρ ἐᾷ μακαρίζειν ἡμᾶς τοῦ πατρὸς τὴν εὐκληρίαν ἡ ἀωρία τῆς ὀρφανίας. ἐκείνῳ κρεῖττον ἦν τὸ σὺν Χριστῷ εἶναι διὰ τῆς ἀναλύσεως, ἀλλ' ἡμῖν χαλεπὸν τὸ διαζευχθῆναι τῆς πατρικῆς προστασίας. ἰδοὺ γάρ, βουλῆς καιρός, καὶ ὁ συμβουλεύων σιγᾷ· πόλεμος ἡμᾶς περιεστοίχισται, πόλεμος
GNO 442 | αἱρετικός, καὶ ὁ στρατηγῶν οὐκ ἔστιν· κάμνει ταῖς ἀρρωστίαις τὸ κοινὸν σῶμα τῆς ἐκκλησίας, καὶ τὸν ἰατρὸν οὐχ εὑρίσκομεν. ὁρᾶτε ἐν ποταποῖς τὰ ἡμέτερα. ἐβουλόμην, εἴ πως οἷόν τε ἦν, τονώσας ἐμαυτοῦ τὴν ἀσθένειαν συναναβῆναι τῷ ὄγκῳ τῆς συμφορᾶς καί τινα ῥῆξαι φωνὴν κατ' ἀξίαν τοῦ πάθους, καθάπερ οἱ γενναῖοι πεποιήκασιν οὗτοι μεγαλοφώνως τὴν ἐπὶ τῷ πατρὶ συμφορὰν ὀδυρόμενοι. ἀλλὰ τί πάθω; πῶς βιάσωμαι γλῶσσαν εἰς ὑπηρεσίαν τοῦ λόγου καθάπερ τινὶ πέδῃ βαρείᾳ τῇ συμφορᾷ πεδηθεῖσαν; πῶς

---

[1]As bishop of the ancient Church of Antioch, and as a key member of the newly assembled Council of Constantinople, Meletius clearly had "apostolic" stature in his own time—something to which Gregory alludes repeatedly in his oration. He also may be alluding here to his hearers' surroundings in the great basilica of the Holy Apostles in the imperial capital, a church built by Constantine and dedicated about 330; at this time, it served as the main church of the bishop of Constantinople, and

A Funeral Oration for Meletius, Bishop of Antioch (*Oratio funebris in Meletium episcopum*)

1 The new apostle, selected to be one of the apostles, has now enlarged the number of the apostles for us;[1] for the saints have drawn up to themselves one like them—the athletes [of God] have lifted up an athlete, the crowned victors one now crowned also, the pure in heart one sanctified in soul, the servants of the Word the Word's proclaimer. How blessed our father is to share the apostles' company and to be freed to be with Christ—but how wretched we are! Our untimely state of being orphans will not let us call ourselves blessed by our father's good fortune. For him, it was better to pass away and be with Christ[2]—but for us it is bitter to be separated from his fatherly leadership. Why? It is the moment for a council, yet our fellow-member has fallen silent. War hems us in, a war of heresy, and there is no one to be our general. Our common body, the Church, lies ill and weak, and we have no doctor with us. You can see what difficulties our affairs are in!

My desire, if somehow I prove up to the challenge, is to counteract my own weakness and climb up on this mound of misfortune, to break out in words worthy of our suffering, just as these noble brethren have done, bewailing loudly the harsh fate of their father. Yet what do I feel? How can I force my tongue to serve the word, when it is fettered, one might say, with the heavy shackle of

remained throughout antiquity the burial-site of many eastern emperors and patriarchs. It had originally been intended to house relics of all the Apostles, but at this point only those of the Apostle Andrew and of Paul's disciples, Timothy and Titus, were actually enshrined there.

[2]See Phil 1.23.

ἀνοίξω στόμα τῇ ἀφασίᾳ κεκρατημένον; πῶς προῶμαι φωνὴν εἰς πάθη καὶ θρήνους ἐκ συνηθείας κατολισθαίνουσαν; πῶς ἀναβλέψω τοῖς τῆς ψυχῆς ὀφθαλμοῖς τῷ τῆς συμφορᾶς γνόφῳ κεκαλυμμένοις; τίς μοι διασχὼν τὴν βαθεῖαν ταύτην καὶ σκοτεινὴν τῆς λύπης νεφέλην πάλιν ἐξ αἰθρίας λαμπρὰν ἀναδείξει τὴν τῆς εἰρήνης ἀκτῖνα; πόθεν δὲ καὶ ἀναλάμψει ἡ ἀκτὶς τοῦ φωστῆρος ἡμῶν καταδύντος; ὢ κακῆς σκοτομήνης ἀνατολὴν φωστῆρος οὐκ ἐλπιζούσης.

Ὡς ἀπεναντίον ἡμῖν ἐν τῷ παρόντι τόπῳ νῦν τε καὶ πρώην οἱ
λόγοι γίνονται. τότε γαμικῶς ἐχορεύομεν, νῦν ἐλεεινῶς ἐπὶ τῷ
GNO 443 πένθει στενάζομεν. τότε ἐπιθαλάμιον, | νῦν ἐπιτάφιον ᾄδομεν.
μέμνησθε γὰρ ὅτε τὸν πνευματικὸν γάμον ὑμᾶς εἱστιάσαμεν τῷ
PG 853 καλῷ νυμφίῳ συνοικίζοντες τὴν παρθένον, ὑμᾶς, καὶ | τὰ τῶν λόγων
ἕδνα κατὰ δύναμιν ἡμῶν εἰσηνεγκάμεθα εὐφραίνοντες ἐν τῷ μέρει
καὶ εὐφραινόμενοι. ἀλλὰ νῦν εἰς θρῆνον ἡμῖν ἡ χαρὰ μεθηρμόσθη
καὶ ἡ τῆς εὐφροσύνης περιβολὴ σάκκος ἐγένετο. ἢ τάχα σιωπᾶν ἔδει
τὸ πάθος καὶ ἔνδον ἀποκλείειν τῇ σιωπῇ τὴν ἀλγηδόνα, ὡς ἂν μὴ
διοχλοίημεν τοὺς υἱοὺς τοῦ νυμφῶνος οὐκ ἔχοντες τὸ φαιδρὸν τοῦ
γάμου ἔνδυμα ἀλλὰ μελανειμονοῦντες τῷ λόγῳ; ἐπειδὴ γὰρ ἀπήρθη
ἀφ᾽ ἡμῶν ὁ καλὸς νυμφίος, ἀθρόως τῷ πένθει κατεμελάνθημεν,
καὶ οὐκ ἔστι συνήθως καταφαιδρῦναι τὸν λόγον τὴν κοσμοῦσαν
ἡμᾶς στολὴν τοῦ φθόνου ἀποσυλήσαντος. πλήρεις ἀγαθῶν πρὸς
ὑμᾶς ἀπηντήσαμεν· γυμνοὶ καὶ πένητες ἀφ᾽ ὑμῶν ὑποστρέφομεν.
ὀρθὴν εἴχομεν ὑπὲρ κεφαλῆς τὴν λαμπάδα πλουσίῳ τῷ φωτὶ
καταλάμπουσαν· ταύτην ἐσβεσμένην ἀνακομίζομεν εἰς καπνὸν καὶ

[3]Gregory may to be alluding to Meletius' role as the leading voice in the empire's eastern provinces, the "sun" who guided the rest of the bishops in their struggles to understand the Mystery of God after Nicaea.

[4]Apparently alluding to 2 Corinthians 11.2, Gregory compares Meletius' arrival in the capital as president of the newly convened council to the arrival of the bridegroom at a wedding. Presumably the bride, here as in Paul's words to the Corinthians, is the Christian community itself, and the true Bridegroom of the Church is Christ, whom Meletius represents.

misfortune? How shall I open my mouth, when it is overcome by a loss of words? How shall I produce language lofty enough for our sufferings and grief, when it is deflated by what all of us share? How shall I look up with the eyes of my soul, when they are covered by the fog of misfortune? Who will divide for me this deep, dark cloud of grief, to show me again the ray of peace shining brightly in the heavens? Where will the light of our sun shine again for us, now that it has set? What a sad, moonless night it is, that no longer hopes for sunrise in the East![3]

2 Words come to us in this place in such opposite ways, now and just a few days ago! Then we were dancing in procession, as at a wedding; now we groan miserably with grief. Then we were singing a bridal anthem, today a dirge. Remember when we celebrated that spiritual marriage, bringing you home as a virgin bride to live with your handsome bridegroom;[4] we brought our wedding gifts of words, as much as we were able,[5] giving and receiving joy in turn. But now our joy has been transformed into lament, the cloak of celebration has been turned to sackcloth. Or should we, perhaps, be silent about our grief and lock our sadness away inside us by saying nothing, so that we, who no longer wear the bright wedding garment but are verbally dressed in black, might not upset the guests of the Bridegroom?[6] For since the handsome bridegroom has been taken from us,[7] we are all darkened by grief together; there is no normal way for us to brighten up our speech, since misfortune[8] has torn away from us the robe we were wearing. We came to meet each other, fully conscious of our blessings; now we turn away from each other, naked and poor. We held up, high over our heads, the lamp shining richly with light; today we carry it forward, its light reduced to smoke

[5]This may be a reference to another oration of Gregory's, *De deitate adversus Evagrium*, which some have suggested was delivered a few weeks earlier.

[6]Literally, the "sons of the bridal chamber" (Lk 5.34).

[7]See Mt 9.15.

[8]Literally, "envy" or "malice" (φθόνος, *phthonos*). This word is used widely in classical Greek to denote the ill will—here perhaps that of the Evil Spirit—that apparently lies behind many of the misfortunes people suffer.

κόνιν διαλυθέντος τοῦ φέγγους. εἴχομεν τὸν θησαυρὸν τὸν μέγαν ἐν ὀστρακίνῳ τῷ σκεύει· ἀλλ' ὁ μὲν θησαυρὸς ἀφανής, τὸ δὲ ὀστράκινον σκεῦος κενὸν τοῦ πλούτου τοῖς δεδωκόσιν ἐπανασῴζεται. τί ἐροῦσιν
GNO 444 οἱ ἀποστείλαντες; τί ἀποκρινοῦνται οἱ ἀπαιτούμε|νοι; ὢ πονηροῦ ναυαγίου. πῶς ἐν μέσῳ τῷ λιμένι τῆς ἐλπίδος ἡμῶν ἐναυαγήσαμεν; πῶς ἡ μυριοφόρος ὁλκὰς αὐτῷ πληρώματι καταδῦσα γυμνοὺς ἡμᾶς τούς ποτε πλουτοῦντας κατέλιπεν; ποῦ τὸ λαμπρὸν ἱστίον ἐκεῖνο τὸ τῷ ἁγίῳ πνεύματι διὰ παντὸς εὐθυνόμενον; ποῦ τὸ ἀσφαλὲς τῶν ψυχῶν ἡμῶν πηδάλιον, δι' οὗ τὰς τρικυμίας τὰς αἱρετικὰς ἀπαθῶς παρεπλέομεν; ποῦ ἡ ἀμετάθετος τῆς γνώμης ἄγκυρα, ᾗ μετὰ πάσης ἀσφαλείας πεποιθότες ἀνεπαυόμεθα; ποῦ ὁ καλὸς κυβερνήτης ὁ πρὸς τὸν ἄνω σκοπὸν διευθύνων τὸ σκάφος; ἆρα μικρὰ τὰ συμβάντα καὶ μάτην παθαίνομαι; ἢ μᾶλλον οὐκ ἐφικνοῦμαι τοῦ πάθους, κἂν ὑπερφωνήσω τῷ λόγῳ; χρήσατε ἡμῖν, ἀδελφοί, χρήσατε τὸ ἐκ συμπαθείας δάκρυον. καὶ γὰρ ὅτε ὑμεῖς ηὐφραίνεσθε, ἡμεῖς τῆς εὐφροσύνης ὑμῖν ἐκοινωνήσαμεν. οὐκοῦν ἀπόδοτε ἡμῖν τὸ πονηρὸν τοῦτο ἀντάλλαγμα. Χαίρειν μετὰ χαιρόντων, τοῦτο ἡμεῖς ἐποιήσαμεν· Κλαίειν μετὰ κλαιόντων, τοῦτο ὑμεῖς ἀνταπόδοτε.
GNO 445 | ἐδάκρυσέ ποτε ξένος λαὸς ἐπὶ τοῦ πατριάρχου Ἰακὼβ καὶ τὴν ἀλλοτρίαν συμφορὰν ᾠκειώσατο, ὅτε τὸν πατέρα ἐξ Αἰγύπτου οἱ ἀπ' ἐκείνου μετακομίσαντες πανδημεὶ τὴν ἐπ' αὐτῷ συμφορὰν ἐπὶ τῆς ἀλλοτρίας κατωλοφύραντο ἡμέραις τριάκοντα καὶ τοσαύταις νυξὶ τὸν ἐπ' αὐτῷ θρῆνον συμπαρατείνοντες. μιμήσασθε τοὺς ἀλλοφύλους οἱ ἀδελφοὶ καὶ ὁμόφυλοι. κοινὸν ἦν τότε τῶν ξένων καὶ τῶν ἐγχωρίων τὸ δάκρυον· κοινὸν ἔστω καὶ νῦν, ἐπεὶ καὶ τὸ πάθος κοινόν. ὁρᾶτε τοὺς πατριάρχας τούτους· πάντες οὗτοι τέκνα τοῦ ἡμετέρου εἰσὶν Ἰακώβ. ἐξ ἐλευθέρας οἱ πάντες. οὐδεὶς νόθος

---

[9]A contrast, perhaps, between the joyful procession at the opening of the council, at which Meletius, as president, may even have been carried on a throne, and his present funeral procession.

[10]2 Cor 4.7.

[11]An apparent reference to the return of Meletius' body to Antioch.

[12]Gen 50.1–14. After going to Egypt with his whole household to be reunited with his son Joseph, the aged Jacob died there. Genesis tells us he was mourned for

and ash.[9] We carried in the great treasure in its earthen vessel;[10] but the treasure has vanished, while the earthen vessel, empty of its riches, is being brought back to those who gave it to us.[11] What shall those who are sending it say? What will those who demand it back reply? A terrible shipwreck! Our ship has gone down, right in the harbor of our hope! The vessel filled with myrrh, sinking under its own fullness, has left us, once rich, now empty-handed!

3 Where is that shining sail, once constantly carried forward by the Holy Spirit? Where is the safe rudder of our souls, by which we have made a straight course past the tidal waves of heresy? Where is that immoveable anchor of the will, in which we can trust with complete safety and find rest? Where is the trusty helmsman, who directs our boat toward the goal ahead? Are these misfortunes small—am I speaking emotionally without cause? Or rather, am I failing to hit the mark of our suffering, even if I outdo everyone with the volume of my words?

Lend us, brothers—lend us a tear out of sympathy. After all, when you were rejoicing, we shared your joy with you. So give us this sad repayment! To "rejoice with those who rejoice": this is what we have done; to "weep with those who weep" is something you can give back to us (Rom 12.15). In days of old, a foreign people wept for the patriarch Jacob, and made the fate of a stranger its own, when his descendants carried their father back with them from Egypt, and the whole multitude bewailed his death in a foreign land, extending their dirges for thirty days and as many nights.[12] Imitate these foreigners, my brothers and compatriots! Tears were then common to strangers and natives; let them be so now, as well, since we share the same sorrow. You see these patriarchs: these are all children of our own Jacob. All are from a free mother; no one is illegitimate,

a total of seventy days, by Egyptian custom, forty days of which were required for embalming. His descendants then conveyed his body back to Palestine, accompanied by many of Pharaoh's household staff, and buried him in the tomb Jacob had prepared in the cave of Machpelah near Mamre. Gregory suggests there is a parallel for him and his fellow bishops in Constantinople in their own mourning for the deceased bishop of Antioch.

οὐδὲ ὑπόβλητος. οὐδὲ γὰρ ἦν θέμις ἐκείνῳ δουλικὴν δυσγένειαν
ἐπεισάγειν τῇ εὐγενείᾳ τῆς πίστεως. οὐκοῦν καὶ ὑμέτερος ἐκεῖνος
πατήρ, διότι τοῦ πατρὸς ἦν τοῦ ὑμετέρου πατήρ. |

PG 856 Ἠκούσατε ἀρτίως τοῦ Ἐφραὶμ καὶ τοῦ Μανασσῆ, οἷα καὶ ὅσα
περὶ τοῦ πατρὸς διηγήσαντο, ὡς ὑπερβαίνει λόγον τὰ θαύματα. δότε
κἀμοί τι περὶ τούτων εἰπεῖν· καὶ γὰρ ἀκίνδυνον τὸ μακαρίζειν λοιπόν·
οὐκέτι φοβοῦμαι τὸν φθόνον· τί γάρ με χεῖρον ἐργάσεται; οὐκοῦν
γνῶτε τίς ὁ ἀνήρ. Εὐγενὴς τῶν ἀφ' ἡλίου ἀνατολῶν, Ἄμεμπτος,
δίκαιος, ἀληθινός, θεοσεβής, ἀπεχόμενος ἀπὸ παντὸς πονηροῦ
GNO 446 πράγματος (οὐ γὰρ δὴ | ζηλοτυπήσει ὁ μέγας Ἰώβ, εἰ ταῖς περὶ
αὐτοῦ μαρτυρίαις καὶ ὁ μιμητὴς ἐκείνου ἐγκαλλωπίζοιτο). ἀλλ'
ὁ τὰ καλὰ πάντα βλέπων φθόνος εἶδε καὶ τὸ ἡμέτερον ἀγαθὸν
πικρῷ ὀφθαλμῷ, καὶ ὁ ἐμπεριπατῶν τῇ οἰκουμένῃ καὶ δι' ἡμῶν
περιεπάτησε πλατὺ τὸ ἴχνος τῆς θλίψεως ταῖς εὐπραγίαις ἡμῶν
ἐναπερείσας. οὐ βοῶν καὶ προβάτων ἀγέλας διελυμήνατο, πλὴν
εἰ μὴ ἄρα τις κατὰ τὸ μυστικὸν εἰς τὴν ἐκκλησίαν μεταλάβοι τὸ
ποίμνιον· πλὴν οὐκ ἐν τούτοις ἡμῖν παρὰ τοῦ φθόνου ἡ βλάβη, οὐδὲ
ἐν ὄνοις καὶ καμήλοις τὴν ζημίαν εἰργάσατο, οὐδὲ τραύματι σαρκὸς
τὰς αἰσθήσεις ἐδρίμυξεν, ἀλλ' αὐτῆς ἡμᾶς τῆς κεφαλῆς ἀπεσύλησεν.
τῇ δὲ κεφαλῇ συναπῆλθε τὰ τίμια ἡμῶν αἰσθητήρια. οὐκέτι ἔστιν ὁ
ὀφθαλμὸς ὁ τὰ οὐράνια βλέπων, οὐδὲ ἡ ἀκοή <ἡ> τῆς θείας φωνῆς
ἐπαΐουσα, οὐδὲ ἡ γλῶσσα ἐκείνη, τὸ ἁγνὸν ἀνάθημα τῆς ἀληθείας.
ποῦ ἡ γλυκεῖα τῶν ὀμμάτων γαλήνη; ποῦ τὸ φαιδρὸν ἐπὶ τοῦ χείλους
μειδίαμα; ποῦ ἡ εὐπροσήγορος δεξιὰ τῇ τοῦ στόματος εὐλογίᾳ τοὺς

---

[13]Gregory seems here to be alluding to Meletius' own fundamental orthodoxy, in a career marked by turbulent disputes and factionalism over the reception of the Nicene faith, especially in the Church of Antioch. His last comment probably refers to the fact that Meletius had been a mentor to Gregory of Nazianzus, and had proposed, early in 379, that Gregory go to Constantinople—still officially presided over by a Homeian bishop—as pastor of the small Nicene community. It was in this capacity that Gregory of Nazianzus unexpectedly found himself the canonical bishop, after Theodosius' accession, and thus president of the council after Meletius' sudden death.

[14]Genesis 48 tells the story of Joseph, who brings his two young sons, Ephraim and Manasseh, to visit his dying father Jacob, and of Jacob adopting them as his own

no one adopted. For it was never his practice to introduce the lowly offspring of slaves into the noble family of the faith. So he is your father, because he was the father of your father![13]

4 You have just heard Ephraim and Manasseh—how many great stories they told about their father, so that the wonders surpassed the counting.[14] Allow me, then, to say something about these things; for there is no harm now in speaking of him as blessed, nor am I afraid of partisan envy—how can it do me any harm? Know, then, who this man was. He was a noble person from the East, "blameless, righteous, truthful, God-fearing, who kept himself from every evil action" (Job 1.1, LXX var.) (for the great Job will surely not be jealous, if his imitator, too, is adorned with the titles given to him). But envy, which never misses anything good, looks on our welfare, too, with malevolent eye; and he who prowls about the world[15] also walks among us, planting his broad and testing footprint even on our successes. He has not destroyed our flocks of cattle and goats, unless indeed one wants to understand "flock" in a mystical way, as referring to the Church; no, the damage done to us by the force of malice does not consist in this, nor has it worked its harm in donkeys and camels, nor wounded our senses by some attack on the flesh.[16] Rather, he has torn off from us our very head. Along with that head, our most valuable organs of sensation have left us. There is no longer an eye, contemplating heavenly things, nor an ear listening attentively for the voice of God, nor that tongue, the sacred monument to the truth. Where is the sweet calm of his eyes? Where is the bright smile on his lips? Where is that right hand, readily extended in welcome, shaking others' hands along with the blessings of his mouth?

sons, and blessing Ephraim in first place (i.e., by laying his right hand on him), even though he is the younger of the two (Gen 48.13–19). This seems to be a veiled reference to panegyrics for Meletius just given by two Antiochene representatives at the Council of 381.

[15]1 Pet 5.8.

[16]For Job's sufferings, to which the Church of Antioch's suffering is being compared here, see Job 1.14–17; 2.4–7.

δακτύλους συνεπισείουσα; προάγομαι δὲ ὡς ἐπὶ σκηνῆς ἀναβοῆσαι
τὴν συμφοράν. ἐλεῶ σε, ὦ ἐκκλησία· πρὸς σὲ λέγω τὴν Ἀντιόχου
GNO 447 πόλιν· | ἐλεῶ σε τῆς ἀθρόας ταύτης μεταβολῆς. πῶς ἀπεκοσμήθη τὸ
κάλλος; πῶς ἀπεσυλήθη ὁ κόσμος; πῶς ἐξαίφνης ἀπερρύη τὸ ἄνθος;
ὄντως Ἐξηράνθη ὁ χόρτος, καὶ τὸ ἄνθος ἐξέπεσεν. τίς ὀφθαλμὸς
πονηρός, τίς βασκανία κακὴ κατὰ τῆς ἐκκλησίας ἐκείνης ἐκώμασεν;
οἷα ἀνθ' οἵων ἠλλάξατο. ἐξέλιπεν ἡ πηγή. ἐξηράνθη ὁ ποταμός.
πάλιν εἰς αἷμα μετεποιήθη τὸ ὕδωρ. ὢ δυστυχοῦς ἀγγελίας ἐκείνης
τῆς διαγγελούσης τῇ ἐκκλησίᾳ τὸ πάθος. τίς ἐρεῖ τοῖς τέκνοις ὅτι
ἀπωρφανίσθησαν; τίς ἀπαγγελεῖ τῇ νύμφῃ ὅτι ἐχήρευσεν; ὢ τῶν
κακῶν. τί ἐξέπεμψαν; καὶ τί ὑποδέχονται; κιβωτὸν προέπεμψαν
καὶ σορὸν ὑποδέχονται. κιβωτὸς γὰρ ἦν, ἀδελφοί, ὁ τοῦ θεοῦ
ἄνθρωπος· κιβωτός, περιέχων ἐν ἑαυτῷ τὰ θεῖα μυστήρια. ἐκεῖ ἡ
στάμνος ἡ χρυσῆ, πλήρης τοῦ θείου μάννα, πλήρης τῆς οὐρανίου
τροφῆς. ἐν ἐκείνῃ αἱ πλάκες τῆς διαθήκης ἐν ταῖς πλαξὶ τῆς καρδίας
ἐγγεγραμμέναι πνεύματι θεοῦ ζῶντος, οὐ μέλανι· οὐδὲν γὰρ τῇ
GNO 448 καθαρότητι τῆς | καρδίας ζοφῶδες καὶ μέλαν ἐνεκέκαυτο νόημα·
ἐν ἐκείνῃ ἡ ῥάβδος τῆς ἱερωσύνης ἡ ἐν ταῖς χερσὶ ταῖς ἐκείνου
βλαστήσασα. καὶ εἴ τι ἄλλο τὴν κιβωτὸν ἔχειν ἀκούομεν, πάντα τῇ
ψυχῇ τοῦ ἀνδρὸς περιείληπτο. |

PG 857 Ἀλλ' ἀντ' ἐκείνων τί; σιωπάτω ὁ λόγος. σινδόνες καθαραὶ καὶ
τὰ ἐκ σηρῶν ὑφάσματα, μύρων καὶ ἀρωμάτων δαψίλεια, γυναικὸς
φιλοτιμία κοσμίας τε καὶ εὐσχήμονος· εἰρήσεται γάρ, ὡς ἂν καὶ
ταῦτα γένοιτο εἰς μαρτυρίαν αὐτῇ, ὃ περὶ τὸν ἱερέα ἐποίησεν

---

[17]Is 40.7 (LXX).

[18]See Ex 7.17–21, one of the plagues of Egypt.

[19]Gregory's depiction of this moment of bereavement for the Church of Antioch suggests that the news of Meletius' death may not yet have reached the city—the shock seems to be something still in the future for them. Hence Gregory's concern over its possible effect.

[20]Literally, "the divine mysteries." Gregory seems to be referring to the holy objects originally at the center of Israel's worship, not to the liturgical acts that later honored them. See Ex 25.10–16; Heb 9.4.

5 I will continue to lament our loss out loud, as if I were on stage. I pity you, O Church! I speak directly to you, city of Antioch: I pity you in this time of intense change! How your beauty has been defaced! How your ornament has been stolen! How suddenly your flower has faded! Truly, "the grass has dried up and the flower fallen"![17] What evil eye, what wicked conspiracy has begun its malign mischief against that community! What a change has taken place! The spring has been exhausted, the river has run dry; water has again turned to blood![18] What miserable news this is, announcing the return of suffering to the Church![19] Who will tell the children that they have become orphans? Who will break the news to the bride that she is a widow? What an evil situation! What did they send us—and what will they receive in return? They sent us an ark as a gift, and they are receiving a coffin. For he was an ark, my sisters and brothers, this man of God: an ark containing within itself the holy signs.[20] There was contained the golden vessel full of divine manna, full of food from heaven. In this vessel were the tables of the covenant, engraved not by ink but by the Spirit of the living God, on the tablets of the heart[21]—for no murky, dark thoughts discolored the purity of his mind. In it was the sacred staff, which blossomed in his own hands.[22] And if there was anything else we hear of, which the ark contained, all of it was embraced by this man's soul.

But what have we received in exchange for this? Let our words fall silent! Clean winding-sheets and woven cloth from worms,[23] an abundant supply of myrrh and spices, marks of reverence from a woman of decency and elegance;[24] for it will be said that all of this,

[21]See 2 Cor 3.3.

[22]See Num 17.17–25 (LXX)—in the Hebrew text, Num 17.1–11; here Aaron's rod sprouts blossoms, not in his own hands but in the sanctuary, where it has been left overnight.

[23]Is Gregory suggesting here that the work of worms, begun in Meletius' silk burial garments, points to the further participation of worms in his material decay?

[24]Drawing on the Gospel story of the woman who anointed Jesus' head with precious ointment in preparation for his burial, the allusion here seems to refer ironically to the Church of Constantinople, which has prepared the body of the deceased Meletius for burial at home.

δαψιλῶς τὴν ἀλάβαστρον τοῦ μύρου τῆς τοῦ ἱερέως κεφαλῆς καταχέασα. ἀλλὰ τὸ ἐν τούτοις διασῳζόμενον, τί; ὀστέα νεκρὰ καὶ πρὸ τοῦ θανάτου προμεμελετηκότα τὴν νέκρωσιν, τὰ λυπηρὰ τῶν συμφορῶν ἡμῶν μνημόσυνα. ὢ οἵα φωνὴ πάλιν ἐν Ῥαμὰ ἀκουσθήσεται· Ῥαχὴλ κλαίουσα οὐχὶ τὰ τέκνα ἑαυτῆς ἀλλὰ τὸν ἄνδρα καὶ οὐ προσιεμένη παράκλησιν. ἄφετε, οἱ παρακαλοῦντες,
GNO 449 ἄφετε. μὴ κατισχύσητε | παρακαλέσαι. βαρὺ πενθείτω ἡ χήρα. αἰσθέσθω τῆς ζημίας, ἣν ἐζημίωται· καίτοι οὐκ ἀμελέτητός ἐστι τοῦ χωρισμοῦ ἐν τοῖς ἀγῶσι τοῦ ἀθλητοῦ προεθισθεῖσα φέρειν τὴν μόνωσιν. Μέμνησθε πάντως ὅπως ὑμῖν ὁ πρὸ ἡμῶν λόγος τοὺς ἀγῶνας τοῦ ἀνδρὸς διηγήσατο, ὅτι διὰ πάντων τιμῶν τὴν ἁγίαν τριάδα καὶ ἐν τῷ ἀριθμῷ τῶν ἀγώνων τὴν τιμὴν διεσώσατο τρισὶ πειρασμῶν προσβολαῖς ἐναθλήσας. ἠκούσατε τὴν ἀκολουθίαν τῶν πόνων, οἷος ἐν πρώτοις, οἷος ἐν μέσοις, ἐν τελευταίοις οἷος

---

[25]See Mk 14.3.

[26]In Greek, a participial form of προμελετάω (*promeletaō*), probably intended as a play on Meletius' name.

[27]See Jer 38.15 (LXX; Hebrew 31.15); Mt 2.18 (thus comparing Meletius to Jacob).

[28]Greek: ἀμελέτητος (*ameletētos*); again, an apparent play on Meletius' name.

[29]Unfortunately, we have no record of who this speaker was or of what he said.

[30]Although he had apparently been ordained bishop for the city of Sebaste in his native Armenia as early as 358–59, Meletius spent much of the next twenty years in various forms of politically motivated exile. According to the *Epitome* of the *Church History* of the fifth-century anti-Nicene historian Philostorgius (5.5), Meletius was forced to resign from the see of Sebaste after a few months, because of resistance on the part of the local people ("Struggle No. 1"?), who apparently still cherished the memory of his charismatic predecessor, Eustathius—known for his insistence that the Holy Spirit was itself a created gift of God. Installed as bishop of the metropolitan see of Antioch by the Emperor Constantius II in 360, as a reputed moderate on Trinitarian issues, Meletius was again sent into exile after a few months, perhaps because his irenic personality made him seem, to the "Homoean" Emperor and his advisors, too friendly to the defenders of Nicaea ("Struggle No. 2"?). Allowed to return to his see by Emperor Julian in 361, Meletius found himself confronted with a city now split into three ideologically competing Christian communities: Nicenes, "Eunomian" Arians,

too, will come to serve as a memorial to her—what she has done in honor of this holy one by generously pouring out an alabaster jar of myrrh on his sacred head.[25] But amidst all these things, what remains? Dead bones, limbs that had prepared[26] in advance for death—sad reminders of all our fate. O, what a voice will be heard once again in Ramah: Rachel weeping no longer for her own children,[27] but for her husband—and uttering no word of consolation. Cease your efforts, you consolers—give up! May your strength to console us fail! May the widow grieve deeply! May she feel the loss that has been inflicted on her! And yet she is not without experience[28] of separation, being trained to bear isolation during his athletic contests. Remember, at least, how the oration before ours[29] set out for you the man's struggles: how he always honored the Holy Trinity, and even in the number of his struggles preserved its honor by fighting against the challenges of three trials.[30]

6 You have heard the results of his labors, how he behaved in the first struggle, how in the second, and how in the final one. I think

and the more "mainstream," but less doctrinally specific, group under his own leadership. After the accession of the anti-Nicene Emperor Valens in 364, Meletius again found himself officially marginalized ("Struggle No. 3"?), and was forced to step down again as bishop in May 365; he lived in a low-grade "exile" in the suburbs of the city, however, for the next six years, apparently continuing to take a quiet but significant role in the pastoral leadership of the "mainstream" Church of Antioch. In the summer of 371, however, Valens became suspicious of his influence and insisted he go into strict exile once more, banishing him back to rural Armenia. At Valens's death in the fall of 378, he returned to Antioch a third time, now recognized as a veteran "moderate" in the struggles over Nicaea (see Epiphanius, *Panarion* 73.34.2–3). The following January, the new emperor, Theodosius I—himself a committed Nicene Christian—invited Meletius to come to Constantinople to crown him (Theodoret, *Ecclesiastical History* 3.6). Through all these difficulties, Meletius' personal reputation steadily grew to be that of a holy man, charitable and welcoming to all, great in his humility, who insisted that the Church's long and varied tradition of faith and worship was more inclusive than the theology of any particular contemporary faction. For details, see my article, "The Enigma of Meletius of Antioch," 129–38. Gregory portrays Meletius here in the image of a warrior husband or champion athlete, repeatedly drawn away from his spouse—the faithful Church of Antioch—to do battle with his opponents; his spouse continues to be faithful to him, and to wait for his return.

ἦν. περιττὴν κρίνω τὴν ἐπανάληψιν τῶν εἰρημένων καλῶς, ἀλλὰ
τοσοῦτον εἰπεῖν μόνον ἴσως οὐκ ἄκαιρον· ὅτε τὸ πρῶτον εἶδεν ἡ
σώφρων ἐκκλησία ἐκείνη τὸν ἄνδρα, εἶδε πρόσωπον ἀληθῶς ἐν
εἰκόνι θεοῦ μεμορφωμένον, εἶδεν ἀγάπην πηγάζουσαν, εἶδε χάριν
περικεχυμένην τοῖς χείλεσιν, ταπεινοφροσύνης τὸν ἀκρότατον
ὅρον, μεθ' ὃν οὐκ ἔστιν ἐπινοῆσαι τὸ πλέον· κατὰ τὸν Δαβὶδ τὴν
πραότητα, κατὰ τὸν Σολομῶντα τὴν σύνεσιν, κατὰ τὸν Μωϋσέα τὴν
ἀγαθότητα, κατὰ τὸν Σαμουὴλ τὴν ἀκρίβειαν, κατὰ τὸν Ἰωσὴφ τὴν
σωφροσύνην, κατὰ τὸν Δανιὴλ τὴν σοφίαν, κατὰ τὸν μέγαν Ἠλίαν
GNO 450 ἐν τῷ ζήλῳ τῆς πίστεως, κατὰ τὸν ὑψηλὸν Ἰω|άννην ἐν τῇ ἀφθορίᾳ
τοῦ σώματος,· εἶδε τοσούτων ἀγαθῶν συνδρομὴν περὶ μίαν ψυχήν·
ἐτρώθη τῷ μακαρίῳ ἔρωτι ἐν τῇ ἁγνῇ καὶ ἀγαθῇ φιλοφροσύνῃ τὸν
νυμφίον ἑαυτῆς ἀγαπήσασα. ἀλλὰ πρὶν τὴν ἐπιθυμίαν ἐμπλῆσαι,
πρὶν ἀναπαῦσαι τὸν πόθον, ἔτι τῷ φίλτρῳ ζέουσα, κατελείφθη
μόνη τῶν πειρασμῶν τὸν ἀθλητὴν ἐπὶ τοὺς ἀγῶνας καλούντων.
καὶ ὁ μὲν ἐνήθλει τοῖς ὑπὲρ τῆς ἀληθείας ἱδρῶσιν, ἡ δὲ ὑπέμενεν
ἐν σωφροσύνῃ τὸν γάμον φυλάσσουσα. χρόνος ἦν ἐν τῷ μέσῳ
πολὺς καί τις μοιχικῶς κατεπεχείρει τῆς ἀχράντου παστάδος. ἀλλ'
ἡ νύμφη οὐκ ἐμιαίνετο. καὶ πάλιν ἐπάνοδος καὶ πάλιν φυγὴ καὶ ἐκ
τρίτου ὡσαύτως, ἕως διασχὼν τὸν αἱρετικὸν ζόφον ὁ κύριος καὶ τὴν
ἀκτῖνα τῆς εἰρήνης ἐπιβαλὼν ἔδωκεν ἀνάπαυσίν τινα τῶν μακρῶν
πόνων ἐλπίζειν. ἀλλ' ἐπειδὴ πάλιν εἶδον ἀλλήλους καὶ ἀνενεώθησαν
εὐφροσύναι καὶ θυμηδίαι πνευματικαὶ καὶ πάλιν ἀνεφλέχθη ὁ
πόθος, εὐθὺς διακόπτει τὴν ἀπόλαυσιν ἡ ἐσχάτη αὕτη ἀποδημία.
PG 860 | ἦλθε νυμφοστολήσων ὑμᾶς καὶ οὐ διήμαρτε τοῦ σπουδάσματος.
GNO 451 ἐπέθηκε τῇ καλῇ συζυγίᾳ τοὺς τῆς εὐλογίας στεφάνους. | ἐμιμήσατο
τὸν δεσπότην τὸν ἴδιον. ὡς ἐν Κανᾶ τῆς Γαλιλαίας ὁ κύριος, οὕτως

---

[31]For David, see Ps 131.1; for Samuel, see: 1 Kg 2.35 (LXX); 12.3–5 (LXX); for Daniel, see: Dan 1.17, 19–20; 5.11–12; for Elijah, see 3 Kg 19.10 (LXX); for John, apparently referring to John the Baptist, known for his austere lifestyle, see Mt 3.4; 11.8; Lk 7.26.

[32]During the 360s and 370s, as we have mentioned, the Christians of Antioch were divided into three main parties—strict Arians, proponents of an equally strict Nicene understanding of God, and the main Church body under Meletius, each

repetition of what was so well said before should be limited, but perhaps it is not out of place to add just this much: when that chaste Church first laid eyes on her spouse, it saw a face truly formed in God's image, it saw love streaming forth as from a spring, it saw "grace was poured forth on his lips" (Ps 44.2), the perfect definition of humility; after him, it will be impossible to imagine anything greater—meekness like that of David, understanding like Solomon's, goodness like Moses', faithful observance like Samuel's, prudence like Joseph's, wisdom like Daniel's, a jealousy for the faith like that of the great Elijah, incorruptible purity of body like that of the lofty John.[31] It saw all these good qualities clustering together around a single soul; it was "wounded by a blessed longing" (Song 2.5), loving its bridegroom with a pure and healthy open-heartedness. But before it could fulfill its desires, before it could still its longing, while still inflamed by his spell, it was left abandoned as trials called its athlete to battle. And he struggled on in his labors on behalf of the truth, while his Church simply endured, preserving its marriage-vow in chastity. Things remained undecided for a long time; people made adulterous assaults against the spotless bridal chamber.[32] Still, the bride was not defiled. Again there was an attack, and again exile for a third time, in the same way, until the Lord, lifting the cloud of heresy and sending down a ray of peace, gave the Church reason to hope for some kind of rest from its great labors. But when at last they had seen each other again, and the spirit of gladness and spiritual joy was revived, when yearning was again enkindled, suddenly this last departure has put celebration to an end. He [i.e., the Lord] came to take you as his bride, and he did not fail in this undertaking; he placed crowns of blessing on this beautiful union.[33] He [i.e., Meletius] imitated his own Master. As the Lord did in Cana of Galilee, so

with its own bishop and each using a different basilica as its liturgical focal point. As the Apollinarian faction grew in importance in the Eastern Mediterranean region the 370s, they also established a headquarters, with their own bishop, in Antioch.

[33]The heart of the eastern Christian celebration of marriage is the crowning of the bride and groom, suggesting the eschatological significance of their nuptial union.

καὶ ἐνταῦθα ὁ μιμητὴς τοῦ κυρίου. τὰς γὰρ Ἰουδαϊκὰς ὑδρίας τοῦ αἱρετικοῦ ὕδατος πεπληρωμένας πλήρεις τοῦ ἀκηράτου οἴνου ἐποίησεν ἐν τῇ δυνάμει τῆς πίστεως μεταποιήσας τὴν φύσιν. ἔστησεν ἐν ὑμῖν πολλάκις κρατῆρα νηφάλιον τῇ γλυκείᾳ ἑαυτοῦ φωνῇ δαψιλῶς οἰνοχοήσας τὴν χάριν. πολλάκις ὑμῖν προεθήκατο τὴν λογικὴν πανδαισίαν. ὁ μὲν εὐλογῶν καθηγεῖτο, οἱ δὲ καλοὶ οὗτοι μαθηταὶ διηκόνουν τοῖς ὄχλοις λεπτοποιοῦντες τὸν λόγον. καὶ ἡμεῖς ηὐφραινόμεθα τὴν τοῦ γένους ὑμῶν δόξαν οἰκείαν ποιούμενοι.

Ὡς καλὰ μέχρι τούτου τὰ διηγήματα. ὡς μακάριον ἦν τούτοις ἐναπολῆξαι τὸν λόγον. ἀλλὰ μετὰ ταῦτα τί; Καλέσατε τὰς θρηνούσας, ὁ Ἰερεμίας φησίν. οὐ γὰρ ἔστιν ἄλλως φλεγομένην καρδίαν καταπεφθῆναι ὑπὸ τοῦ πάθους οἰδαίνουσαν, μὴ στεναγμοῖς καὶ δακρύοις κουφιζομένην. Τότε παρεμυθεῖτο τὸν χωρισμὸν ἡ τῆς ἐπανόδου ἐλπίς, νυνὶ δὲ τὸν ἔσχατον ἡμῶν χωρισμὸν ἀπεσχίσθη. χάσμα μέγα μεταξὺ αὐτοῦ τε καὶ τῆς ἐκκλησίας κατὰ τὸ μέσον
GNO 452 ἐστήρικται. | ὁ μὲν ἐν τοῖς κόλποις τοῦ Ἀβραὰμ ἀναπαύεται, ὁ δὲ διακομίζων τὴν σταγόνα τοῦ ὕδατος, ἵνα καταψύξῃ τῶν ὀδυνωμένων τὴν γλῶσσαν, οὐκ ἔστιν. οἴχεται τὸ κάλλος ἐκεῖνο, σιγᾷ ἡ φωνή, μέμυκε τὰ χείλη, ἀπέπτη ἡ χάρις, διήγημα γέγονεν ἡ εὐκληρία. ἐλύπει ποτὲ καὶ τὸν Ἰσραηλίτην λαὸν Ἠλίας ἀπὸ γῆς πρὸς τὸν θεὸν ἀνιπτάμενος. ἀλλὰ παρεμυθεῖτο τὸν χωρισμὸν Ἐλισσαῖος τῇ μηλωτῇ τοῦ διδασκάλου κοσμούμενος. νυνὶ δὲ τὸ τραῦμα ὑπὲρ θεραπείαν ἐστίν, ὅτι καὶ Ἠλίας ἀνελήφθη καὶ Ἐλισσαῖος οὐχ ὑπελείφθη. ἠκούσατε τοῦ Ἰερεμίου φωνάς τινας σκυθρωπὰς καὶ γοώδεις, αἷς ἐρημωθεῖσαν τὴν πόλιν Ἱεροσολυμιτῶν κατεθρήνησεν, ὃς ἄλλα τέ τινα περιπαθῶς διεξῆλθε καὶ τοῦτό φησιν· Ὁδοὶ Σιὼν

---

[34] A somewhat obscure reference, possibly suggesting Meletius' work as preacher at the liturgy, or as catechist preparing his congregation for baptism. His concern for preserving the long and varied liturgical tradition of the Church of Antioch may also be supported by the *Apostolic Constitutions*, if the collection was indeed put together under his patronage; see "The Enigma of Meletius of Antioch," 145–47.

[35] Using eucharistic language, and alluding to the story of Jesus and his disciples feeding the crowd with loaves and fish in Matthew 14.14–21 (and its parallel passages), Gregory seems to be referring to Meletius' teaching and preaching in Antioch, in which he would have been assisted by deacons and other ministers. The image of

here he acted as the Lord's imitator. For he changed the Jewish water-jars, full of the water of heresy, into jars of pure wine, transforming their nature by the power of faith. Often he set a vessel of pure water in your midst, and with his sweet voice richly poured out the wine of grace.[34] Often he set the spiritual banquet before you: he led the way by speaking the words of blessing, and these excellent disciples of his assisted by breaking the discourse into small, digestible pieces for the crowd.[35] And we [in Constantinople] have rejoiced as well, making the glory of your race our own!

7 How good it has been to share this story up to this point! How blessed it is to finish our narrative with these details! But what comes next? "Call the mourners," Jeremiah says (Jer 9.16); for there is no other way for a fevered heart, swollen with grief, to be cooled,[36] unless it is relieved by groaning and tears. In the past, hope for his return made separation bearable; but now he has been taken away from us in the final separation. "A great gulf has been fixed" (Lk 16.26) between him and his Church; he rests in the bosom of Abraham, but there is no one to provide a drop of water to cool the tongue of the mourners.[37] That beauty has gone away, that voice is silent, those lips are still, that grace has flown, your good fortune has become a tale from the past. Elijah, too, once grieved the people Israel, when he was lifted up from the earth to God. But Elisha offered consolation for the separation, wrapped in the sheepskin cloak of his teacher.[38] Now the wound is beyond healing, since Elijah has been taken up and no Elisha remains. Listen to some sad and mournful words of Jeremiah, in which he lamented the abandoned city Jerusalem; with deep feeling he recounts some other things, and

skilled oratory as an intellectual banquet, presided over by the speaker, is a common one in late antique rhetoric; see, for example, Andrew of Crete, *Homily I on the Dormition of Mary* 7 (PPS 18:111).

[36]Reading, with manuscript M, κατασβεσθῆναι (*katasbesthēnai*) for Spira's καταπεφθῆναι (*katapephthēnai*).

[37]Cf. Lk 16.22–26. Gregory here places the grieving Church of Antioch in the position of the rich man in Hades, in Jesus' parable: consolation is impossible.

[38]4 Kg 2.11–13 (LXX).

πενθοῦσιν. ταῦτα τότε μὲν εἴρηται, νῦν δὲ πεπλήρωται. ὅταν γὰρ
περιαγγείλῃ τὸ πάθος ἡ φήμη, τότε πλήρεις ἔσονται αἱ ὁδοὶ τῶν
πενθούντων καὶ προχυθήσονται οἱ ὑπ' αὐτοῦ ποιμαινόμενοι τὴν τῶν
Νινευϊτῶν φωνὴν ἐπὶ τοῦ πάθους μιμούμενοι, μᾶλλον δὲ κἀκείνων
ἀλγεινότερον ὀδυνώμενοι. τοῖς μὲν γὰρ ὁ θρῆνος τὸν φόβον ἔλυσεν,
τούτοις δὲ λύσις οὐδεμία τῶν κακῶν ἀπὸ τῶν θρήνων ἐλπίζεται. οἶδά
GNO 453 τινα | τοῦ Ἱερεμίου καὶ ἄλλην φωνὴν ταῖς βίβλοις οὖσαν τῶν ψαλμῶν
ἐναρίθμιον, ἣν ἐπὶ τῇ αἰχμαλωσίᾳ τοῦ Ἰσραὴλ ἐποιήσατο, ὅτε ἐπὶ τῶν
Βαβυλωνίων ποταμῶν καθήμενοι τὴν μνήμην τῶν ἰδίων ἀγαθῶν
ἀπεκλάοντο. φησὶ δὲ ὁ λόγος ὅτι Ἐν ἰτέαις ἐκρεμάσαμεν ἑαυτῶν τὰ
ὄργανα, σιωπὴν ἑαυτῶν τε καὶ τῶν ὀργάνων καταδικάσαντες. ἐμὴν
ποιοῦμαι τὴν ᾠδὴν ταύτην. ἐὰν γὰρ ἴδω τὴν αἱρετικὴν σύγχυσιν
(Βαβυλὼν δέ ἐστιν ἡ σύγχυσις) καὶ ἐὰν ἴδω τοὺς πειρασμοὺς τοὺς
διὰ τῆς συγχύσεως ῥέοντας, ταῦτα ἐκεῖνά φημι τὰ Βαβυλώνια
ῥεύματα, οἷς προσκαθήμενοι κλαίομεν, ὅτι τὸν διάγοντα ἡμᾶς διὰ
τούτων οὐκ ἔχομεν. κἂν τὰς ἰτέας εἴπῃς καὶ τὰ ἐπὶ τούτων ὄργανα,
PG 861 ἐμὸν | καὶ τοῦτο τὸ αἴνιγμα. ὄντως γὰρ ἐν ἰτέαις ὁ βίος. δένδρον
γὰρ ἄκαρπον ἡ ἰτέα ἐστίν. ἡμῶν δὲ ἀπερρύη τῆς ζωῆς ὁ γλυκὺς
καρπός. οὐκοῦν ἰτέαι γεγόναμεν ἄκαρποι ἀργὰ καὶ ἀκίνητα τὰ
τῆς ἀγάπης ὄργανα ἐπὶ τῶν ξύλων κρεμάσαντες. Ἐὰν ἐπιλάθωμαί
σου, φησίν, Ἱερουσαλήμ, ἐπιλησθείη ἡ δεξιά μου. δότε μοι μικρὸν
ὑπαλλάξαι τὸ γεγραμμένον, ὅτι οὐχ ἡμεῖς τῆς δεξιᾶς, ἀλλ' ἡ δεξιὰ
ἡμῶν ἐπιλέλησται, καὶ ἡ γλῶσσα τῷ ἰδίῳ λάρυγγι κολληθεῖσα |
GNO 454 τὰς τῆς φωνῆς διεξόδους ἀπέφραξεν, ἵνα μηκέτι ἡμεῖς τῆς γλυκείας
ἐκείνης φωνῆς πάλιν ἀκούσωμεν.

then says, "The ways of Zion mourn" (Lam 1.4). This was said of old, but now it is fulfilled! For when the news spreads this sorrow abroad, the roads will then be filled with mourners, and those who belonged to his flock will spill forth, imitating the cry of the Ninevites in their own suffering, or grieving even more bitterly than they did.[39] For them, after all, lament was a way to release them from fear; but for these [Antiochenes], no hope of release from their sufferings can be expected as the fruit of mourning.

And I know that another expression of Jeremiah's mourning is found among the books of Psalms—one he made during Israel's captivity, when, seated by the rivers of Babylon, they lamented the memory of their own bygone blessings.[40] The text says, "We hung our harps upon the willows in the midst of her" (Ps 136.2), passing a judgment on their own and their instruments' silence. I will make this song my own: for if I look on the confusion made by heretics (and "Babylon" stands for confusion! [see Gen 11.9]), and if I contemplate the trials that flow for us from this confusion, I call these things "the waters of Babylon;" we sit down by them and weep, because we do not have the one who led us across them. And if you speak of the willows and the instruments on them, this, too, refers in figures to each of us. Truly, human life is signified by the willows: for the willow is a tree without fruit, and the sweet fruit of our life has flowed away from us. So we have become willows without fruit, hanging on these trees our instruments of love, which now are idle and motionless. "If I forget you, O Jerusalem," it says, "let my right hand be forgotten!" (Ps 136.5) Allow me to make a small alteration in the text, to the effect that it is not we who will forget our right hand, but our own right hand that will forget us; and that tongue, adhering to its own throat, will be kept from speaking his words, so that we cannot again hear that sweet voice!

[39]See Jon 3.5–8.

[40]Psalm 136 (LXX). Although this Psalm—without ascription in the Hebrew text—is attributed to David in the Septuagint, the older Latin translation in the Vulgate ascribes it to both David and Jeremiah, suggesting there may have been early versions of the Psalter that ascribed it to Jeremiah, as Gregory does here.

Ἀλλ' ἀποψήσασθέ μοι τὰ δάκρυα. αἰσθάνομαι γὰρ πέρα τοῦ
δέοντος ἐπὶ τῷ πάθει γυναικιζόμενος. οὐκ ἀπήρθη ἀφ' ἡμῶν ὁ
νυμφίος, μέσος ἡμῶν ἕστηκεν, κἂν ἡμεῖς μὴ βλέπωμεν. ἐν τοῖς
ἀδύτοις ὁ ἱερεύς· εἰς τὰ ἐνδότερα τοῦ καταπετάσματος, ὅπου
πρόδρομος ὑπὲρ ἡμῶν εἰσῆλθε Χριστός. κατέλιπε τὸ τῆς σαρκὸς
παραπέτασμα. οὐκέτι ὑποδείγματι καὶ σκιᾷ τῶν ἐπουρανίων
λατρεύει, ἀλλ' εἰς αὐτὴν βλέπει τὴν τῶν πραγμάτων εἰκόνα. οὐκέτι
δι' ἐσόπτρου καὶ δι' αἰνίγματος, ἀλλ' αὐτοπροσώπως ἐντυγχάνει
τῷ θεῷ, ἐντυγχάνει δὲ ὑπὲρ ἡμῶν καὶ τῶν τοῦ λαοῦ ἀγνοημάτων.
ἀπέθετο τοὺς δερματίνους χιτῶνας· οὐδὲ γάρ ἐστι χρεία τοῖς ἐν
GNO 455 παραδείσῳ διάγουσι τῶν τοιούτων χιτώνων· ἀλλ' | ἔχει ἐνδύματα,
ἃ τῇ καθαρότητι τοῦ βίου ἑαυτῷ ἐξυφήνας ἐπεκομίσατο. τίμιος
ἐναντίον κυρίου τοῦ ὁσίου ὁ θάνατος, μᾶλλον δὲ οὐχὶ θάνατος,
ἀλλὰ ῥῆξίς ἐστι δεσμῶν. Διέρρηξας γάρ, φησίν, τοὺς δεσμούς μου.
ἀπελύθη ὁ Συμεών, ἠλευθερώθη τῶν δεσμῶν τῶν τοῦ σώματος. ἡ
παγὶς συνετρίβη, τὸ δὲ στρουθίον ἀπέπτη. κατέλιπε τὴν Αἴγυπτον,
τὸν ἰλυώδη βίον. ἐπέρασεν οὐχὶ τὴν ἐρυθρὰν ἐκείνην, ἀλλὰ τὴν
μέλαιναν ταύτην καὶ ζοφώδη τοῦ βίου θάλασσαν. εἰσῆλθεν εἰς τὴν
γῆν τῆς ἐπαγγελίας, ἐπὶ τοῦ ὄρους προσφιλοσοφεῖ τῷ θεῷ. ἐλύσατο
τὸ ὑπόδημα τῆς ψυχῆς, ἵνα καθαρᾷ τῇ βάσει τῆς διανοίας τῆς ἁγίας
GNO 456 γῆς ἐπιβατεύσῃ, ἐν ᾗ καθορᾶται | θεός. ταύτην ἔχοντες, ἀδελφοί,
τὴν παράκλησιν ὑμεῖς οἱ τὰ ὀστᾶ τοῦ Ἰωσὴφ ἐπὶ τὴν χώραν τῆς
εὐλογίας μετακομίζοντες ἀκούσατε τοῦ Παύλου παρεγγυῶντος·
Μὴ λυπεῖσθε ὡς καὶ οἱ λοιποὶ οἱ μὴ ἔχοντες ἐλπίδα. εἴπατε τῷ
ἐκεῖ λαῷ, διηγήσασθε τὰ καλὰ διηγήματα. εἴπατε τὸ ἀπιστούμενον

---

[41]See Heb 6.19–20.

[42]See Heb 10.1.

[43]Gregory often uses this image from Genesis to signify the state of fallen humanity.

[44]Lk 2.29.

[45]See Ps 123.7.

8 But wipe away my tears—for I feel that I am showing womanly emotion beyond what is fitting. The bridegroom has not been taken away from us, but stands in our midst, even if we cannot see him. The priest in is the sanctuary; he has entered within the veil, where Christ the forerunner entered on our behalf.[41] He has left behind him the curtain of the flesh. He no longer offers worship in the pattern and shadow of heavenly things, but gazes on the very image of the things themselves.[42] He no longer intercedes before God "in a mirror and mysteriously" (1 Cor 13.12), but face to face—and he intercedes for us, and for the acts of ignorance of the people. He has taken off the "garments of skin" (Gen 3.21),[43] for there is no need of such clothing among those living in paradise. But he has clothing, which he wove by the purity of his life, and has brought with him. "Precious in the sight of the Lord is the death of his saint" (Ps 115.6)—or rather, it is not death, but is the breaking of bonds. "For you have broken my bonds asunder" (Ps 115.7) as [the Psalm] says. Symeon is allowed to depart,[44] freed from the body's chains. The trap is broken, and the bird has flown away.[45] He has left Egypt and life in the mud; he has crossed not that Red Sea, but the dark and cloudy sea of life. He has entered into the land of promise, and on the mountaintop he leads the philosophic life before God.[46] He has loosened the sandal of his soul, so that he might tread with pure step on the holy ground of understanding, where God is seen directly.[47]

9 Having this consolation, my brothers and sisters—you who now bear the bones of Joseph to the land of blessing[48]—hear Paul when he exhorts you, "Do not grieve like the rest, who have no hope" (1 Thess 4.13). Tell this to the people there, recount this marvelous

[46]In the fourth century, the "philosophic life" was a frequent way of speaking about the lifestyle of ascetics and contemplatives, focused as far as possible on God himself.

[47]See Ex 3.5, the account of Moses before the burning bush. To remove one's sandals was for Gregory a symbol of taking off the "skin" of earthly existence, in order to contemplate God. See *Life of Moses* 1.22–26.

[48]Gen 50.24–25; Ex 13.19; Josh 24.32. Gregory seems now to be addressing the party which will accompany Meletius' body back to Antioch.

θαῦμα, πῶς εἰς θαλάσσης ὄψιν καταπυκνωθέντες ὁ μυριάνθρωπος δῆμος ἓν ἦν κατὰ τὸ συνεχὲς σῶμα οἱ πάντες οἷόν τι ὕδωρ περὶ τὴν τοῦ σκηνώματος πομπὴν πελαγίζοντες· πῶς ὁ καλὸς Δαβὶδ πολυμερῶς καὶ πολυτρόπως εἰς μυρίας τάξεις ἑαυτὸν καταμερίσας ἐν ἑτερογλώσσοις καὶ ὁμογλώσσοις περὶ τὸ σκῆνος ἐχόρευεν· πῶς ἑκατέρωθεν οἱ τοῦ πυρὸς ποταμοὶ τῇ συνεχείᾳ τῶν λαμπάδων οἷόν τις ὑδάτων ὁλκὸς ἀδιασπάστως ῥέοντες, ἕως οὗ δυνατὸν ἦν ὀφθαλμῷ λαβεῖν, παρετείνοντο. εἴπατε τοῦ λαοῦ παντὸς τὴν προθυμίαν, τῶν ἀποστόλων τὴν συσκηνίαν· πῶς τὰ σουδάρια τῶν χρωτῶν αὐτοῦ εἰς φυλακτήρια τῶν πιστῶν διετίλλετο. προσκείσθω τῷ διηγήματι βασι-|
PG 864 λεὺς σκυθρωπάζων ἐπὶ τῷ πάθει καὶ θρόνων ἐξανιστάμενος, καὶ
GNO 457 πόλις ὅλη τῇ πομπῇ | τοῦ ἁγίου συμμεταβαίνουσα, καὶ παρακαλεῖτε ἀλλήλους ἐν τοῖς λόγοις τούτοις. καλῶς ὁ Σολομὼν ἰατρεύει τὴν λύπην. κελεύει γὰρ οἶνον τοῖς ἐν λύπῃ διδόναι, πρὸς ὑμᾶς τοῦτο λέγων, τοὺς τοῦ ἀμπελῶνος ἐργάτας. δότε οὖν τὸν ὑμέτερον οἶνον τοῖς λυπουμένοις, οὐ τὸν τῆς μέθης ἐργάτην ἀλλὰ τὸν τὴν καρδίαν εὐφραίνοντα. ζωροτέρῳ τῷ κράματι καὶ ἀφθονωτέραις δεξιοῦσθε τοῦ λόγου ταῖς κύλιξιν, ὥστε ἡμῖν πάλιν εἰς εὐφροσύνην περιστραφῆναι τὸ πένθος ἐν Χριστῷ Ἰησοῦ τῷ κυρίῳ ἡμῶν, ᾧ ἡ δόξα εἰς τοὺς αἰῶνας. ἀμήν.

story! Tell them the incredible wonder of how a crowd of many thousands of people, brought together in one continuous body as wide as the sea, surged ocean-like around the procession with his remains; [49] how David the beautiful, speaking "in many and various ways" (Heb 1.1), divided himself into countless companies, among people of the same and of differing languages, and danced around the ark of his body;[50] how rivers of fire, from the continuous light of the torches, stretched out and flowed uninterruptedly on both sides, like some massive rush of water, as far as it was possible to see with the naked eye. Tell of the eagerness of the whole population, and of the gathering of the apostles in a single tabernacle;[51] and how the shroud wrapping his remains was plucked at for mementos by the faithful. And add to the account the story of the emperor, looking downcast in his sadness and rising from his throne, and the entire city with him, accompanying the funeral procession of the holy man. "Comfort one another with these words!" (1 Thess 4.18).

Solomon offered an effective cure for grief. He commanded us to offer wine to those in sorrow,[52] addressing this to you, the workers who tend the vine. Give your own wine, then, to those who grieve: not wine that brings on intoxication, but the "wine that gladdens the heart" (Ps 103.15).[53] Take it up unmixed and undiluted, in the generous goblets of the Word, so that our grief may again be converted into joy, in Christ Jesus our Lord, to whom be glory for the ages. Amen.

[49]In the next few sentences, Gregory offers a dramatic narrative of Meletius' funeral liturgy in Constantinople, again made vivid by biblical allusions.

[50]See 2 Sam (LXX: 2 Kg) 6.14–15. Gregory may be alluding here to the unifying effect of the liturgical chanting of the biblical psalms, despite the cultural and linguistic differences of the clergy and people assembled.

[51]Gregory seems to be alluding to the bishops present at the liturgy, and perhaps also to their presence in the church where the relics of the apostles are venerated.

[52]Prov 31.6: "Give strong drink to the one who is perishing, and wine to those in bitter distress."

[53]Gregory seems to be encouraging preachers and those who minister the Eucharist to offer the grieving people of Antioch, as well as his own hearers in Constantinople, the genuine consolation of the orthodox faith.

A Discourse of Consolation for Pulcheria
(*Oratio consolatoria in Pulcheriam*)

A Note on the Text

This oration is a memorial address, or discourse of consolation (παραμυθητικός λόγος, *paramythētikos logos*), delivered by Gregory in memory of the little princess Pulcheria, daughter of Emperor Theodosius I and his wife Flaccilla, who had just died at the age of 6—probably sometime in the late summer of 385, several months before the death of her mother the following winter. Gregory's allusion to a recent earthquake in a "neighboring city," whose anniversary had been observed in the liturgy a day earlier, may well refer to the major shock that had destroyed Nicomedia, the imperial residence some sixty miles to the east, almost thirty years before, on August 24, 358 (see Ammianus Marcellinus, *History* 17.7.1–8; see also Glanville Downey, "Earthquakes in Constantinople and Vicinity, A.D. 342–1454," *Speculum* 3 [1955]: 596–600]). If this is indeed the earthquake Gregory is referring to, this oration can be dated to August 25, 385, and Pulcheria's death would have occurred shortly before. We do not have any information on where it was delivered; but the funeral itself, as Gregory so splendidly describes it (section 3), probably took place in the basilica of the Holy Apostles, where the members of the imperial family were usually buried, and this oration may have been a later part of that same liturgical celebration. For the princess Pulcheria's death and its importance for Theodosius and his family, see Kenneth G. Holum, *Theodosian Empresses: Women and Imperial Dominion in Late Antiquity* (Berkeley: University of California Press, 1982), 21–22. The Greek text used for this translation is the critical edition of Andreas Spira, in GNO IX/1:461–72. I have added section numbers for ease in reference.

GNO IX:461 PG 46:864

ΓΡΗΓΟΡΙΟΥ ΕΠΙΣΚΟΠΟΥ ΝΥΣΣΗΣ ΕΙΣ ΠΟΥΛΧΕΡΙΑΝ ΠΑΡΑΜΥΘΗΤΙΚΟΣ ΛΟΓΟΣ

Οὐκ οἶδα ὅπως τῷ λόγῳ χρήσομαι· διπλῆν τε γὰρ ὁρῶ τὴν ὑπόθεσιν
καὶ σκυθρωπὴν καθ᾽ ἑκάτερον, ὡς μὴ ῥᾴδιον ἔξω δακρύων τὸν
λόγον ἐλθεῖν, ὁτιοῦν ἐξ ἀμφοτέρων ἑλόμενον. ἡ παροῦσα τοῦ
ἔτους περίοδος, καθὼς ἡμῖν χθὲς τοῦτο παρὰ τοῦ ποιμένος
ἐπήγγελται, σκυθρωπῶν πραγμάτων τῶν τῇ γείτονι πόλει ποτὲ
διὰ τοῦ σεισμοῦ συμπεπτωκότων περιέχει τὴν μνήμην. ἃ τίς ἂν
ἀδακρυτὶ διεξέλθοι; ἡ δὲ μεγάλη καὶ περιφανὴς αὕτη καὶ τῆς ὑφ᾽
ἥλιον πάσης προτεταγμένη καλλίπολις ἄλλον σεισμὸν ὑπέστη καὶ
οὐ μικρὸν ἀπεσυλήθη κόσμον, τοῦ ἐν αὐτῇ λάμψαντος φωστῆρος
εἰς προσθήκην τῆς βασιλικῆς εὐκληρίας ἀθρόως ἀφαιρεθεῖσα καὶ
διὰ τοῦτο τῇ κατηφείᾳ τῶν βασιλέων συσκυθρωπάζουσα. τὸ δὲ
λεγόμενον οὐκ ἀγνοεῖτε πάντως οἱ πληροῦντες τὸν σύλλογον
ὁρῶντες αὐτόν τε τὸν τόπον τοῦτον, ἐν ᾧ συνειλέγμεθα, καὶ
τὴν ἐν τῷ τόπῳ κατήφειαν. οὐκ οἶδα τοίνυν πρὸς ποῖον σεισμὸν
τρέψω τὸν λόγον, πρὸς τὸν νῦν ἢ τὸν πάλαι γενόμενον. ἢ καλῶς
ἔχει πρὸς τὸ ὑπερβάλλον τοῦ πάθους στῆναι καὶ καταπραῦναι τῆς
πόλεως τὴν ἰδίαν ἀλγηδόνα λογισμοῖς τισι καταφαρμάσσοντα;
εἰ γὰρ καὶ μὴ πάντες οἱ τοῦ κακοῦ συμμετέχοντες τῷ συλλόγῳ
πάρεισιν, ἀλλὰ διὰ τῶν παρόντων ἴσως καὶ εἰς τοὺς μὴ παρόντας
PG 865 ὁ λόγος δια|δοθήσεται. καὶ γὰρ καὶ τῶν ἰατρῶν ἐκεῖνοι σοφοὶ οἱ
GNO 462 πρὸς τὸ πλεονάζον τῶν ἀλγηδόνων διὰ τῆς τέχνης ἱστά|μενοι,
τῶν δὲ ἧττον ὀδυνηρῶν τὴν θεραπείαν ὑπερτιθέμενοι. ὥσπερ δέ
φασιν οἱ περὶ ταῦτα δεινοί, εἰ δύο κατὰ ταὐτὸν ἑνὶ σώματι πόνοι

A Discourse of Consolation for Pulcheria

1 I do not know how to construct this oration. For I see a double subject, mournful on either side, so that it is not easy to begin speaking without tears, whichever of the two we choose. This present anniversary, as it was proclaimed to us yesterday by our shepherd,[1] holds up before us memories of the sad event of an earthquake that occurred in a nearby city in the past. Who could tell this story without tears? But our own great, renowned city, held up for its beauty before every land under the sun, has undergone another earthquake, is robbed of another world that was no small one[2]—suddenly it is deprived of the star that has been shining in it, to advance the good fortune of the imperial house, and for that reason it shares in the deep grief and sadness of our royal couple. Surely you who are gathered here, seeing the crowd and the place where we have assembled, as well as the grief that is among us, are not unaware of what I am saying. I do not know, then, at which shock I should aim this oration—the one we have just undergone, or the one that happened some years ago.

Is it a good idea, perhaps, to resist the excess of our grief, and to soften the private suffering of the city, by treating them with the medications of argument? For even if not all those touched by this misfortune are present here in our gathering,[3] still perhaps the content of our oration will be passed on by those who are here, to those who are not. Those doctors, after all, are wise who use their art to take a stand against the worst kinds of pain, deferring the treatment of lesser discomforts until later. As the experts in the field tell us, if two disorders coincide in one body at the same time, our perception

[1]Presumably a reference to Nectarius, bishop of Constantinople from 381 to 397.

[2]A moving allusion to the importance of the little princess for the court.

[3]Gregory seems to imply that not all the royal family are part of the gathering where he is preaching.

συμπέσοιεν, μόνου τοῦ ὑπερβάλλοντος τὴν αἴσθησιν γίνεσθαι, ἐν τῷ πλεονάζοντι τῆς ἐπικρατούσης ἀλγηδόνος ἐκκλεπτομένης τῆς ἥττονος, οὕτω καὶ ἐπὶ τοῦ παρόντος βλέπω· τὸ γὰρ νέον τε καὶ ἡμέτερον ἄλγημα τῶν διὰ τῆς μνήμης ἀλγυνόντων ἡμᾶς ἐστιν ἐπικρατέστερον. πῶς γὰρ οὐκ ἄν τις ἐπὶ τοῖς συμβεβηκόσι πάθοι; τίς οὕτως ἀπαθὴς τὴν ψυχήν; τίς οὕτω τὸν τρόπον σιδήρεος, ὡς ἀναλγητὶ τὸ συμβὰν δέξασθαι; ἔγνωτε πάντως τὴν νέαν ταύτην περιστερὰν τὴν ἐντρεφομένην τῇ βασιλικῇ καλιᾷ, τὴν ἄρτι μὲν πτερουμένην ἐν λαμπρῷ τῷ πτερῷ, ὑπερβᾶσαν δὲ τὴν ἡλικίαν ταῖς χάρισιν ὅπως ἀφεῖσα τὴν καλιὰν οἴχεται, ὅπως ἔξω τῶν ὀφθαλμῶν ἡμῶν ἀπέπτη, ὅπως αὐτὴν ἀθρόως ὁ φθόνος τῶν χειρῶν ἡμῶν ἀφήρπασεν, εἴτε περιστερὰν χρὴ λέγειν ταύτην, εἴτε νεοθαλὲς ἄνθος, ὃ οὔπω μὲν ὅλον τῶν καλύκων ἐξέλαμψεν, ἀλλὰ τὸ μὲν ἔλαμπεν ἤδη, τὸ δὲ λάμψειν ἠλπίζετο καὶ ὅμως ἐν τῷ μικρῷ τε καὶ ἀτελεῖ ὑπερέλαμπεν· ὅπως ἀθρόως ἐναπέσβη τῇ κάλυκι καὶ πρὶν εἰς ἀκμὴν προελθεῖν καὶ ὅλον ἄνω διαπετάσαι τὸ ἄνθος, αὐτὸ περὶ ἑαυτὸ κατερρύη καὶ κόνις ἐγένετο, ὃ οὔτε ἐδρέψατό τις οὔτε ἐστεφανώσατο, ἀλλὰ μάτην ἡ φύσις ἐπόνησεν· οὗ τὸ μὲν ἀγαθὸν ἐν ἐλπίσιν ἦν, ὁ δὲ φθόνος ξίφους δίκην πλάγιος ἐμπεσὼν τὴν ἐλπίδα διέκοψεν. σεισμός τις ἦν ἄντικρυς, ἀδελφοί, τὸ γενόμενον, σεισμὸς οὐδὲν τῶν χαλεπῶν συμπτωμάτων φιλανθρωπότερος· οὐ γὰρ ἄψυχον οἰκοδομημάτων κάλλος διελυμήνατο, οὐδὲ εὐανθεῖς γραφὰς ἢ λίθων περικαλλῆ θεάματα εἰς γῆν κατέβαλεν, ἀλλ' αὐτῆς τῆς φύσεως τὸ οἰκοδόμημα λαμπρὸν τῷ κάλλει, ὑπεραστράπτον |
GNO 463 ταῖς χάρισιν, ἀθρόως προσπεσὼν ὁ σεισμὸς οὗτος διέλυσεν. εἶδον ἐγὼ καὶ τὸ ὑψηλὸν ἔρνος, τὸν ὑψίκομον φοίνικα (τὸ βασιλικόν φημι κράτος) τὸν ταῖς βασιλικαῖς ἀρεταῖς οἷόν τισι κλάδοις πάσης

tends to be focused on just one of them, the dominant pain stealing attention from the lesser by its excess. This is how I see things in this present moment: our recent pain, shared just by ourselves, is more powerful than the things that pain us in our memories.

2 For how could one not be pained by what has happened? Who is so insensitive in his soul? Who is so steely at heart as to receive the news of this event without being saddened? Surely you know that this little dove, nurtured in the royal nest, so recently fledged with her bright wings and so far beyond her age in graces—how she has left the nest and gone away; [you know] how she has flown out of our sight, how evil has suddenly snatched her from our hands—whether we should call this child a dove, or a newly-sprouted flower, which had not yet emerged in all its brilliance from the bud. Still, some of the flower's brilliance did shine forth, some was hoped for in future brilliance; even in its small, incomplete way, the flower still dazzled us with its splendor. [You know] how suddenly she was extinguished in the bud, and how, before the flower reached full maturity and could spread out its petals to the sky, it has collapsed into itself and turned to dust. No one could pluck it or weave it into a garland;[4] nature has done its work in vain. The good lay all in our hopes, but treacherous evil[5] has fallen upon it like a sword, and has cut our hope down.

What has happened was obviously an earthquake, my brothers and sisters—an earthquake in no way gentler than that sad event of years ago. It has not knocked down the lifeless beauty of buildings, nor cast to the ground brightly-colored paintings or splendid decorations in stone; but this earthquake, happening so unexpectedly, has destroyed a house built by nature itself, lovely in form, radiant with grace. I myself have watched the lofty tree—the high-branched palm (I mean the imperial power)[6] that towers with its royal virtues,

[4]Gregory refers here to the crowns in the Greek wedding liturgy, and to the sad fact that Pulcheria has died before reaching marriageable age (see *Meletius* 8).

[5]Literally "envy" (φθόνος, *phthonos*)—the classical Greek way of speaking about pitiless fate.

[6]The emperor Theodosius.

ὑπερανεστῶτα τῆς οἰκουμένης καὶ πάντα διαλαμβάνοντα· εἶδον
αὐτὸν τῶν μὲν ἄλλων κρατοῦντα, τῇ δὲ φύσει καμπτόμενον καὶ
πρὸς τὴν ἀποβολὴν τοῦ ἄνθους ἐπικλινόμενον. εἶδον καὶ τὴν
εὐγενῆ κληματίδα τὴν περιειλημμένην τῷ φοίνικι τὴν τὸ ἄνθος
ἡμῖν τοῦτο ὠδίνασαν, οἵας ὑπέστη ἐκ δευτέρου πάλιν ὠδῖνας ἐν
ψυχῇ, οὐκ ἐν σώματι, ὅτε αὐτῆς οὗτος ὁ βλαστὸς ἀπετίλλετο. τίς
ἀστενάκτως τὸ πάθος παρέδραμεν; τίς τὴν τοῦ βίου ζημίαν οὐκ
ὠλοφύρατο; τίς οὐκ ἐπαφῆκε τῷ πάθει δάκρυα; τίς οὐ κατέμιξε τῇ
κοινῇ συνῳδίᾳ τοῦ θρήνου τὰς ἰδίας φωνάς; εἶδον θέαμα ἄπιστον,
ὃ οὐκ ἂν εἰς πίστιν ἔλθοι τοῖς ἀκοῇ παραδεχομένοις τὰ θαύ-|
PG 868 ματα· εἶδον ἐξ ἀνθρώπων πέλαγος τῇ πυκνότητι τῶν συνεστώτων
οἷόν τι ὕδωρ κατὰ πᾶν μέρος τοῖς ὀφθαλμοῖς προφαινόμενον·
πλήρης ὁ ναός, πλῆρες τοῦ ναοῦ τὸ προαύλιον, ἡ ἐκδεχομένη
πλατεῖα, οἱ στενωποί, τὰ ἄμφοδα, ἡ μέση, τὰ πλάγια, ἡ ἐπὶ τῶν
δωμάτων εὐρυχωρία· πᾶν τὸ ὁρώμενον ἀνθρώπων πλήρωμα ἦν,
ὥσπερ πάσης τῆς οἰκουμένης εἰς ταὐτὸν συνδραμούσης ἐπὶ τῷ
πάθει. θέαμα δὲ προέκειτο πᾶσι τὸ ἱερὸν ἄνθος ἐκεῖνο ἐπὶ κλίνης
χρυσῆς κομιζόμενον. πῶς κατηφῆ πάντων ἦν τῶν προσορώντων
τὰ πρόσωπα. πῶς δεδακρυμένα τὰ ὄμματα. χεῖρες ἀλλήλαις
συναρασσόμεναι. στεναγμοὶ πρὸς τούτοις τὴν ἐγκάρδιον ὀδύνην
καταμηνύοντες. οὔ μοι ἔδοξε κατὰ τὴν ὥραν ἐκείνην (τάχα δὲ
οὐδὲ τοῖς ἄλλοις τῶν τότε παρόντων) τὴν ἐκ φύσεως χάριν ὁ
χρυσὸς ἀποστίλβειν. ἀλλὰ καὶ αἱ τῶν λίθων αὐγαὶ καὶ τὰ ἐκ χρυσοῦ
GNO 464 ὑφάσματα καὶ αἱ τοῦ ἀργύρου μαρμαρυγαὶ καὶ τὸ ἐκ τοῦ | πυρὸς
φῶς πολύ τε καὶ ἄφθονον κατὰ τὰ πλάγια ἑκατέρωθεν τῇ συνεχείᾳ
τῶν ἐκ τοῦ κηροῦ λαμπάδων παρατεινόμενον, πάντα τῷ πένθει
συνεμελαίνετο καὶ πάντα μετεῖχε τῆς κοινῆς κατηφείας. τότε καὶ
ὁ μέγας Δαβὶδ τὰς ἰδίας ὑμνῳδίας τοῖς θρήνοις ἔχρησε καὶ ἀντὶ
τῆς φαιδρᾶς χοροστασίας μεταλαβὼν τὴν γοεράν τε καὶ πένθιμον
ἐξεκαλεῖτο τοὺς θρήνους τοῖς μέλεσιν, πάσης δὲ κατὰ τὸν καιρὸν

---

[7]His wife, the empress Flaccilla.

[8]Greek, "the *Mesē*" (= "middle way"). This was the main thoroughfare in Constantine's capital, starting in front on the Church of Hagia Sophia and running to the western extremity of the city. It was extended as the city was expanded, and is

as with branches, over the whole world and draws everything together; I have seen this one who rules over others, bowed down by the weight of nature, bending low over his fallen blossom. I have also seen the noble vine,[7] which clings to the palm-tree, the one who bore this flower for us, undergoing a kind of second childbirth in her soul, not in her body, as this blossom was plucked away from her. Who can pass by such sorrow without a groan? Who can fail to grieve at this loss of life? Who has not shed a tear at their suffering? Who has not mingled his own voice with the common chorus of laments?

3 I have seen an unbelievable spectacle, which would not sound credible to those who know these wonders only by hearsay. I have seen a sea of people, appearing before our eyes on every side, crowded together like some body of water in their density: the church is full, the forecourt of the church also full, the adjoining square, the alleys, the side streets, the main boulevard,[8] the neighboring streets, the broad spaces on the roofs of buildings. Everywhere you looked, there was a crowd of human beings, as if all the human world had rushed together because of this sad news. And the sight that lay before us all was that sacred flower, borne in on a golden litter! How sorrowful were all the onlookers' faces! How tear-filled their eyes! Hands struck against one another; groans, too, that gave still further signs of grief in their hearts! At that moment, it did not seem to me—and perhaps not to the others present—that even gold would shine with its natural beauty. And so it was: the shining of the stones and the vestments of gold, the flashing of silver and the abundant light of the flames offered by the crowded candles on all sides—everything was darkened by grief, everything shared in the common sadness. At that moment, the great David provided his own hymnody for the laments; taking up the sound of a dirge and mourning in place of light-hearted choral song, he brought forth hymns of sadness in his

still today the main street of the ancient center of Istanbul. The Church of the Holy Apostles, the city's main Christian sanctuary, was located just off the *Mesē*, some two miles to the northwest of Hagia Sophia and the royal palace.

ἐκεῖνον ἡδονῆς τῶν ψυχῶν ἀπελαθείσης μόνον ἦν ἐν ἡδονῇ τοῖς ἀνθρώποις τὸ δάκρυον.

Ἐπειδὴ τοίνυν τοσοῦτον ἡττήθη τοῦ πάθους ὁ λογισμός, καιρὸς ἂν εἴη τὸ κεκμηκὸς τῆς διανοίας διὰ τῆς τῶν λογισμῶν συμβουλῆς ὡς ἔστι δυνατὸν ἀναρρώννυσθαι. κίνδυνος γὰρ οὐ μικρὸς παρακούσαντας ἐν τούτῳ τῆς τοῦ Ἀποστόλου φωνῆς συγκατακριθῆναι τοῖς ἀνελπίστοις. φησὶ γάρ, καθὼς τοῦ ὑπαναγινώσκοντος ἀρτίως ἠκούσαμεν, Μὴ δεῖν ἐπὶ τῶν κεκοιμημένων λυπεῖσθαι· μόνων γὰρ τοῦτο τῶν οὐκ ἐχόντων ἐλπίδα τὸ πάθος εἶναι. ἀλλ' εἴποι τις ἄν, οἶμαι, τῶν μικροψυχοτέρων ἀδύνατα κελεύειν τὸν θεῖον Ἀπόστολον καὶ ὑπερβαίνειν τὴν φύσιν τοῖς ἐπιτάγμασιν. πῶς γάρ ἐστι δυνατὸν ὑπεραρθῆναι τοῦ πάθους τὸν ἐν τῇ φύσει ζῶντα καὶ μὴ κρατηθῆναι τῇ λύπῃ ἐπὶ τοιούτῳ θεάματι, ὅταν μὴ καθ' ὥραν ἐν γήρᾳ συμπέσῃ ὁ θάνατος, ἀλλ' ἐν τῇ πρώτῃ ἡλικίᾳ κατασβεσθῇ μὲν τῷ θανάτῳ ἡ ὥρα, καλυφθῇ δὲ τοῖς βλεφάροις ἡ τῶν ὀμμάτων ἀκτίς, μεταπέσῃ δὲ εἰς ὠχρότητα τῆς παρειᾶς τὸ ἐρύθημα, κρατηθῇ δὲ τῇ σιωπῇ τὸ στόμα, μελαίνηται δὲ τὸ ἐπὶ τοῦ χείλους ἄνθος, χαλεπὸν δὲ μὴ μόνον τοῖς γεννησαμένοις τοῦτο δοκῇ, ἀλλὰ καὶ παντὶ τῷ πρὸς
GNO 465 τὸ πάθος βλέποντι; τί οὖν πρὸς τούτοις ἡμεῖς; οὐχ | ἡμέτερον ἐροῦμεν, ἀδελφοί, λόγον, ἀλλὰ τὴν ἀναγνωσθεῖσαν ἡμῖν ἐκ τοῦ Εὐαγγελίου ῥῆσιν παραθησόμεθα. ἠκούσατε γὰρ λέγοντος τοῦ κυρίου· Ἄφετε τὰ παιδία καὶ μὴ κωλύετε αὐτὰ ἔρχεσθαι πρός με· τῶν γὰρ τοιούτων ἐστὶν ἡ βασιλεία τῶν οὐρανῶν. οὐκοῦν
PG 869 εἰ καὶ σοῦ ἀπεφοίτησε τὸ παιδίον, | ἀλλὰ πρὸς τὸν δεσπότην ἀπέδραμεν. σοὶ τὸν ὀφθαλμὸν ἔκλεισεν, ἀλλὰ τῷ φωτὶ τῷ αἰωνίῳ διήνοιξεν. τῆς σῆς ἀπέστη τραπέζης, ἀλλὰ τῇ ἀγγελικῇ προσετέθη. ἔνθεν τὸ φυτὸν ἀνεσπάσθη, ἀλλὰ τῷ παραδείσῳ ἐνεφυτεύθη. ἐκ βασιλείας εἰς βασιλείαν μετέστη. ἐξεδύσατο τὸ τῆς πορφύρας

poetry. All joy, in that moment, was driven out of souls; only tears were a source of joy to the people there.

4 Since, then, our reasoning is so much overcome by sadness, it would be a good time to strengthen the weakness of our thinking, as far as we can, with the help of arguments. For there is no small danger that those who, in this situation, fail to hear the Apostle's voice will be condemned along with the hopeless. For he says, as we have just heard the lector read, that "we should not grieve for those who have fallen asleep," for this is the sorrow only of "those who have no hope" (1 Thess 4.13).[9] But I suppose someone may say that the divine Apostle is commanding the impossible for limited minds, is going beyond nature with his commands. How is it possible, after all, for someone living within nature's bounds to be raised above sorrow, and not to be crushed with grief at a spectacle such as this, when death attacks not an aged person at an appropriate time, but when time itself is quenched by death in earliest youth—when the light of the eyes is covered over, the ruddy hue of the cheeks falls pale, the mouth held shut by silence, the bloom on the lips blackened? Does this not seem a hard thing, not only for parents but for everyone who gazes on their sorrow?

5 And what shall we say about this? We will not speak our own words, my brothers and sisters, but we will lay before you the saying of the Gospel that was just read to us. For you heard the Lord say, "Let the children come to me, and do not prevent them, for of such is the Kingdom of heaven" (Mt 19.14). So, then, even if this little one has wandered away from you, surely she has run away to the Lord. As far as you are concerned, she has closed her eyes, but she has opened them to the light of eternity. She has departed from your table, but has joined the table of the angels. The shoot has been uprooted from here, but has been planted in the garden of paradise. She has moved from one kingdom to another. She has taken off the bright garment

[9]This text and the following Gospel passage apparently had been read as part of the memorial liturgy.

ἄνθος, ἀλλὰ τῆς ἄνω βασιλείας τὴν περιβολὴν ἐνεδύσατο. εἴπω σοι τὴν ὕλην τοῦ θείου ἐνδύματος; οὐ λίνον ἐστὶν οὐδὲ ἔριον οὐδὲ τὰ ἐκ σηρῶν νήματα. ἄκουσον τοῦ Δαβίδ, ὅθεν ἐξυφαίνεσθαι λέγει τῷ θεῷ τὰ ἐνδύματα· Ἐξομολόγησιν καὶ μεγαλοπρέπειαν ἐνεδύσω, ἀναβαλλόμενος φῶς ὡς ἱμάτιον. ὁρᾷς οἷα ἀνθ' οἵων ἠλλάξατο; λυπεῖ σε τὸ τοῦ σώματος κάλλος μηκέτι φαινόμενον, οὐ γὰρ ὁρᾷς αὐτῆς τὸ ἀληθινὸν τῆς ψυχῆς κάλλος, ᾧ νῦν ἐν τῇ πανηγύρει τῶν οὐρανίων ἀγάλλεται. ὡς καλὸς ἐκεῖνος ὁ ὀφθαλμὸς ὁ τὸν θεὸν βλέπων. ὡς ἡδὺ τὸ στόμα τὸ ταῖς θείαις ὑμνῳδίαις καλλωπιζόμενον.

Ἐκ στόματος γάρ, φησίν, νηπίων καὶ θηλαζόντων κατηρτίσω αἶνον. ὡς καλαὶ αἱ χεῖρες αἱ μηδέποτε τὸ κακὸν ἐνεργήσασαι. ὡς ὡραῖοι οἱ πόδες οἱ μὴ ἐπιβάντες κακίας, μηδὲ τῇ ὁδῷ τῶν ἁμαρτωλῶν τὸ ἴχνος ἑαυτῶν ἐπιστήσαντες. ὡς καλὴ πᾶσα τῆς ψυχῆς ἐκείνης ἡ ὄψις, οὐ λίθων αὐγαῖς κεκοσμημένη, ἀλλ'
GNO 466 ἁπλότητι καὶ ἀκακίᾳ ἐκλάμπουσα. ἀλλὰ λυπεῖ σε τυχὸν | τὸ μὴ εἰς γῆρας ἐλθεῖν. τί γάρ, εἰπέ μοι, καλὸν ἐνορᾷς τῷ γήρᾳ; ἆρα καλὸν τὸ κνυζοῦσθαι τὰ ὄμματα, τὸ ῥυσοῦσθαι τὴν παρειάν, τὸ ἀπορρεῖν τοὺς ὀδόντας τοῦ στόματος καὶ ψελλισμὸν ἐμποιεῖν τῇ γλώσσῃ, τὸ ὑποτρέμειν τῇ χειρὶ καὶ εἰς γῆν κύπτειν, καὶ ὑποσκάζειν τῷ ποδὶ καὶ χειραγωγοῖς ἐπερείδεσθαι καὶ παρανοεῖν τῇ καρδίᾳ καὶ παραφθέγγεσθαι τῇ φωνῇ, οἷα τῇ ἡλικίᾳ ταύτῃ κατ' ἀνάγκην συμβαίνει πάθη; καὶ ὑπὲρ τούτου ἀγανακτοῦμεν, ὅτι μὴ ἀφίκετο εἰς τὴν τῶν τοιούτων πεῖραν; καὶ μὴν συγχαίρειν προσήκει ἐκείνοις, ὧν ἡ ζωὴ τὴν τῶν σκυθρωπῶν πεῖραν οὐ παρεδέξατο καὶ οὔτε ἐνταῦθα τῶν λυπηρῶν ᾔσθετο οὔτε τι τῶν ἐκεῖ σκυθρωπῶν ἐπιγνώσεται. ἡ γὰρ τοιαύτη ψυχὴ ἡ οὐκ ἔχουσα ἐφ' ὅτῳ εἰς κρίσιν ἔλθῃ, γέενναν οὐ φοβεῖται, κρίσιν οὐ δέδοικεν, ἄφοβος διαμένει καὶ ἀκατάπληκτος, οὐδενὸς πονηροῦ συνειδότος τὸν τῆς κρίσεως φόβον ἐπάγοντος. ἀλλ' ἔδει, φησίν, αὐτὴν εἰς μέτρον ἡλικίας ἐλθεῖν

[10] In the ancient world, purple was the distinctive color of royalty, mainly because genuine purple dye was the rarest and most expensive coloring agent available. For a full discussion of the costly and elaborate ancient process of making purple dye out

of purple,[10] but has put on the robe of the Kingdom on high. Shall I tell you the material of this divine garment? It is not linen or wool, or woven silk from worms. Hear David when he describes the garments woven for God: "You are clothed with praise and majesty: covering yourself with light as with a garment" (Ps 103.1–2). Do you see what an exchange she has made? It pains you that her physical beauty no longer can be seen, for you cannot see the true beauty of her soul, in which she now rejoices at the heavenly festival.

How beautiful is that eye, which now gazes on God! How sweet the mouth, beautified by heavenly hymns! For "out of the mouths of babes and infants," Scripture says, "you have perfected praise" (Ps 8.2). How beautiful the hands that have never been responsible for evil! How lovely the feet that never moved toward evil, nor "stood in the way of sinners" (Ps 1.1). How beautiful is the whole appearance of that soul, adorned not with shining gems, but radiant with simplicity and innocence. Or does it grieve you, perhaps, that she will never reach old age? Tell me, what beauty do you see in age? Is it good when eyes grow bleary, when the cheek becomes shriveled, when the teeth fall out of the mouth and stammering invades the tongue, when one shakes with the hand and bends over toward the ground, when one limps a little with the foot and leans for support on helpers, when one thinks mistakenly with the mind and speaks mistakenly with the voice—all disabilities that necessarily accompany old age? And beyond this, should we be troubled over the fact that she has not had the chance to experience the things of this world? It would be more fitting, surely, for us to congratulate those whose life has had no share in the experience of misfortunes, and has not sensed any of this life's griefs, nor is destined to share in the misfortunes of the next world. Such a soul, which has nothing for which it needs to come to judgment, need not fear Gehenna, has no dread of judgment, endures fearless and undaunted, conscious in itself of nothing evil that might arouse fear of judgment.

of small Mediterranean snails, see Gerhard Steigerwald, "Die antike Purpurfärberei nach dem Bericht Plinius' des Älteren in seiner 'Naturalis Historia'," *Traditio* 42 (1986): 1–57.

καὶ νυμφικῷ θαλάμῳ ἐμφαιδρυνθῆναι. ἀλλ' ἐρεῖ σοι πρὸς τοῦτο ὁ ἀληθινὸς νυμφίος, ὅτι κρείττων ἡ οὐρανία παστάς, προτιμότερος ἐκεῖνος ὁ θάλαμος, ἐν ᾧ χηρείας φόβος οὐκ ἔστιν. τίνος οὖν, εἰπέ μοι, τῶν καλῶν ἀπεστέρηται τὸν σάρκινον τοῦτον ἐκδυσαμένη βίον; εἴπω σοι τὰ τοῦ βίου καλά; λῦπαι καὶ ἡδοναί, θυμοὶ καὶ φόβοι, ἐλπίδες καὶ ἐπιθυμίαι. ταῦτά ἐστι καὶ τὰ τοιαῦτα, οἷς κατὰ τὴν παροῦσαν ζωὴν συμπεπλέγμεθα. τί οὖν κακὸν πέπονθεν ἡ τοσούτων ἀπαλλαγεῖσα τυράννων; ἕκαστον γὰρ πάθος, ὅταν ἐπικρατῇ τῆς ψυχῆς, τύραννος ἡμῶν γίνεται τοὺς λογισμοὺς
PG 872 δουλωσάμενος. ἢ λυπεῖ ἡμᾶς, ὅτι μὴ κατεπονήθη διὰ | ὠδίνων, ὅτι
GNO 467 μὴ συνετρίβη διὰ φροντίδων | παιδοτροφίας, ὅτι μὴ τὰς ὁμοίας ἀλγηδόνας ἐδέξατο, ἃς ἐπ' αὐτῆς οἱ γεγεννηκότες ὑπέμειναν; ἀλλὰ τὰ τοιαῦτα μακαρισμῶν οὐκ ὀδυρμῶν ἐστιν ἄξια. τὸ γὰρ ἐν μηδενὶ γενέσθαι κακῷ κρεῖττον ἢ κατὰ τὴν ἀνθρωπίνην φύσιν ἐστίν. οὕτως καὶ ὁ σοφὸς Σολομὼν ἐν τῇ ἰδίᾳ γραφῇ μακαρίζει πρὸ τοῦ περιόντος τὸν κατοιχόμενον καὶ ὁ μέγας Δαβὶδ θρήνου καὶ οἰμωγῆς ἀξίαν τὴν ἐν σαρκὶ διαγωγὴν εἶναί φησιν. καίτοι γε ἀμφότεροι λαμπροὶ κατὰ τὴν βασιλείαν ὑπάρχοντες, πάντων κατ' ἐξουσίαν τῶν κατὰ τὸν βίον ἡδέων μετέχοντες, οὐδὲν πρὸς τὴν παροῦσαν ἀπόλαυσιν ἐπεκλίθησαν, ἀλλὰ τῶν ἀπορρήτων ἀγαθῶν τῶν ἐν τῇ ἀσωμάτῳ ζωῇ προκειμένων τὴν ἐπιθυμίαν ἔχοντες συμφορὰν ἐποιοῦντο τὴν ἐν σαρκὶ ζωήν. ἤκουσα πολλαχῇ τοῦ Δαβὶδ ἐν ταῖς ἱεραῖς ψαλμῳδίαις ἔξω γενέσθαι τῆς τοιαύτης ἀνάγκης ἐπιθυμοῦντος, ἐν οἷς φησι νῦν μέν, ὅτι Ἐπιποθεῖ καὶ ἐκλείπει ἡ ψυχή μου εἰς τὰς αὐλὰς τοῦ κυρίου, νῦν δέ, ὅτι Ἐξάγαγε ἐκ φυλακῆς τὴν ψυχήν μου. ὡσαύτως δὲ καὶ ὁ Ἰερεμίας κατάρας ἀξίαν κρίνει τὴν ἡμέραν ἐκείνην τὴν ἄρξασαν αὐτῷ τῆς τοιαύτης ζωῆς. καὶ πολλάς ἐστι τοιαύτας τῶν παλαιῶν ἁγίων φωνὰς ἐν τῇ

6 Someone will say she should have come to full maturity, and to have shared in the glory of the bridal chamber. But the true Bridegroom will say to you in reply that the heavenly chamber is better still: that room is still more honorable, where there is no fear of widowhood. Of what blessing, I ask you, will she be deprived, now that she has put off this life in the flesh? Shall I tell you about the blessings of life? Griefs and pleasures, courageous moments and fears, hopes and fleshly yearnings. These, and other things like them, are what we engage with during the present life. What evil, then, has she suffered in being freed from these tyrants? Each passion, after all, when it gains power over the soul, becomes our master, making slaves of our thoughts. Or are we sad that she has not been troubled by the pains of childbirth, that she is not worried about the concerns of child-rearing, that she has not undergone the same suffering that her parents have endured over her? Such things, surely, are worthy of congratulation, not of lament! Not to be involved in any misfortune is beyond what human nature has a right to expect. So wise Solomon, in his own writing, calls the one who has departed more blessed than the one who survives,[11] and the great David says that life in the flesh is worthy of lament and groaning.[12] And yet although both of these men led brilliant lives as kings, sharing as far as possible in all the joys we can experience in life, they did not rest their hopes on present enjoyment; but cherishing a desire for the unspeakable good laid up in a life apart from the body, they considered existence in the flesh a misfortune. I have often heard David, in the sacred texts of the Psalms, desiring to be outside this present round of necessity—now saying "My soul longs and faints for the courts of the Lord" (Ps 83.2), now "Bring my soul out of prison" (Ps 141.7). So Jeremiah judges the day that began this life for him as deserving a curse.[13] And it is possible to find many sayings like these preserved in Holy Scripture,

[11]See Eccl 4.2.

[12]An allusion, perhaps, to psalms of lament, such as Ps 88.47–49 (LXX), Ps 140.7–8 (LXX), etc.

[13]Jer 20.14–18.

θείᾳ γραφῇ φερομένας εὑρεῖν, οἳ δι' ἐπιθυμίαν τῆς ὄντως ζωῆς τὴν
ἐν σαρκὶ διαγωγὴν ἐβαρύνοντο.

Οὕτως καὶ ὁ μέγας ποτὲ Ἀβραὰμ προθύμως τῷ θεῷ διὰ θυσίας
προσῆγε τὸν ἠγαπημένον υἱόν, εἰδὼς ὅτι πρὸς τὸ κρεῖττόν τε καὶ
θειότερον γενήσεται τῷ παιδὶ ἡ μετάστασις. ὅσοι δὲ τῆς ἱστορίας
GNO 468 ἐμπείρως ἔχετε, πάντως οὐκ ἀγνοεῖτε | τὰ περὶ αὐτοῦ διηγήματα.
τί γάρ φησιν ἡ γραφή; ὅτι νέῳ μὲν ὄντι τῷ Ἀβραὰμ θεόθεν περὶ
τοῦ παιδὸς ἐπαγγελία γίνεται, παρεληλυθότι δὲ τὴν ἀκμὴν καὶ
ἤδη καταμαρανθέντι ὑπὸ τοῦ χρόνου, ὅτε παύεται ἡ φύσις ἑαυτὴν
αὔξουσα οὐκέτι τοῦ γήρως ταῖς ὁρμαῖς ὑπακούοντος, τότε παρὰ
τὰς ἀνθρωπίνας ἐλπίδας εἰς πέρας ἡ ὑπόσχεσις ἄγεται, καὶ τίκτεται
παῖς ὁ Ἰσαάκ· καὶ συμμέτρου διαγεγονότος χρόνου, οἷόν τι ἔρνος
ἀναδραμὼν εἰς κάλλος καὶ μέγεθος, ἡδὺς ἦν τοῖς ὀφθαλμοῖς τῶν
γονέων τῷ τῆς νεότητος κάλλει λαμπόμενος. τότε προσάγεται τῷ
Ἀβραὰμ ἡ τῆς ψυχῆς δοκιμασία καὶ βάσανος, εἰ ἀκριβῶς ἐν τῇ τῶν
ὄντων φύσει διαγιγνώσκει τὸ κάλλιον, εἰ μὴ πρὸς τὴν παροῦσαν
βλέπει ζωήν, καί φησι πρὸς αὐτὸν ὁ θεός· ἀνένεγκε τὸν υἱόν σου
διὰ θυσίας εἰς ὁλοκάρπωσιν. οἴδατε πάντως ὅσοι πατέρες ἐστὲ καὶ
παῖδας ἔχετε καὶ τὴν πρὸς τὰ τέκνα στοργὴν παρὰ τῆς φύσεως
ἐδιδάχθητε, ὅπως εἰκὸς διατεθῆναι τὸν Ἀβραάμ, εἰ πρὸς τὴν
παροῦσαν μόνην ἀφεώρα ζωήν, εἰ δοῦλος τῆς φύσεως ἦν, εἰ ἐν τῷ
παρόντι βίῳ τὸ γλυκὺ τῆς ζωῆς ἐλογίζετο. τί δὲ περὶ ἐκείνου φημί,
καταλιπὼν τὴν γυναῖκα, τὸ ἀσθενέστερον μέρος τῆς ἀνθρωπίνης
φύσεως; εἰ μὴ πεπαίδευτο κἀκείνη ὑπὸ τοῦ ἀνδρὸς τὰ θειότερα,
εἰ μὴ ἠπίστατο τὴν κεκρυμμένην ζωὴν εἶναι τῆς φαινομένης
ἀμείνονα, οὐκ ἂν ἐπέτρεπε τῷ ἀνδρὶ τοιαῦτα κατὰ τοῦ παιδὸς

written by the ancient saints, who because of a desire for the true life found involvement in the flesh wearisome.

7 So the great Abraham[14] also once willingly brought forward his beloved son in sacrifice to God, knowing that the transferal would be for the boy a step toward something better and more divine. And as many of you as have experienced the story will surely not be unaware of the details of what is said there about him. What does Scripture say? That when Abraham was young, the promise about the child was made to him by God, but that when he had passed the prime of life and was already diminished in his powers by time—when nature had stopped expanding its forces, no longer obeying the drives of old age—then, contrary to human hope, the promise was brought to fulfillment and his son Isaac was born. And when a proper measure of time had gone by, he grew, like a young shoot, to full beauty and size, and was sweet to his parents' eyes in the splendor of youthful good looks. Then the heart-searching test was laid on Abraham, to see if he recognized what is more beautiful in the nature of things, and was not simply looking toward the present life; God said to him: "Offer your son in sacrifice as a whole-burnt offering" (Gen 22.1–2). Surely you who are parents and have children, and have been taught by nature to love your children deeply, realize how Abraham probably would have been inclined, if he had been looking toward this present life alone—if he had been a slave to nature, if he reckoned the sweetness of existence to lie in this present life.

8 And why do I simply speak of him, leaving out his wife—the weaker part of human nature? If she, too, had not been educated by her husband in more divine considerations, if she had not known that the hidden life is superior to the one that is seen, she would not have allowed her husband to carry out such plans against their

[14]Spira, the editor, has pointed out close textual echoes between the following passage on Abraham and Sarah (through the end of section 8) and Gregory's discourse *On the Godhead of the Son and the Holy Spirit* (GNO X/2:131.1–136.15). In the absence of a reliable chronology for most of Gregory's works, it is difficult to know with certainty which piece "borrows" from which.

ἐνεργῆσαι· πάντως γὰρ τοῖς μητρικοῖς συγκινηθεῖσα σπλάγχνοις
PG 873 περιεχύθη τῷ | τέκνῳ καὶ ταῖς ὠλέναις αὐτὸν ἐμπλεξαμένη πρὸ
αὐτοῦ τὴν καιρίαν ἐδέχετο. ἆρ' οὐκ εἶπεν ἂν πρὸς τὸν Ἀβραὰμ
ταῦτα τὰ ῥήματα; φεῖσαι τοῦ παιδός, ἄνερ, μὴ πονηρὸν γένῃ
GNO 469 τοῦ βίου διήγημα, μὴ μῦθος τῷ μετὰ | ταῦτα χρόνῳ γενώμεθα,
μὴ φθονήσῃς τῷ υἱῷ τῆς ζωῆς, μὴ στερήσῃς αὐτὸν τῆς γλυκείας
ἀκτῖνος· θάλαμος τέκνοις οὐ τάφος παρὰ πατέρων σπουδάζεται,
στέφανος γαμικὸς οὐ ξίφος φονικόν, γαμήλιος λαμπὰς οὐ πῦρ
ἐπιτάφιον· ταῦτα λῃσταὶ καὶ πολέμιοι, οὐ πατέρων χεῖρες ἐπὶ τῶν
τέκνων ἐργάζονται· εἰ δὲ χρὴ πάντως γενέσθαι τὸ κακόν, μὴ ἴδοι
Σάρρας ὀφθαλμὸς νεκρούμενον τὸν Ἰσαάκ· ἰδοὺ δι' ἀμφοτέρων
ὦσον τὸ ξίφος, ἀπ' ἐμοῦ τῆς δειλαίας ἀρξάμενος· μία τοῖς δυσὶν
ἀρκέσει πληγή, κοινὸν ἐπ' ἀμφοτέρων γενέσθω τὸ χῶμα, μία
στήλη τὴν κοινὴν συμφορὰν τραγῳδείτω. ταῦτα πάντως ἂν καὶ
τὰ τοιαῦτα διεξῄει ἡ Σάρρα, εἰ μὴ ἐκεῖνα τοῖς ὀφθαλμοῖς ἔβλεπεν,
ἅπερ ἡμῖν ἐστιν ἀθέατα. ᾔδει γὰρ ὅτι τὸ τέλος τῆς ἐν σαρκὶ ζωῆς
ἀρχὴ τοῦ θειοτέρου βίου τοῖς μεταστᾶσι γίνεται· καταλείπει σκιάς,
καταλαμβάνει ἀλήθειαν, ἀφίησιν ἀπάτας καὶ πλάνας καὶ θορύβους,
καὶ εὑρίσκει ἐκεῖνα τὰ ἀγαθά, ἃ ὑπὲρ ὀφθαλμόν τε καὶ ἀκοὴν καὶ
καρδίαν ἐστίν· οὔτε ἔρως αὐτὸν ἀνιάσει οὔτε ἐπιθυμία ῥυπαρὰ
διαστρέψει, οὐχ ὑπερηφανία χαυνώσει, οὐκ ἄλλο τι πάθος τῶν
λυπούντων τὴν ψυχὴν ἐνοχλήσει, ἀλλὰ πάντα γίνεται αὐτῷ ὁ θεός.
διὰ τοῦτο προθύμως δίδωσι τῷ θεῷ τὸν παῖδα. τί δὲ ὁ μέγας Ἰώβ;
ὅτε αὐτῷ γυμνωθέντι πάντων τῶν περιόντων ἀθρόως, πρὶν ἐπὶ
ταῖς προλαβούσαις πληγαῖς τὴν ψυχὴν ἀναλέξασθαι, ἡ τελευταία
κατεμηνύθη πληγή, πῶς ἐδέξατο τὴν ἐπὶ τοῖς παισὶ συμφοράν;
τρεῖς αὐτῷ θυγατέρες ἦσαν, καὶ παῖδες ἑπτά. μακαριστὸς ἦν τῆς
εὐπαιδίας· τοσοῦτοι γὰρ ὄντες εἷς ἦσαν οἱ πάντες τῇ μετ' ἀλλήλων
GNO 470 στοργῇ οὐ διῃρημένως καθ' | ἑαυτὸν ἕκαστος βιοτεύοντες,

son. For surely, moved by a mother's compassion, she would have embraced the child and wrapped him in her arms, letting herself be bound with the cord rather than him. Would she not have said words like these to Abraham: "Spare the child, my husband! Do not become a negative case-study for how to live! Let us not be made a cautionary tale for times to come! Do not begrudge our son a share in life, do not deprive him of the sweet light of day! The bridal chamber, not the tomb, is what parents desire for their children; the crown of marriage, not the deadly sword; the wedding-torch, not the funeral fire! These are the things bandits and enemies do, not the hands of fathers toward their children! If this evil must come about, let Sarah's eyes not look on Isaac's corpse! Come, thrust the sword through both of us, beginning with my wretched self! Let one blow suffice for us both, let a common burial mound cover both of us, a single monument narrate in sad detail our common fate!" Surely Sarah would have made such a plea as this, if she were not gazing with her eyes on those things that to us are invisible. For she knew that the end of this life in the flesh is the beginning of a more divine life for those who have made the transition there. [Isaac] leaves shadows behind, and lays hold of truth; he sends away deceit and error and confusion, and finds those blessings that lie beyond eye and ear and heart;[15] passionate love will not distress him, nor will sordid fleshly desire torture him, nor arrogance puff him up, nor any other passion that causes grief beset his soul, but God will be all to him.[16] For this reason, she gives her son readily to God.

9 And what of the great Job? When he had suddenly been stripped of all his possessions, and when, before he could recover his soul from the blows that gone before, the final blow is told to him, how did he receive the news of the destruction that had come upon his children? He had three daughters and seven sons. He was extremely blessed in his family; numerous as they were, they were all one in love for each other. Each did not live a separate life for himself, but

[15]See 1 Cor 2.9 (quoting Is 64.4).

[16]1 Cor 15.28.

ἀλλὰ πάντες παρ' ἀλλήλους φοιτῶντες διὰ τῆς ἐγκυκλίου φιλοφροσύνης διετέλουν εὐφραίνοντες ἀλλήλους ἐν τῷ μέρει καὶ εὐφραινόμενοι. καὶ δῆτα καὶ τότε κατὰ περίοδον παρὰ τῷ πρεσβυτέρῳ τῶν ἀδελφῶν ἦν τὸ συμπόσιον· πλήρεις οἱ κρατῆρες, πλήρης τῶν ἐδωδίμων ἡ τράπεζα, ἐν χερσὶν αἱ κύλικες, θεάματα ὡς εἰκὸς ἐπὶ τούτοις καὶ ἀκροάματα καὶ πᾶσαι θυμηδίαι συμποτικαί· προπόσεις, φιλοφροσύναι, παίγνια, μειδιάματα· πάντα ὅσα εἰκὸς ἐν συνόδῳ νέων ἐφ' ἑστίας ἁβρύνεσθαι. τί οὖν ἐπὶ τούτοις; ἐν ἀκμῇ τῆς ἀπολαύσεως τῶν ἡδίστων ἐπισεισθέντος αὐτοῖς τοῦ ὀρόφου τάφος τῶν δέκα παίδων τὸ συμπόσιον γίνεται, καὶ τοῖς αἵμασι τῶν νέων ὁ κρατὴρ καταμίγνυται, καὶ τὰ ἐδώδιμα τῷ ἐκ τῶν σωμάτων λύθρῳ κατεμολύνετο. τοιαύτης συμφορᾶς τῷ Ἰὼβ ἀγγελθείσης (θέασαί μοι τῷ λόγῳ τὸν ἀθλητήν, οὐχ ἵνα θαυμάσῃς μόνον τὸν νικητήν, μικρὸν γὰρ τὸ ἐκ τοῦ θαύματος κέρδος, ἀλλ' ἵνα ζηλώσῃς
PG 876 ἐν τοῖς ὁμοίοις τὸν ἄνδρα καί σοι γένηται παιδοτρίβης | ὁ ἀθλητής, τῷ καθ' ἑαυτὸν ὑποδείγματι πρὸς ὑπομονὴν καὶ ἀνδρείαν τὴν ψυχὴν ἀλείφων ἐν καιρῷ τῆς τῶν πειρασμῶν συμπλοκῆς), τί οὖν ἐποίησεν ὁ ἀνήρ; ἆρά τι δυσγενὲς καὶ μικρόψυχον ἢ εἶπε τῷ ῥήματι ἢ διὰ σχήματος ἐνεδείξατο ἢ παρειὰν ἀμύξας τοῖς ὄνυξιν ἢ τρίχας τῆς κεφαλῆς ἀποτίλας ἢ κόνιν καταπασάμενος ἢ τὰ στήθη ταῖς χερσὶ μαστιγώσας ἢ ἐπὶ γῆν ἑαυτὸν ῥίψας ἢ θρηνῳδοὺς ἑαυτῷ περιστήσας ἢ ἀνακαλῶν τὰ τῶν κατοιχομένων ὀνόματα καὶ ἐποιμώζων τῇ μνήμῃ; οὐκ ἔστι τούτων οὐδέν. ἀλλ' ὁ μὲν τῶν κακῶν μηνυτὴς τὴν κατὰ τοὺς παῖδας συμφορὰν διηγήσατο, ὁ δὲ ὁμοῦ τε ἤκουσε καὶ εὐθὺς περὶ τῆς τῶν ὄντων ἐφιλοσόφει φύσεως, πόθεν

---

[17]By rhetorical elaboration or *ekphrasis*, Gregory here turns the simple statement of Job 1.18 that Job's children were at one of the brothers' houses, drinking wine, into the scene of a classical Greek *symposion*.

[18]In classical Greek athletic contests, the trainer was seen less as a coach in our

each visited the others; and because of their general unity of spirit they continued to give joy to each other, and to receive it in turn. Well, then—at one point, in the course of things, there was a dinner party at the house of the eldest brother. The mixing bowls were full, the table laden with delicacies, cups were in everyone's hands; beyond this were probably other joyful sights and sounds, and all the things that cause gladness at a party: toasts, warm feelings, jests, smiles—everything that is likely to contribute to celebration in a gathering of young people at home.[17] And what happened at that moment? At the peak of their enjoyment of the festivities, the roof was shaken down on them, and the party became the tomb of Job's ten children; the wine in the bowl was mixed with the young people's blood, and the food on the table was polluted by gore from their bodies.

When news of this disaster was announced to Job, what did the man do? (Imagine with me that athlete, not just that you might admire the victor—for there is little benefit in admiration—but that you might imitate the man in similar situations: that the athlete might become your trainer, anointing your soul by his example of patience and courage in the time of your own contest against trials.)[18] What did the man do? Did he say a word that was mean-spirited or small-minded, or show this by his expression? Did he tear at his cheeks with his nails, or pull out the hair from his head, or smear himself with dust, or beat his chest with his hands, or throw himself on the ground, or surround himself with singers of dirges? Did he call on the names of the departed, or lament them by recalling their lives?[19] There is no mention of any of this! Rather, the messenger brought him the bad news of the disaster that had taken his children, and he, as soon as he heard it, immediately began to reflect[20] on the nature of things, pointing out where all things come from and by

modern sense, but prepared the athlete physically for competition by massaging his body and anointing him with oil.

[19]These are classical Greek expressions of mourning, which apparently continued to be common well into Christian times among the near relatives of the dead.

[20]Greek: "began to philosophize."

τὰ ὄντα λέγων καὶ παρὰ τίνος εἰς γένεσιν ἄγεται καὶ τίνα εἰκὸς τῶν
ὄντων ἐπιστατεῖν· Ὁ κύριος ἔδωκεν, ὁ κύριος ἀφείλετο. ἐκ θεοῦ,
GNO 471 φησί, τοῖς ἀνθρώποις | ἡ γένεσις, καὶ πρὸς αὐτὸν ἡ ἀνάλυσις· ὅθεν
παρῆκται, πρὸς ἐκεῖνο καὶ ἀναλύεται. θεὸς οὖν ὁ τοῦ διδόναι τὴν
ἐξουσίαν ἔχων, ὁ αὐτὸς ἔχει καὶ τοῦ ἀφαιρεῖσθαι τὴν ἐξουσίαν·
ἀγαθὸς ὢν ἀγαθὰ βουλεύεται, σοφὸς ὢν τὸ συμφέρον ἐπίσταται.
Ὡς τῷ κυρίῳ ἔδοξεν (ἔδοξε δὲ πάντως καλῶς), οὕτως καὶ ἐποίησεν·
Εἴη τὸ ὄνομα κυρίου εὐλογημένον.

Ὁρᾷς πόσον τὸ ὕψος τῆς τοῦ ἀθλητοῦ μεγαλοφυΐας· τὸν τῆς
θλίψεως καιρὸν εἰς ἐπίσκεψιν τῆς περὶ τῶν ὄντων φιλοσοφίας
μετέστησεν. ᾔδει γὰρ ἀκριβῶς, ὅτι ἡ ὄντως ζωὴ δι᾽ ἐλπίδος
ἀπόκειται, ἡ δὲ παροῦσα ζωὴ οἱονεὶ σπέρμα τῆς μελλούσης ἐστίν.
πολὺ δὲ διενήνοχε τῶν παρόντων τὰ προσδοκώμενα, ὅσον διαφέρει
ὁ στάχυς τοῦ κόκκου ὅθεν ἐκφύεται. ὁ νῦν βίος ἀναλογεῖ πρὸς
τὸν κόκκον, ὁ δὲ προσδοκώμενος βίος ἐν τῷ κάλλει τοῦ στάχυος
δείκνυται· Δεῖ γὰρ τὸ φθαρτὸν τοῦτο ἐνδύσασθαι ἀφθαρσίαν, καὶ
τὸ θνητὸν τοῦτο ἐνδύσασθαι ἀθανασίαν. πρὸς ταῦτα βλέπων ὁ
Ἰὼβ συγχαίρει τοῖς τέκνοις τῆς εὐκληρίας, ὡς θᾶττον ἐκλυθεῖσι
τῶν τοῦ βίου δεσμῶν. τεκμήριον δὲ ὅτι τῆς ἐπαγγελίας τοῦ θεοῦ
τὸ διπλάσιον ἀντὶ τῶν ἀφαιρεθέντων πάντων ὑποσχομένης, ἐν
τοῖς ἄλλοις ἅπασι διπλασιασθείσης τῆς ἀντιδόσεως, μόνων τῶν
τέκνων τὸν διπλασιασμὸν οὐκ ἐζήτησεν, ἀλλὰ δέκα μόνα ἀντὶ
τῶν ἀφαιρεθέντων δέδοται. ἐπειδὴ δὲ αἱ τῶν ἀνθρώπων ψυχαὶ
εἰς ἀεὶ διαμένουσιν, τούτου χάριν τῶν ἀπολλυμένων διπλασίαν
δέχεται τὴν ἀντίδοσιν, ἐπὶ δὲ τῶν τέκνων τὰ ἐπιγενόμενα τοῖς
προγεννηθεῖσι συναριθμεῖται ὡς πάντων τῷ θεῷ ζώντων, καὶ
οὐδὲν τοῦ προσκαίρου θανάτου τοὺς κατοιχομένους πρὸς |
GNO 472 τὸ εἶναι κωλύοντος. οὐδὲ γὰρ ἄλλο τί ἐστιν ἐπ᾽ ἀνθρώπων ὁ
θάνατος, εἰ μὴ κακίας καθάρσιον. ἐπειδὴ γὰρ οἷόν τι σκεῦος

whom they are brought into being, and who seems to be in command of all things: "The Lord gave, the Lord has taken away" (Job 1.21). From God, he says, comes our human origin, and to him our end is directed: from whence [life] comes, there also it goes. God, then, is the one who has the power to give, and he has also the power to take away. Since he is good, he plans our good; since he is wise, he knows what is best. As seemed right to the Lord—and surely what seems right to him is for the best—so he has done. "May the name of the Lord be blessed!" (Job 1.21).

Do you see how lofty the athlete's nobility is? He transformed the moment of trial into a chance to examine in depth the nature of things.[21] For he knew precisely that our real life is stored up for us in hope, and that this present life is a kind of seed of the life to come. What we look forward to differs greatly from the present—as much as the ear of wheat differs from the grain from which it springs. This present life resembles the grain, the life we look forward to is revealed in the beauty of the ear.[22] "For this perishable nature must put on the imperishable, and this mortal nature must put on immortality" (1 Cor 15.53). Considering this, Job rejoiced in the good fortune of his children, in that they had been quickly freed from the fetters of life. The proof of this is that when the message of God promised him double restoration of all that had been taken away, the return was double in all other things, but he did not ask for twice as many children—only ten were given, in place of the ten who had been taken away. But since the souls of human beings remain forever, for this reason he *did* receive the double of those who perished: those children who came later were counted along with those born before them, since all live to God, and an untimely death offers no hindrance to the existence of those who have passed away. For death is nothing else for human beings than a cleansing of our troubles.

[21]Literally, "into an examination of the philosophical understanding of things."

[22]This comparison of the difference between present and the risen body with that between a sown grain and the future ear of wheat is one Gregory uses frequently. See *On the Dead* 14; *On Holy Pascha* 12; *On the Soul and the Resurrection* (GNO III/3:117.21—119.18; PPS 12:117–18).

ἀγαθῶν δεκτικὸν τὸ κατ' ἀρχὰς ἡ φύσις ἡμῶν παρὰ τοῦ θεοῦ
PG 877 τῶν ὅλων | κατεσκευάσθη, τοῦ δὲ ἐχθροῦ τῶν ψυχῶν ἡμῶν δι' ἀπάτης ἡμῖν τὸ κακὸν παρεγχέαντος τὸ ἀγαθὸν χώραν οὐκ ἔσχεν, τούτου ἕνεκεν, ὡς ἂν μὴ διαιωνίζοι ἡμῖν ἡ ἐμφυεῖσα κακία, προνοίᾳ κρείττονι θανάτῳ τὸ σκεῦος πρὸς καιρὸν διαλύεται, ἵνα τῆς κακίας ἐκρυείσης ἀναπλασθῇ τὸ ἀνθρώπινον καὶ ἀμιγὲς κακίας τῷ ἐξ ἀρχῆς ἀποκαταστῇ βίῳ. τοῦτο γάρ ἐστιν ἡ ἀνάστασις, ἡ εἰς τὸ ἀρχαῖον τῆς φύσεως ἡμῶν ἀναστοιχείωσις. εἰ οὖν ἀμήχανόν ἐστιν ἀναστοιχειωθῆναι πρὸς τὸ κρεῖττον τὴν φύσιν χωρὶς ἀναστάσεως, θανάτου δὲ μὴ προηγησαμένου ἀνάστασις γενέσθαι οὐ δύναται, ἀγαθὸν ἂν εἴη ὁ θάνατος, ἀρχὴ καὶ ὁδὸς τῆς πρὸς τὸ κρεῖττον μεταβολῆς ἡμῖν γενόμενος. οὐκοῦν ἐκβάλωμεν, ἀδελφοί, τὴν λύπην τὴν περὶ τῶν κεκοιμημένων, ἣν μόνοι ὑπομένουσιν οἱ μὴ ἔχοντες ἐλπίδα. ἐλπὶς δέ ἐστιν ὁ Χριστός· ᾧ ἡ δόξα καὶ τὸ κράτος εἰς τοὺς αἰῶνας τῶν αἰώνων. ἀμήν.

10 Since, then, our nature was created from the beginning by the God of all things as a vessel capable of receiving what is good, but the enemy of our souls has deceitfully poured evil into us, so that the good has no more room, for this reason—so that the evil instilled into us might not remain forever—the vessel is shattered by death for a time by a beneficent providence, so that the evil might flow away and what is human might be shaped anew and be restored, unmingled with evil, to the life it had in the beginning.[23] For this is the resurrection: the formation of our nature once again in its original condition. If, then, it is impossible that nature be formed anew for the better apart from resurrection, and resurrection cannot take place unless death precedes it, death must be a good thing—it must become for us the beginning and the way toward a change for the better. Let us, then, cast away our grief, brothers and sisters, "for those who have fallen asleep," which only they experience "who have no hope" (1 Thess 4.13). Our hope is Christ—to whom be glory and power for the ages of ages! Amen.

[23]Gregory uses this same image of death as God's way of shattering the earthenware vessel of our humanity, in order to reshape it in its original beauty, in his *Catechetical Discourse* 8.3–7 (GNO III/4:29.13—31.21; PPS 60:83–85).

A Funeral Oration for the Empress Flaccilla
(*Oratio funebris in Flaccillam*)

A Note on the Text

This funeral address, generally following the traditional form of a classical *epitaphios logos*, was given by Gregory, apparently at the request of the Patriarch Nectarius (see p. 138, n. 2 below), shortly after the death of the Empress Flaccilla, probably in the winter of 386.[1]

Aelia Flavia Flaccilla (356–86) was a Spanish woman of aristocratic background, whom Theodosius, a successful military officer and himself a Spaniard, married shortly before his victory over the forces of Valens at Adrianople in Thrace, which then led his armies to acclaim him as Eastern emperor. Like Theodosius, Flaccilla was deeply committed to Nicene Christianity. She bore Theodosius three children: Arcadius—later eastern emperor (d. 408)—around 377; Pulcheria in 379, who died as a child in the summer of 385; and Honorius—later emperor in the West (d. 423)—on September 9, 384. Flaccilla herself died some six months after Pulcheria, in a place called Skotoume or Skotoumis in Thrace—a spa where she had gone to drink the healing waters during her final illness; her body was brought back to Constantinople for burial. This oration,

[1]For the date of her death, see Claudian, *De quarto consulatu Honorii* 158, 165–68, passages that suggest Flaccilla was still alive when the baby Honorius—born in 384—was designated consul for 386. Cf. Ambrose, *De obitu Theodosii* 401; Theodoret, *Ecclesiastical History* 5.19; also A. H. M. Jones, J. R. Martindale, and J. Morris, *The Prosopography of the Later Roman Empire* I (Cambridge: Cambridge University Press, 1971), 341–42.

like that for her daughter Pulcheria, was probably delivered in the Church of the Holy Apostles, where the imperial family were buried. Given the title and status of *Augusta* by Theodosius shortly after he acceded to imperial office, Flaccilla was known for her strong faith and her Christian virtues, as Gregory emphasizes; see also Theodoret, *Ecclesiastical History* 5.18. She is recognized as a saint by the Orthodox Church, and is commemorated on September 14 (as is her husband Theodosius, commemorated on January 17). For a discussion of her life and career, and of the iconographic honors shown to her on coins and in statuary during the reign of Theodosius I, see Kenneth G. Holum, *Theodosian Empresses: Women and Imperial Dominion in Late Antiquity* (Berkeley: University of California Press, 1982), 21–44.

The Greek text of the oration translated here is that of the critical edition by Andreas Spira, in GNO IX/1:475–90. I have added section numbers for ease in reference.

GNO IX:475
PG 46:877

ΓΡΗΓΟΡΙΟΥ ΕΠΙΣΚΟΠΟΥ ΝΥΣΣΗΣ ΕΠΙΤΑΦΙΟΣ ΕΙΣ ΠΛΑΚΙΛΛΑΝ ΒΑΣΙΛΙΣΣΑΝ

Ὁ πιστὸς καὶ φρόνιμος οἰκονόμος (ἐκ γὰρ τῶν ἀνεγνωσμένων ἀπὸ τοῦ θείου εὐαγγελίου προοιμιάζομαι), ὃν κατέστησεν ὁ κύριος ἐπὶ τῆς οἰκετίας ταύτης τοῦ διδόναι ἐν καιρῷ τοῖς οἰκονομουμένοις τὸ σιτομέτριον, καλῶς ἐν τῷ πρὸ τούτου χρόνῳ καταδικάσας τὴν ἀφωνίαν τοῦ λόγου, καλῶς τοῦ μεγέθους τῆς συμφορᾶς ἐπαισθόμενος καὶ τιμήσας τῇ ἡσυχίᾳ τὸ πένθος, οὐκ οἶδ' ὅπως ἐν τῷ παρόντι συλλόγῳ πάλιν ἐπανάγει τῇ ἐκκλησίᾳ τὸν λόγον αὐτὸς ἀναλύων τὴν ἰδίαν κατὰ τοῦ λόγου ψῆφον· καίτοι γε σφόδρα θαυμάζων τῆς συνέσεως ἐν πολλοῖς τὸν διδάσκαλον ἐν τούτῳ μάλιστα πλέον ὑπερεθαύμασα ὡς καλῶς ἐν τῇ συμφορᾷ τὸν λόγον κατασιγάσαντα. προσφυὲς γάρ μοι δοκεῖ καὶ κατάλληλον εἶναι τοῖς πενθοῦσι φάρμακον ἡ σιγὴ τὸ διοιδοῦν τῆς ψυχῆς χρόνῳ καὶ
PG 880 κατηφείᾳ δι' ἡσυχίας ἐκπέττουσα. ὡς εἴ γέ τις ἔτι τὴν | ψυχὴν τοῦ
GNO 476 πάθους ὑποθερμαίνοντος ἀνακινοίη τὸν λόγον, | δυσαλθέστερον
τὸ τῆς λύπης τραῦμα γενήσεται τῇ μνήμῃ τῶν ἀλγεινῶν οἷόν τίσιν ἀκάνθαις ἐπιξαινόμενον. εἰ δὲ μὴ λίαν ἐστὶ τολμηρὸν κἀμέ τι τῶν τοῦ διδασκάλου προσδιορθώσασθαι, τάχα καλῶς ἔσχε μέχρι τοῦ νῦν κατακρατεῖν ἡμῶν τὴν ἡσυχίαν, ὡς ἂν μὴ πρὸς τὸ πάθος ὁ λόγος καθελκυσθεὶς τὴν ἀκοὴν ἀνιάσειεν. οὔπω γὰρ τοσοῦτος ὁ ἐν τῷ μέσῳ χρόνος ὥστε προσεθίσαι τῷ κακῷ τὴν διάνοιαν· ἔτι νέον ἐν τῇ ψυχῇ τὸ πάθος (τάχα δὲ καὶ ἀεὶ νέον ἔσται τῷ βίῳ τὸ ἄλγημα), ἔτι ταράσσεται ἡμῶν ἡ καρδία καὶ καθάπερ τις θάλασσα

A Funeral Oration for the Empress Flaccilla

1 "The trustworthy and prudent steward" (for I begin from what we have heard read in the holy Gospel), "whom the master has set over this household to give those he oversees their measure of food at the right time" (Mt 24.45; Lk 12.42),[2] has, in these recent days, properly judged the weakness of human speech—has rightly perceived the greatness of this misfortune, and has honored our grief in silence. Yet now, for some reason, he has restored words again to the Church in our present gathering, overruling his own decision against speaking. And though I greatly admire our teacher for his understanding on many accounts, I have come to admire him still more in these recent days, for rightly bringing all speech to silence in a time of misfortune. Silence seems to me, at least, a natural and appropriate medicine for those who are grieving, helping them soothe the things that fester in the soul, over time and through sadness, by holding their peace. So that if someone should give free motion to words while suffering still heats the soul, the wound of sorrow is made still more deadly by painful memories, as if scraped by thorns. And if it is not rash for me to offer a correction to the decisions of our teacher, perhaps it would be a good thing for him to impose silence on us even now, lest, in addition to our grief, my words, when dragged out of me, give pain to my hearers. For the intervening time has not been long enough to let our minds become accustomed to this misfortune; grief is still fresh in our souls (and this particular pain will perhaps always remain fresh throughout our lives); our hearts are still disturbed, and, like the sea, are churned from their depths

[2]Gregory appears to apply these images of steward and teacher here to Nectarius, bishop of Constantinople, who would have been in charge of the liturgical rites of the empress's burial, and who has apparently invited the renowned bishop of Nyssa to deliver the official funeral address.

κυματουμένη τῇ λαίλαπι τῆς συμφορᾶς ἐκ βυθῶν ἀναστρέφεται, ἔτι διοιδοῦσιν οἱ λογισμοὶ πρὸς τὴν μνήμην τῶν κακῶν ἀναζέοντες. ἀστατούσης οὖν τῷ τοιούτῳ κλύδωνι τῆς ψυχῆς πῶς ἔστι προαγαγεῖν ἐπ᾽ εὐθείας τὸν λόγον οἱόν τινι καταιγίδι τῷ πάθει τῆς λύπης ἐγχειμαζόμενον; ἀλλ᾽ ἐπειδὴ χρὴ κελεύοντι πείθεσθαι, οὐκ οἶδα ὅπως τῷ λόγῳ χρήσομαι· οὐ γὰρ εὑρίσκω τῆς διανοίας τοῦ διδασκάλου καταστοχάσασθαι. ἢ τάχα βούλεταί τι καὶ τῷ πάθει χαρίσασθαι καὶ τοῖς ἐμπαθεστέροις τῶν λόγων ἀνακινῆσαι τῇ ἐκκλησίᾳ τὸ δάκρυον; καὶ εἰ ταῦτα διανοεῖται, ὀρθῶς κατά γε τὴν ἐμὴν κρίσιν καὶ τοῦτο ποιεῖ· δεῖ γὰρ πάντως, ὥσπερ τὴν ἀπόλαυσιν τῶν ἀγαθῶν προθυμούμεθα, οὕτω καὶ πρὸς τὰ λυπηρὰ τῶν συμπιπτόντων οἰκείως ἔχειν· τοῦτο γὰρ καὶ ὁ Ἐκκλησιαστὴς συμβουλεύει· Καιρός, φησί, τοῦ γελάσαι καὶ καιρὸς τοῦ κλαῦσαι. μανθάνομεν γὰρ διὰ τούτων ὅτι δεῖ καταλλήλως τῷ ὑποκειμένῳ καὶ τὴν ψυχὴν διατίθεσθαι· κατὰ ῥοῦν τὰ πράγματα φέρεται; εὔκαιρον τὸ εὐφραίνεσθαι· μετέπεσε τὸ φαιδρὸν εἰς κατήφειαν;
GNO 477 μεταβάλλειν προσήκει | καὶ τὴν εὐθυμίαν εἰς δάκρυον. ὥσπερ γὰρ ὁ γέλως σημεῖον τῆς ἔνδον φαιδρότητος γίνεται, οὕτω καὶ ὁ ἐν τῇ καρδίᾳ πόνος ὑπὸ τῶν θρήνων διερμηνεύεται καὶ γίνεται τῶν τῆς ψυχῆς τραυμάτων ὥσπερ αἷμα τὸ δάκρυον. τοῦτο καὶ ἡ Παροιμία Σολομῶντός φησιν ὅτι Καρδίας εὐφραινομένης πρόσωπον θάλλει, τῆς ψυχῆς δὲ ἐν λύπαις οὔσης σκυθρωπάζει. οὐκοῦν ἀνάγκη πᾶσα τῇ διαθέσει τῆς καρδίας συσκυθρωπάσαι τὸν λόγον. καὶ εἴθε δυνατὸν ἦν τοιούτους ἐξευρεῖν τινας λόγους, οἵους ὁ μέγας Ἰερεμίας τῇ συμφορᾷ ποτε τῶν Ἰσραηλιτῶν ἐπεθρήνησεν. ἐκείνων γὰρ ἄξια τὰ παρόντα μᾶλλον ἢ εἴ τι τῶν ἀρχαίων ἐν σκυθρωποῖς μνημονεύεται. χαλεπὰ τὰ τοῦ Ἰὼβ διηγήματα· ἀλλὰ τί χρὴ πρὸς τοσοῦτον κακὸν ἀντεξαγαγεῖν μιᾶς οἰκίας εὐαρίθμητα πάθη; κἂν τὰ μεγάλα καὶ κοινότερα τῶν κακῶν διεξέλθῃς, σεισμοὺς καὶ πολέμους καὶ ἐπικλύσεις καὶ χάσματα, μικρὰ καὶ ταῦτα εἰ πρὸς τὰ

into waves by the storm of misfortune; our thoughts are still in ferment, boiling up at the memory of our sufferings. With our souls still restless, then, on these waves, how is it possible to produce a straightforward oration, such that it can weather the passion of grief like some winter squall?

2 But since one must obey an order, I will try as best I can to put our feelings into words. I do not have the resources to guess at the mind of our teacher. Is it possible, perhaps, that he wishes that some concession be made to emotion, and hopes to stir up tears in the church among those who are sensitive to speech? If this is his thinking, then in my judgment he is acting rightly. For surely, just as we yearn in advance to enjoy good things, we must also take steps to deal with the sad things that befall us. This is what Ecclesiastes advises, after all: "There is a time," he says, "to laugh and a time to weep" (Eccl 3.4). We learn from this that we must dispose our soul in a way suited to the subject. Are things flowing along easily? It is time to rejoice! Have bright days turned to dark ones? It is appropriate to transform their good feelings to tears. For just as a laugh is a sign of the cheerful mood within, so pain in the heart is expressed by laments, and the tear becomes the blood that flows from the wounds of the soul. A proverb of Solomon says this: "When the heart is joyful, the face blooms; but when the soul is grieving it looks sad" (Prov 15.13).[3] So we are forced to make our words mournful, to accord with the feelings of our hearts.

If only it were possible to find some words like those the great Jeremiah once uttered in lament, in the time of the Israelites' disaster. For our present misfortune is worthy of them, more than if some ancient event were simply being recalled in words of mourning. The story of Job is hard; but why must we lay out the sufferings of one household, so easily recounted, in comparison with a misfortune as great as this? Even if you were to list the major evils of everyday life—earthquakes and wars and floods and collapses of the

[3]The reference to "the soul" is not in the LXX text.

παρόντα κρίνοιτο. διὰ τί; ὅτι οὐ πάσης ἀθρόως τῆς οἰκουμένης ἡ
κατὰ πόλεμον ἅπτεται συμφορά, ἀλλὰ τὸ μέν τι πολεμεῖται αὐτῆς,
τὸ δὲ εἰρηνεύεται. μέρος τι πάλιν ἢ σκηπτὸς ἐπέφλεξεν ἢ τὸ ὕδωρ
PG 881 ἐπ|έκλυσεν ἢ κατεπόθη τῷ χάσματι. τὸ δὲ παρὸν κακὸν πάσης
ἀθρόως τῆς οἰκουμένης ἐστὶ πληγή· οὐκ ἔστιν ἔθνος ἓν ἢ πόλιν
μίαν ἀπολοφύρασθαι, ἀλλ' ἁρμόζει τάχα τὴν τοῦ Ναβουχοδονοσὸρ
προέσθαι φωνήν, ἣν πρὸς τοὺς ὑποχειρίους πεποίηται· Ὑμῖν λέγω,
λαοί, φυλαί, γλῶσσαι. μᾶλλον δὲ συγχωρήσατέ μοι προσθεῖναί
GNO 478 τι τῷ Ἀσσυρίῳ κηρύγματι καὶ μεγαλοφωνότερον | ἀνακηρῦξαι
τὴν συμφορὰν καὶ εἰπεῖν, ὡς ἄν τις ἐπὶ σκηνῆς ἀναβοήσας εἴποι·
ὦ πόλεις καὶ δῆμοι καὶ ἔθνη καὶ σύμπασα γῆ καὶ τῆς θαλάσσης
ὅσον τε πλόϊμον καὶ ὅσον οἰκούμενον, ὦ πάσης τῆς καθ' ἡμᾶς
οἰκουμένης ὅσον τῷ σκήπτρῳ τῆς βασιλείας εὐθύνεται, ὦ πάντες
οἱ πανταχόθεν ἄνθρωποι, κοινῇ τῷ πάθει ἐπιστενάξατε, κοινῇ
τοῦ θρήνου τὴν συνῳδίαν στήσασθε, κοινῇ τὴν πάντων ζημίαν
ἀπολοφύρασθε. ἢ βούλεσθε, καθὼς ἂν οἷός τε ὦ, καὶ τὴν ζημίαν
ὑμῖν διηγήσωμαι; ἤνεγκεν ἐν τῇ καθ' ἡμᾶς γενεᾷ ἡ ἀνθρωπίνη
φύσις ἐκβᾶσα τοὺς ἰδίους ὅρους καὶ τὰ συνήθη μέτρα νικήσασα,
ἤνεγκεν ἡ φύσις, μᾶλλον δὲ ὁ τῆς φύσεως κύριος, ἀνθρωπίνην
ψυχὴν ἐν γυναικείῳ τῷ σώματι ὑπὲρ πάντα σχεδὸν τὰ προλαβόντα
τῆς ἀρετῆς ὑποδείγματα, ἐν ᾗ πᾶσα μὲν σώματος πᾶσα δὲ ψυχῆς
ἀρετὴ συνδραμοῦσα θαῦμα ἄπιστον ἔδειξε τῇ ἀνθρωπίνῃ ζωῇ,
πόσων ἀγαθῶν συνδρομὴν μία ψυχὴ ἐν ἑνὶ ἐχώρησε σώματι. καὶ
ὡς ἂν μάλιστα καταφανὲς ἅπασι γένοιτο τῆς γενεᾶς τὸ εὐτύχημα,
ἐπὶ τὸν ὑψηλὸν θρόνον τῆς βασιλείας ἀνάγεται, ὅπως ἡλίου δίκην
ἐκ τοῦ ὑψηλοῦ ἀξιώματος πᾶσαν τὴν οἰκουμένην ταῖς ἀκτῖσι τῶν
ἀρετῶν καταλάμψειεν. καὶ τῷ κατὰ θείαν ψῆφον τῆς οἰκουμένης
ἁπάσης προτεταγμένῳ εἰς βίου τε καὶ βασιλείας κοινωνίαν
συναρμοσθεῖσα μακαριστὸν ἐποίει δι' ἑαυτῆς τὸ ὑπήκοον, ὄντως,

earth[4]—these, too, are small things when compared to the present situation. Why? Because the disaster of war does not lay hold of the whole world at once, but part of it is at war, part is at peace. A bolt of lightning, again, only sets part on fire, water floods only a part, only part is swallowed up by a sinkhole. But this present evil is a blow to the whole world at once. It is impossible for just one ethnic group or one city to grieve; perhaps one ought, instead, to quote the words of Nebuchadnezzar, which he spoke to his subjects: "I say to you, peoples, tribes, languages . . ." (Dan 3.4). Or rather, allow me to add something to the Assyrian edict, to proclaim this misfortune in a still clearer voice, and say, as one might cry out loudly on stage: O cities and peoples and tribes, all the earth and whatever part of the sea is navigable, wherever people live; O whatever place, on our whole inhabited earth, is under the direction of the scepter of Empire; O all people everywhere—let us lament our suffering together, join together in the chorus of mourning, weep together over the loss we all suffer!

3 With your permission, may I sketch out our loss for you, as much as I am able? In our own generation, human nature has succeeded in transcending its own boundaries and overcoming its accustomed measures; human nature—or rather, the Lord of nature—has produced a human soul, in a female body, that has surpassed almost all previous examples of virtue. In it, all perfections of body and soul came together, to reveal an incredible marvel for human life: how many virtues one soul has succeeded in bringing together within one body. And that this extraordinary achievement might be obvious to everyone in our generation, she has been led up to the exalted throne of empire, so that she might shine like the sun on the whole world from this high office with the rays of virtue. Being joined to share life and rule with him who has, by divine decree, been set over the whole world, she has, on her own, made obedience a blessed thing—becoming truly what Scripture calls a "helpmate" to him for

[4]Literally, "yawning holes."

GNO 479 καθώς φησιν ἡ γραφή, βοηθὸς | αὐτῷ πρὸς πᾶν ἀγαθὸν γινομένη. εἰ φιλανθρωπίας ἦν ὁ καιρός, ἢ συνέτρεχεν αὐτῷ πρὸς τὸ ἀγαθὸν τοῦτο ἢ καὶ προέτρεχεν· ἴσος ἦν ὁ ζυγὸς ἑκατέρωθεν τῇ τῆς φιλανθρωπίας ῥοπῇ. μαρτυρεῖ δὲ τῷ λόγῳ τά τε πρότερα ἀριθμὸν νικῶντα καὶ τὰ ἐπὶ τοῦ παρόντος κηρύγματα, ἃ νῦν παρὰ τοῦ κήρυκος τῆς ἀληθείας ἠκούσαμεν. εἰ τὸ εὐσεβὲς ἐπιζητεῖς, κοινὸς ἦν ἀμφοτέρων ὁ πρὸς εὐσέβειαν δρόμος, εἰ τὸ προνοητικόν, εἰ τὸ δίκαιον, εἰ ἄλλο τι τῶν πρὸς τὸ κρεῖττον σπουδαζομένων, πάντα ἐν ἁμίλλῃ ἦν ἀλλήλους νικᾶν ἐν ταῖς εὐποιΐαις φιλονικούντων καὶ οὐκ ἦν ὁ ἡττώμενος. ἴση τις ἦν ἀμφοτέρων ἡ ἐπ᾽ ἀλλήλοις χάρις· ἡ μὲν ἀρετῆς ἆθλον εἶχε τὸν τῆς οἰκουμένης προτεταγμένον, ὁ δὲ μικρὰν ἡγεῖτο γῆς τε καὶ θαλάττης τὴν ἐξουσίαν συγκρίσει τοῦ κατ᾽ αὐτὴν εὐτυχήματος. ἴσας ἀλλήλοις ἀντιπαρεῖχον τὰς εὐφροσύνας ἀλλήλους τε βλέποντες καὶ ὑπ᾽ ἀλλήλων ὁρώμενοι· ὁ μὲν τοιοῦτος ὢν οἷός ἐστι (ποῖον γὰρ ἄν τις κάλλος ὑπὲρ τὸ φαινόμενον δείξειεν; καὶ εἴη γε διαρκέσαι καὶ εἰς ἐκγόνων ζωὴν τὸ ὁρώμενον), τὴν δέ, οἵα τις ἦν, οὐκ ἔστιν ὑποδεῖξαι τῷ λόγῳ· οὐ γὰρ περιλέλειπταί τι αὐτῆς δι᾽ ἀκριβείας παρὰ τῆς τέχνης ὁμοίωμα, ἀλλ᾽ εἰ καί τι γέγονεν ἐν γραφαῖς ἢ ἐν πλάσμασιν, πάντα τῆς ἀληθείας ἐστὶν ἐνδεέστερα. |

PG 884 Τοιαῦτα καὶ μέχρι τούτου τὰ διηγήματα. τὰ δὲ ἐπὶ τούτοις οἷα·
GNO 480 πάλιν βοᾶν ἀναγκάζομαι καί μοι σύγγνωτε | ὑπερβοῶντι τὸ πάθος· ὦ Θρᾴκη τὸ φευκτὸν ὄνομα, ὦ δυστυχὲς ἔθνος ἐκ συμφορῶν γνωριζόμενον, ὦ πρότερον μὲν πολεμίῳ πυρὶ ταῖς τῶν βαρβάρων ἐπιδρομαῖς δῃωθεῖσα, νῦν δὲ τὸ κεφάλαιον τῆς κοινῆς συμφορᾶς ἐν ἑαυτῇ δεξαμένη. ἐκεῖθεν τὸ ἀγαθὸν ἀναρπάζεται, ἐκεῖ ὁ φθόνος κατὰ τῆς βασιλείας ἐκώμασεν, ἐκεῖ γέγονεν τὸ τῆς οἰκουμένης

---

[5]Gen 2.18. For Flaccilla's extraordinary charitable activities, see also Theodoret, *Ecclesiastical History* 5.18.

[6]Greek: φιλανθρωπία (*philanthrōpia*).

[7]Gregory seems to be alluding to a passage of Scripture about the need for mercy, which has just been proclaimed to the congregation. Spira, the editor of the Greek text, suggests it may also be a reference to the pardon Theodosius is later reported in the oration (sec. 10) to have given to a condemned man, in memory of Flaccilla.

achieving all good things.[5] If a moment for public generosity[6] arose, she either collaborated with him in good projects or led the way in them. The pair was equal in the inclination of both toward charity. And countless reports about past years, as well as about the present, confirm in words what we have now just heard from the herald of truth.[7] If you are looking for piety, both of them shared a common inclination to it; if you are looking for careful planning, for justice, for any other characteristic of those eager to seek out the better way—all of these things were part of their competition, as they tried to outdo each other in doing good; and neither was defeated! Their delight in each other was equal: she considered the one who was set over the world as her prize of virtue; he considered authority over land and sea to be small, in comparison with the good fortune of having her. They shared with one another the delight of seeing and being seen by one another: he, being the sort of person *he* is (for what beauty might one point to there, beyond mere appearance? May what we see in him last into the life of his descendants!); and she—it is impossible to express in words what kind of person *she* was! For there is no likeness of her left that accurately represents her by art; and if there is some portrait in a painting or a statue, all are deficient in comparison to the truth.

4 Such, and within these limits, is my description. But beyond this, let me speak thus—again I am forced to cry out loud! (Please forgive me if I exaggerate my feelings!) O Thrace, name to be shunned![8] O unfortunate nation known for its disasters! O land once ravaged by enemy fire during barbarian invasions, but now taking on itself the chief role in our common misfortune! There goodness has been snatched away, there malice[9] has been let loose against the Empire,

[8]Gregory is referring to the fact that Flaccilla has died in Thrace, the European province just to the northwest of Asia Minor and Constantinople. As a border-province, it had been the scene of many battles during the previous few centuries of Roman imperial history.

[9]Literally, "envy" (φθόνος, *phthonos*). In classical Greek literature, it was customary to speak of inexplicable misfortune as the work of a kind of personified malicious Envy.

ναυάγιον, ἐκεῖ καθάπερ ἐν κλύδωνι τῷ προβόλῳ προσπταίσαντες
τῷ τῆς λύπης βυθῷ κατεδύημεν. ὢ πονηρᾶς ἐκδημίας ἐκείνης, ἣ
τὴν ὑποστροφὴν οὐκ ἀπέδωκεν, ὢ πικρῶν ὑδάτων, ὧν τὰς πηγὰς
ἐπεπόθησεν, ὡς οὐκ ὤφελεν, ὢ χωρίον, ἐν ᾧ τὸ πάθος ἐγένετο, διὰ
τὸ πάθος τῇ σκοτομήνῃ ἐπώνυμον. (ἀκούω γὰρ κατὰ τὴν πάτριον
αὐτῶν γλῶσσαν Σκοτούμην τὸν τόπον ἐπονομάζεσθαι.) ἐκεῖ
ἐσκοτίσθη ὁ λύχνος, ἐκεῖ κατεσβέσθη τὸ φέγγος, ἐκεῖ αἱ ἀκτῖνες τῶν
ἀρετῶν ἠμαυρώθησαν. οἴχεται τῆς βασιλείας τὸ ἐγκαλλώπισμα, τὸ
τῆς δικαιοσύνης πηδάλιον, ἡ τῆς φιλανθρωπίας εἰκών, μᾶλλον δὲ
αὐτὸ τὸ ἀρχέτυπον. ἀφῃρέθη τῆς φιλανδρίας ὁ τύπος, τὸ ἁγνὸν τῆς
σωφροσύνης ἀνάθημα, ἡ εὐπρόσιτος σεμνότης, ἡ ἀκαταφρόνητος
ἡμερότης, ἡ ὑψηλὴ ταπεινοφροσύνη, ἡ πεπαρρησιασμένη αἰδώς, ἡ
σύμμικτος τῶν ἀγαθῶν ἁρμονία. οἴχεται ὁ τῆς πίστεως ζῆλος, ὁ τῆς
ἐκκλησίας στῦλος, ὁ τῶν θυσιαστηρίων κόσμος, ὁ τῶν πενομένων
πλοῦτος, ἡ πολυαρκὴς δεξιά, ὁ κοινὸς τῶν καταπονουμένων λιμήν.
πενθείτω ἡ παρθενία, θρηνείτω ἡ χηρεία, ὀδυρέσθω ἡ ὀρφανία,
γνώτωσαν τί εἶχον ὅτε οὐκ ἔχουσιν. μᾶλλον δὲ τί χρή με κατὰ μέρη
καὶ τάξεις διαιρεῖν τὸν θρῆνον; στεναζέτω πᾶσα ἡ γενεὰ βύθιον ἐκ
GNO 481 μέσης καρδίας τὸν στεναγμὸν | ἀναπέμπουσα. συμπενθείτω καὶ ἡ
ἱερωσύνη αὐτὴ τὸν κοινὸν κόσμον τοῦ φθόνου ἀποσυλήσαντος.
ἆρα μὴ τολμηρὸν τὸ τοῦ προφήτου εἰπεῖν; τὸ Ἵνα τί ἀπώσω, ὁ
θεός, εἰς τέλος, καὶ διωργίσθη ὁ θυμός σου ἐπὶ πρόβατα νομῆς
σου; ποίων ἁμαρτημάτων τὰς δίκας ἐκτιννύομεν; ὑπὲρ τίνος ταῖς
ἐπαλλήλοις τῶν συμφορῶν μαστιζόμεθα; ἢ τάχα διὰ τὸ πλεονάσαι
τὴν ἀσέβειαν τῶν ποικίλων αἱρέσεων αὕτη καθ᾽ ἡμῶν ἡ ψῆφος
ἐκράτησεν; ὁρᾶτε γὰρ οἵοις κακοῖς ἐν βραχεῖ συνηνέχθημεν χρόνῳ.
οὔπω ἐπὶ τῇ προτέρᾳ πληγῇ ἀναπνεύσαντες, οὔπω τὸ δάκρυον τῶν

there the world's shipwreck has happened; there, as if swept against a boulder by a flood, we have drowned in the depths of grief. What a wicked journey that was, that allowed no return; what bitter waters, at whose springs she drank, though they offered no cure! O town, in which our suffering began, named "dark night"[10] because of our suffering! (For I hear that in the language of that country the place is named "Skotoumē.") There our lamp has become dark, there our light has gone out, there the rays of virtue are dimmed. The adornment of the Empire has left us, the rudder of justice, the image of benevolence—or rather its archetype! The model of spousal love has been taken away, the chaste monument of self-control, the accessible shrine of sanctity, the gentleness no one could despise, the lofty humility, the modesty that was able to speak out, the harmony that mingled all blessings. Zeal for the faith is gone, the pillar of the Church, the ornament of sacrificial altars, the wealth of the poor, the right hand that reached out to so many in need, the common refuge for the downtrodden. Let virgins mourn, let widows lament, let orphans weep; let them realize what they had, now that they have it no longer!

5 But why should I divide up my lament into orderly sections? Let the whole nation emit a deep groan, from the depth of its heart! Let the rank of priests, too, grieve with them, since the evil one[11] has stolen our common ornament! Would it be rash to speak out in the words of the prophet, "Why have you cast us off forever? Why was your wrath kindled against the sheep of your pasture?" (Ps 73.1) For what sins are we paying the penalty? For what are we being beaten, in the exchange of indignities? Is it perhaps that this divine decree is in force against us because so many different wicked heresies have spread? For you see in what misfortunes we are surrounded, within a short time. We have not yet drawn our breath in response to that

[10]Greek: Σκοτομήνη (*Skotomēnē*), "overshadowed," "Shadow-Land." As he explains, Gregory is playing on the name "Skotoumē," the Thracian spa where Flaccilla died while seeking a cure. Its location is unknown.

[11]Literally, "malice," or "envy" (φθόνος, *phthonos*). Cf. Wis 2.24.

ὀφθαλμῶν ἀποψήσαντες πάλιν ἐν τοσαύτῃ γεγόναμεν συμφορᾷ· τότε τὸ νεοθαλὲς ἄνθος ἀπωδυράμεθα, νῦν αὐτὸ τὸ ἔρνος, ἀφ' οὗ τὸ ἄνθος ἐβλάστησεν, τότε τὴν ἐλπισθεῖσαν ὥραν, νῦν τὴν ἀκμάσασαν, τότε τὸ προσδοκώμενον ἀγαθόν, νῦν τὸ ἐν πείρᾳ γενόμενον.

Ἆρά μοι συγγνώσεσθε, ἀδελφοί, εἴ τι διὰ τὸ πάθος
παραληρήσαιμι; τάχα, καθώς φησιν ὁ ἀπόστολος, καὶ αὐτὴ ἡ κτίσις
τῷ ἡμετέρῳ κακῷ συνεστέναξεν. ὑπομνήσω δὲ τῶν γεγονότων
ὑμᾶς καὶ οἶμαι τοὺς πολλοὺς τοῖς λεγομένοις συνθήσεσθαι· ὅτε
χρυσῷ καὶ πορφυρίδι κεκαλυμμένη ἐπὶ τὴν πόλιν ἡ βασιλὶς |
PG 885 ἐκομίζετο (κλίνη δὲ ἦν ἡ κομίζουσα) καὶ πᾶσα ἀξία καὶ ἡλικία
πᾶσα προχεθεῖσα τοῦ ἄστεος ἅπαν ἐστενοχώρει ἀπὸ πλήθους
τὸ ὕπαιθρον πάντων ἐκ ποδῶν καὶ τῶν ὑπερεχόντων τοῖς
GNO 482 ἀξιώμασι προπομπευόντων | τοῦ πάθους (μέμνησθε πάντως
ὅπως ὁ ἥλιος ταῖς νεφέλαις τὰς ἀκτῖνας ἑαυτοῦ συνεκάλυψεν, ὡς ἂν μὴ ἴδοι τάχα καθαρῷ τῷ φωτὶ μετὰ τοιούτου σχήματος εἰσελαύνουσαν τὴν βασιλίδα τῇ πόλει, οὐκ ἐπὶ ἅρματός τινος ἢ χρυσοδέτου ἀπήνης κατὰ τὸν βασίλειον κόσμον τοῖς δορυφόροις ἀγαλλομένην, ἀλλ' ἐν σορῷ κεκαλυμμένην, ἐπικρυπτομένην τὸ εἶδος ἐκείνῳ τῷ σκυθρωπῷ προκαλύμματι, θέαμα δεινόν τε καὶ ἐλεεινόν, δακρύων ἀφορμὴν προκειμένην τοῖς ἐντυγχάνουσιν, ἣν ἅπας τῶν συνειλεγμένων ὁ δῆμος ὁ ἔπηλύς τε καὶ ὁ ἐγχώριος οὐκ εὐφημίαις, ἀλλὰ θρήνοις εἰσιοῦσαν ἐδέχετο), τότε καὶ ὁ ἀὴρ πενθικῶς ἐσκυθρώπασεν οἷον ἱμάτιόν τι πενθικὸν τὸν ζόφον περιβαλλόμενος, ἀλλὰ καὶ αἱ νεφέλαι καθὼς δυνατὸν αὐταῖς ἦν ἐπεδάκρυον ἁπαλὰς ψεκάδας ἀντὶ δακρύων ἐπαφιεῖσαι τῷ πάθει. ἢ ταῦτα μὲν ὄντως λῆρός ἐστι καὶ οὐδὲ λέγειν ἄξιον; εἰ γάρ τι καὶ γέγονεν ἐν τῇ κτίσει τοιοῦτον οἷον ἐπισημῆναι τὴν συμφοράν, οὐ παρὰ τῆς κτίσεως γέγονε πάντως, ἀλλὰ παρὰ τοῦ δεσπότου τῆς

first blow,[12] nor wiped away the tears yet from our eyes, and we are again in such great sorrow. Then we bitterly lamented the loss of the newly-sprung blossom, but now the shoot itself, from which the blossom sprouted. Then we lamented the loss of the full maturity we hoped for, but now ripeness itself. Then it was a hoped-for blessing, but now it is one we know from experience.

6 Will you forgive me, brothers and sisters, if I speak foolishly because of our sorrow? Perhaps, as the Apostle says, "all creation groans" along with our misfortune (Rom 8.22). I will remind you of what has happened, and I know most of you will agree with the details of what I say.[13] When the empress was carried to the city, covered with gold and purple (for she was brought on a bier), and people of every rank and age poured out from the city, all the open fields were crowded by the number of people, with all the foot soldiers and the superior officers leading the procession of grief. Surely you remember how the sun cloaked its rays in the clouds, so that it might not see, perhaps, in the pure light, the empress entering the city in such a form: not in a chariot or a gold-trimmed wagon, resplendent with a detail of guards in the royal insignia, but covered up in a coffin, her form veiled by that gloomy pall—a dreadful and pitiful sight, an obvious cause of tears to all who saw it. The whole crowd that had gathered, visitors and city-folk, took all this in not with cheers but with laments, as the procession came into the city—at that moment the air, too, put on a sad and grieving face, wrapping mist around itself like a kind of mourning-cloak; the clouds, too, wept in the way it was possible for them, releasing gentle raindrops on our sorrow. Is this all foolishness, not worthy of mention? If something occurred in nature so as to mark this misfortune, surely it did not come about from nature itself, but from the Lord of nature, paying honor

[12]Gregory refers here to the death of Flaccilla's six-year-old daughter, the princess Pulcheria, the previous summer.

[13]Gregory draws on his rhetorical skills here to paint a poignant, vivid descriptive scene, known as an *ekphrasis*, of Flaccilla's funeral procession as it reached Constantinople a few days before her burial.

κτίσεως τιμῶντος δι᾽ ὧν ἐποίει τῆς ὁσίας τὸν θάνατον· Τίμιος γάρ,
φησίν, ἐναντίον κυρίου ὁ θάνατος τῶν ὁσίων αὐτοῦ. εἶδον δὲ ἐγὼ
τότε ἕτερον θέαμα τῶν εἰρημένων παραδοξότερον· εἶδον διπλοῦν
ὄμβρον τὸν μὲν ἐκ τοῦ ἀέρος τὸν δὲ ἐκ τῶν δακρύων ἐπὶ τὴν γῆν
καταρρέοντα καὶ οὐκ ἦν ὁ ἐξ ὀφθαλμῶν ὑετὸς τοῦ ἐκ τῶν νεφῶν
ἐνδεέστερος· ἐν γὰρ τοσαύταις μυριάσι τῶν συμπαρόντων οὐκ ἦν
ὀφθαλμὸς ὁ μὴ καταβρέχων τὴν γῆν ταῖς τῶν δακρύων σταγόσιν.

Ἀλλ᾽ οὐ καλῶς τάχα τῆς τοῦ διδασκάλου γνώμης ἐστοχασάμεθα
GNO 483 πλέον ἢ ἔδει τοῖς σκυθρωποῖς ἐμβαθύναντες. | ἴσως γὰρ βούλεται
θεραπεῦσαι μᾶλλον ἢ ἀνιᾶσαι τὴν ἀκοήν, ἡμεῖς δὲ τὸ ἐναντίον
νῦν πεποιήκαμεν, ὥσπερ ἂν εἴ τις ἰατρὸς τραυματίαν λαβὼν μὴ
μόνον ἀμελοίη τῆς θεραπείας, ἀλλὰ καὶ βρωτικοῖς τισι φαρμάκοις
προσεπιτρίβοι τὸν ὀδυνώμενον. οὐκοῦν ἐπαντλητέον τὸν ἐλαιώδη
λόγον τῇ διοιδούσῃ πληγῇ· οἶδε γὰρ καὶ ἡ εὐαγγελικὴ ἰατρεία
τῇ στύψει τοῦ οἴνου καταμιγνύειν τὸ ἔλαιον. ἐπικλίνωμεν οὖν
ὑμῖν παρὰ τῆς γραφῆς λαβόντες τὸν τοῦ ἐλαίου καμψάκην, ὥς
ἐστι δυνατόν, τὸ σκυθρωπὸν τῶν εἰρημένων εἰς παραμυθίαν
παλινῳδήσαντες. ἀλλά μοι μηδεὶς ἀπιστείτω τῷ λεγομένῳ κἂν
παράδοξον ᾖ· ἔστιν, ἀδελφοί, τὸ ἀγαθὸν ὃ ζητοῦμεν, ἔστι καὶ
οὐκ ἀπόλωλεν. μᾶλλον δὲ μικρότερον εἶπον τῆς ἀληθείας· οὐ
μόνον γὰρ ἔστι τὸ ἀγαθόν, ἀλλὰ καὶ ἐν ὑψηλοτέροις ἢ πρότερον.
τὴν βασιλίδα ζητεῖς; ἐν τοῖς βασιλείοις τὴν διαγωγὴν ἔχει. ἀλλ᾽
PG 888 ὀφθαλμῷ | γνῶναι τοῦτο ποθεῖς; οὐκ ἔξεστί σοι βασιλίδος θέαν
περιεργάζεσθαι, φοβερὰ περὶ αὐτὴν ἡ τῶν δορυφόρων φρουρά, οὐ
τούτων λέγω τῶν δορυφόρων οἷς σίδηρος τὸ ὅπλον ἐστίν, ἀλλὰ
τῶν τῇ φλογίνῃ ῥομφαίᾳ καθωπλισμένων ὧν τὸ εἶδος ἀνθρώπων
ὄψις οὐχ ὑποδέχεται. ἐν τοῖς ἀπορρήτοις τῆς βασιλείας ἡ οἴκησις·
GNO 484 τότε ὄψει ὅταν καὶ σὺ προκύψῃς | τοῦ σώματος, οὐ γὰρ ἔστιν

[14]Again, presumably the Patriarch Nectarius.

[15]See Lk 10.34. The Samaritan who cared for the wounded stranger knew how to use both wine and oil to cleanse a wound and to soothe the pain. Gregory is marking a transition here from the first part of his discourse, which uses classical rhetorical

through the things he has made to the death of a holy woman—for Scripture says, "Precious in the sight of the Lord is the death of his saints" (Ps 115.6). And then I saw another sight, still more wonderful than what I have mentioned: I saw a twofold rainstorm, one from the sky and the other from tears, both flowing down on the ground, and the rain from our eyes was no less intense than that from the clouds! For among so many thousands who had gathered, there was not an eye that did not moisten the earth with the drops of its tears.

7 But perhaps it is not good that we have guessed at the intention of our teacher,[14] deepening his thoughts with gloom more than is proper. Perhaps he wishes to heal rather than to cause pain to our hearing. But we have just done the opposite—as if a doctor, receiving a wounded man, were not only to neglect treating his wound, but were to make him suffer more pain by the drugs he gives him to consume. So we must pour the oil of words on this swelling wound. For the medicine of the Gospel is able to mix oil with the stinging effect of the wine.[15] Let us sit down together, then, and take a bottle of oil from the Scripture, to reverse the sadness of what we have said, as far as possible, and change it into consolation. But let no one be distrustful of what is said here, even if it sounds mysterious. And what is it that is proclaimed? It is the Good we seek, my brothers and sisters; it is real, and has not perished![16] Or rather, I have understated the truth: the Good is not only real, but lies in a higher state than what went before it. Do you seek our empress? She lives in a royal palace. But do you yearn to see this with your eyes? It is impossible for you to attain for yourself a vision of the empress, for the guard mounted around her is formidable—I am not talking about the kind of guard who have iron spears, but those armed with a flaming sword, whose form human eyesight cannot attain. Her dwelling is in an ineffable part of the Kingdom; you will see it yourself only when you, too, emerge from your body—for it is not possible to come into

forms to evoke the hearers' grief, to the second, scriptural part, which lays before them the comforting considerations of Christian faith.

[16]Following the reading of manuscripts APΛ, which seems to offer better sense.

ἄλλως ἐντὸς τῶν ἀδύτων τῆς βασιλείας γενέσθαι μὴ διασχόντα τὸ τῆς σαρκὸς παραπέτασμα.

Ἢ κρεῖττον οἴει τὸ διὰ σαρκὸς μετέχειν τοῦ βίου; οὐκοῦν παιδευσάτω σε ὁ θεῖος ἀπόστολος ὁ τῶν ἀρρήτων τοῦ παραδείσου μετεσχηκὼς μυστηρίων. τί λέγει περὶ τῆς ὧδε ζωῆς τάχα ἐκ τοῦ κοινοῦ τῶν ἀνθρώπων φθεγγόμενος;

Ταλαίπωρος ἐγὼ ἄνθρωπος· τίς με ῥύσεται ἀπὸ τοῦ σώματος τοῦ θανάτου τούτου; διὰ τί τοῦτο λέγει; ὅτι Τὸ ἀναλῦσαι καὶ σὺν Χριστῷ εἶναι πολλῷ κρεῖττον εἶναί φησιν. τί δὲ ὁ μέγας Δαυὶδ ὁ τοσαύτῃ δυναστείᾳ κομῶν ὁ πάντα πρὸς ἡδονὴν καὶ κατ' ἐξουσίαν εἰς ἀπόλαυσιν ἔχων; οὐ στενοχωρεῖται τῷ βίῳ; οὐ φυλακὴν ὀνομάζει τὴν ὧδε ζωήν; οὐ βοᾷ πρὸς τὸν κύριον· Ἐξάγαγε ἐκ φυλακῆς τὴν ψυχήν μου; οὐ πρὸς τὴν παράτασιν τῆς ζωῆς δυσχεραίνει Οἴμοι, λέγων, ὅτι ἡ παροικία μου ἐμακρύνθη; ἢ οὐκ ᾔδεισαν διακρῖναι οἱ ἅγιοι τὸ καλὸν ἐκ τοῦ χείρονος καὶ διὰ τοῦτο προτιμοτέραν ᾤοντο τῇ ψυχῇ τὴν ἀπὸ τοῦ σώματος ἔξοδον; σὺ δὲ τί καλόν, εἰπέ μοι, παρὰ τὸν βίον ὁρᾷς; κατανόησον ἐν τίσιν ἡ ζωὴ θεωρεῖται. οὐ λέγω σοι τὴν τοῦ προφήτου φωνὴν ὅτι Πᾶσα σὰρξ χόρτος· σεμνύνει γὰρ ἐκεῖνος μᾶλλον τῷ ὑποδείγματι τὴν τῆς φύσεως ἡμῶν ἀθλιότητα· τάχα γὰρ κρεῖττον ἦν χόρτον εἶναι μᾶλλον ἢ ὅπερ ἐστίν· διὰ τί; ὅτι οὐδεμίαν ὁ χόρτος ἐκ φύσεως ἀηδίαν ἔχει, ἡ δὲ σὰρξ ἡμῶν ὀσμῆς ἐστιν ἐργαστήριον ἅπαν τὸ ληφθὲν εἰς διαφθορὰν ἀχρειοῦσα. |
GNO 485 τὸ δὲ τὸν ἅπαντα χρόνον ὑποκεῖσθαι τῇ τῆς γαστρὸς λειτουργίᾳ ποίας τιμωρίας οὐκ ἔστιν ἀνιαρώτερον; ὁρᾶτε γὰρ τοῦτον τὸν διηνεκῆ φορολόγον, τὴν γαστέρα λέγω, ὅσην ἐπάγει καθ' ἡμέραν τὴν ἀνάγκην τῆς ἐπαιτήσεως, ᾧ κἂν ποτε πλέον τοῦ τεταγμένου προκαταβάλωμεν, οὐδὲν τοῦ ἐφεξῆς χρέους προεξετίσαμεν. οὐ καθ' ὁμοιότητα τῶν ἐν τῷ μυλῶνι ταλαιπωρούντων ζῴων κεκαλυμμένοις τοῖς ὀφθαλμοῖς τὴν τοῦ βίου μύλην περιερχόμεθα ἀεὶ διὰ τῶν ὁμοίων περιχωροῦντες καὶ ἐπὶ τὰ αὐτὰ ἀναστρέφοντες;

the inner part of the Kingdom in any other way than by removing the veil of the flesh.

8 Do you think it is better to share in the life available through flesh? Let the holy Apostle teach you, who shared in the secret mysteries of paradise.[17] What does he say about this present life, speaking surely from our common human experience? "Wretched man that I am! Who will save me from the body of this death?" (Rom 7.24) Why does he say this? Because, he says, "to be dissolved and to be with Christ is far better" (Phil 1.23). And what does great David say, who enjoyed such power, who had access to every pleasure and could indulge himself in them at will? Is he not cramped by this life? Does he not call life here a confinement? Does he not cry out to the Lord, "Bring my soul out of prison" (Ps 141.7).[18] Does he not complain about the length of life, saying "Woe is me, for my sojourn is prolonged!" (Ps 119.5) Or did the holy ones not know how to distinguish good from evil, and did they therefore think it was preferable for the soul to depart from the body? You tell me what you see that is beautiful in the course of this existence! Consider where the force of life is to be seen. I will not repeat for you the prophet's word, that "all flesh is grass" (Is 40.6); for he is signifying by his image here rather the wretchedness of our nature. Perhaps it would be better [for flesh] to be grass than what it is. Why? Because grass has nothing naturally unpleasant about it, but our flesh is the place where smell is produced, discarding as corruption everything it has taken in. And what torture is more unendurable than always to be subject to the needs of the stomach? Do you see the work of this constant tax-collector—I mean the stomach—how it daily forces its demands on us? And if we sometimes contribute in advance more than we have been assessed, we still have made no headway against the next levy! Are we not like animals laboring in the mill? With eyes shut, we walk around the mill of life, always circling through similar events and coming round to the same place? Shall I tell you what this cyclic pattern is?

[17]See 2 Cor 12.2–4.

[18]See *Funeral Oration on Pulcheria* 6 (p. 130).

εἴπω σοι τὴν κυκλικὴν ταύτην περίοδον; ὄρεξις, κόρος, ὕπνος, ἐγρήγορσις, κένωσις, πλήρωσις· ἀεὶ ἀπ᾽ ἐκείνων ταῦτα καὶ ἀπὸ τούτων ἐκεῖνα καὶ πάλιν ταῦτα καὶ οὐδέποτε κύκλῳ περιϊόντες παυόμεθα, ἕως ἂν ἔξω τοῦ μυλῶνος γενώμεθα. καλῶς ὁ Σολομὼν πίθον τετρημένον καὶ οἶκον ἀλλότριον ὀνομάζει τὸν ὧδε βίον. ὄντως γὰρ ἀλλότριος οἶκος καὶ οὐχ ἡμέτερος, ὅτι οὐκ ἐφ᾽ ἡμῖν
PG 889 | ἐστιν ἢ ὅτε βουλόμεθα ἢ ἐφ᾽ ὅσον ἐπιποθοῦμεν ἐν αὐτῷ εἶναι· ἀλλὰ καὶ εἰσαγόμεθα ὡς οὐκ οἴδαμεν καὶ ἐξοικιζόμεθα ὅτε οὐκ οἴδαμεν. τὸ δὲ τοῦ πίθου αἴνιγμα νοήσεις ἐὰν εἰς τὸ ἀπλήρωτον τῶν ἐπιθυμιῶν ἀποβλέψῃς. ὁρᾷς πῶς ἐπαντλοῦσιν ἑαυτοῖς οἱ ἄνθρωποι τὰς τιμάς, τὰς δυναστείας, τὰς δόξας καὶ πάντα τὰ τοιαῦτα; ἀλλ᾽ ὑπορρεῖ τὸ βαλλόμενον καὶ οὐ παραμένει τῷ ἔχοντι· ἡ μὲν γὰρ περὶ τὴν δόξαν καὶ τὴν δυναστείαν καὶ τὴν τιμὴν σπουδὴ πάντοτε ἐνεργεῖται, ὁ δὲ τῆς ἐπιθυμίας πίθος μένει ἀπλήρωτος. τί
GNO 486 δὲ ἡ φιλοχρηματία; | οὐκ ἀληθῶς πίθος τετρημένος ἐστὶν ὅλῳ τῷ πυθμένι ῥέων ᾧ κἂν πᾶσαν ἐπαντλήσῃς τὴν θάλασσαν πληρωθῆναι φύσιν οὐκ ἔχει;

Τί οὖν λυπηρὸν εἰ τῶν τοῦ βίου κακῶν ἡ μακαρία κεχώρισται καὶ ὥσπερ τινὰ λήμην τὸν τοῦ σώματος ῥύπον ἀποβαλοῦσα καθαρᾷ τῇ ψυχῇ πρὸς τὴν ἀκήρατον ζωὴν μετανίσταται, ἐν ᾗ ἀπάτη οὐ πολιτεύεται, διαβολὴ οὐ πιστεύεται, κολακεία χώραν οὐκ ἔχει, ψεῦδος οὐ καταμίγνυται, ἡδονή τε καὶ λύπη καὶ φόβος καὶ θράσος καὶ πενία καὶ πλοῦτος καὶ δουλεία καὶ κυριότης καὶ πᾶσα ἡ τοιαύτη τοῦ βίου ἀνωμαλία ὡς πορρωτάτω τῆς ζωῆς ἐκείνης ἐξώρισται; Ἀπέδρα ἐκεῖθεν, καθώς φησιν ὁ προφήτης, ὀδύνη καὶ λύπη καὶ στεναγμός. ἀντὶ δὲ τούτων τί; ἀπάθεια, μακαριότης, κακοῦ παντὸς ἀλλοτρίωσις, ἀγγέλων ὁμιλία, τῶν ἀοράτων θεωρία, θεοῦ μετουσία, εὐφροσύνη τέλος οὐκ ἔχουσα. ἆρ᾽ οὖν λυπεῖσθαι προσήκει περὶ τῆς βασιλίδος μαθόντας οἷα ἀνθ᾽ οἵων ἠλλάξατο; κατέλιπε βασιλείαν γηΐνην, ἀλλὰ τὴν οὐράνιον κατέλαβεν·

Appetite, satiety, sleeping, waking, emptying, filling; this one comes from that one and that from this, and then this again—and we never stop going around in a circle, until we come to be outside the mill!

Solomon was right to call life here in the world "a leaky cask and a stranger's house" (Prov 23.27, LXX).[19] Truly it is a stranger's house and not our own, since it is not our decision to be in it when we choose, or for how long we desire; we come to it in a way we do not understand, and leave it at a moment we do not know. And you will understand the image of the wine-cask if you consider how our fleshly desires are never satisfied. Do you see how people drink in honors for themselves, and power, titles, and all such things? But what we lay up for ourselves passes away, and does not endure for the one who has it; for our eager pursuit of glory and power and honor is always in operation, but the wine-cask of our desires remains half-full. And what is greed? Is it not truly a leaky cask, with its contents flowing out of the whole bottom? If you were to pour in the whole sea, it could still not naturally be filled!

9 What is there to mourn, then, if this blessed one is released from the evils of this life, and casting off the filth of the body like a smudge in the eye, moves on with purified soul to the uncontaminated life: where deceit is not practiced, slander is not believed, flattery has no place, lies are not mingled with speech—where pleasure and pain and fear and rashness and poverty and wealth and servitude and lordship, and all the inconsistency of this life, are removed as far as possible from that life to come? "Mourning and sorrow and groaning," as the Prophet says, "have fled from there!" (Is 35.10) And what will take their place? Freedom from suffering, blessedness, removal from all evil, familiarity with angels, contemplation of invisible things, a share in God, joy that has no end. Is it appropriate for people to grieve for our empress, when they have learned what she has left behind and received in exchange? She has left an earthly kingdom, but has received the Kingdom of heaven; she has put off a

[19]Gregory uses the same text from Proverbs in *On the Dead* 21.

ἀπέθετο τὸν ἐκ λίθων στέφανον, ἀλλὰ τὸν τῆς δόξης περιεθή-|
GNO 487 κατο· ἀπεδύσατο τὴν πορφυρίδα, ἀλλὰ Χριστὸν ἐνεδύσατο. τοῦτό
ἐστι τὸ βασιλικὸν ὄντως καὶ τίμιον ἔνδυμα. τὴν ὧδε πορφύραν
ἀκούω αἵματι κόχλου τινὸς θαλασσίας φοινίσσεσθαι, τὴν δὲ ἄνω
πορφύραν τὸ τοῦ Χριστοῦ αἷμα λάμπειν ποιεῖ· εἶδες ὅσον ἐν τῷ
ἐνδύματι τὸ διάφορον. βούλει πεισθῆναι ὅτι ἐν ἐκείνοις ἐστίν;
ἀνάγνωθι τὸ εὐαγγέλιον· Δεῦτε οἱ εὐλογημένοι τοῦ πατρός μου
(φησὶ ταῦτα πρὸς τοὺς δεξιοὺς ὁ κριτής), κληρονομήσατε τὴν
ἡτοιμασμένην ὑμῖν βασιλείαν· τὴν παρὰ τίνος ἡτοιμασμένην; ἣν
ἑαυτοῖς, φησί, διὰ τῶν ἔργων προητοιμάσασθε. πῶς; ἐπείνων,
ἐδίψων, ξένος ἤμην, γυμνός, ἀσθενής, ἐν φυλακῇ· Ἐφ᾽ ὅσον
ἐποιήσατε ἑνὶ τούτων τῶν ἐλαχίστων, ἐμοὶ ἐποιήσατε. εἰ οὖν ἡ
περὶ ταῦτα σπουδὴ βασιλείας πρόξενος γίνεται, ἀριθμήσατε, εἴπερ
δυνατόν ἐστιν ἐξαριθμήσασθαι, πόσοι τοῖς ἐνδύμασι τοῖς παρ᾽
αὐτῆς ἐσκεπάσθησαν, πόσοι τῇ μεγάλῃ ἐκείνῃ δεξιᾷ διετράφησαν,
πόσοι τῶν κατακλείστων οὐκ ἐπισκέψεως μόνον, ἀλλὰ καὶ
παντελοῦς ἀφέσεως ἠξιώθησαν. εἰ δὲ τὸ ἐπισκέψασθαι τὸν
κατάκλειστον προξενεῖ βασιλείαν, τὸ ἐλευθερῶσαι τῆς τιμωρίας
δηλαδὴ πλείονος τιμῆς ἄξιον, εἴπερ τι βασιλείας ἔστιν ἀνώτερον.
ἀλλ᾽ οὐ μέχρι τούτων ἐστὶν ἐκείνης ὁ ἔπαινος. παρέρχεται γὰρ
PG 892 καὶ τὰ προσ|τεταγμένα τοῖς κατορθώμασιν. πόσοι δι᾽ ἐκείνην
τὴν τῆς ἀναστάσεως χάριν ἐφ᾽ ἑαυτῶν ἐγνώρισαν, οἳ τοῖς νόμοις
ἀποθανόντες καὶ τὴν ἐπὶ θανάτῳ ψῆφον δεξάμενοι πάλιν δι᾽ αὐτῆς
εἰς τὴν ζωὴν ἀνεκλήθησαν. ἐν ὀφθαλμοῖς τῶν εἰρημένων ἡ μαρτυρία.
GNO 488 | εἶδες παρὰ τὸ θυσιαστήριον ἀπογνὸν τὴν σωτηρίαν μειράκιον,
εἶδες γύναιον ἐπὶ κατακρίσει ἀδελφοῦ ὀδυρόμενον, ἤκουσας τοῦ τὰ
ἀγαθὰ τῇ ἐκκλησίᾳ κηρύσσοντος, ὅπως τῇ μνήμῃ τῆς βασιλίδος ἡ

crown made of stones, but put on one formed of glory; she has taken off a robe of purple, but has clothed herself in Christ. This is truly the royal and precious garment! I understand that a purple robe here is made red with the blood of some shellfish from the sea,[20] but the blood of Christ is what makes the purple robe of heaven glow. You can see how much difference there is between these garments!

10 Do you want to be persuaded that she is in that place? Read the Gospel: "Come, you who are blessed by my Father," the Judge says to those on the right, "inherit the Kingdom that has been prepared for you" (Mt 25.34). A Kingdom prepared by whom? Which you have prepared for yourselves, he says, by your works. How? "I was hungry . . . I was thirsty . . . I was a stranger, naked, sick, in prison. What you have done for one of these least ones, you have done for me" (Mt 25.35–36, 40). If, then, eagerness for these things is the guarantee of the Kingdom, count—if it is possible to count—how many have been wrapped in clothes that she has given, how many were fed by her powerful right hand, how many prisoners were found deserving not only of her visits, but of complete release. And if visiting the prisoner is a pointer toward the Kingdom, surely to free someone from punishment is worthy of greater honor—if there is anything higher than the Kingdom! But her praise must not stop with these things. For the commandments given us in the Law have passed away. How many have come to recognize the grace of the resurrection in their own lives through her, who, dying in accord with the laws and receiving the sentence of death, were called back to life again through her? The testimony to what I am saying is before your eyes. You see, next to the altar, a young man who once despaired of survival; you see a young woman who once lamented the condemnation of her brother; you heard someone proclaiming an act of benevolence in church:

[20]See G. Steigerwald (above, *p.* 129, n. 10), for detailed information about the production of purple dye in the ancient world. It seems to have produced a color closer to what we would identify as scarlet than what modern people recognize as purple.

σκυθρωπὴ τοῦ θανάτου ψῆφος εἰς ζωὴν ἀναλύεται. ἆρα καὶ μόνον ταῦτα; τὴν δὲ ταπεινοφροσύνην ποῦ θήσομεν ἣν προτιμοτέραν ἡ γραφὴ ποιεῖται παντὸς τοῦ κατ' ἀρετὴν κατορθώματος; ἥτις συνηνιοχοῦσα τῷ μεγάλῳ βασιλεῖ τὴν τοσαύτην ἀρχὴν πάσης δυναστείας ὑποκυπτούσης, τοσούτων ἐθνῶν ὑποτελούντων, γῆς τε καὶ θαλάττης ἐκ τῶν οἰκείων ἑκατέρας δωροφορούσης οὐκ ἔδωκε πάροδον καθ' ἑαυτῆς τῷ τύφῳ ἀεὶ πρὸς ἑαυτὴν οὐκ εἰς τὰ ἔξω ἑαυτῆς ἀποβλέπουσα. διὰ τοῦτο τοῦ μακαρισμοῦ γίνεται κληρονόμος διὰ τῆς προσκαίρου ταπεινοφροσύνης τὸ ἀληθινὸν ὕψος ἐμπορευσαμένη. εἴπω τι καὶ τῆς φιλανδρίας τεκμήριον; ἔδει πάντως διαλυομένης τῆς σωματικῆς συζυγίας καὶ τὰ τίμια τῶν προσόντων αὐτοῖς ἀγαθῶν ἐλθεῖν εἰς διαίρεσιν. πῶς οὖν ἐποιήσατο τὴν διανομήν; τριῶν ὄντων τέκνων (ταῦτα γὰρ τῶν ἀγαθῶν τὰ κεφάλαια) τοὺς ἄρρενας τῷ πατρὶ προσκατέλιπεν, ὥστε εἶναι
GNO 489 αὐτοὺς τῆς βασιλείας | ἐρείσματα, τῆς δὲ ἰδίας μερίδος μόνην τὴν θυγατέρα πεποίηται. ὁρᾷς πῶς εὐγνώμων τε καὶ φιλόστοργος ἐν τοῖς τιμίοις τὸ πλέον τῷ ἀνδρὶ συγχωρήσασα.

Ἀλλ' ὃ μάλιστα παρ' ἡμῶν λέγεσθαι χρὴ τοῦτο προσθεὶς καταπαύσω τὸν λόγον. τὸ τῶν εἰδώλων μῖσος κοινὸν πάντων ἐστὶ τῶν μετεχόντων τῆς πίστεως, ἀλλ' ἐκείνης ἐξαίρετον τὸ τὴν Ἀρειανὴν ἀπιστίαν ὁμοίως τῇ εἰδωλολατρίᾳ βδελύττεσθαι. τοὺς γὰρ ἐν τῇ κτίσει τὸ θεῖον εἶναι νομίζοντας οὐδὲν ἔλαττον ἀσεβεῖν ᾤετο τῶν εἰδωλοποιούντων τὰς ὕλας, καλῶς καὶ εὐσεβῶς τοῦτο κρίνουσα· ὁ γὰρ τὸ κτίσμα προσκυνῶν, κἂν ἐπ' ὀνόματι τοῦ Χριστοῦ τοῦτο ποιῇ, εἰδωλολάτρης ἐστὶ Χριστὸν ὄνομα τῷ εἰδώλῳ τιθέμενος. διὰ τοῦτο μαθοῦσα ὅτι οὐκ ἔστι θεὸς πρόσφατος,

---

[21] Apparently Theodosius pardoned a condemned criminal in memory of his departed wife.

[22] Mt 18.4.

[23] See Lk 14.11.

how, in memory of the empress, the grim sentence of death has been transformed into life.[21]

11 And is this all? Where shall we put her humility, which Scripture says is more precious than every act of virtue?[22] As she drove in the chariot along with the great emperor, as every ruler bowed down before such great power, as so many tribes paid tribute, as earth and sea both offered gifts from what is theirs—she gave no place, on her own part, to arrogance, always keeping her eyes on herself and not gazing out toward the great scene beyond. Therefore she has become the heir of a blessing, gaining true exaltation in exchange for her humility in this world.[23] And shall I offer a proof of her love for her husband? Surely when a couple's bodily union is broken, the privileges of owning the possessions that belong to them also come into a state of dissolution. How, then, has she made distribution of her goods? Since there were three children (for that is the number of blessings there were),[24] she left the two boys to their father, so that they might be the support of his empire; but she has taken as her own share only their daughter![25] Do you see how generous and loving she is toward her husband, giving him the greater share of their precious possessions!

12 But when I have added what most deserves to be said, I shall bring these words to an end. Hatred of idols is the common duty of those who share the faith; her outstanding trait was to loathe the Arian distortion of faith as if it were idolatry. For she considered that those who think the divine is to be included among creatures are no less impious than those who make idols out of wood; and she judged rightly and piously in this! For the one who worships a creature, even if he does this in the name of Christ, is an idolater who puts the name of Christ onto his idol. For this reason, learning that there is no God

[24]A distant allusion, perhaps, to the "three gifts that abide" in 1 Cor 13.13: faith, hope, and charity.

[25]Pulcheria, the six-year-old daughter of Theodosius and Flaccilla, died a few months before her mother. Their two sons, Arcadius and Honorius, survived to rule the empire

μίαν προσεκύνει θεότητα τὴν ἐν πατρὶ καὶ υἱῷ καὶ πνεύματι ἁγίῳ δοξαζομένην. ταύτῃ ἐνηυξήθη τῇ πίστει, ταύτῃ ἐνήκμασεν, ταύτῃ τὸ πνεῦμα παρακατέθετο, ὑπὸ ταύτης προσήχθη τῷ κόλπῳ τοῦ πατρὸς τῆς πίστεως Ἀβραὰμ παρὰ τὴν τοῦ παραδείσου πηγὴν (ἧς ἡ ῥανὶς ἐπὶ τοὺς ἀπίστους οὐκ ἔρχεται), ὑπὸ τὴν σκιὰν τοῦ ξύλου GNO 490 τῆς ζωῆς τοῦ πεφυτευμένου παρὰ τὰς διεξόδους τῶν | ὑδάτων ὧν καὶ ἡμεῖς ἀξιωθείημεν ἐν Χριστῷ Ἰησοῦ τῷ κυρίῳ ἡμῶν· ᾧ ἡ δόξα εἰς τοὺς αἰῶνας τῶν αἰώνων. ἀμήν.

who is later in time,[26] she worshiped one divinity, which is glorified in Father and Son and Holy Spirit. In this faith she prayed fervently, in this she flourished, to this she entrusted her spirit; by this she was brought safely to the bosom of Abraham, the father of faith, by the spring of paradise (whose drops do not reach as far as the faithless), under the shade of the tree of life—that tree planted by those springs of water of which we too hope to be found worthy, in Christ Jesus our Lord, to whom be glory for the ages of ages. Amen!

[26]Arius was famous for his insistence that the Son, as begotten of the Father, had a beginning that was in some sense temporal, leading to the admission that he and his associates acknowledged that "there was [a time] when he was not." See Arius' letter to Eusebius of Nicomedia, from 321–22: in H. G. Opitz, *Athanasius Werke* III/1, Urkunde 1 (Leipzig: De Gruyter, 1934), 1–3.

Bibliography

Aelian. *Variae Historiae*. English translation: *Aelian: Historical Miscellany*. Translated by N. G. Wilson. Loeb Classical Library 486. Cambridge, MA: Harvard University Press, 1997.

Alexandre, Monique. "Le *De mortuis* de Grégoire de Nysse." *Studia Patristica* 10 (1970): 35–43.

Ambrose. *On the Death of Satyrus*. NPNF^2 10:159–97.

Ambrose. *De obitu Theodosii*. English translation: *Oration on the Death of Theodosius I*. Pages 174–203 in *Ambrose of Milan: Political Letters and Speeches*. Translated by J. H. W. G. Liebeschuetz. Translated Texts for Historians, vol. 43. Liverpool University Press, 2005.

Ammianus Marcellinus. *History: Books 14–19*. Translated by J. C. Rolfe. Loeb Classical Library 300. Cambridge, MA: Harvard University Press, 1950.

Andrew of Caesarea. *Commentary on the Apocalypse*. Translated by Eugenia Scarvelis Constantinou. Fathers of the Church 123. Washington, DC: The Catholic University of America, 2011.

Andrew of Crete. *Homily 1 on the Dormition of Our Most Holy Lady, the Mother of God*. Pages 103–106 in *On the Dormition of Mary*. Translated by Brian E. Daley, S.J. PPS 18. Crestwood, NY: St Vladimir's Seminary Press, 1997.

Apostolic Constitutions. ANF 7:387–505.

Aristotle. *Categories*. Pages 3–24 in *The Complete Works of Aristotle: The Revised Oxford Translation*. Edited by Jonathan Barnes, vol. 1. Princeton/Bollingen Series 71:2. Princeton: Princeton University Press, 1984. (Hereafter *Complete Works of Aristotle* 1.)

Aristotle. *On the Soul*. *Complete Works of Aristotle* 1:641–92.

Aristotle. *On the Heavens*. *Complete Works of Aristotle* 1:447–511.

Aristotle. *Nicomachean Ethics*. *Complete Works of Aristotle* 2:1729–1867

Aristotle. *On the History of Animals*. *Complete Works of Aristotle* 1:774–993.

Arius. *Letter to Eusebius of Nicomedia.* Pages 1–3 in H. G. Opitz, *Athanasius Werke* III/1, Urkunde 1. Leipzig: De Gruyter, 1934.

Athenagoras. *On the Resurrection.* ANF 2:149–62.

Augustine. *Confessions.* NPNF[1] 1:29–207.

Augustine. *De Genesi ad litteram.* English Translation: *St. Augustine: The Literal Meaning of Genesis, Volume 1: Books 1–6* and *Volume 2: Books 7–10.* Translated by John Hammond Taylor, S.J. Ancient Christian Writers 41 and 42. Mahwah, NJ: Paulist Press, 1982.

Augustine. *Enchiridion.* NPNF[1] 3:229–76.

Augustine. *Ennarations on the Psalms.* NPNF[1] 8 (passim).

Augustine. *On the City of God.* NPNF[1] 2:1–511.

Augustine. *Sermon 362.* Pages 77–126 in John A. Mourant. *Augustine On Immortality.* Villanova, PA: Augustinian Institute, Villanova University, 1969.

Claudian. *De quarto consulatu Honorii.* English translation: *Panegyric on the Fourth Consulship of the Emperor Honorius.* Pages 286–335 in *Claudian: Volume 1.* Translated by Maurice Platnauer. Loeb Classical Library 135. Cambridge, MA: Harvard University Press, 1922.

Clement of Alexandria. *Protrepticus.* English translation: *Exhortation to the Heathen.* ANF 2:171–206.

Courcelle, Pierre. *Connais-toi toi-même: de Socrate à saint Bernard.* 3 vols. Paris: Études augustiniennes, 1974–1975.

Cyril of Jereusalem. *Catechetical Orations.* English translation: *Lectures on the Christian Sacraments.* Translated by Maxwell E. Johnson, PPS 57. Yonkers, NY: St Vladimir's Seminary Press, 2017.

Daly, Brian E. "'Heavenly Man' and 'Eternal Christ': Apollinarius and Gregory of Nyssa on the Personal Identity of the Savior." *Journal of Early Christian Studies* 10 (2002): 469–88.

Daly, Brian E. "Divine Transcendence and Human Transformation: Gregory of Nyssa's Anti-Apollinarian Christology." *Studia Patristica* 32 (1997): 87–95. Reprinted in Sarah Coakley, ed. *Re-Thinking Gregory of Nyssa.* Oxford: Blackwell 2003.

Daly, Brian E. "The Enigma of Meletius of Antioch." In *Tradition and the Rule of Faith in the Early Church; Essays in Honor of Joseph T. Lienhard, SJ.*, edited by Ronnie J. Rombs and Nigel G. Wilson, 128–150. Washington: The Catholic University of America Press, 2010.

Downey, Glanville. "Earthquakes in Constantinople and Vicinity, A.D. 432–1454." *Speculum* 3 (1955): 596–600.

Gavrilyuk, Paul, and Sarah Coakley, eds. *The Spiritual Senses: Perceiving God in Western Christianity.* Cambridge: Cambridge University Press, 2012.

Gill, Joseph. *The Council of Florence*. Cambridge, 1959.

Gorman, Michael J. *Abortion in the Early Church: Christian, Jewish and Pagan Attitudes in the Greco-Roman World.* New York: Paulist Press, 1982.

Gregory of Nazianzus. *Epistula* 11. Pages 90–92 in *Gregory of Nyssa: The Letters: Introduction, Translation and Commentary*. Translated by Anna M. Silvas. Supplements to Vigiliae Christianae 83. Leiden: Brill, 2007.

Gregory of Nyssa. *A Discourse on the Dead. De mortuis.* Edited by Gunther Heil. GNO IX:28–93.

Gregory of Nyssa. *A funeral Oration for the Empress Flaccilla. Oratio funeris in Flacillam Imperatricem.* Edited by Andreas Spira. GNO IX/1:475–90.

Gregory of Nyssa. *Contra Eunomium*. Edited by Werner Jaeger. GNO I and II.

Gregory of Nyssa. *De deitate adversus Evagrium*. Edited by E. Gebhardt. GNO IX/1:331–341.

Gregory of Nyssa. *De hominis opificio.* [PG 44:124–256]

Gregory of Nyssa. *De tridui spatio.* [Edited by E. Gebhardt. GNO IX/1:273–306.]

Gregory of Nyssa. *Discorso sui defunti di Gregorio di Nissa: Edizione critica con introduzione, traduzione, note, e indici.* Edited by Giuseppe Lozza. Turin: Società Editrice Internazionale, 1991.

Gregory of Nyssa. *Homilies on Ecclesiastes. Homiliae in Ecclesiasten.* Edited by Paul Alexander. GNO V:277–442. English translation: *Gregory of Nyssa: Homilies on Ecclesiastes, An English Version with Supporting Studies, Proceedings of the Seventh International Colloquium on Gregory of Nyssa (St Andrews, 5–10 September 1990).* Edited by Stuart George Hall. Berlin: Walter de Gruyter, 1993.

Gregory of Nyssa. *In sanctum Pascha III*. Edited by Ernst Gebhardt. GNO IX: 245–70. Earlier translation by Stuart G. Hall. *The Easter Sermons of Gregory of Nyssa.* Patristic Monographs Series 9, 5–23. Winchendon, MA: Philadelphia Patristic Foundation, 1981.

Gregory of Nyssa. *Life of Moses. Grégoire de Nysse. La vie de Moïse*. Edited by J. Daniélou. SC 1-*ter.* Paris: Éditions du Cerf, 1968: 44–326. English translation: *Gregory of Nyssa: The Life of Moses*. Translated by Abraham Malherbe and Everett Ferguson. Classics of Western Spirituality. Mahwah, NJ: Paulist Press, 1978

Gregory of Nyssa. *On Perfection. De perfectione.* Edited by Werner Jaeger. GNO VIII/1:173–214. English translation: Pages 24–44 in Rowan A. Greer. *One Path for All: Gregory of Nyssa on the Christian Life and Human Destiny*. Eugene, OR: Cascade Books, 2015.

Gregory of Nyssa. *On the Godhead of the Son and the Holy Spirit. De deitate filii et spiritu sancti.* Edited by E. Rhein. GNO X/2:1–144.

Gregory of Nyssa. On *the Song of Songs. In Canticum canticorum*. Edited by Hermann Langerbeck. GNO VI. English translation: *Gregory of Nyssa: Homilies on the Song of Songs*. Translated by Richard A. Norris, Jr. Atlanta, GA: Society of Biblical Literature, 2012.

Gregory of Nyssa. *On the Soul and the Resurrection. De anima et resurrectione.* Edited by Andreas Spira. GNO III/3. PG 46:11–160. *On the Soul and the Resurrection.* Translated by Catharine P. Roth. PPS 12. Crestwood, NY: St Vladimir's Seminary Press, 1992.

Gregory of Nyssa. *Oratio catechetica.* Edited by Ekkehard Mühlenberg. GNO III/4. *Catechetical Discourse: A Handbook for Catechists*. Translated by Ignatius Green. PPS 60. Yonkers, NY: St Vladimir's Seminary Press, 2019.

Gregory of Nyssa. *Oratio consolatoria in Pulcheriam.* Edited by Andreas Spira. GNO IX/1:461–72. PG 46:864–877.

Gregory of Nyssa. *On Infants Taken Away before Their Time. De infantibus praemature abreptis*. Edited by Hadwiga Hörner. GNO III/2:61–99. Previously translated by W. Moore and H. A. Wilson. *On Infants' Early Deaths*. NPNF^2 5:372–82.

Gregory of Nyssa. *On Virginity. De virginitate*. GNO VIII/1:215–343. English translation: Pages 1–75 in *St. Gregory of Nyssa: Ascetical Works.* Translated by Virgina Woods Callaghan. Fathers of the Church 58. Washington, DC: The Catholic University of America, 1967.

Hesiod. *Theogony*. Pages 123–86 in *Hesiod*. Translated by Richard Lattimore. Ann Arbor, MI: The University of Michigan Press, 1959.

Hippolytus. *Against Plato, on the Cause of the Universe.* ANF 5:221–23.

Holum, Kenneth G. *Theodosian Empresses: Women and Imperial Dominion in Late Antiquity.* Berkeley: University of California Press, 1982.

Homer. *Iliad.* English translation: *The Iliad of Homer*. Translated by Richard Lattimore. The University of Chicago, 1951.

Hübner, Reinhard. "Gregor von Nyssa und Markell von Ancyra." In *Écriture et culture philosophique dans las pensée de Grégoire de Nysse*, edited by Marguerite Harl, 199–229. Leiden: Brill, 1971.

Irenaeus. *Against Heresies.* ANF 1:315–567.

John Chrysostom. *Homilies on the Rich Man and Lazarus.* English translation: *On Wealth and Poverty.* Translated by Catharine P. Roth. PPS 9. Second edition. Yonkers, NY: 2020.

Jones, A. H. M *The Prosopography of the Later Roman Empire 1.* Cambridge: Cambridge University Press, 1971.

Justin Martyr. *Dialogue with Trypho*. ANF 1:194–270.

Lactantius. *Institutes.* ANF 7:9–255.

Le Goff, Jacques. *La naissance du Purgatoire.* Paris: Gallimard, 1981. English: *The Birth of Purgatory*. Translated by Arthur Goldhammer. Chicago: University of Chicago Press, 1984.

Libanius. *Libanius: Autobiography and Selected Letters,* vol. 2. Translated A. E. Norman. Loeb Classical Library 479. Cambridge, MA: Harvard University Press, 1992.

Lienhard, Joseph T. "The Exegesis of I Cor. 15.24–28 from Marcellus of Ancyra to Theodoret of Cyrus." *Vigiliae Christianae* 17 (1983): 349–59.

Lozza, Giuseppe. *See* Gregory of Nyssa. *Discorso sui defunti.*

Maraval, Pierre. Maraval, Pierre. "Chronology of Works." *Brill Dictionary,* 153–169.

Marcellus of Ancyra. *Fragments.* In *Eusebius: Gegen Marcell.* Edited by E. Klostermann and G. C. Hansen. Berlin: Akademie Verlag, 1972.

Mateo-Seco, Lucas. "Tunics of Hide." Pages 768–70 in *The Brill Dictionary of Gregory of Nyssa*.

Menander Rhetor. *Menander Rhetor: A Commentary*. Edited and translated by Donald A. Russell and Nigel G. Wilson. Oxford: Oxford University Press, 1981.

Methodius. *On the Resurrection.* [Extant fragments:] ANF 6:364–78.

Nemesius of Emesa. *De natura hominis.* Edited by M. Morani. Leipzig: Teubner, 1987. English Translation: *Nemesius of Emesa: On the Nature*

of Man. Translated by R. W. Sharples and P. J. van der Eijk. Translated Texts for Historians 49. Liverpool University Press, 2008.

Origen. *Homilies on Exodus*. English translation: *Origen: Homilies on Genesis and Exodus.* Translated by Ronald E. Heine. Fathers of the Church 71. Washington, DC: The Catholic University of America, 1982.

Origen. *Origen: On First Principles, Volumes 1 and 2*. Edited and translated by John Behr. Oxford University Press, 2017.

Ostroumev, Ivan. *The History of the Council of Florence.* London, 1861.

Overstreet, R. Larry. "The Greek Concept of the 'Seven Stages of Life' and its New Testament Significance." *Bulletin for Biblical Research* 19 (2009): 537–63.

Paulinus of Nola. *Epistula* 23. English translation: Pages 1–49 in *Letters of St. Paulinus of Nola, Volume II: Letters 23–51*. Ancient Christian Writers 36. Westminster, MD: The Newman Press, 1967.

Philo. *De opificio mundi*. English translation: On the Creation. Pages 3–24 in *The Words of Philo: Complete and Unabridged, New Updated Version.* Translated by C. D. Yonge. Peabody, MA: Hendrickson Publishers, 1993 [revised reprinted edition].

Philostorgius. *Philostorgius: Church History.* Translated by Philip R. Amidon, S.J. Writings from the Greco-Roman World 23. Atlanta, GA: Society of Biblical Literature, 2007.

Plato. *Gorgias*. Pages 791–869 in *Plato: Complete Works*. Edited by John M. Cooper. Indianapolis, IN: Hackett Publishing Company, 1997. (Hereafter *Plato: Complete Works*.)

Plato. *Protagoras*. Pages 746–90 in *Plato: Complete Works.*

Plato. *Republic*. Pages 971–1223 in *Plato: Complete Works.*

Plutarch. *Regum et imperatorum apophthegmata*. English translation: Sayings of Kings and Commanders. Pages 8–194 in *Plutarch's Moralia in Fifteen Volumes, Volume 3: 172a–263c*. Translated by Frank Cole Babbit. Loeb Classical Library 245. Cambridge, MA: Harvard University Press, 1931.

Plutarch. *Life of Artaxerxes*. Pages 128–203 in *Plutarch: Lives, Volume 11*. Translated by Bernadotte Perren. Loeb Classical Library 103. Cambridge, MA: Harvard University Press, 1926.

Scott, Alan B. *Origen and the Life of the Stars: The History of an Idea*. Oxford: Oxford University Press, 1991.

Shakespeare, William. *As You Like It*. Pages 217–42 in *Shakespeare: Complete Works*. Edited by W. J. Craig. Oxford University Press, 1905.

Sorabji, Richard. *Matter, Space and Motion: Theories in Antiquity and Their Sequel*. Ithaca: Cornell University Press, 1988.

Steigerwald, Gerhard. "Die antike Purpurfäberei nach dem Bericht Plinius' des Älteren in seiner 'Naturalis Historia.'" *Traditio* 42 (1986): 1–57.

Tatian. *Diatesseron*. ANF 9:33–129.

Tertullian. *Apology*. ANF 3:17–55.

Tertullian. *On the Soul*. ANF 3:181–235.

Tertullian. *On the Resurrection of the Flesh*. ANF 3:545–94.

Tetz, Martin. "Zur Theologie des Markell von Ankyra I. Eine Markellische Schrift 'De incarnatione et contra Arianos.'" *Zeitschrift für Kirchengeschichte* 75 (1964): 215–270.

Theodoret. *Ecclesiastical History*. NPNF[2] 3:33–159.

Theodosius. *Codex Theodosianus*. English translation: *The Theodosian Code and Novels and the Sirmondian Constitutions*. Translated by Clyde Pharr. New York: Greenwood Press, 1969.

Vanhoye, Albert. "Interrogation johannique et exégèse de Cana (Jn 2.4)." *Biblica* 55 (1974): 157–67.

POPULAR PATRISTICS SERIES

1 *On the Priesthood* – St John Chrysostom
2 *Sermons from the Life of Saint John Chrysostom*
6 *On the Holy Icons* – St Theodore the Studite
7 *On Marriage and Family Life* – St John Chrysostom
8 *On the Divine Liturgy* – St Germanus
9 *On Wealth and Poverty* – St John Chrysostom
10 *Hymns on Paradise* – St Ephrem the Syrian
11 *On Ascetical Life* – St Isaac of Nineveh
12 *On the Soul and Resurrection* – St Gregory of Nyssa
13 *On the Unity of Christ* – St Cyril of Alexandria
14 *On the Mystical Life*, vol. 1 – St Symeon the New Theologian
15 *On the Mystical Life*, vol. 2 – St Symeon the New Theologian
16 *On the Mystical Life*, vol. 3 – St Symeon the New Theologian
17 *On the Apostolic Preaching* – St Irenaeus
18 *On the Dormition* – Early Patristic Homilies
19 *On the Mother of God* – Jacob of Serug
21 *On God and Man* – Theological Poetry of St Gregory of Nazianzus
23 *On God and Christ* – St Gregory of Nazianzus
24 *Three Treatises on the Divine Images* – St John of Damascus
25 *On the Cosmic Mystery of Christ* – St Maximus the Confessor
26 *Letters from the Desert* – Barsanuphius and John
27 *Four Desert Fathers* – Coptic Texts
28 *Saint Macarius the Spiritbearer* – Coptic Texts
29 *On the Lord's Prayer* – Tertullian, Cyprian, Origen
30 *On the Human Condition* – St Basil the Great
31 *The Cult of the Saints* – St John Chrysostom
32 *On the Church: Select Treatises* – St Cyprian of Carthage
33 *On the Church: Select Letters* – St Cyprian of Carthage
34 *The Book of Pastoral Rule* – St Gregory the Great
35 *Wider than Heaven* – Homilies on the Mother of God
36 *Festal Orations* – St Gregory of Nazianzus
37 *Counsels on the Spiritual Life* – Mark the Monk
38 *On Social Justice* – St Basil the Great
39 *The Harp of Glory* – An African Akathist
40 *Divine Eros* – St Symeon the New Theologian
41 *On the Two Ways* – Foundational Texts in the Tradition
42 *On the Holy Spirit* – St Basil the Great
43 *Works on the Spirit* – Athanasius and Didymus
44 *On the Incarnation* – St Athanasius
45 *Treasure-House of Mysteries* – Poetry in the Syriac Tradition
46 *Poems on Scripture* – St Gregory of Nazianzus
47 *On Christian Doctrine and Practice* – St Basil the Great
48 *Light on the Mountain* – Homilies on the Transfiguration
49 *The Letters* – St Ignatius of Antioch
50 *On Fasting and Feasts* – St Basil the Great
51 *On Christian Ethics* – St Basil the Great
52 *Give Me a Word* – The Desert Fathers
53 *Two Hundred Chapters on Theology* – St Maximus the Confessor
54 *On the Apostolic Tradition* – Hippolytus
55 *On Pascha* – Melito of Sardis
56 *Letters to Olympia* – St John Chrysostom
57 *Lectures on the Christian Sacraments* – St Cyril of Jerusalem
58 *The Testament of the Lord*
59 *On the Ecclesiastical Mystagogy* – St Maximus the Confessor
60 *Catechetical Discourse* – St Gregory of Nyssa
61 *Hymns of Repentance* – St Romanos the Melodist
62 *On the Orthodox Faith* – St John of Damascus
63 *Headings on Spiritual Knowledge* – Isaac of Nineveh
64 *On Death and Eternal Life* – St Gregory of Nyssa
65 *The Prayers of Saint Sarapion* – Saint Sarapion of Thmuis

ST VLADIMIR'S SEMINARY PRESS
1-800-204-2665 • www.svspress.com

We hope this book has been enjoyable and edifying for your spiritual journey toward our Lord and Savior Jesus Christ.

One hundred percent of the net proceeds of all SVS Press sales directly support the mission of St Vladimir's Orthodox Theological Seminary to train priests, lay leaders, and scholars to be active apologists of the Orthodox Christian Faith. However, the proceeds only partially cover the operational costs of St Vladimir's Seminary. To meet our annual budget, we rely on the generosity of donors who are passionate about providing theological education and spiritual formation to the next generation of ordained and lay servant leaders in the Orthodox Church.

Donations are tax-deductible and can be made at www.svots.edu/donate. We greatly appreciate your generosity.

To engage more with St Vladimir's Orthodox Theological Seminary, please visit:

www.svots.edu
online.svots.edu
www.svspress.com
www.instituteofsacredarts.com

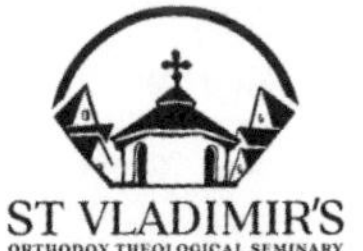